LORD CHESTERFIELD'S LETTERS

PHILIP DORMER STANHOPE, 4th Earl of Chesterfield, was born in 1694, the grandson of George Savile, Marquis of Halifax. Brought up to be bilingual in English and French, he spent a year at Cambridge before travelling in the Low Countries. In 1715 he was made gentleman of the bedchamber to George, Prince of Wales, and became an under-age MP for St Germans, Cornwall, moving to Paris later the same year. After his return he became acquainted with Pope, Addison, and Arbuthnot, and sat in Parliament as the member for Lostwithiel, moving to the Lords on his father's death in 1726. From this time he was active in opposition. He accepted the embassy at The Hague in 1728, where he met Elizabeth du Bouchet, the mother of his son, Philip Stanhope, born in 1732. In 1737 he began the thirty-year correspondence with Stanhope on which his fame now rests. He became Lord-Lieutenant of Ireland and ambassador extraordinary to The Hague in 1744, and Secretary of State in 1746. It was during this period in high office that Johnson approached him with the plan for his Dictionary, Chesterfield's neglect of which became notorious. His resignation in 1748 marked the end of his political career except as an occasional orator and mediator. Deafness made his long retirement increasingly solitary. Polite in the face of death in March 1773, with his last words he offered a chair to his friend Dayrolles. He was succeeded by his godson, another pupil by correspondence, and a year after his death his letters began to be published.

PHYLLIS M. JONES edited the 1929 World's Classics selection of Chesterfield's letters.

DAVID ROBERTS has taught for the British Council and at universities in Britain and Japan, where he is now Visiting Lecturer at Osaka University. His publications include *The Ladies* (OUP, 1989) and the introduction to Defoe's *A Journal of the Plague Year* in Oxford World's Classics.

OXFORD WORLD'S CLASSICS

*For almost 100 years Oxford World's Classics have brought
readers closer to the world's great literature. Now with over 700
titles—from the 4,000-year-old myths of Mesopotamia to the
twentieth century's greatest novels—the series makes available
lesser-known as well as celebrated writing.*

*The pocket-sized hardbacks of the early years contained
introductions by Virginia Woolf, T. S. Eliot, Graham Greene,
and other literary figures which enriched the experience of reading.
Today the series is recognized for its fine scholarship and
reliability in texts that span world literature, drama and poetry,
religion, philosophy and politics. Each edition includes perceptive
commentary and essential background information to meet the
changing needs of readers.*

OXFORD WORLD'S CLASSICS

LORD CHESTERFIELD

Letters

826
C525

Edited with an Introduction and Notes by
DAVID ROBERTS

Oxford   New York
OXFORD UNIVERSITY PRESS

Oxford University Press, Great Clarendon Street, Oxford OX2 6DP

Oxford New York

Athens Auckland Bangkok Bogotá Buenos Aires Calcutta
Cape Town Chennai Dar es Salaam Delhi Florence Hong Kong Istanbul
Karachi Kuala Lumpur Madrid Melbourne Mexico City Mumbai
Nairobi Paris São Paulo Singapore Taipei Tokyo Toronto Warsaw
and associated companies in Berlin Ibadan

Oxford is a registered trade mark of Oxford University Press

First published as a World's Classics paperback 1992
Reissued as an Oxford World's Classics paperback 1998

British Library Cataloguing in Publication Data

Data available

Library of Congress Cataloging in Publication Data
Chesterfield, Philip Dormer Stanhope, Earl of, 1694–1773.
[Correspondence]
Lord Chesterfield's letters / edited with an introduction by David Roberts.
p. cm.—(Oxford world's classics)
Includes bibliographical references and index.
1. Chesterfield, Philip Dormer Stanhope, Earl of, 1694–1773—
Correspondence. 2. Statesmen—Great Britain—Correspondence.
3. Authors, English—18th century—Correspondence.. I. Roberts,
David, 1960– . II. Title. III. Series.
DA501.C5A4 1992 941.07'0'092—dc20 92-7195
ISBN 0-19-283715-X

1 3 5 7 9 10 8 6 4 2

Printed in Great Britain by
The Bath Press, Bath

ACKNOWLEDGEMENTS

THE apparatus of this edition needs some apology, since it is both extensive and limited. The learning Chesterfield displays in his letters is extraordinarily wide and sometimes out of focus, and I hope the present edition goes further than its predecessors in making his obscurities accessible to modern readers. There have, regrettably, been occasions when calculated guesses or mere blanks were all that the most intensive enquiries could turn up—these things of darkness I acknowledge mine. Chesterfield had his own cheerfully acerbic view of new editions and their compilers: 'the last editions are always the best, if the editors are not blockheads, for they may profit of the former'. Although I have profited particularly from Bonamy Dobrée's heroic six-volume edition of the letters, my chief debts are to the friends, relations, and correspondents whose generous assistance has on more occasions than I wish to count saved me from blockheadedness. Those who have supplied or helped me to find information are Dr Peter Davidson, Ms Annemiek Scholten, Dr Albert van der Heide, and members of the Sir Thomas Browne Institute, University of Leiden; Professor Roy Foster of Hertford College, Oxford; Dr Tom Bartlett of University College, Galway; Ms Petra Hesse of the Leipzig University Archive; Mr Horst Flechsig of the Leipzig Theaterhochschule; Dr Bernd Neumann of Kyoto University; Mr Simon Rees; Mrs Elizabeth Roberts; Mr Michael Walling; and Mr Stephen Wood, Keeper of the Department of Armed Forces History, National Museum of Scotland. None of these kind people is responsible for any errors which remain. Simon Rees also saved me from the sort of débâcle which can only befall a certified computer blockhead. My greatest debt is to my wife, who assisted with proofreading and surrendered to Chesterfield and his son much of the time I should have been spending with ours.

D.R.

CONTENTS

INTRODUCTION

IN the summer of 1773 there came to the attention of Edward
Gibbon a bundle of manuscript letters from a recently deceased
earl to his illegitimate son. Gibbon recalled the episode to his
friend Holroyd on 10 September: 'I forgot to tell you, that I
have declined the publication of Lord Chesterfield's Letters.
The public will see them, and upon the whole, I think, with
pleasure; but the family were strongly against it.' A month later
came another refusal. Horace Walpole informed an intermediary appointed by the owner of the letters that he too declined to
prepare them for the press: he would not offend the families of
people mentioned in them, or the memory of his own father,
whom Chesterfield had opposed as first minister, and he
certainly would not publish without the consent of the author's
family.[1] Personal memoirs often give offence, but Walpole's
knowledge of Chesterfield himself suggested that these letters,
which he probably had not read, must be a special case. In fact
the author's family was not unanimous in opposing publication; had they known what vices were soon to be associated
with the name of Chesterfield, they might have been. His
widow, ever complaisant, favoured the publication of letters so
'elegant' and 'instructive'; it was left to his executors to oppose
James Dodsley's plan to bring them out in two suitably
'elegant' royal quarto volumes. The story of the injunction
which they brought against Dodsley neatly sums up Chesterfield's current reputation as a man more reviled than read, for
having been advised by the judge to go away and read the
volumes they were intending to prohibit, the executors
returned after six days to waive their objections, 'tho there are
some things in [the letters] which it might have been better to
have omitted'.[2] If this whimper which ended the dress rehearsal
of the scandal of Lord Chesterfield's letters bodes ill for the

[1] Letter to Lady Louisa Lennox, 14 Oct. 1773.
[2] Letter of Beaumont Hotham and Lovel Stanhope to Mrs Eugenia
Stanhope, 29 Mar. 1774, quoted by S. L. Gulick, 'The Publication of Lord
Chesterfield's Letters to his Son' *PMLA* 51 (1936).

modern reader thirsting for the manners of dancing masters and the morals of whores, it also gives little hint of what one contemporary was to call the 'torrent of obloquy' which greeted their eventual publication in 1774, eight months after Gibbon had forecast that they would be read, upon the whole, with pleasure.

They were certainly read. Chesterfield himself, reportedly asked by his daughter-in-law whether he did not think the letters 'would form a fine system of education if published', agreed but thought there was 'too much Latin in them' for general use.[3] His readers were not so easily deterred. Eleven editions had appeared in England and Ireland by 1800, the year of a six-volume Viennese edition; by then the letters had also been printed in Paris, Amsterdam, and Leipzig, where the six-volume collection of 1775–7 was described with amoral Continental enthusiasm in a new-book listing as simply 'very well worth reading'. For those who could not afford the guinea each Dodsley charged for his two volumes, the letters could be borrowed from one of the new library societies established in the early 1770s, in the records of which they sometimes appeared among the ten most popular books. Often the English editions bore titles which promised nothing but wholesome improvement: *The Principles of Politeness* (1775); *The Fine Gentleman's Etiquette* (1776); *Some Advices on Men and Manners* (also 1776). It was no doubt these successive breaches of advertising standards together with the wide readership enjoyed by the letters which, no less than their scandalous content, unleashed the torrent of printed commentaries and allusions, most of them adequately summarized by the subtitle of a publication of 1791, *The Contrast: or an antidote against the pernicious principles disseminated in the letters of the late Earl of Chesterfield.*

Those principles proved easy to caricature: self-interest above morality, adultery above marriage, cynicism above patriotism, breeding above all. Chesterfield badgers his son to find a mature society beauty who will 'polish' him; tells him to seem trustworthy but never to trust; advises him that his

---

[3] See Gulick, ibid. 170.

dancing master is more important than his Aristotle. He favours smutty repartee with 15-year-old girls; prefers deceitful high-society liaisons, sometimes two or more at a time, to affairs of the heart; encourages the boy to enjoy his father's old flames (little wonder that his son's sometime travelling companion, Lord Eliot, should have remarked 'that it was strange that a man who shewed he had so much affection for his son as Lord Chesterfield did, by writing so many long and anxious letters to him, almost all of them when he was Secretary of State, which certainly was a proof of great goodness of disposition, should endeavour to make his son a rascal'[4]). It was not only a matter of personal morality. To Chesterfield the vaunted British parliamentary system seemed a display of shabby theatricals, and the apex of modern civilization the Court of Berlin; he had a *précieux* preference for everything French, and enthused more over Voltaire than Shakespeare. To cap it all, he neglected to assist the lexicographic labours of that embodiment of dogged English virtue, Dr Samuel Johnson.

In 1774 it was likely that above the 'general murmur of abhorrence' described by Blake's sometime patron, William Hayley, there would be heard cries of 'irreligious', 'profligate', 'unpatriotic', and 'Frenchified fop' (the latter dies hard—a recent account of Chesterfield's year as Lord-Lieutenant of Ireland marks him down as 'egregiously francophile'[5]). However propitious the times were for James Dodsley, they could hardly have been worse for the reputation of his late author. For nearly fifteen of the past thirty-four years Britain had been at war with France: victories against the French at the end of the Seven Years War (1756–63) had boosted patriotic sentiments beyond Britain's legal and political institutions to encompass a conviction of her supremacy in the world. Chesterfield was not only proud of having made 'personal friends' out

[4] James Boswell, *The Life of Samuel Johnson*, Everyman edn., 2 vols. (London, 1906), ii. 547.
[5] Hayley, *Two Dialogues; containing a comparative view of ... Chesterfield and Dr Samuel Johnson* (1787), 172; and Bruce P. Lenman, 'Scotland and Ireland, 1742–1789', in J. Black (ed.), *British Politics and Society from Walpole to Pitt 1742–1789* (Basingstoke, 1990), 86.

of 'national enemies' in times of war; some of his central moral
concepts were French imports suspected as late as Jane Austen's *Emma* of sacrificing virtue to appearance. '"No, Emma,"'
says Mr Knightley of Frank Churchill, '"your amiable young
man can be amiable only in French, not in English. He may be
very *aimable*, have very good manners, and be very agreeable;
but he can have no English delicacy towards the feelings of
other people: nothing really amiable about him".'[6] Even
French appreciation of Britain's political institutions might
exceed Chesterfield's. His friend Montesquieu praised the
precious balance of the constitution, the Lords protecting the
Commons from the King and the King from the Commons, so
honouring the bedrock of common political thinking since the
Glorious Revolution. Although Chesterfield declared himself a
man of 1689 principles, he also viewed the upper house as
merely 'a hospital for incurables', a view scandalous not
because it was unique but because it came from within—'Lord
Chesterfield has let us all behind the scenes: he invites us to see
the peer dress for public exhibition,' complained one critic. For
David Hume the 'true sage and patriot' was also characterized
by other notably un-Chesterfieldian qualities: 'The softest
benevolence, the most sublime love of virtue, all these animate
successively his transported bosom.'[7] Such transports ooze
through the sentimental best-seller of the 1770s, Henry Mac-
kenzie's *The Man of Feeling*, and the host of other popular
fictions, philosophical as well as literary, which seconded its
advocacy of instinct over calculation, of natural over acquired
gentility, of 'feminine' intensities of pity and distress over
hypocritical masculine designings: far indeed from Chesterfield's dismissal of women as 'children of a larger growth', and
still further from his pervasive Machiavellian warning 'to be
upon your own guard, and yet, by a seeming natural openness,
to put people off theirs'. No less shocking to readers who
expected enlightenment in the true gentleman's etiquette was

[6] Letter to his son, 29 Sept. 1752 (not in this edn.); Austen, *Emma*, ed. D.
Lodge and J. Kinsley (Oxford, 1971), 134–5.
[7] Vicesimus Knox, quoted by Paul Langford, *A Polite and Commercial People*
(Oxford, 1989), 590; Hume quoted from A. R. Humphreys, 'Friend of
Mankind', *Review of English Studies*, 24 (1948).

the mile-wide gap between Chesterfield's principles and those of the state religion, together with his benign advice to observe the usual ceremonies when in Catholic countries for the sake of 'complaisance'. While many mistrusted the enthusiasms of the burgeoning evangelical movement, few would have preferred Chesterfield's cooler alternative view of religion as a subject unfit for polite conversation.

If there were plenty of reasons why the letters should have been disliked and caricatured when they were published, their success was not merely *de scandale*. The famed breadth of Chesterfield's achievements promised, and delivered, a fusion of the polite, the political, and the learned which far exceeded the agenda of comparable publications. Where favourable epithets were bestowed, they stressed the totality of the Chesterfieldian ethos, lending the hackneyed language of courtesy literature a fresh significance—'a perfect knowledge of mankind', 'a complete gentleman', sang the editor of the *Monthly Review* in April 1774. To an unusual degree, the letters assume the perfectibility of their addressee, their obsession with 'attention' urging an infallible mastery of languages, politics, and *politesse*, of the body and of the face, which not even laughter must be allowed to discompose. That drive for discipline and its panoptic enforcement by which Michel Foucault characterized the late eighteenth-century social order finds here one of its clearest yet least recognized expositions: to Stanhope's eternal vigil of self-observation was added his father's trans-European network of friends and associates, ready to watch narrowly and relate faithfully of his progress. Chesterfield's status, and his ambitions for his son, gave to his educational programme a political import unignorable in the years when he was read most often, up to the end of the century. If the letters were believed by some to hold up the peerage to public scorn, they also gave a reassuring picture of a patriciate at once tolerant, industrious, vigilant, and above all capable. In all these matters mention of the word 'France' was, for once, to Chesterfield's advantage.

The curricular advice contained in the letters was welcome for some of the same reasons. Chesterfield's advocacy of classical education stressed freedom from pedantry, recognition of the rival claims of modern languages and history, and a rigour of method to facilitate the performance of small tasks as well as great ones. Above all, this anticipation of modern civil service selection criteria emphasized not the insouciant acquisition of gentlemanly accomplishments but competence and self-reliance in social, political, and business dealings. As such it was likely to recommend itself to a generation of reformers seeking, like the headmaster of Tonbridge School, Vicesimus Knox, to restore the classics as a training-ground for professional and commercial life and not as the preserve of idle young noblemen; Knox's own *Liberal Education* (1781) was reprinted nine times in as many years. Stanhope's grand tour of Europe was likewise planned according to practical concerns which, refreshingly, balanced the usual diet of polite society and amateur art criticism with introductions to diplomats and studies of constitutional and economic affairs. 'Never be proud of your rank or birth, but be as proud as you please of your character,' wrote Chesterfield to a second pupil by correspondence, his godson and heir. That this advice was less necessary in the more celebrated case of his natural son indicates that the very fact of the boy's illegitimacy shaped a system of education in which success was achieved, as Chesterfield observed in quoting the classical Tacitus to professional effect, by being equal to business and not too grand for it. A ready stick with which to threaten Stanhope ('you neither have, nor can have, a shilling in the world but from me'), his birth also fostered a vision of success through ability, not rank.

To accidents of physiology rather than conception Chesterfield's most earnest apologists have always turned, and seldom convincingly: the letters had been written 'for a very private and very particular purpose', complained one; they were intended not as a system of education but as correctives to an individual who combined intelligence, reserve, clumsiness, squatness, and portliness in unique proportions.[8] This objection would have more force if Chesterfield had not repeated to his heir all the advice he had given his son, and still more did not his style tend less to conversation than to declamation. It

[8] Hayley, *Two Dialogues*, 173.

was Lord Hervey who observed that although Chesterfield was a fine parliamentary orator, 'he never made any figure in a reply, nor was his manner of speaking like debating, but declaiming'.[9] The shapely moral abstractions of his letters likewise give little room for the voice they were intended to cultivate; without this quality they would have been less plausible as the 'system of education' which Dodsley was the first to lay before the general public. Yet to sense the actual addressee, the 'very private and very particular' person to whom the letters were written, is to recognize a dramatic interest even in their habitual codification of Stanhope's behaviour in the 'harmony and roundness' of his father's highly self-involved epistolary style. Chesterfield, aware that the correspondence lacked intimacy, employed different tactics to nurture it, blaming his son being one of them. He declares a wish to be 'upon the footing of an intimate friend, and not of a parent'; he changes abruptly from 'Dear Boy' to 'Dear Friend' in his son's eighteenth year; his coarse quips bespeak a strained and possibly alienating familiarity; and in a passage which hints at the reticence with which young Stanhope responded to these formidable yet insinuating parental missives, he encourages his son to be less laconic in mentioning the trivial incidents of each day, summing up his frustration in a complaint which was never to receive full redress—'in short, let me see more of You in your letters'. No one who had been told of his father's 'Arguses, with an hundred eyes each, who will watch you narrowly, and relate to me faithfully' could respond to that friendly overture with much alacrity; equally, no one who had been told that his father could better bear him in letters than in person could for very long lament the pathos of a filial relationship largely constructed, given Stanhope's frequent absences abroad, upon the formalities of correspondence. A month after complaining of Stanhope's reticence in replying, Chesterfield was promising to be 'more regular and methodical' in his own letters. The boy must have trembled.

The subject on which Stanhope felt least able to speak led, by degrees, to the unusual circumstances in which the letters were

---

[9] Hervey, *Memoirs of George II*, ed. J. W. Croker, 2 vols. (1848), ii. 341.

published. Here, at least, Chesterfield's allies were on firm
ground. At the time when he was being exhorted to have affairs
with two French ladies, one for the sake of 'attachment' and the
other for 'gallantry', Stanhope was becoming enamoured of an
illegitimate Irish girl, Eugenia Peters, his lasting attachment
and marriage to whom were unknown to Chesterfield until
after his son's death. It was then that Eugenia proposed
publication of the letters as 'a fine system of education'; we
have only her word that her father-in-law demurred because
there was 'too much Latin in them'. Finding that Chesterfield's
will provided only for her two sons, she approached Gibbon
and Horace Walpole before selling the copyright to Dodsley
for no less than fifteen hundred guineas; little wonder that she
was accused of taking advantage of Chesterfield's death for
personal gain. If she felt any resentment at being excluded from
his estate, she could not have exacted a better revenge upon his
name.

Proper consideration of a less intimate relationship may erect
a further barrier against Chesterfield-bashing. The intertwining
of his name with Johnson's which occurs in every history of
English Literature has, with the falsifications which usually
attend it, established Chesterfield as the enemy of writers, the
patron who in the words of Johnson's celebrated letter, 'looks
with unconcern on a man struggling for life in the water, and,
when he has reached ground, encumbers him with help'.[10] The
truth is that the roll-call of writers indebted to Chesterfield for
actual or proffered assistance is long and distinguished, including Fielding, Berkeley, Gibbon, Voltaire, Montesquieu, Garrick, and James Thomson. Pope's appreciation of his patronage
was so keen that he preferred to think of him simply as a
friend.[11] Chesterfield also assisted and sought the company of
dozens of minor British and French poets, dramatists, historians, and scientists, not because he was flattered by their
fulsome dedicatory epistles, but because his social instincts, for
all the superficial accomplishments recommended by the let-

---

[10] Boswell, *Life of Johnson*, i. 155–7. Chesterfield also appears as a negligent
patron in Smollett's *Roderick Random* (1748) and *Peregrine Pickle* (1751).

[11] Pope, 'Epilogue to the Satires', ii. 84–93.

ters, were strongly meritocratic: 'I used to think myself in company as much above me, when I was with Mr Addison and Mr Pope, as if I had been with all the Princes in Europe,' he observed. Johnson's charge of patronly negligence, untrue in general, is only partly true in the particular case of the dictionary episode. Chesterfield was regarded as an authority on English usage; Thomas Sheridan appealed to him to establish an academy 'for the correcting, ascertaining and fixing' of the language, while the author of a grammar of 1785 attributed changes in pronunciation to his influence.[12] It was natural for Johnson to approach him, in 1747, to hand over the plan for his dictionary, receive the benefits of Chesterfield's knowledge and exquisite politeness, and ten pounds for his pains. Subsequently, however, it was alleged that Chesterfield so far neglected his trust as to turn the impoverished editor from his door, an assertion of which there is no proof. Chesterfield might well have had prior commitments, for at this time he was one of the two Secretaries of State and not, perhaps, much concerned with whatever duties patronage demanded; after his resignation in 1748 his own resentments led to his partial withdrawal from society to a recently acquired house in Blackheath. A reference of 1752 to French and Italian dictionaries (p. 179 of this edition) suggests that he had at worst simply forgotten about Johnson's project. When its publication was announced in 1754, Chesterfield wrote two articles in the *World* which nominated Johnson the worthy and necessary 'dictator' of a language beset by 'tolerance, adoption, and naturalization', sins from which his own prose, rich in original and early borrowings from French, is scarcely free. No doubt these protestations were an atonement for prior neglect, but Johnson chose to regard them as hollow and penned his letter of complaint, which Chesterfield demurely left on a table for the admiration of visitors. It is likely that Johnson was stung not only by the belatedness of his former patron's support, but by a gratuitous allusion to his manners, of which he was unjustifiably vain: Chesterfield said he had 'a greater

---

[12] Sheridan, *British Education* (1756), p. xvi; John Walker, *A Critical Pronouncing Dictionary and Expositor of the English Language* (1785), 111.

opinion of [Johnson's] impartiality and severity as a judge, than of his gallantry as a fine gentleman'. Perhaps Chesterfield felt confirmed in this opinion when, in an incident rarely included in English accounts of the episode (but popular in German ones), Johnson refused to accept an apology conveyed by one of the earl's friends.[13] If the full story implicates Johnson rather than exculpating Chesterfield, it reflects the view of one contemporary in whose mind their names were, as for modern readers, inseparably linked: 'my hand would have shrunk from Johnson, as from a hedge-hog, and from Chesterfield . . . as an eel too slippery to be held.'[14]

Johnson's famous judgement on the letters, that 'they teach the morals of a whore, and the manners of a dancing-master',[15] is more tenable than his alleged innocence in the dictionary episode, as long as it is not taken literally. Chesterfield is unequivocal in condemning 'low pleasures' ('I will, by no means, pay for whores, and their never-failing consequences, surgeons'), while one of his first principles is that a proper accommodation of the ego to society entails the study of 'established follies to which people of sense are sometimes obliged to conform', dancing being one of them. Here, however, as so often in the letters, the terms of social accommodation are stated with a cynicism which, apart from its conceivably counter-productive effect on the son, gives purchase for the wider charges of faithlessness, dissimulation, and superficiality implied in Johnson's rebuke, and confirmed in Boswell's footnote to it. Manners fulfil for Chesterfield an ideal not of civilized or even socialized conduct, but of ready self-advancement: they are tools for achieving private ends, preferable to violence for reasons of efficacy rather than morality. Every second writer on the letters wonders at Chesterfield's omission of Castiglione's *Book of the Courtier* from the list of recommended reading in Italian, but the real wonder is that he did not include *The Prince*, so pervasive are the name and spirit of

---

[13] See Sir John Hawkins, *Life of Johnson* (1787), 191; and, for example, the review of Chesterfield's Letters in *Neue Bibliothek der schönen Wissenschaften*, 16 (1774), 327–8.

[14] Hayley, *Two Dialogues*, 235.

[15] Boswell, *Life of Johnson*, i. 159.

Machiavelli in his disquisitions upon society, courts, and power. His ethos—and this is no doubt one reason why people used to read him so avidly—is one of success. The letters are often spoken of as proto-Wildean celebrations of style over sincerity, as elegant adumbrations of society values, but they are more frequently concerned with the rewards due to individual merit and the quickest means of attaining them. The injunctions against bad conduct have accordingly less to say about turpitude or even breaches of the polite order than about risks to personal advancement. Boswell was wrong to accuse Chesterfield of 'inculcating the base practice of dissimulation', for Chesterfield regards all dissimulation as a grave political and social mistake. He is content that the line between diplomatic concealment and lying is a clear one, while being sharply aware of the vigilance required not to cross it ('The prudence and necessity of often concealing the truth, insensibly seduces people to violate it'); but he expresses no view of outright deceit which represents it as other than simply contrary to career interests. While he refers more often to the Bible than one might expect, he does so in a way which scarcely threatens the autonomous demands of the social and political circles in which his son moved: 'do as you would wish to be done by', as he puts it, admits a tolerance of prevailing suspicion and concealment. His general reticence about what he calls 'Religion and Morality', highly exclusive terms in his vocabulary, is offered as a gesture of paternal trust which must have raised a few laughs in 1774: 'I cannot possibly suspect you as to either of them', he observes with a dose of what Dickens's Sir John Chester, in *Barnaby Rudge*, calls his 'captivating hypocrisy'.

Stanhope's illegitimacy, which contributed to his father's ethic of competence and self-reliance, gave an extra twist to this guide to the art of success through pleasing, and to its first readers yet another shock. Chesterfield was discreet about his relationship to the boy, advising, if only to ensure a cordial reception, that he be introduced abroad as a nephew, but in the letters there was no disguising his promotion of Stanhope's claims to the highest offices of state. 'I dare not call him Father, nor he without shame own me as his Issue,' wrote a *Spectator* correspondent in 1711; attitudes had not changed enough by

1791 to prevent Boswell from saying of the letters that he could 'by no means approve of confounding the distinction between lawful and illicit offspring, which is, in effect, insulting the civil establishment of our country', although he also thought it 'laudable to be kindly attentive to those, of whose existence we have ... been the cause'.[16] The insult which Boswell detected was a dangerous one in 1791, for in the previous year the National Assembly in Paris had abolished hereditary titles and with them primogeniture, the aim being, in the words of Tom Paine's *The Rights of Man*, 'to exterminate the monster Aristocracy, root and branch'. No such aim could be expected of Chesterfield; nor, however, is there much evidence that he was tender of the sensibilities of people who thought as Boswell did. He was, to judge from his warmly adoptive relationships with younger men and his relentless pedagogic instincts, a man with a drive for fatherhood; yet he was also negligent of his aristocratic duty to produce an heir. Affairs with younger women whom he never thought of as potential spouses sustained him until the age of 39, when for gain and influence he married a woman of 40, herself the illegitimate daughter of George I. As a child, he had been ignored by his father and then deprived of estates which he, as the eldest son, should have inherited; in later life the warmth of his paternal affection was as evident as the strength of his contempt for those who took pride in their birth ('there are twenty fools in the House of Lords who could out-descend you in pedigree', he advised his heir). It was not, it seems, only the arrival of young Stanhope, or the subsequent setbacks his birth guaranteed would occur, which led Chesterfield to scorn the 'civil establishment of our country'; rather, a long-standing disregard for the root and branch of the aristocracy, and a scepticism about all institutional behaviour, made his son's very illegitimacy a tool to combat hypocrisy in the name of merit. With his sympathy for the villains of literature, for those, like Turnus in the *Aeneid*, opposed to the divinely ordained state of things, Chesterfield would no doubt have agreed with Shakespeare's Edmund that 'legitimacy' was an affront to those who might, but for the plague of custom, grow and prosper.

[16] Ibid. i. 159; *Spectator* no. 203 (23 Oct. 1711).

Custom was, however, a plague virulent enough to obstruct Stanhope's progress, his first application for an important diplomatic post meeting a curt refusal from the King: 'he is a bastard,' said George II. Nevertheless he rose to residencies at Hamburg and Dresden which made his diplomatic career, terminated by premature death at the age of 36, very far from the failure which some have called it. His political career was another matter: two brief periods as an MP, a maiden speech for connoisseurs of ineptitude to savour, and a failed attempt to buy a seat in the year of his death. He asked to be allowed to abandon politics in favour of diplomacy, but his father would not consent. Part of the problem was that the frustrations and compromised distinctions of Chesterfield's own career coloured, or tainted, the way he viewed his son's: anxious that Stanhope surpass his own achievements, he yet encouraged him in a spirit of bitter disillusionment. Chesterfield himself spent two-thirds of his political life in opposition to the divinely ordained state of things which Robert Walpole's twenty-year hold on power must often have seemed, while his years of success were not exemplary. His triumphs—as ambassador to The Hague and as Lord-Lieutenant of Ireland—were in appointments often given to deserving people whom the King or his senior ministers disliked too much to have close to home. His finest speeches were personal successes which augured no great changes of policy: his 'Patriot', libertarian opposition to Walpole's Theatre Licensing Act of 1737 failed to avert a measure which in his view threatened the entire liberty of the press; while his harmonious oration introducing the Calendar Bill of 1752 was a rational exercise for one who had already been four years in retirement. His term in high office as Secretary of State had lasted little more than a year because, ironically in view of his later reputation, he could not put up with the duplicity of his colleagues or flatter the King sufficiently to gain his own relatives preferment. The period in opposition of this sly, attentive courtier was lengthened by the fact that George II grew to hate him, and that partly because he had won the favour of a former royal mistress and married the King's half-sister, both designed to increase his influence. It is not therefore surprising that for all his defiant optimism about

Stanhope's future ('you may very probably come in time to be
Secretary of State'), for all his allusions to the heroic exploits of
Julius Caesar, the political viewpoint he imparts in the letters is
one of either contemptuous disagreement with current trends
or weary impatience with the whole system ('I have seen all the
coarse pullies and dirty ropes, which exhibit and move all the
gaudy machines'). Nor is it surprising that the two people
whom Chesterfield perhaps admired most, and whose works he
constantly urged his son to read, should have been for much of
their lives political exiles—Bolingbroke and Voltaire. Boswell
thought it a sign of Chesterfield's tenderness that he wrote so
many letters to his son as Secretary of State; but this was also
the time when his faith was weakest in the career to which he
was committing the boy. Soon after his resignation, it was the
bitter recollections of another unsuccessful politician, Cardinal
de Retz, which he recommended to Stanhope as 'the best
Memoirs that I know of'. His readings of history likewise
dwell on base motives—the jealousy of Luther, the grudges of
Caesar's assassins—which accord with the pessimism of his
favoured moralist, La Rochefoucauld. No wonder Stanhope
later expressed his wish to give up politics for diplomacy, given
the burdens of being, by birth and education, in opposition.

   To his father, part of the pity of Stanhope's failure was that it
occurred just when the principles on which his education was
founded had their best chance of success. In the 1760s there
were six different administrations, and Chesterfield saw in the
turmoil opportunities for the young and ambitious at the
expense of the old and discredited. The break-up of the Whig
Old Corps and the collapse of the Tories gave capable individuals the prospect of power irrespective of ideological
grouping, a situation which Chesterfield had favoured since the
1740s, and which sat easily with the virtues of unopinionated
toleration and personal aptitude preached by his letters. That
Stanhope could not take advantage of this change was due
partly to premature disillusionment, and more immediately to
the return of 'nabob' MPs from the Indies who, to Chesterfield's disgust, snapped up parliamentary seats at dramatically
inflated prices. The former Secretary of State duly wondered at
'the present state of this country', disclaiming any understand-

ing of a complex political scene in which his own talents might have flourished more effectively than they had done twenty years earlier, and contemplating with aptly variable degrees of irony the Ciceronian motto which was to recur to him through twenty-five years of retirement: *otium cum dignitate*, leisure with honour.

That retirement, wrote one biographer, Samuel Shellabarger, brought the best out of Chesterfield: 'all that was wise and just and refined in him progressively triumphed'. Appropriately, many readers and editors have been charmed by his letters as the expression of a consummately leisured, civilized world-view—an apt tribute to his widow's reasons for wishing to see them published, but, even supposing a consensus on the justice of the word 'civilized', too refined for the decades of business, ambition, and disaffection which pervade them. Never one to turn his gaze from the baser springs of human conduct, ever confident of the perfectibility of his pupils, Chesterfield himself might have preferred to view his letters in terms which increasingly command the interest of modern students of eighteenth-century literature: as a book of tough political self-fashioning, geared with remarkable range and prescience to the historical situation of the aristocracy, if not to the abilities and provenance of their addressee. Viewed in this light, the letters better justify the status accorded by the present edition, a broad selection which was made, fittingly, to reflect the extent both of Chesterfield's career and of his devotion to letter-writing. Diplomatic dispatches, political commentaries, and greetings to old friends sit alongside his incurably fond, intrusive, and arch letters to his son and godson, which in fact account for only one-seventh of his published epistolary output. The effect, paradoxically, is to show the depth of his obsession with Stanhope and his successor, reports of whose progress or failings appear often in his musings to friends over diplomatic or political developments. Just as a whole life of political and social training informed Chesterfield's educational principles, so his pupils in turn informed that life wholly.

NOTE ON THE TEXT

THE text of this edition has been reproduced from that of the 1929 World's Classics volume, which was prepared from Lord Mahon's edition, 5 vols. (1845–53). Occasional footnotes have been removed and typographical errors corrected. The text has been checked against that of the standard modern edition, by Bonamy Dobrée, 6 vols. (1932).

SELECT BIBLIOGRAPHY

PLACE of publication for books is London except as otherwise stated.

A guide to early editions of Chesterfield is S. L. Gulick, 'A Chesterfield Bibliography to 1800', *Publications of the Bibliographical Society of America*, 29 (1935); Gulick's 'The Publication of Lord Chesterfield's Letters to his Son', *Publications of the Modern Language Association*, 51 (1936), is an invaluable account of the first edition's complicated history.

Under the title of *The Art of Pleasing*, fourteen of Chesterfield's letters to his godson and heir appeared, before those to his son, in the *Edinburgh Magazine*, 1–2 (1774). *Letters to his Son Philip Stanhope* came out in 2 vols. in 1774, both in London and Dublin, and in 4 vols. later the same year. The most important early edition is *Miscellaneous Works*, ed. J. O. Justamond, 2 vols. (1777), and 3 vols. (Dublin, 1777), with intermittent notes and a memoir of Chesterfield by Matthew Maty, together with Chesterfield's pieces for the *World* on Johnson's Dictionary. This edition was enlarged in 1778 to include sixteen 'Characters of great personages' and the letters to George Faulkner, which in 1777 had been published separately as part of a collection of letters to some of his Irish acquaintance. A further *Miscellaneous Works* (3 vols.) appeared in 1778, including political tracts and poems, edited by B. Way. Important editions since then include *Letters*, ed. Lord Mahon, 5 vols. (1845–53); *Letters to his Godson and Successor*, ed. the Earl of Carnarvon (1890), which includes 44 letters to his godson's father, Arthur Stanhope; *Letters to his Son*, ed. Charles Strachey and Annette Calthrop, 2 vols. (1901), reissued in 1 vol. (1932); *Letters to Lord Huntingdon*, ed. A. F. Steuart (1923); *Letters to his Son and Others*, ed. R. K. Root for the Everyman library (1929, last reprinted in 1986); and the present selection by Phyllis M. Jones (Oxford, 1929). Chesterfield's correspondence with the Duke of Newcastle was edited by R. Lodge for the Camden Society in 1930. By far the most comprehensive edition is that of Bonamy Dobrée, 6 vols. (1932), which also contains a detailed survey of Chesterfield life. To Dobrée's 2629 letters S. L. Gulick, *Unpublished Letters of Lord Chesterfield* (Berkeley, Calif., 1937), added 26 more; a further five appear in C. Price's 'Five Unpublished Letters', *Life and Letters*, 59 (1948). The most recent additions to the field are a selection by J. Harding (1973) and a Bantam edition, *Dear Boy* (1989), introduced by Catherine Cookson, which prints snippets of Chesterfield's worldly wisdom in the best eighteenth-century manner. Of Chesterfield's other works, extracts from his speech against the

Theatre Licensing Act may be found in *Restoration and Georgian England, 1660–1788. Theatre in Europe: A Documentary History*, ed. David Thomas (Cambridge, 1989).

Among biographies of Chesterfield, Willard Connely's *The True Chesterfield* (1939) is the most detailed but also the most diffuse; Samuel Shellabarger's *Lord Chesterfield and his World* (Boston, 1951) is crisp but lacking in treatment of the godson; W. H. Craig's *Life of Chesterfield* (1907) is strong on political matters. Biographical articles include F. C. Nelick, 'Lord Chesterfield's Adoption of Philip Stanhope', *Philological Quarterly*, 38 (1959); Benjamin Boyce, 'Johnson and Chesterfield Once More', *Philological Quarterly*, 32 (1953); and Willard Connely's 'Chesterfield's Sons and Grandsons', *Times Literary Supplement*, 11 (Nov. 1939). Stanhope's education is examined in S. M. Brewer, *Design for a Gentleman* (1963) and A. P. Cappon, 'The Earl of Chesterfield as Educator', *University Review*, 31 (1965).

Useful accounts of the reception of Chesterfield's letters are Roger Coxon's *Chesterfield and his Critics* (1925), S. L. Gulick's *The Publication and Reception of Chesterfield's Letters to his Son* (Berkeley, Calif., 1933), and R. W. Nelson's 'The Reputation of Lord Chesterfield in Great Britain and America, 1730–1936' (Northwestern University Dissertation, 1938). His thought on various matters is helpfully discussed by V. Heltzel, *Chesterfield and the Tradition of the Ideal Gentleman* (1925) and 'Chesterfield and the Anti-Laughter Tradition', *Modern Philology*, 26 (1928); F. L. Lucas, in *Search for Good Sense* (1958); Melvyn R. Watson, 'Chesterfield and Decorum', *Modern Language Notes*, 62 (1947); J. Churton Collins, in *Essays and Studies* (1895); and J. H. Neumann, 'Chesterfield and the Standard of Usage in English', *Modern Language Quarterly*, 7 (1946).

Among recent work on eighteenth-century society and politics, the following are especially useful in understanding and appreciating Chesterfield: Paul Langford, *A Polite and Commercial People* (Oxford, 1989) and *The Excise Crisis* (Oxford, 1975); John Cannon, *Aristocratic Century* (Cambridge, 1984); Jeremy Black, *The British and the Grand Tour* (Beckenham, 1985); and Roy Porter, *English Society in the Eighteenth Century* (1982). Chesterfield's viceroyalty in Ireland is viewed harshly by Bruce P. Lenman, 'Scotland and Ireland 1742–1789', in Jeremy Black (ed.), *British Politics and Society from Walpole to Pitt 1742–1789* (Basingstoke, 1990). Narratives of the political events recorded in the letters may be found in Basil Williams, *The Whig Supremacy* (Oxford, 1939), and Keith Perry, *British Politics and the American Revolution* (Basingstoke, 1990).

A CHRONOLOGY OF
LORD CHESTERFIELD

1694   Born 22 Sept., son of Philip Stanhope, 3rd Earl of Chesterfield, and Elizabeth Savile, daughter of the Marquis of Halifax. Educated under the guidance of his maternal grandmother.

1713   Enters Trinity Hall, Cambridge.

1714   Leaves Cambridge to tour Flanders, where he meets the Duke and Duchess of Marlborough.

1715   Made Gentleman of the Bedchamber to George, Prince of Wales, and Whig MP for St Germans, Cornwall, before his 21st birthday. His maiden speech denounces all supporters of the Treaty of Utrecht as traitors; advised that his election as a minor might be called into question, he flees to Paris.

1717   Returns to London, becoming friendly with Pope, Arbuthnot, and the Prince of Wales's mistress, Henrietta Howard, which makes him the enemy of the Prince's wife, Caroline.

1722   MP for Lostwithiel, supporting the King's interest in a motion to increase the size of the army.

1723   Made Captain of the gentlemen-pensioners, but loses his seat in the Commons.

1725   Refuses Walpole's offer of a Knighthood of the Bath, openly criticizing those who accepted, including his brother William. Walpole then strips him of the Captaincy of the gentlemen-pensioners, initiating his period in opposition.

1726   Succeeds to his father's title on 27 Jan.

1727   After George I's death, Chesterfield moves the Lords' address of condolence and congratulation to George II, and becomes Lord of the Bedchamber.

1728   Nominated Privy Councillor and ambassador to The Hague, where he gains the confidence of the Dutch ministers by his discretion, efficiency, and hospitality.

1730   Elected Knight of the Garter and made Lord Steward of the Household.

1731   Signs the Second Treaty of Vienna in The Hague, promising Britain's support for the accession of Maria Theresa to the Austrian throne.

1732   Resigns from the embassy because of ill-health. A governess,
        Elizabeth du Bouchet, gives birth to his son, Philip Stanhope.

1733   Organizes opposition to Walpole's excise bill, for which he is
        dismissed as Lord Steward, putting an end to his friendship
        with George II. Marries the King's half-sister, Petronilla von
        der Schullenberg, and begins keeping a mistress, Fanny Shir-
        ley.

1734   Writes for *Fog's Journal* against Walpole.

1737   Speech against Walpole's Theatre Licensing Act. Begins his
        correspondence with Philip Stanhope.

1741   Signs Carteret's unsuccessful petition for Walpole's dismissal,
        travelling to the Continent for seven months and visiting
        Bolingbroke and others.

1742   Declares himself still in opposition after Walpole's fall, arguing
        against Carteret's pro-Hanoverian policies.

1744   Appointed ambassador-extraordinary to The Hague to per-
        suade the Dutch to join the War of the Austrian Succession.

1745   Travels to Dublin as the new Lord-Lieutenant of Ireland.

1746   Appointed Secretary of State for the Northern Department.

1747   Approached by Johnson with the plan of his Dictionary.
        Stanhope begins his travels on the Continent.

1748   Resigns on 6 Feb. after disagreements with Newcastle over the
        conduct of the war. Acquires his late brother's house in
        Blackheath.

1751   Proposes and carries the reform of the calendar. Stanhope
        employed in the British embassy in Paris, and visits Chester-
        field for four months.

1753   Begins writing for the *World*, his two pieces on Johnson's
        Dictionary appearing the following year.

1754   Stanhope (then 22) elected MP for Liskeard.

1755   Last speech in the Lords, denouncing subsidy treaties with the
        German states. Receives Johnson's letter about the Dictionary.
        Elected to the Academy of Inscriptions in Paris. His godson
        and heir, another Philip Stanhope, born. Stanhope's disastrous
        maiden speech.

1756   Stanhope made HM Resident at Hamburg.

1757   Reconciles Pitt to Newcastle, initiating the ministry which
        brought success in the Seven Years War.

1761 Stanhope elected MP for St Germans. Chesterfield begins the correspondence with his godson and heir.

1763 Stanhope made envoy at Ratisbon.

1764 Stanhope made HM Resident at Dresden.

1768 Death of Stanhope in Avignon, on leave for ill-health.

1772 Chesterfield's health breaks down and he leaves Blackheath to be near his physician.

1773 Death of Chesterfield on 24 March.

1. TO LORD TOWNSHEND*

SECRETARY OF STATE

Private

HAGUE, AUGUST 31, N.S. 1728

MY LORD,

I cannot omit returning your Lordship my thanks for the honour of your letter *apart*, of the 13th August, O.S It gave me the utmost satisfaction to see the very friendly manner in which your Lordship not only forgave, but even approved, the liberty I had taken, and flatters me with the continuance of your friendship and protection, which I shall always be equally solicitous to deserve and proud to obtain. It is upon this friendship that I rely when I venture to make, and persuade myself your Lordship will (at least) pardon, the following request. By the death of the Duke of York* there are now two Garters vacant, that probably will not long remain so, and your Lordship knows by the former applications I have troubled you with on that score, how desirous and ambitious I am of that honour. Your Lordship knows too, that, though it is at all times a mark of honour and his Majesty's favour, yet it can never be of so much (or indeed of any real) use to me, as now, that I have the honour to be in the station I am in. In the first place, the thing itself is much more considered abroad than in England; in the second place, such a mark of favour is much more necessary for those who have the honour of being employed abroad, than for those who have the advantage of being at home; and I am sure every body will agree that I can never have it so advantageously for myself, (especially

in this country) as at a time when it must be known to
be entirely owing to your Lordship's friendship and
recommendation. It may possibly be owning a great
weakness when I confess to your Lordship that I
would rather have this one mark of his Majesty's and
your favour than any one other thing that your Lordship can recommend to, or the King dispose of; but
at the same time I hope it may in some measure excuse
the great earnestness with which I beg leave to recommend this request to your protection, which, if it is
possible any thing can, will add to the obligations I
already have to your Lordship, and to the very great
respect with which I have the honour to be, etc.

2. TO LORD TOWNSHEND

Private

HAGUE, NOVEMBER 30, N.S., 1728

MY LORD,

I trouble your Lordship with this letter *apart*, to inform you of the contents of a letter the Pensionary
received about a week ago from General Keppell, and
which he communicated to me in the utmost confidence.* Mr. Keppell tells him that the Queen of Prussia,
upon receiving the Queen of England's letter (of which
your Lordship sent me a copy), was 'in such joy, that
she immediately communicated it to him, together
with all the steps that had been taken in that affair;
that she had told him she was persuaded it would not
only bring back the King to a right way of thinking,
but even make him continue firm in it. He adds the
greatest commendations imaginable of that Princess,
and speaks of the match as a thing that he expects will
be attended with the best consequences.*

After having talked over this affair with the Pensionary, he asked me whether what he had seen in the newspapers was true, that the Prince of Orange was to have one of the vacant Garters.* I told him I knew nothing of it, but that I thought it seemed natural enough, considering the regard the King had for that name and family, and that there had hardly ever been a Prince of Orange without it. He said that was very true, if people would but consider it rightly, but that he doubted they would draw other consequences from it, which might have an ill effect; that his coming here (which by the way is put off till Christmas, upon the account of the ill news of his Governor)* had already given an alarm which would be very much increased, if it were accompanied with that mark of the King's favour and distinction; that in the present situation of this Republic he did not know which was the most dangerous, to have a Stadtholder or not; that if the Stadtholder had not power sufficient to reform the abuses the Republic groaned under, he would be useless, and that if he had he might commit as many of his own. He concluded with saying that this was not a time to determine either way. Notwithstanding the confidence I live in with the Pensionary, I have always avoided any conversation with him upon the affair of the Stadtholder; being firmly convinced that he will be against one while there is any possibility of carrying on the Government without one; and he had never spoke to me so much on that subject as in this conversation; however, I avoided entering into it upon this occasion by saying that I was not enough informed of the nature of this Government to be able to judge whether a Stadtholder would prove advantageous or prejudicial to it, but that I was persuaded if the Prince of Orange had the Garter it was without any further view, and only as a mark of the consideration the King had for him and his family.

After this I went to M. de Linden*and told him part of the conversation that had passed between the Pensionary and myself about the Prince's having the Garter, and asked his opinion upon it. He said he thought it highly improper that the Prince should have it, till other things were ready to go along with it; that he was sure it would give an unnecessary alarm, which might prove prejudicial to some things which are now secretly transacting in favour of that Prince here; and which I will inform your lordship of more fully hereafter.

M. de Linden is the only person here to whom I ever speak upon this subject; he is both an honest and an able man, has the same fondness for the Prince that he could have were he his own son; and as he has the utmost confidence in me, and informs me of every step that is taken in that Prince's affairs, I can with great safety open myself to him whenever occasion shall require it.

I hope your Lordship will do me the justice to believe that I have no view of my own in submitting these considerations to your judgment. I shall neither have the Garter the more nor the less, the sooner nor the later, for the Prince of Orange's having it or not; but I thought myself obliged for his sake to lay this matter before your Lordship, that you may act in it as you think proper. I own I have his interest a good deal at heart, and hope not to be altogether useless to him during my stay here.

Your Lordship will give me leave to take this opportunity of recommending myself again to your friendship and protection in an affair which I believe is yet pretty remote, but which probably will happen, which is this: If when the match shall be agreed upon between Prince Frederick and the Princess Royal of Prussia, an Ambassador is to be sent to Berlin upon that extraordinary occasion, that your Lordship will be so good as to recommend me to his Majesty's consideration upon that account, for which I ask no extraordinaries nor additional allowance; so that it will be a considerable saving to the King. I would not be mistaken and be thought to desire to quit this place, but as I take it for granted such a commission would be very short, it would require very little absence from hence.

After so long a letter I will not trouble your Lordship with any professions of my gratitude for the past marks of your friendship, nor of my endeavours to deserve the continuance of it; I will only assure you that it is impossible to be with greater truth and respect

Your Lordship's, etc.

3. TO LORD TOWNSHEND
Very Private

HAGUE, DECEMBER 14, N.S., 1728

MY LORD,

I cannot express how sensible I am of His Majesty's great goodness and the confidence he is pleased to show he has in me, by not only entrusting me with, but even employing me in, an affair of such secrecy and importance as that contained in your Lordship's very private letter of the 29th November, o.s., which I have just now received. I wish I were as able as I am desirous to execute his Majesty's commands to his satisfaction; but, sensible of my own inabilities, I must beg that his

Majesty's indulgence will in favour of my known zeal for his service, excuse what may be wanting on my part, in the means of pursuing it.

I must more particularly beg your Lordship to solicit his Majesty's indulgence towards me upon this occasion, since I take the liberty of delaying to obey his Majesty's commands till I have first laid before your Lordship my reasons for so doing; and till I have received further instructions upon them.

I must inform your Lordship then, in the first place, that I believe it is possible that some things might be communicated to the Pensionary in confidence, which he would not tell the Greffier;* but I am firmly persuaded there is no one thing in the world that could be communicated to the Greffier that he would not immediately tell the Pensionary; and therefore I submit it to your Lordship whether such a distinguished confidence in the one would not very much exasperate the other, when he should come to know it, which he certainly would immediately. The Pensionary is extremely averse to the thoughts of that match already, and I doubt this would make him much more so. In talking to me some time ago upon that subject, he told me he would much rather see the match made between Don Carlos and the Arch-Duchess, than between the Princess Royal and the Prince of Orange.* I must observe to your Lordship too, that the sentiments of the Pensionary and Greffier upon the affair of the Stadtholder are extremely changed since your Lordship has seen them; when they inclined to a Stadtholder, Mr. Slingelandt was then but Treasurer, and was opposed and thwarted by the then Pensionary in almost everything; but now that Mr. Slingelandt is Pensionary, and Messrs. Vander Haym and Teinhoven*

(both relations and creatures of the Greffier's) Treasurer
and Secretary of State, the Pensionary and Greffier
have the whole management of affairs in their own
hands, and think they may lose, but cannot get, by
a Stadtholder, and consequently, while they can possibly carry on affairs without one, will, in my opinion,
be as much against one, as any two people in the
Republic. Should this opinion of mine be true, as I
have a good deal of reason to believe it is, if I had communicated this affair to the Greffier, I am persuaded he
would have given me no answer till he had first consulted the Pensionary upon it; and I am equally persuaded that they would both have done their utmost
endeavours to prevent it; that match being considered
by everybody, and with reason, as the sure forerunner
of the Stadtholdership.

Your Lordship will now give me leave to acquaint
you with what passed a month ago between M. de
Linden and myself, in conversation upon this subject.
I asked M. de Linden when he thought there was any
prospect of the Prince of Orange's being Stadtholder
of the Province of Holland? He told me certainly not
of two years at soonest; that it could not be attempted
till he had taken his place in the Council of State as
Stadtholder of Gueldres, which he could not do till
next September, not being of age for that Province till
then.* I then asked him, whether in case a marriage that
had been talked of for that Prince should take place,
it would promote or obstruct his arriving at that
dignity? He said it would certainly promote it; and
indeed I think it is pretty clear that it will, from the
dread that all the Anti-Stadtholder party have of that
match; which would undoubtedly give spirit and
vigour to all the Prince's friends, and extremely deject

the opposite party. He told me afterwards in the utmost secrecy, that there was now a design carrying on of getting that Prince chosen Stadtholder of another Province; which would give him a majority of the Seven Provinces, and extremely facilitate his election in this; that the stroke was to be struck in March next; but that the whole depended upon the secrecy of the affair, and upon a little money properly distributed. Upon which I gave him some hopes, but no promises, that they might meet with some assistance from England as to the last particular. By all that I have been able to observe here, and I have omitted no opportunity of informing myself upon that subject, I think there is no reason to doubt but that that Prince will inevitably be one day Stadtholder of this Province; but how soon, I believe it is impossible for anybody to guess. The Army are nine in ten for him, and the common people unanimously so; his greatest enemies are the town of Amsterdam and the chief Burgomasters of the other towns, whose oppressions, rapines and extortions are now grown so flagrant and grievous, and daily increase so much, that they must, before it is very long, reduce the honest and thinking part of the Republic to fly to a Stadtholder as the only remedy. Or should that fail, the common people themselves, who groan under the oppressions and abuses of the magistrates, will by a general insurrection, impose one upon them. I know that a person in the Government has written to Sir Matthew Decker to acquaint him, that should any steps be taken in favour of the Prince of Orange, that the town of Amsterdam, together with the Nobles and eleven other towns of this Province, would immediately declare the Prince of Nassau-Seigen Stadtholder; and possibly Sir Matthew may have acquainted your Lordship with this; but you need have no apprehensions of it, for I know it to be a poor artifice of Mr. Buys to deter the Prince of Orange's party from stirring in his favour, and it was wrote into England in the same view.*

After having said all this, I don't know whether I may take the liberty of offering most humbly my poor opinion upon this affair; but I am persuaded that however erroneous it may be, your Lordship will at least do me the justice to believe it meant for his Majesty's service.

I should think therefore that if his Majesty is determined to give the Princess Royal to the Prince of Orange, it had better be communicated jointly to the Pensionary and Greffier, as a thing determined, than proposed to them as a thing doubtful; for upon the supposition I go upon, that they will both be extremely averse to it, they will be less offended if it be done without, than against, their consent. I submit it likewise to your Lordship, whether anything of the Stadtholdership should be mentioned to them or no; for I am sure it will startle them extremely, and whether it is mentioned or no, it will undoubtedly be sooner or later the necessary consequence of the match.

I ask a thousand pardons for presuming to communicate my poor thoughts upon this subject, and still more for not immediately executing his Majesty's orders; but I thought it my duty in an affair of this very great importance, to suggest to your Lordship's consideration everything that could occur to me; hoping that the little delay of this messenger's going and coming can be of no great consequence. I am sure it is impossible for anybody to have anything more at heart than I have the success of this affair, and however mistaken I may be now, I am sure of being set right by his Majesty's further orders, which I shall have from your Lordship by the return of this messenger.

I am, with the greatest truth.

4. TO GEO. TILSON,* ESQ.

Private

HAGUE, DECEMBER 12, N.S., 1730

SIR,

I beg you will acquaint Lord Harrington that I don't answer his last letter *apart* in expectation of his next, that I may give him but one trouble.

I am sorry the answer from the court of Vienna is not satisfactory at first, for I am persuaded it will be so at last, but it is asking too much of the Emperor to ask him to do what none of his family ever could do, *agir de bonne grace.* For my own part I see no other way of getting out of this scrape. I think it is pretty plain France will not help us out of it, at least, without drawing us into a worse. Monsieur Fénelon takes immense pains to persuade the people here of *la droiture scrupuleuse*, as he calls it, of his Court, but to very little purpose. I know 'tis a bold word, but I really think him the silliest Minister in Europe.*

The King of Prussia in the oath he prepared for the Prince to swallow, among many other things, has made him swear that he will never believe the doctrine of Predestination!* A very unnecessary declaration in my mind for any body who has the misfortune of being acquainted with him to make, since he himself is a living proof of free-will, for Providence can never be supposed to have pre-ordained such a creature!

I find I shall have the pleasure of seeing you soon in

England. Without pretending to be fatigued with business, I have had enough on't to desire no more, and to be very glad to be quiet in St. James's Square,* where I shall always have a pleasure in assuring you that I am with real esteem, etc.

5. TO DEAN SWIFT

HAGUE, DECEMBER 15, N.S., 1730

SIR,

You need not have made any excuse to me for your solicitation; on the contrary, I am proud of being the first person, to whom you have thought it worth the while to apply since those changes, which, you say, drove you into distance and obscurity. I very well know the person you recommend to me, having lodged at his house a whole summer at Richmond.* I have always heard a very good character of him, which alone would incline me to serve him; but your recommendation, I can assure you, will make me impatient to do it. However, that he may not again meet with the common fate of Court-suitors, nor I lie under the imputation of making Court-promises, I will exactly explain to you how far it is likely I may be able to serve him.

When first I had this office, I took the resolution of turning out nobody; so that I shall only have the disposal of those places that the death of the present possessors will procure me. Some old servants, that have served me long and faithfully, have obtained the promises of the first four or five vacancies; and the early solicitations of some of my particular friends have tied me down for about as many more. But, after having satisfied these engagements, I do assure you,

Mr. Launcelot shall be my first care. I confess, his prospect is more remote than I could have wished it; but, as it is so remote, he will not have the uneasiness of a disappointment, if he gets nothing; and if he gets something we shall both be pleased.

As for his political principles, I am in no manner of pain about them. Were he a Tory, I would venture to serve him, in the just expectation that, should I ever be charged with having preferred a Tory, the person, who was the author of my crime, would likewise be the author of my vindication.

I am, with real esteem, etc.

6. TO HIS SON

24TH JULY, 1739

MY DEAR BOY:

I was pleased with your asking me, the last time I saw you, why I had left off writing; for I looked upon it as a sign that you liked and minded my letters. If that be the case, you shall hear from me often enough; and my letters may be of use, if you will give attention to them; otherwise it is only giving myself trouble to no purpose; for it signifies nothing to read a thing once, if one does not mind and remember it. It is a sure sign of a little mind to be doing one thing, and at the same time to be either thinking of another, or not thinking at all. One should always think of what one is about; when one is learning, one should not think of play; and when one is at play, one should not think of one's learning. Besides that, if you do not mind your book while you are at it, it will be a double trouble to you, for you must learn it all over again.

One of the most important points of life is Decency;

which is to do what is proper, and where it is proper; for many things are proper at one time, and in one place, that are extremely improper in another; for example, it is very proper and decent that you should play some part of the day; but you must feel that it would be very improper and indecent, if you were to fly your kite, or play at ninepins, while you are with Mr. Maittaire. It is very proper and decent to dance well; but then you must dance only at balls, and places of entertainment; for you would be reckoned a fool, if you were to dance at church, or at a funeral. I hope, by these examples, you understand the meaning of the word *Decency*; which in French is *Bienséance*; in Latin *Decorum*; and in Greek Πρεπον. Cicero says of it, *Sic hoc Decorum, quod elucit in vitâ, movet approbationem eorum quibuscum vivitur, ordine et constantiâ et moderatione dictorum omnium atque factorum.* By which you see how necessary Decency is, to gain the approbation of mankind. And, as I am sure you desire to gain Mr. Mattaire's* approbation, without which you will never have mine; I dare say you will mind and give attention to whatever he says to you, and behave yourself seriously and decently, while you are with him; afterwards play, run, and jump, as much as ever you please.

7. TO HIS SON

NOVEMBER 20, 1739

DEAR BOY:

As you are now reading the Roman History, I hope
you do it with that care and attention which it deserves.
The utility of History consists principally in the examples it gives us of the virtues and vices of those who
have gone before us; upon which we ought to make
the proper observations. History animates and excites
us to the love and the practice of virtue; by showing us
the regard and veneration that was always paid to great
and virtuous men in the times in which they lived, and
the praise and glory with which their names are per-
petuated and transmitted down to our times. The
Roman History furnishes more examples of virtue and
magnanimity, or greatness of mind, than any other.
It was a common thing to see their Consuls and Dic-
tators (who, you know, were their chief Magistrates)
taken from the plough, to lead their armies against
their enemies; and, after victory, returning to their
plough again, and passing the rest of their lives in
modest retirement; a retirement more glorious, if possible, than the victories that preceded it! Many of their
greatest men died so poor, that they were buried at the
expence of the publick.

Curius, who had no money of his own, refused a
great sum that the Samnites offered him, saying,
that he saw no glory in having money himself, but
in commanding those that had. Cicero relates it thus:
*Curio ad focum sedenti magnum auri pondus Samnites
cum attulissent, repudiati ab eo sunt. Non enim aurum
habere praeclarum sibi videri, sed iis, qui haberent aurum,
imperare.*[*] And Fabricius, who had often commanded

the Roman armies, and as often triumphed over their enemies, was found by his fireside, eating those roots and herbs which he had planted and cultivated himself in his own field. Seneca tells it thus: *Fabricius ad focum coenat illas ipsas radices, quas, in agro repurgando, triumphalis Senex vulsit.* Scipio, after a victory he had obtained in Spain, found among the prisoners a young Princess of extreme beauty, who, he was informed, was soon to have been married to a man of quality of that country. He ordered her to be entertained and attended with the same care and respect as if she had been in her father's house; and, as soon as he could find her lover, he gave her to him, and added to her portion the money that her father had brought for her ransom. Valerius Maximus says, *Eximiae formae virginem accersitis parentibus, et sponso inviolatam tradidit, et Iuvenis, et Coelebs, et Victor.* This was a most glorious example of moderation, continence, and generosity, which gained him the hearts of all the people of Spain; and made them say, as Livy tells us, *Venisse Diis simillimum iuvenem, vincentem omnia, tum armis, tum benignitate, ac beneficiis.*

Such are the rewards that always crown virtue; and such the characters that you should imitate, if you would be a great and a good man, which is the only way to be a happy one! Adieu!

8. TO HIS SON

DEAR BOY, THURSDAY

You will seldom hear from me without an admonition to think. All you learn, and all you can read, will be of little use, if you do not think and reason upon it yourself. One reads to know other people's thoughts; but if we take them upon trust, without examining and comparing them with our own, it is really living upon other people's scraps, or retailing other people's goods. To know the thoughts of others is of use, because it suggests thoughts to one's self, and helps one to form a judgment; but to repeat other people's thoughts, without considering whether they are right or wrong, is the talent only of a parrot, or at most a player.

If *Night* were given you as a subject to compose upon, you would do very well to look what the best authors have said upon it, in order to help your own invention; but then you must think of it afterwards yourself, and express it in your own manner, or else you would be at best but a plagiary. A plagiary is a man who steals other people's thoughts, and puts them off for his own. You will find, for example, the following account of Night in Virgil:

> Nox erat, et placidum carpebant fessa soporem
> Corpora per terras; sylvaeque et saeva quierant
> Aequora: cum medio volvuntur sidera lapsu;
> Cum tacet omnis ager, pecudes, pictaeque volucres,
> Quaeque lacus late liquidos, quaeque aspera dumis
> Rura tenent, somno positae sub nocte silenti,
> Lenibant curas, et corda oblita laborum.*

Here you see the effects of Night: that it brings rest to men when they are wearied with the labours of the day; that the stars move in their regular course; that flocks and birds repose themselves, and enjoy the quiet of the Night. This, upon examination, you would find to be all true; but then, upon consideration too, you would find, that it is not all that is to be said upon Night; and many more qualities and effects of Night would occur to you. As, for instance, though Night is in general the time of quiet and repose, yet it is often the time too for the commission and security of crimes, such as robberies, murders and violations which generally seek the advantage of darkness, as favourable for the escape of the guilty. Night too, though it brings rest and refreshment to the innocent and virtuous, brings disquiet and horror to the guilty. The consciousness of their crimes torments them, and denies them sleep and quiet. You might, from these reflections, consider what would be the proper epithets to give to Night; as for example, if you were to represent Night in its most pleasing shape, as procuring quiet and refreshment from labour and toil, you might call it the *friendly* Night, the *silent* Night, the *welcome* Night, the *peaceful* Night: but if, on the contrary, you were to represent it as inviting to the commission of crimes, you would call it the *guilty* Night, the *conscious* Night, the *horrid* Night; with many other epithets, that carry along with them the idea of horror and guilt: for an epithet to be proper must always be adapted (that is, suited) to the circumstances of the person or thing to which it is given. Thus Virgil, who generally gives Eneas the epithet of Pious, because of his piety to the Gods, and his duty to his father, calls him *Dux* Eneas, where he represents him making love to Dido, as a proper epithet for him in that situation; because making love becomes a General much better than a man of singular piety.

Lay aside, for a few minutes, the thoughts of play, and think of this seriously.

Amoto quaeramus seria ludo.*

Adieu!

You may come to me on Saturday morning, before you go to Mr. Maittaire.

9. TO HIS SON

DEAR BOY:

I have often told you in my former letters (and it is most certainly true), that the strictest and most scrupulous honour and virtue can alone make you esteemed and valued by mankind; that parts and learning can alone make you admired and celebrated by them; but that the possession of lesser talents was most absolutely necessary towards making you liked, beloved, and sought after in private life. Of these lesser talents, good-breeding is the principal and most necessary one, not only as it is very important in itself; but as it adds great lustre to the more solid advantages both of the heart and the mind. I have often touched upon good-breeding to you before; so that this letter shall be upon the next necessary qualification to it, which is a genteel easy manner, and carriage, wholly free from those old tricks, ill habits, and awkwardnesses, which even many very worthy and sensible people have in their behaviour. However trifling a genteel manner may sound, it is of very great consequence towards pleasing in private life, especially the women, whom, one time or other, you will think worth pleasing; and I have known many a man, from his awkwardness, give people such a dislike of him at first, that all his merit could not get the better of it afterwards. Whereas a genteel manner prepossesses people in your favour, bends them towards you, and makes them wish to like you.

Awkwardness can proceed but from two causes; either from not having kept good company, or from not having attended to it. As for your keeping good

company, I will take care of that; do you take care to
observe their ways and manners, and to form your own
upon them. Attention is absolutely necessary for this,
as indeed it is for every thing else; and a man without
attention is not fit to live in the world. When an awkward fellow first comes into a room, it is highly probable that his sword gets between his legs, and throws
him down, or makes him stumble, at least; when he
has recovered this accident, he goes and places himself
in the very place of the whole room where he should
not; there he soon lets his hat fall down, and, in taking
it up again, throws down his cane; in recovering his
cane, his hat falls a second time, so that he is a quarter
of an hour before he is in order again. If he drinks tea
or coffee, he certainly scalds his mouth, and lets either
the cup or the saucer fall, and spills either the tea or
coffee in his breeches. At dinner, his awkwardness distinguishes itself particularly, as he has more to do;
there he holds his knife, fork, and spoon differently
from other people, eats with his knife, to the great
danger of his mouth, picks his teeth with his fork, and
puts his spoon, which has been in his throat twenty
times, into the dishes again. If he is to carve, he can
never hit the joint; but, in his vain efforts to cut
through the bone, scatters the sauce in every body's
face. He generally daubs himself with soup and grease,
though his napkin is commonly stuck through a but-
ton-hole, and tickles his chin. When he drinks, he
infallibly coughs in his glass, and besprinkles the company. Besides all this, he has strange tricks and gestures; such as snuffing up his nose, making faces,
putting his fingers in his nose, or blowing it and looking afterwards in his handkerchief, so as to make the
company sick. His hands are troublesome to him,

when he has not something in them, and he does not know where to put them; but they are in perpetual motion between his bosom and his breeches: he does not wear his clothes, and in short does nothing like other people. All this, I own, is not in any degree criminal; but it is highly disagreeable and ridiculous in company, and ought most carefully to be avoided, by whoever desires to please.

From this account of what you should not do, you may easily judge what you should do; and a due attention to the manners of people of fashion, and who have seen the world, will make it habitual and familiar to you.

There is, likewise, an awkwardness of expression and words, most carefully to be avoided; such as false English, bad pronunciation, old sayings, and common proverbs; which are so many proofs of having kept bad and low company. For example, if, instead of saying that tastes are different, and that every man has his own peculiar one, you should let off a proverb, and say, That what is one man's meat is another man's poison: or else, Every one as they like, as the good man said when he kissed his cow; everybody would be persuaded that you had never kept company with any body above footmen and housemaids.

Attention will do all this, and without attention nothing is to be done; want of attention, which is really want of thought, is either folly or madness. You should not only have attention to everything, but a quickness of attention, so as to observe, at once, all the people in the room, their motions, their looks, and their words, and yet without staring at them, and seeming to be an observer. This quick and unobserved observation is of infinite advantage in life, and is to be acquired with care; and, on the contrary, what is called absence, which is a thoughtlessness, and want of attention about what is doing, makes a man so like either a fool or a madman, that, for my part, I see no real difference. A fool never has thought; a madman has lost it; and an absent man is, for the time, without it.

Adieu! Direct your next to me, *chez Monsieur Chabert, Banquier, à Paris*; and take care that I find the improvements I expect at my return.

10. TO G. BUBB DODINGTON,* ESQ.

SPA, SEPTEMBER 8, 1741

SIR,

Having at last found a safe way of sending you this letter, I shall, without the least reserve, give you my thoughts upon the contents of yours of the 30th of May, o.s.

By the best judgment I can form of the list of this present Parliament, and I have examined it very carefully, we appear to be so strong, that I think we can but just be called the minority; and I am very sure that such a minority, well united and well conducted, might soon be a majority. But,

Hoc opus hic labor est.*

It will neither be united nor well conducted. Those who should lead it will make it their business to break and divide it; and they will succeed; I mean Carteret and Pulteney.* Their behaviour for these few years has, in my mind, plainly shown their views and their negotiations with the Court: but, surely, their conduct at the end of last Session puts that matter out of all dispute. They feared even the success of that minority, and took care to render it as insignificant as possible. Will they then not be much more apprehensive of the success of this: and will not both their merit and their reward be much the greater for defeating it? If you tell me that they ought rather to avail themselves of these numbers, and, at the head of them, force their way where they are so impatient to go, I will agree with you, that in prudence they ought; but the fact is, they reason quite differently, desire to get in with a few, by negotiation, and not by victory with numbers, who, they fear, might presume upon their strength, and grow troublesome to their generals.

On the other hand, Sir Robert must be alarmed at our numbers, and must resolve to reduce them before they are brought into the field. He knows by experience where and how to apply for that purpose; with this difference only, that the numbers will have raised the price, which he must come up to. And this is all the fruit I expect from this strong minority. You will possibly ask me, whether all this is in the power of Carteret and Pulteney? I answer, yes—in the power of Pulteney alone. He has a personal influence over many, and an interested influence over more. The silly, half-witted, zealous Whigs consider him as the only support of Whigism; and look upon us as running headlong into Bolingbroke and the Tories. The interested Whigs, as Sandys, Rushout and Gibbon,* with many others, are as impatient to come into Court as he can be; and, persuaded that he has opened that door a little, will hold fast by him to squeeze in with him, and think they can justify their conduct to the public, by following their old leader, under the colours (though false ones) of Whigism.

What then, is nothing to be done? Are we to give

it up tamely, when the prospect seems so fair? No; I am for acting, let our numbers be what they will. I am for discriminating, and making people speak out; though our numbers should, as I am convinced they will, lessen considerably by it. Let what will happen, we cannot be in a worse situation than that we have been in for these last three or four years. Nay, I am for acting at the very beginning of the Session, and bringing our numbers the first week; and points for that purpose, I am sure, are not wanting. Some occur to me now, many more will, I dare say, occur to others; and many will, by that time, present themselves.

For example, the Court generally proposes some servile and shameless tool of theirs to be Chairman of the Committee of Privileges and Elections.* Why should not we, therefore, pick out some Whig of a fair character, and with personal connections, to set up in opposition? I think we should be pretty strong upon this point. But as for opposition to their Speaker, if if be Onslow, we shall be but weak; he having, by a certain decency of behaviour, made himself many personal friends in the minority. The affair of Carthagena* will of course be mentioned; and there, in my opinion, a question, and a trying one too, of censure, lies very fair, that the delaying of that expedition so late last year was the principal cause of our disappointment. An Address to the King, desiring him to make no peace with Spain, unless our undoubted right of navigation in the West Indies, without molestation or search, be clearly, and in express words, stipulated; and till we have acquired some valuable possession there, as a pledge of the performance of such stipulation: such a question would surely be a popular one, and distressful enough to the Ministry.

I entirely agree with you, that we ought to have meetings to concert measures some time before the meeting of the Parliament; but that, I likewise know, will not happen. I have been these seven years endeavouring to bring it about, and have not been able; fox-hunting, gardening, planting, or indifference having always kept our people in the country, till the very day before the meeting of the Parliament. Besides, would it be easy to settle who should be at those meetings? If Pulteney and his people were to be chose, it would only be informing them beforehand, what they should either oppose or defeat; and if they were not there, their own exclusion would in some degree justify, or at least colour, their conduct. As to our most flagitious House, I believe you agree there is nothing to be done in it; and for such a minority to struggle with such a majority, would be much like the late King of Sweden's attacking the Ottoman army at Bender,* at the head of his cook and his butler.

These are difficulties, the insurmountable difficulties, that I foresee; and which make me absolutely despair of seeing any good done. However, I am entirely at the service of you and the rest of my friends who mean the public good. I will either fight or run away, as you shall determine. If the Duke of Argyle* sounds to battle, I will follow my leader; if he stays in Oxfordshire, I'll stay in Grosvenor Square. I think it is all one which we do as to our House; yours must be the scene of action, if action there be; and action, I think, there should be, at least for a time, let your numbers be what you will.

I leave this place to-morrow, and set out for France; a country which, in my conscience, I think as free as our own: they have not the form of freedom, as we

have. I know no other difference. I shall pass a couple
of months in rambling through the Southern Provinces,
and then return to England, to receive what commands
you may leave for, etc.

11. TO HIS SON

BATH, JUNE 28, 1742

DEAR BOY,

Your promises give me great pleasure; and your performance of them, which I rely upon, will give me still
greater. I am sure you know that breaking of your
word is a folly, a dishonour, and a crime. It is a folly,
because nobody will trust you afterwards; and it is
both a dishonour and a crime, truth being the first duty
of religion and morality; and whoever has not truth,
cannot be supposed to have any one good quality, and
must become the detestation of God and man. Therefore I expect, from your truth and your honour, that
you will do that, which, independently of your promise, your own interest and ambition ought to incline
you to do; that is to excel in every thing you undertake.
When I was of your age, I should have been ashamed if
any boy of that age had learned his book better, or
played at any play better than I did; and I would not
have rested a moment till I had got before him. Julius
Caesar, who had a noble thirst of glory, used to say, that
he would rather be the first in a village, than the second
in Rome; and he even cried when he saw the statue of
Alexander the Great, with the reflection of how much
more glory Alexander had acquired, at thirty years old,
than he at a much more advanced age.* These are the
sentiments to make people considerable; and those

who have them not, will pass their lives in obscurity and contempt; whereas, those who endeavour to excel all, are at least sure of excelling a great many. The sure way to excel in any thing, is only to have a close and undissipated attention while you are about it; and then you need not be half the time that otherwise you must be: for long, plodding, puzzling application, is the business of dulness; but good parts attend regularly, and take a thing immediately. Consider, then, which you would choose; to attend diligently while you are learning, and thereby excel all other boys, get a great reputation, and have a great deal more time to play; or else not mind your book, let boys even younger than yourself get before you, be laughed at by them for a dunce, and have no time to play at all: for, I assure you, if you will not learn, you shall not play. What is the way, then, to arrive at that perfection which you promise me to aim at? It is, first, to do your duty towards God and man; without which every thing else signifies nothing: secondly, to acquire great knowledge; without which you will be a very contemptible man, though you may be a very honest one; and, lastly, to be very well bred; without which you will be a very disagreeable, unpleasing man, though you should be an honest and a learned one.

Remember then these three things, and resolve to excel in them all; for they comprehend whatever is necessary and useful for this world or the next: and in proportion as you improve in them you will enjoy the affection and tenderness of,

Yours.

12. TO THE REV. DR. CHENEVIX*

HAGUE, APRIL 27, N.S. 1745

DEAR DOCTOR,

I told you at first not to reckon too much upon the success of my recommendation, and I have still more reason to give you the same advice now, for it has met with great difficulties, merely as mine, and I am far from knowing yet how it will end. Pray, give no answer whatsoever to anybody, that either writes or speaks to you upon that subject, but leave it to me, for I make it my own affair, and you shall have either the Bishopric of Clonfert, or a better thing, or else I will not be Lord Lieutenant. I hope to be in England in about a fortnight, when this affair must and shall be brought to a decision. Good-night to you!

Yours, etc.

13. TO BISHOP CHENEVIX

HAGUE, MAY 12, N.S. 1745

MY GOOD LORD,

Now you are what I had positively declared you should be—a Bishop; but it is Bishop of Killaloe, not Clonfert, the latter refusing the translation. Killaloe, I am assured, is better. I heartily wish you joy, and could not refuse myself that pleasure, though I am in the greatest hurry imaginable, being upon my journey to Helvoet-Sluys for England. Adieu!

Yours, etc.

14. TO DAVID MALLET,* ESQ.

DUBLIN CASTLE, NOVEMBER 27, 1745

SIR,

I have just now received the favour of your letter of the 20th, which adds to my shame, for not having sooner acknowledged your former. The truth is, that the business of this place, such as it is, is continual; and as I am resolved to do it while I am here, it leaves me little or no time to do things I should like much better; assuring you of my regard and friendship is one of those things, but though one of the most agreeable, I believe the least necessary.

I cannot comprehend the consternation which 8,000 of your countrymen have, I find, thrown seven millions of mine into; I, who at this distance, see things only in their plain natural light, am, I confess, under no apprehensions; I consider a Highlander (with submission to you) as Rowe does a Lord, who when opposed to a man, he affirms to be but a man; from which principle I make this inference, that 49,000 must beat 8,000; not to mention our sixteen new regiments, which must go for something, though in my opinion not for much.* I have with much difficulty quieted the fears here, which were at first very strong, partly by contagion from England, and partly from old prejudices, which my good subjects are far from being yet above. They are in general still at the year 1689,* and have not shook off any religious or political prejudice that prevailed at that time. However, I am very glad I am among them; for in this little sphere, a little may do a great deal of good, but in England they must be much stronger shoulders than mine that can do any good at that bulky machine. Pray let me hear from you as often and as minutely as you have leisure; most correspondents, like most very learned men, suppose that one knows more than one does, and therefore don't tell one half what they could, so one never knows so much as one should.

                                            I am, etc.

15. TO HIS SON

SIR,

I most thankfully acknowledge the honour of two or three letters from you, since I troubled you with my last; and am very proud of the repeated instances you give me of your favour and protection, which I shall endeavour to deserve.

I am very glad that you went to hear a trial in the Court of King's Bench; and still more so, that you made the proper animadversions upon the inattention of many of the people in the Court. As you observed very well the indecency of that inattention, I am sure you will never be guilty of any thing like it yourself. There is no surer sign in the world of a little, weak mind, than inattention. Whatever is worth doing at all, is worth doing well; and nothing can be well done without attention. It is the sure answer of a fool, when you ask him about any thing that was said or done where he was present, that 'truly he did not mind it'. And why did not the fool mind it? What had he else to do there, but to mind what was doing? A man of sense sees, hears, and retains, every thing that passes where he is. I desire I may never hear you talk of not minding, nor complain, as most fools do, of a treacherous memory. Mind, not only what people say, but how they say it; and, if you have any sagacity, you may discover more truth by your eyes than by your ears. People can say what they will, but they cannot look just as they will; and their looks frequently discover, what their words are calculated to conceal. Observe, therefore, people's looks carefully, when they speak not only to you, but to each other. I have often guessed, by people's faces, what they were saying, though I could not hear one word they said. The most material knowledge of all, I mean the knowledge of the world, is never to be acquired without great attention; and I know many old people, who, though they have lived long in the world, are but children still as to the knowledge of it, from their levity and inattention. Certain forms, which all people comply with, and certain arts, which all people aim at, hide, in some degree, the truth, and give a general exterior resemblance to almost every body. Attention and sagacity must see through that veil, and discover the natural character. You are of an age now, to reflect, to observe and compare characters, and to arm yourself against the common arts, at least, of the world. If a man, with whom you are but barely acquainted, to whom you have made no offers, nor given any marks of friendship, makes you, on a sudden, strong professions of his, receive them with civility, but do not repay them with confidence: he certainly means to deceive you; for one man does not fall in love with another at sight. If a man uses strong protestations or oaths, to make you believe a thing, which is of itself so likely and probable that the bare saying of it would be sufficient, depend upon it he lies, and is highly interested in making you believe it; or else he would not take so much pains.

In about five weeks, I propose having the honour of laying myself at your feet: which I hope to find grown longer than they were when I left them. Adieu.

16. TO THE DUKE OF NEWCASTLE*
Private

MY LORD,   DUBLIN CASTLE, MARCH 11, 1746

My office letter to your Grace by this post being, as I hope, the last that I shall trouble you with from hence this season, contains variety of matters, and those of some importance, with regard to this country. Your Grace will therefore give me leave to explain them to you, with that truth which, wherever I am concerned, I desire his Majesty should most minutely know.

The Council door has not been opened of some years, I think seven or eight, and crowds are pressing at it, as it is really a Board of consequence here, being part of the Legislature.* Some new members are really wanting, it being sometimes difficult to make up a quorum; but the greatest difficulty of all was, where to stop. I have at last reduced the number to eight, of which I don't reckon above five effective, which is about the number wanted at the Board.

The Earl of Kildare applied to me early and strongly; his rank and estate in this country, I thought, left me no room to hesitate, and I readily promised him my recommendation.

The Earl of Kerry is of a great family, has a great estate, and is a kind of a sovereign in the wild county of Kerry; a very honest man, and very zealous for his Majesty's Government. He is ambitious of the title, more than of the thing itself; for his ill state of health, which is a palsy, will seldom or never let him attend. I think he very well deserves that mark of his Majesty's favour.

Lord Ikerren is son-in-law to the Speaker—has a very good estate, is a very honest man; and, the truth is, the Speaker makes it a point.

The Lords Massarene and Powerscourt are men of good sense and good estates, and will be of use at the Board. They are both what we call here *Castle-men*— that is they meddle with no cabals nor parties; but they belong to the Lord-Lieutenant, and as such, in my humble opinion, deserve the favour of the Government in this case; and the more so, as they ask for nothing else.

Lord Limerick applies himself much to the business of this country, promotes the manufactures, and is in that way so efficient a man, that it seems as much the desire of most people, as his own, that he should have a place at that Board.

Lord Hillsborough has a very considerable estate in this country, and his relations here, particularly Mr. Hill, his uncle, have credit and influence. They make it their request; and I look upon his admission there to be more nominal than real, as I believe he will be more in England than here.

Lord Viscount Fitzwilliam, who likewise will, I believe, seldom take his seat, I fairly confess I recommend, at the earnest instances of his relations in England, though he has a very good estate here, and is a most unexceptionable person.

I assure your Grace I have no favourite among them, and my recommendation proceeds singly from the motives I have mentioned.

The Earl of Grandison's application for a Viscountship for his daughter, Lady Betty Mason, seems to me so reasonable with regard to him, and of so little consequence to anybody else, that I own I have given him some reason to hope for that mark of his Majesty's favour. His estate here is at least eight thousand pounds a year. Mr. Mason, who married his daughter, has four; all which will centre in the son by that daughter. Lord Grandison's present Viscountship goes at his death to Lord Jersey. This request of his, therefore, seems to be a very common, and, so far at least a pardonable, piece of human vanity, often indulged in other cases, and I hope will be so in this.

The new Barrack Patent is a thing of absolute necessity for his Majesty's military service here. I should be a great deal too tedious if I were to state to your Grace a tenth part of that affair. I will therefore only say, that this new Patent, together with some other regulations I am making here, is the only probable method of preventing for the future the enormous abuses of the Barrack Board.*

The Dublin Society* is really a very useful establishment. It consists of many considerable people, and has been kept up hitherto by voluntary subscriptions. They give premiums for the improvement of lands, for plantations, for manufactures. They furnish many materials for those improvements in the poorer and less cultivated parts of this kingdom, and have certainly done a great deal of good. The bounty they apply for to his Majesty is five hundred pounds a year, which, in my humble opinion, would be properly bestowed; but I entirely submit it.

As to the applications of the Earls of Cavan and Rosse, and Lord Mayo,* all I can say for them is, that they have nothing of their own—that they are part of the furniture of this House of Lords, which if his Majesty thinks proper to put in a little better repair, he will at the same time do a real act of compassion.

The few small pensions are too trifling to mention; they are the usual charities of the Government, and at the same time lay some obligations upon more considerable people who solicit them; and the establishment can very well bear them.

Having now finished, as I hope, all my recommendations for some time, I must beg leave to assure your

Grace that they are, every one of them the recommendations of his Majesty's Lord-Lieutenant only, and that I am neither directly nor indirectly, in my private capacity, concerned in any one of them. I have neither retainer, friend, nor favourite among them.

I have one request more to trouble your Grace with, which indeed concerns myself singly, and that is, that your Grace will be pleased to apply to his Majesty for his gracious permission for me to return to England, to lay myself at his feet. I shall by that time have been here near eight months, during which time I have endeavoured to carry on his Majesty's service. If I have failed it must have been only from want of abilities; for my zeal, I am sure, was not wanting, and I must, with the warmest and most respectful gratitude, acknowledge that his Majesty's indulgence to all my recommendations has given me all the credit and weight I was capable of receiving.

I am, with the greatest truth and respect, etc.

P.S. I have received the honour of your Grace's letter of the 5th, relating to the embargo,* and have given the proper orders thereupon.

17. TO HIS SON

DUBLIN CASTLE, APRIL 5, 1746

DEAR BOY,

Before it is very long, I am of opinion that you will both think and speak more favourably of women than you do now. You seem to think that from Eve downwards they have done a great deal of mischief. As for that Lady, I give her up to you: but, since her time, history will inform you, that men have done much more mischief in the world than women; and, to say the truth, I would not advise you to trust either, more than is absolutely necessary. But this I will advise you to, which is, never to attack whole bodies of any kind; for, besides that all general rules have their exceptions, you unnecessarily make yourself a great number of enemies, by attacking a *corps* collectively. Among women, as among men, there are good as well as bad; and it may be full as many, or more, good than among men. This rule holds as to lawyers, soldiers, parsons, courtiers, citizens, etc. They are all men, subject to the same passions and sentiments, differing only in the manner, according to their several educations; and it would be as imprudent as unjust to attack any of them by the lump. Individuals forgive sometimes; but bodies and societies never do. Many young people think it very genteel and witty to abuse the Clergy; in which they are extremely mistaken; since, in my opinion, parsons are very like other men, and neither the better nor the worse for wearing a black gown. All general reflections, upon nations and societies, are the trite, thread-bare jokes of those who set up for wit without having any, and so have recourse to common-place. Judge of individuals from your own knowledge of them, and not from their sex, profession, or de-nomination.

Though at my return, which I hope will be very soon, I shall not find your feet lengthened, I hope I shall find your head a good deal so, and then I shall not much mind your feet. In two or three months after my return, you and I shall part for some time; you must go to read men as well as books, of all languages and nations. Observation and reflection will then be very necessary for you. We will talk this matter over fully when we meet; which I hope will be in the last week of this month; till when, I have the honour of being

> Your most faithful servant.

18. TO THOMAS PRIOR,* ESQ.

LONDON, JUNE 14, 1746

SIR,

I thank you for the favour of your letter, with the inclosed scheme for carrying on the war; which if others approved of as much as I do, and the present situation of the war permitted, would be soon put in execution.

As you are one of the few in Ireland, who always think of the public, without any mixture of private, interest; I do not doubt but that you have already thought of some useful methods of employing the King's bounty to the Dublin Society. The late additional tax upon glass*here, as it must considerably raise the price of glass-bottles imported into Ireland, seems to point out the manufacturing them there; which consideration, with a small premium added to it, would, in my mind, set up such a manufacture. Fine writing and printing paper, we have often talked of together; and the specimen you gave me, before I left Dublin, proves, that nothing but care and industry is wanting, to bring that manufacture to such a perfection as to prevent the exportation of it from Holland, and through Holland from France; nay, I am convinced that you might supply England with a great deal if you pleased, that is, if you would make it, as you could do, both good and cheap. Here is a man who has found out a method of making starch of potatoes, and, by the help of an engine of his own invention, to make a prodigious quantity of it in a day.* But here is an Act of Parliament which strictly prohibits the making starch of any thing but flour. Have you such an Act of Parliament in Ireland? If you have not, and that you import your starch from England, as I take it for granted that you do, for you import everything that you can, it would be well worth this man's while to go to Ireland, and advantageous for you that he should; his starch being to my knowledge and experience full as good, and abundantly cheaper than any other.

These are the sorts of jobs that I wish people in Ireland would attend to with as much industry and care, as they do to jobs of a very different nature. These honest arts would solidly increase their fortunes, and improve their estates, upon the only true and permanent foundation, the public good. Leave us and your regular forces in Ireland to fight for you; think of your manufactures at least as much as of your militia, and be as much upon your guard against Poverty as against Popery; take my word for it, you are in more danger of the former than of the latter.

I hope my friend, the Bishop of Meath,* goes on prosperously with his Charter-schools. I call them his, for I really think that without his care and perseverance they would hardly have existed now. Though their operation is sure, yet, being slow, it is not suited to the Irish taste of *the time present only*; and I cannot help saying, that, except in your claret, which you are very solicitous should be two or three years old, you think less of two or three years hence than any people under the sun. If they would but wish themselves as well as I wish them; and take as much pains to promote their own true interest, as I should be glad to do to contribute to it, they would in a few years be in a very different situation from that which they are in at present. Go on, however, you and our other friends; be not weary of well-doing, and though you cannot do all the good you would, do all the good you can.

When you write to the most worthy Bishop of Cloyne, pray assure him of my truest regard and esteem, and remember me to my honest and indefatigable friend in good works, Dr. Madden;* and be persuaded yourself, that I am, with sincere friendship and regard,

Your most faithful humble servant.

19. TO THOS. PRIOR, ESQ.

LONDON, SEPTEMBER 23, 1746

SIR,

A long and dangerous illness has hindered me from acknowledging, till now, your last letters; and though I am a great deal better, I still feel, by extreme weakness, the shock which that illness has given to a constitution too much shattered before.

Pray be under no kind of uneasiness as to the accident that happened to my letter, for I assure you that I am under none myself. I confess, the printing of a letter carelessly and inaccurately written, in the freedom and confidence of a friendly correspondence, is not very agreeable, especially to me, who am so idle and negligent in my familiar letters, that I never wrote one over twice in my life, and am consequently often guilty both of false spelling and false English; but as to my sentiments with regard to Ireland, I am not only willing, but desirous, that all Ireland should know them. I very well recollect the two paragraphs in my letter, which might be objected to by many people; but I recollect them without retracting them. I repeat it again, that there are not many people there, who, like you, employ their thoughts, their time, and their labour, merely for the public good, without any private view. The condition of Ireland sufficiently proves that truth. How different would the state of your lands, your trade, your manufactures, your arts and sciences, have been now from what it is, had they been the objects of general, as they have been of your particular, attention! I still less recant what I said about claret, which is a known and melancholy truth; and I could add a great deal more upon that subject.

Five thousand tuns of wine imported *communibus annis* into Ireland, is a sure, but indecent, proof of the excessive drinking of the gentry there, for the inferior sort of people cannot afford to drink wine there, as many of them can here;* so that these five thousand tuns of wine are chiefly employed in destroying the constitutions, the faculties, and too often the fortunes, of those of superior rank, who ought to take care of all the others. Were there to be a contest between public cellars and public granaries, which do you think would carry it? I believe you will allow that a Claret Board, if there were one, would be much better attended than the Linen Board,* *unless when flax-seed were to be distributed*. I am sensible that I shall be reckoned a very shallow politician, for my attention to such trifling objects, as the improvement of your lands, the extension of your manufactures, and the increase of your trade, which only tend to the advantages of the public; whereas an able Lord-Lieutenant ought to employ his thoughts in greater matters. He should think of jobs for favourites, sops for enemies, managing parties, and engaging Parliaments to vote away their own and their fellow-subjects' liberties and properties. But these great arts of Government, I confess, are above me, and people should not go out of their depth. I will modestly be content with wishing Ireland all the good that is possible, and with doing it all the good I can; and so weak am I, that I would much rather be distinguished and remembered by the name of the *Irish Lord-Lieutenant* than by that of the Lord-Lieutenant of Ireland.

My paper puts me in mind that I have already troubled you too long, so I conclude abruptly, with assuring you that I am, with the truest esteem, etc.

20. TO HIS SON

BATH, OCTOBER 4, O.S. 1746

DEAR BOY,

Though I employ so much of my time in writing to you, I confess I have often my doubts whether it is to any purpose. I know how unwelcome advice generally is; I know that those who want it most, like it and follow it least; and I know too, that the advice of parents, more particularly, is ascribed to the moroseness, the imperiousness, or the garrulity of old age. But then, on the other hand, I flatter myself, that as your own reason (though too young as yet to suggest much to you of itself) is, however, strong enough to enable you, both to judge of, and receive plain truths; I flatter myself (I say) that your own reason, young as it is, must tell you, that I can have no interest but yours in the advice I give you; and that, consequently, you will at least weigh and consider it well; in which case, some of it will, I hope, have its

effect. Do not think that I mean to dictate as a Parent;
I only mean to advise as a friend, and an indulgent one
too: and do not apprehend that I mean to check your
pleasures, of which, on the contrary, I only desire to be
the guide, not the censor. Let my experience supply
your want of it, and clear your way, in the progress of
your youth, of those thorns and briars which scratched
and disfigured me in the course of mine. I do not,
therefore, so much as hint to you, how absolutely de-
pendent you are upon me; that you neither have, nor
can have a shilling in the world but from me; and that,
as I have no womanish weakness for your person, your
merit must and will be the only measure of my kindness. I say, I do not hint these things to you, because
I am convinced that you will act right, upon more
noble and generous principles; I mean for the sake of
doing right, and out of affection and gratitude to me.

I have so often recommended to you attention and
application to whatever you learn, that I do not mention them now as duties; but I point them out to
you as conducive, nay, absolutely necessary to your
pleasures; for can there be a greater pleasure, than to
be universally allowed to excel those of one's own age
and manner of life? And, consequently, can there be
any thing more mortifying, than to be excelled by them?
In this latter case, your shame and regret must be
greater than any body's, because every person knows
the uncommon care which has been taken of your
education, and the opportunities you have had of
knowing more than others of your age. I do not confine
the application which I recommend, singly to the view
and emulation of excelling others (though that is a very
sensible pleasure and a very warrantable pride); but
I mean likewise to excel in the thing itself; for in my

mind, one may as well not know a thing at all, as know it but imperfectly. To know a little of anything, gives neither satisfaction nor credit; but often brings disgrace or ridicule.

Mr. Pope says, very truly,

> A little knowledge is a dangerous thing;
> Drink deep or taste not the Castalian spring.*

And what is called a *smattering* of every thing infallibly constitutes a coxcomb. I have often, of late, reflected what an unhappy man I must now have been, if I had not acquired in my youth some fund and taste of learning. What could I have done with myself at this age, without them? I must, as many ignorant people do, have destroyed my health and faculties by sotting away the evenings; or, by wasting them frivolously in the tattle of women's company, must have exposed myself to the ridicule and contempt of those very women; or, lastly, I must have hanged myself, as a man once did, for weariness of putting on and pulling off his shoes and stockings every day. My books, and only my books, are now left me: and I daily find what Cicero says of learning to be true: '*Haec studia* (says he) *adolescentiam alunt, senectutem oblectant, secundas res ornant, adversis perfugium ac solatium praebent, delectant domi, non impediunt foris, pernoctant nobiscum, peregrinantur, rusticantur.*'*

I do not mean, by this, to exclude conversation out of the pleasures of an advanced age; on the contrary, it is a very great and a very rational pleasure, at all ages; but the conversation of the ignorant is no conversation, and gives even them no pleasure: they tire of their own sterility, and have not matter enough to furnish them with words to keep up a conversation.

Let me, therefore, most earnestly recommend to

you, to hoard up, while you can, a great stock of knowledge; for though, during the dissipation of your youth, you may not have occasion to spend much of it; yet, you may depend upon it, that a time will come, when you will want it to maintain you. Public granaries are filled in plentiful years; not that it is known that the next, or the second, or third year will prove a scarce one; but because it is known that, sooner or later, such a year will come, in which the grain will be wanted.

I will say no more to you upon this subject; you have Mr. Harte with you to enforce it; you have reason to assent to the truth of it; so that, in short, 'you have Moses and the Prophets; if you will not believe them, neither will you believe, though one rose from the dead.'* Do not imagine that the knowledge which I so much recommend to you, is confined to books, pleasing, useful, and necessary as that knowledge is: but I comprehend in it the great knowledge of the world, still more necessary than that of books. In truth, they assist one another reciprocally; and no man will have either perfectly, who has not both. The knowledge of the world is only to be acquired in the world, and not in a closet. Books alone will never teach it you; but they will suggest many things to your observation, which might otherwise escape you; and your own observations upon mankind, when compared with those which you will find in books, will help you to fix the true point.

To know mankind well, requires full as much attention and application as to know books, and, it may be, more sagacity and discernment. I am, at this time, acquainted with many elderly people, who have all passed their whole lives in the great world, but with such levity and inattention, that they know no more of it now, than they did at fifteen. Do not flatter yourself, therefore, with the thoughts that you can acquire this knowledge in the frivolous chit-chat of idle companies; no, you must go much deeper than that. You must look into people, as well as at them. Almost all people are born with all the passions, to a certain degree; but almost every man has a prevailing one, to which the others are subordinate. Search every one for that ruling passion;* pry into the recesses of his heart, and observe the different workings of the same passion in different people; and when you have found out the prevailing passion of any man, remember never to trust him where that passion is concerned. Work upon him by it, if you please; but be upon your guard yourself against it, whatever professions he may make you.

I would desire you to read this letter twice over, but that I much doubt whether you will read once to the end of it. I will trouble you no longer now; but we will have more upon this subject hereafter. Adieu.

I have this moment received your letter from Schaffhausen;* in the date of it you forgot the month.

21. TO HIS SON

BATH, OCTOBER 9, O.S. 1746

DEAR BOY:

Your distresses in your journey from Heidleberg to Schaffhausen, your lying upon straw, your black bread, and your broken *berline*,* are proper seasons for the greater fatigues and distresses, which you must expect in the course of your travels; and, if one had a mind to moralize, one might call them the samples of the accidents, rubs, and difficulties, which every man meets with in his journey through life. In this journey, the understanding is the *voiture* that must carry you through; and in proportion as that is stronger or weaker, more or less in repair, your journey will be better or worse; though at best you will now and then find some bad roads, and some bad inns. Take care, therefore, to keep that necessary *voiture* in perfect good repair; examine, improve, and strengthen it every day: it is in the power, and ought to be the care, of every man to do it; he that neglects it, deserves to feel, and certainly will feel, the fatal effects of that negligence.

A propos of negligence; I must say something to you upon that subject. You know I have often told you, that my affection for you was not a weak, womanish one; and, far from blinding me, it makes me but more quicksighted, as to your faults; those it is not only my right, but my duty, to tell you of; and it is your duty and your interest to correct them. In the strict scrutiny which I have made into you, I have (thank God) hitherto not discovered any vice of the heart, or any peculiar weakness of the head; but I have discovered laziness, inattention, and indifference; faults which are only pardonable in old men, who, in the decline of life, when health and spirits fail, have a kind of claim to that sort of tranquillity. But a young man should be ambitious to shine and excel; alert, active, and inde-fatigable in the means of doing it; and, like Caesar, *Nil actum reputans, si quid superesset agendum.** You seem to want that *vivida vis animi,** which spurs and excites most young men to please, to shine, to excel. Without the desire and the pains necessary to be con-siderable, depend upon it, you never can be so; as, without the desire and attention necessary to please, you never can please. *Nullum numen abest, si sit prudentia*,* is unquestionably true with regard to everything except poetry; and I am very sure that any man of common understanding may, by proper culture, care, attention, and labour, make himself whatever he pleases, except a good poet. . . .

What is commonly called an absent man, is commonly either a very weak, or a very affected man; but be he which he will, he is, I am sure, a very disagreeable man in company. He fails in all the common offices of civility; he seems not to know those people to-day, with whom yesterday he appeared to live in intimacy. He takes no part in the general conversation; but, on the contrary, breaks into it from time to time, with some start of his own, as if he waked from a dream. This (as I said before) is a sure indication, either of a mind so weak that it is not able to bear above one object at a time; or so affected, that it would be supposed to be wholly engrossed by, and directed to, some very great and important objects. Sir Isaac Newton, Mr. Locke, and (it may be) five or six more, since the creation of the world, may have had a right to absence, from that intense thought which the things they were investigating required. But if a young man, and a man of the world, who has no such avocations to plead, will claim and exercise that right of absence in company, his pretended right should, in my mind, be turned into an involuntary absence, by his perpetual exclusion out of company. However frivolous a company may be, still, while you are among them, do not show them, by your inattention, that you think them so; but rather take their tone, and conform in some degree to their weakness, instead of manifesting your contempt for them. There is nothing that people bear more impatiently, or forgive less, than contempt; and an injury is much sooner forgotten than an insult. If therefore you would rather please than offend, rather be well than ill spoken of, rather be loved than hated; remember to have that constant attention about you, which flatters every man's little vanity; and the want of which, by mortifying his pride, never fails to excite his resentment, or at least his ill-will. For instance; most people (I might say all people) have their weaknesses; they have their aversions and their likings, to such or such things; so that, if you were to laugh at a man for his aversion to a cat, or cheese, (which are common antipathies), or, by inattention and negligence, to let them come in his way, where you could prevent it, he would, in the first case, think himself insulted, and, in the second, slighted, and would remember both. Whereas your care to procure for him what he likes, and to remove from him what he hates, shows him, that he is at least an object of your attention; flatters his vanity, and makes him possibly more your friend, than a more important service would have done. With regard to women, attentions still below these are necessary, and, by the custom of the world, in some measure due, according to the laws of good-breeding.

My long and frequent letters, which I send you in great doubt of their success, put me in mind of certain papers, which you have very lately, and I formerly, sent up to kites, along the string, which we called messengers; some of them the wind used to blow away, others were torn by the string, and but few of them got up and stuck to the kite. But I will content myself now, as I did then, if some of my present messengers do but stick to you. Adieu!

22. TO THE LORDS JUSTICES OF IRELAND

MY LORDS, GROSVENOR SQUARE, 18 NOV., 1746

His Majesty having done me the honour, most un-expectedly and undeservedly on my part, to appoint me to be one of his Principal Secretaries of State, and having been pleased to appoint the Earl of Harrington to be Lord Lieutenant of Ireland, I cannot take my leave of your Lordships without returning you at the same time my sincerest thanks for your assistance during my residence in Ireland, and for your wise and prudent administration of the government of that Kingdom ever since.

Could anything add to my personal regard and con-sideration for your Lordships, it would be the convic-tion I have that your sentiments and affection for the Kingdom of Ireland correspond with mine.

May your Lordships be able to promote effectually what now I can only wish sincerely—the interest and prosperity of a loyal and a brave people; may Indus-try improve, Trade enrich, and all Happiness attend Ireland.

I am, my Lords, with great respect, your Lordships'
Most faithful and most humble servant.

23. TO HIS SON

LONDON, MARCH 27, O.S. 1747

DEAR BOY,

Pleasure is the rock which most young people split upon: they launch out with crowded sails in quest of it, but without a compass to direct their course, or reason sufficient to steer the vessel; for want of which, pain and shame, instead of pleasure, are the returns of their voyage. Do not think that I mean to snarl at pleasure, like a Stoic, or to preach against it, like a parson; no, I mean to point it out, and recommend it to you, like an Epicurean: I wish you a great deal; and my only view is to hinder you from mistaking it.

The character which most young men first aim at is, that of a man of pleasure; but they generally take it upon trust; and instead of consulting their own taste and inclinations, they blindly adopt whatever those with whom they chiefly converse, are pleased to call by the name of pleasure; and a *man of pleasure*, in the vulgar acceptation of that phrase, means only a beastly drunkard, an abandoned whore-master, and a profligate swearer and curser. As it may be of use to you, I am not unwilling, though at the same time ashamed, to own, that the vices of my youth proceeded much more from my silly resolution of being what I heard called a man of pleasure, than from my own inclinations. I always naturally hated drinking; and yet I have often drunk, with disgust at the time, attended by great sickness the next day, only because I then considered drinking as a necessary qualification for a fine gentleman, and a man of pleasure.

The same as to gaming. I did not want money, and consequently had no occasion to play for it; but I thought play another necessary ingredient in the composition of a man of pleasure, and accordingly I plunged into it without desire, at first; sacrificed a thousand real pleasures to it; and made myself solidly uneasy by it, for thirty the best years of my life.

I was even absurd enough, for a little while, to swear, by way of adorning and completing the shining character which I affected; but this folly I soon laid aside, upon finding both the guilt and the indecency of it.

Thus seduced by fashion, and blindly adopting nominal pleasures, I lost real ones; and my fortune impaired, and my constitution shattered, are, I must confess, the just punishment of my errors.

Take warning then by them; choose your pleasures for yourself, and do not let them be imposed upon you. Follow nature and not fashion: weigh the present enjoyment of your pleasures against the necessary consequences of them, and then let your own common sense determine your choice.

Were I to begin the world again, with the experience which I now have of it, I would lead a life of real, not of imaginary pleasure. I would enjoy the pleasures of the table, and of wine; but stop short of the pains inseparably annexed to an excess in either. I would not, at twenty years, be a preaching missionary of abstemiousness and sobriety; and I should let other people do as they would, without formally and sententiously rebuking them for it: but I would be most firmly resolved not to destroy my own faculties and constitution; in complaisance to those who have no regard to their own. I would play to give me pleasure, but not to give me pain; that is, I would play for trifles, in mixed companies, to amuse myself, and conform to custom; but I would take care not to venture for sums which, if I won, I should not be the better for; but, if I lost, should be under a difficulty to pay; and when paid, would oblige me to retrench in several other articles. Not to mention the quarrels which deep play commonly occasions.

I would pass some of my time in reading, and the

rest in the company of people of sense and learning, and chiefly those above me; and I would frequent the mixed companies of men and women of fashion, which, though often frivolous, yet they unbend and refresh the mind, not uselessly, because they certainly polish and soften the manners.

These would be my pleasures and amusements, if I were to live the last thirty years over again: they are rational ones; and moreover, I will tell you, they are really the fashionable ones: for the others are not, in truth, the pleasures of what I call people of fashion, but of those who only call themselves so. Does good company care to have a man reeling drunk among them? or to see another tearing his hair, and blaspheming, for having lost, at play, more than he is able to pay? or a whore-master with half a nose, and crippled by coarse and infamous debauchery? No; those who practise, and much more those who brag of them, make no part of good company; and are most unwillingly, if ever, admitted into it. A real man of fashion and pleasures observes decency: at least neither borrows nor affects vices; and if he unfortunately has any, he gratifies them with choice, delicacy, and secrecy.

I have not mentioned the pleasures of the mind (which are the solid and permanent ones), because they do not come under the head of what people commonly call pleasures; which they seem to confine to the senses. The pleasure of virtue, of charity, and of learning, is true and lasting pleasure; with which I hope you will be well and long acquainted. Adieu!

24. TO SOLOMON DAYROLLES,* ESQ.

DEAR DAYROLLES,

I received by the last mail your letter of the 7th, N.S. and though I have very little time to-night, yet I would not omit acquainting you that the hints, which I gave you in one of my former letters, concerning the 30,000 Russians,* are now useless. The Prince of Orange writ to me two posts ago to propose the taking of the Russian troops jointly in the service of the Maritime Powers, that is that the Dutch were to take 10,000 into their pay, and we the 20,000 into ours. Nay, more, they would even, I believe, have contributed their fourth part to our 20,000 over and above their own 10,000; but upon mature and *wise* deliberation, it was thought proper to put off this affair till September to wait for events *en attendant*, which God knows, in my mind, we have done but too long already. I represented the distance of the Court of Petersburg, and the necessity of immediately beginning whatever negotiation you would have concluded at that Court even by next spring, but in vain, for the old spirit of delay and indecision prevailed. I fear this delay will be very disagreeable to the Prince of Orange, who I dare say thought that the proposal would have been very welcome here.

I thank you for the account which you sent me from Lausanne, though I can't say that it gives me great comfort. I shall hint nothing of it to the boy, while he stays at Lausanne, that he may neither accuse nor suspect anybody there of being my informer; but, as soon as he is at Leipsig, he shall receive *des mercuriales** upon all those points.

I own I am in great pain for the Dutch frontier, Bergen-op-zoom, Breda, or Bois-le-duc, but chiefly the two first, being, I am convinced, the object of the French, which, if they succeed in, the consequence is but too plain. Pray tell me what you take to be the whole force of Prince Saxe Hildbourghausen's corps.*

Burn this letter as soon as you have read it, and don't mention the former part of it to anybody living.

Yours faithfully.

(Separate and Secret Postscript, first printed in Lord Mahon's edition.)

When you deliver my office letter to the Prince of Orange, I dare say he will talk to you about the Russian affair, which it relates to. I dare say, too, that he will be disappointed in finding his proposal so coldly received here, and put off for so long. He will probably express something of this kind to you, which when he does, you will just hint, that you believe that my opinion was for taking the Russians immediately; because you know, that while we are in war, I am for making it vigorously, and with superior force, and not consuming ourselves, by inferior and ineffectual armies.

In the course of this conversation, take an opportunity of showing him my enclosed letter, which I have calculated for that purpose, and in which I have inserted the Lausanne affair, to prevent the least suspicion. But when you do show it, do it with seeming difficulty, and as a mark of your unbounded confidence in the Prince; and enjoin him the strictest secrecy, especially that I may never know that you showed it to him.

Both the King and I thought the measure a right

one, and that we should get all the force we could; but we can neither of us do what we have a mind to do, and the resolutions of those who neither know how to make war nor peace are to prevail.

Good night, once more!

25. TO HIS SON

LONDON, OCTOBER 9, O.S. 1747

DEAR BOY:

People of your age have, commonly, an unguarded frankness about them; which makes them the easy prey and bubbles of the artful and the experienced: they look upon every knave or fool, who tells them that he is their friend, to be really so; and pay that profession of simulated friendship with an indiscreet and unbounded confidence, always to their loss, often to their ruin. Beware, therefore, now that you are coming into the world, of these proffered friendships. Receive them with great civility, but with great incredulity too; and pay them with compliments, but not with confidence. Do not let your vanity and self-love make you suppose that people become your friends at first sight, or even upon a short acquaintance. Real friendship is a slow grower; and never thrives, unless ingrafted upon a stock of known and reciprocal merit. There is another kind of nominal friendship among young people, which is warm for the time, but, by good luck, of short duration. This friendship is hastily produced, by their being accidentally thrown together, and pursuing the same course of riot and debauchery. A fine friendship, truly; and well cemented by drunkenness and lewdness. It should rather be called a conspiracy against morals and good manners, and be punished as such by the civil magistrate. However, they have the impudence and folly to call this confederacy a friendship. They lend one another money, for bad purposes; they engage in quarrels, offensive and defensive, for their accomplices; they tell one another all they know, and often more too, when, of a sudden, some accident disperses them, and they think no more of each other, unless it be to betray and laugh at their imprudent confidence. Remember to make a great difference between companions and friends; for a very complaisant and agreeable companion may, and often does, prove a very improper and a very dangerous friend. People will, in a great degree, and not without reason, form their opinion of you, upon that which they have of your friends; and there is a Spanish proverb,* which says very justly, *Tell me whom you live with, and I will tell you who you are.* One may fairly suppose, that a man, who makes a knave or a fool his friend, has something very bad to do or to conceal. But, at the same time that you carefully decline the friendship of knaves and fools, if it can be called friendship, there is no occasion to make either of them your enemies, wantonly, and unprovoked; for they are numerous bodies: and I would rather choose a secure neutrality, than alliance, or war, with either of them. You may be a declared enemy to their vices and follies, without being marked out by them as a personal one. Their enmity is the next dangerous thing to their friendship. Have a real reserve with almost everybody; and have a seeming reserve with almost nobody; for it is very disagreeable to seem reserved, and very dangerous not to be so. Few people find the true medium; many are ridiculously mysterious and reserved upon trifles; and many imprudently communicative of all they know.

The next thing to the choice of your friends, is the choice of your company. Endeavour, as much as you can, to keep company with people above you: there you rise, as much as you sink with people below you; for (as I have mentioned before) you are whatever the company you keep is. Do not mistake, when I say company above you, and think that I mean with regard to their birth: that is the least consideration; but I mean with regard to their merit, and the light in which the world considers them.

There are two sorts of good company; one, which is called the *beau monde*, and consists of those people who have the lead in courts, and in the gay part of life; the other consists of those who are distinguished by some peculiar merit, or who excel in some particular and valuable art or science. For my own part, I used to think myself in company as much above me, when I was with Mr. Addison and Mr. Pope,* as if I had been with all the Princes in Europe. What I mean by low company, which should by all means be avoided, is the company of those, who, absolutely insignificant and contemptible in themselves, think they are honoured by being in your company, and who flatter every vice and every folly you have, in order to engage you to converse with them. The pride of being the first of the company is but too common; but it is very silly, and very prejudicial. Nothing in the world lets down a character more than that wrong turn.

You may possibly ask me, whether a man has it always in his power to get into the best company? and how? I say, Yes, he has, by deserving it; provided he is but in circumstances which enable him to appear upon the footing of a gentleman. Merit and good-breeding will make their way everywhere. Knowledge

will introduce him, and good-breeding will endear him
to the best companies; for, as I have often told you,
politeness and good-breeding are absolutely necessary
to adorn any, or all other good qualities or talents.
Without them, no knowledge, no perfection whatever,
is seen in its best light. The scholar, without good-
breeding, is a pedant; the philosopher, a cynic; the
soldier, a brute; and every man disagreeable.

I long to hear, from my several correspondents at
Leipsig, of your arrival there, and what impression you
make on them at first; for I have Arguses,* with an hundred eyes each, who will watch you narrowly, and
relate to me faithfully. My accounts will certainly be
true; it depends upon you, entirely, of what kind they
shall be. Adieu.

26. TO HIS SON

LONDON, OCTOBER 16, O.S. 1747

DEAR BOY,

The art of pleasing is a very necessary one to possess;
but a very difficult one to acquire. It can hardly be
reduced to rules; and your own good sense and observation will teach you more of it than I can. Do as
you would be done by, is the surest method that I
know of pleasing. Observe carefully what pleases you
in others, and probably the same things in you will
please others. If you are pleased with the complaisance
and attention of others to your humours, your tastes,
or your weaknesses, depend upon it the same complaisance and attention, on your part to theirs, will
equally please them. Take the tone of the company
that you are in, and do not pretend to give it; be serious,
gay, or even trifling, as you find the present humour of

the company; this is an attention due from every individual to the majority. Do not tell stories in company; there is nothing more tedious and disagreeable; if by chance you know a very short story, and exceedingly applicable to the present subject of conversation, tell it in as few words as possible; and even then, throw out that you do not love to tell stories, but that the shortness of it tempted you. Of all things, banish the egotism out of your conversation, and never think of entertaining people with your own personal concerns or private affairs; though they are interesting to you they are tedious and impertinent to everybody else; besides that, one cannot keep one's own private affairs too secret. Whatever you think your own excellencies may be, do not affectedly display them in company; nor labour, as many people do, to give that turn to the conversation, which may supply you with an opportunity of exhibiting them. If they are real, they will infallibly be discovered, without your pointing them out yourself, and with much more advantage. Never maintain an argument with heat and clamour, though you think or know yourself to be in the right; but give your opinion modestly and coolly, which is the only way to convince; and, if that does not do, try to change the conversation, by saying, with good-humour, 'We shall hardly convince one another; nor is it necessary that we should, so let us talk of something else.'

Remember that there is a local propriety to be observed in all companies; and that what is extremely proper in one company, may be, and often is, highly improper in another.

The jokes, the *bons mots*, the little adventures, which may do very well in one company, will seem flat and

tedious when related in another. The particular characters, the habits, the cant of one company, may give
credit to a word, or a gesture, which would have none
at all if divested of those accidental circumstances.
Here people very commonly err; and fond of something that has entertained them in one company, and
in certain circumstances, repeat it with emphasis in
another, where it is either insipid, or, it may be, offensive, by being ill-timed or misplaced. Nay, they often
do it with this silly preamble: 'I will tell you an excellent thing'; or, 'the best thing in the world.' This
raises expectations, which, when absolutely disappointed, make the relator of this excellent thing look,
very deservedly, like a fool.

If you would particularly gain the affection and
friendship of particular people, whether men or
women, endeavour to find out their predominant excellency, if they have one, and their prevailing weakness, which everybody has; and do justice to the one,
and something more than justice to the other. Men
have various objects in which they may excel, or at
least would be thought to excel; and, though they love
to hear justice done to them, where they know that
they excel, yet they are most and best flattered upon
those points where they wish to excel, and yet are
doubtful whether they do or not. As, for example:
Cardinal Richelieu, who was undoubtedly the ablest
statesman of his time, or perhaps of any other, had the
idle vanity of being thought the best poet too: he
envied the great Corneille his reputation, and ordered
a criticism to be written upon the *Cid.** Those, therefore, who flattered skilfully, said little to him of his
abilities in state affairs, or at least but *en passant*, and
as it might naturally occur. But the incense which

they gave him, the smoke of which they knew would turn his head in their favour, was as a *bel esprit* and a poet. Why? Because he was sure of one excellency, and distrustful as to the other. You will easily discover every man's prevailing vanity, by observing his favourite topic of conversation; for every man talks most of what he has most a mind to be thought to excel in. Touch him but there, and you touch him to the quick. The late Sir Robert Walpole (who was certainly an able man) was little open to flattery upon that head; for he was in no doubt himself about it; but his prevailing weakness was, to be thought to have a polite and happy turn to gallantry;—of which he had undoubtedly less than any man living: it was his favourite and frequent subject of conversation; which proved, to those who had any penetration, that it was his prevailing weakness. And they applied to it with success.

Women have, in general, but one object, which is their beauty; upon which, scarce any flattery is too gross for them to swallow. Nature has hardly formed a woman ugly enough to be insensible to flattery upon her person; if her face is so shocking, that she must in some degree be conscious of it, her figure and air, she trusts, make ample amends for it. If her figure is deformed, her face, she thinks, counterbalances it. If they are both bad, she comforts herself that she has graces; a certain manner; a *je ne sçais quoi*, still more engaging than beauty. This truth is evident, from the studied and elaborate dress of the ugliest women in the world. An undoubted, uncontested, conscious beauty is, of all women, the least sensible of flattery upon that head; she knows that it is her due, and is therefore obliged to nobody for giving it her. She must be flattered upon her understanding; which, though she may possibly not doubt of herself, yet she suspects that men may distrust.

Do not mistake me, and think that I mean to recommend to you abject and criminal flattery: no; flatter nobody's vices or crimes: on the contrary, abhor and discourage them. But there is no living in the world without a complaisant indulgence for people's weaknesses, and innocent, though ridiculous vanities. If a man has a mind to be thought wiser, and a woman handsomer, than they really are, their error is a comfortable one to themselves, and an innocent one with regard to other people; and I would rather make them my friends, by indulging them in it, than my enemies, by endeavouring (and that to no purpose) to undeceive them.

There are little attentions likewise, which are infinitely engaging, and which sensibly affect that degree of pride and self-love, which is inseparable from human nature; as they are unquestionable proofs of the regard and consideration which we have for the persons to whom we pay them. As, for example, to observe the little habits, the likings, the antipathies, and the tastes of those whom we would gain; and then take care to provide them with the one, and to secure them from the other; giving them, genteelly, to understand, that you had observed they liked such a dish, or such a room; for which reason you had prepared it: or, on the contrary, that having observed they had an aversion to such a dish, a dislike to such a person, etc., you had taken care to avoid presenting them. Such attention to such trifles flatters self-love much more than greater things, as it makes people think themselves almost the only objects of your thoughts and care.

These are some of the *arcana* necessary for your

initiation in the great society of the world. I wish I had known them better at your age; I have paid the price of three and fifty years for them, and shall not grudge it, if you reap the advantage. Adieu.

27. TO HIS SON

LONDON, DECEMBER 18, O.S. 1747

DEAR BOY,

As two mails are now due from Holland, I have no letters of yours or Mr. Harte's to acknowledge; so that this letter is the effect of that *scribendi cacoethes*,* which my fears, my hopes, and my doubts, concerning you give me. When I have wrote you a very long letter upon any subject, it is no sooner gone, but I think I have omitted something in it, which might be of use to you; and then I prepare the supplement for the next post: or else some new subject occurs to me, upon which I fancy that I can give you some informations, or point out some rules which may be advantageous to you. This sets me to writing again, though God knows whether to any purpose or not; a few years more can only ascertain that. But, whatever my success may be, my anxiety and my care can only be the effects of that tender affection which I have for you; and which you cannot represent to yourself greater than it really is. But do not mistake the nature of that affection, and think it of a kind that you may with impunity abuse. It is not natural affection, there being in reality no such thing; for, if there were, some inward sentiment must necessarily and reciprocally discover the parent to the child, and the child to the parent, without any exterior indications, knowledge, or acquaintance whatsoever; which never happened since the creation of the world, whatever poets, romance, or novel writers, and such sentiment-mongers, may be pleased to say to the contrary. Neither is my affection for you that of a mother, of which the only, or at least the chief objects, are health and life: I wish you them both most heartily; but, at the same time, I confess they are by no means my principal care.

My object is to have you fit to live; which, if you are not, I do not desire that you should live at all. My affection for you then is, and only will be, proportioned to your merit, which is the only affection that one rational being ought to have for another. Hitherto I have discovered nothing wrong in your heart or your head: on the contrary, I think I see sense in the one, and sentiments in the other. This persuasion is the only motive of my present affection; which will either increase or diminish, according to your merit or demerit. If you have the knowledge, the honour, and probity which you may have, the marks and warmth of my affection shall amply reward them; but if you have them not, my aversion and indignation will rise in the same proportion; and, in that case, remember, that I am under no farther obligation, than to give you the necessary means of subsisting. If ever we quarrel, do not expect or depend upon any weakness in my nature, for a reconciliation, as children frequently do, and often meet with, from silly parents; I have no such weakness about me: and, as I will never quarrel with you but upon some essential point, if once we quarrel, I will never forgive. But I hope and believe, that this declaration (for it is no threat) will prove unnecessary. You are no stranger to the principles of virtue; and, surely, whoever knows virtue must love it. As for knowledge, you have already enough of it, to engage you to acquire more. The ignorant only either despise it, or think that they have enough: those who have the most, are always the most desirous to have more, and know that the most they can have is, alas! but too little.

Reconsider from time to time, and retain the friendly advice which I send you. The advantage will be all your own.

28. TO HIS SON

BATH, FEBRUARY 22, O.S. 1748

DEAR BOY,

Every excellency, and every virtue, has its kindred vice or weakness; and if carried beyond certain bounds, sinks into the one or the other. Generosity often runs into profusion, œconomy into avarice, courage into rashness, caution into timidity, and so on;—insomuch that, I believe, there is more judgment required, for the proper conduct of our virtues, than for avoiding their opposite vices. Vice in its true light, is so deformed, that it shocks us at first sight, and would hardly ever seduce us, if it did not, at first, wear the mask of some virtue. But virtue is, in itself, so beautiful, that it charms us at first sight; engages us more and more upon farther acquaintance; and as with other beauties, we think excess impossible; it is here that judgment is necessary, to moderate and direct the effects of an excellent cause. I shall apply this reasoning, at present, not to any particular virtue, but to an excellency, which, for want of judgment, is often the cause of ridiculous and blameable effects; I mean, great learning; which, if not accompanied with sound judgment, frequently carries us into error, pride, and pedantry. As, I hope, you will posses that excellency in its utmost extent, and yet without its too common failings, the hints, which my experience can suggest, may probably not be useless to you.

Some learned men, proud of their knowledge, only speak to decide, and give judgment without appeal; the consequence of which is, that mankind, provoked by the insult, and injured by the oppression, revolt; and in order to shake off the tyranny, even call the lawful authority in question. The more you know, the modester you should be: and (by-the-bye) that modesty is the surest way of gratifying your vanity. Even where you are sure, seem rather doubtful; represent, but do not pronounce, and if you would convince others, seem open to conviction yourself.

Others, to show their learning, or often from the prejudices of a school education, where they hear nothing else, are always talking of the ancients, as something more than men, and of the moderns, as something less. They are never without a classic or two in their pockets; they stick to the old good sense; they read none of the modern trash; and will show you, plainly, that no improvement has been made, in any one art or science, these last seventeen hundred years. I would by no means have you disown your acquaintance with the ancients: but still less would I have you brag of an exclusive intimacy with them. Speak of the moderns without contempt, and of the ancients without idolatry; judge them all by their merits, but not by their ages; and if you happen to have an Elzevir classic* in your pocket, neither show it nor mention it.

Some great scholars, most absurdly, draw all their maxims, both for public and private life, from what they call parallel cases in the ancient authors; without considering that in the first place, there never were, since the creation of the world, two cases exactly parallel; and in the next place, that there never was a case stated, or even known, by any historian, with every one of its circumstances; which, however, ought to be known, in order to be reasoned from. Reason upon the case itself, and the several circumstances that attend it, and act accordingly; but not from the authority of ancient poets, or historians. Take into your consideration, if you please, cases seemingly analogous; but take them as helps only, not as guides. We are really so prejudiced by our education, that, as the ancients deified their heroes, we deify their madmen; of which, with all due regard for antiquity, I take Leonidas and Curtius* to have been two distinguished ones. And yet a solid pedant would, in a speech in parliament, relative to a tax of twopence in the pound upon some commodity or other, quote those two heroes as examples of what we ought to do and suffer for our country. I have known these absurdities carried so far by people of injudicious learning, that I should not be surprised, if some of them were to propose, while we are at war with the Gauls, that a number of geese should be kept in the Tower, upon account of the infinite advantage which Rome received *in a parallel case*, from a certain number of geese in the Capitol. This way of reasoning, and this way of speaking, will always form a poor politician, and a puerile declaimer.

There is another species of learned men who, though less dogmatical and supercilious, are not less impertinent. These are the communicative and shining pedants, who adorn their conversation, even with women, by happy quotations of Greek and Latin; and who have contracted such a familiarity with the Greek and Roman authors, that they call them by certain names or epithets denoting intimacy. As *old* Homer; that *sly rogue* Horace; *Maro*, instead of Virgil; and *Naso*, instead of Ovid. These are often imitated by coxcombs, who have no learning at all; but who have got some names and some scraps of ancient authors by heart, which they improperly and impertinently retail in all companies, in hopes of passing for scholars. If, therefore, you would avoid the accusation of pedantry on one hand, or the suspicion of ignorance on the other, abstain from learned ostentation. Speak the language of the company you are in; speak it purely, and unlarded with any other. Never seem wiser, nor more learned, than the people you are with. Wear your learning, like your watch, in a private pocket: and do not merely pull it out and strike it; merely to show that you have one. If you are asked what o'clock it is, tell it; but do not proclaim it hourly and unasked, like the watchman.

Upon the whole, remember that learning (I mean Greek and Roman learning) is a most useful and necessary ornament, which it is shameful not to be master of; but, at the same time, most carefully avoid those errors and abuses which I have mentioned, and which too often attend it. Remember, too, that great modern knowledge is still more necessary than ancient; and that you had better know perfectly the present, than the old state of Europe; though I would have you well acquainted with both.

I have this moment received your letter of the 17th, N.S. Though, I confess, there is no great variety in your present manner of life, yet materials can never be wanting for a letter; you see, you hear, or you read something new every day; a short account of which, with your own reflections thereupon, will make out a letter very well. But since you desire a subject, pray send me an account of the Lutheran establishment in Germany; their religious tenets, their church government, the maintenance, authority, and titles of their clergy.

Vittorio Siri,* complete, is a very scarce and very dear book here; but I do not want it. If your own library grows too voluminous, you will not know what to do with it, when you leave Leipsig. Your best way will be, when you go away from thence, to send to England, by Hamburg, all the books that you do not absolutely want. Yours.

29. TO SOLOMON DAYROLLES, ESQ.

BATH, FEBRUARY 23, O.S. 1748

Me voici, mon cher enfant, enjoying liberty and idleness, but attended with a great cold, which I got upon the road, in the coldest weather, and the deepest snow that I ever remember. This has hindered me from drinking the waters hitherto; but that is no great matter, as I came here more for the sake of quiet, and absence from London, while I was the only subject of conversation there, than for any great occasion that I had for the waters.

Without affectation, I feel most sensibly the comforts of my present free and quiet situation;* and if I had much vanity in my composition, of which I really think that I have less than most people, even that vanity would be fully gratified, by the voice of the public upon this occasion. But, upon my word, all the busy tumultuous passions have subsided in me; and that not so much from philosophy, as from a little reflection upon a great deal of experience. I have been behind the scenes, both of pleasure and business. I have seen all the coarse pullies and dirty ropes, which exhibit and move all the gaudy machines; and I have seen and smelt the tallow-candles which illuminate the whole decoration, to the astonishment and admiration of the ignorant audience.

Since my resignation, my brother, as you will have seen in the newspapers, is appointed Commissioner of the Admiralty,* which he never would have been as long as I had continued in, the resolution being taken to exclude all those who might otherwise have been supposed to have come in upon my interest. As I retire without quarrelling, and without the least intention to oppose, I saw no reason why my brother should decline this post; and I advised him to accept of it, and the rather as it was the King's own doing.

George Stanhope* too, I am told, is now to have the rank of Colonel given him, which I could never procure him; so that it seems I have a much better interest out of place than I had in.

All goes well at Leipsig; the boy applies and improves more than I expected. Count and Countess Flemming, who saw him there, and who carried him to the Duchess of Courland's, gave me a very good account of him; and assured me, that he was by no means the awkward English oaf, but *passablement décrotté.** He shall stay there a year longer, and then go to Turin. If you should accidentally hear, or can procure, any memoirs of his private character, pray let me know them.

Remember the cautions which I gave you in one of

my former letters. When Lord Sandwich goes to the Congress, you will have a great deal to do, and play a considerable part, at the Hague; which I know you are able to acquit yourself of very well. This, I think, will put you *en train d'être Monsieur l'Envoyé*, upon Lord Sandwich's return to his post here, which will be before it is very long; for, however little peace is at present intended, necessity will soon make it by the means of the *Maréchaux de Saxe et Lowendahl*; and then, being upon the place, I think you may reasonably ask, and probably obtain, the character and appointments of Envoy.*

The more to facilitate this point, make your court as much as possible to the Prince of Orange,

> 'Et sachez qu'en ceci
> La femme est comprise aussi.'*

For a word dropped in a private letter from *sister* to *sister*, may be of great use upon that occasion.

May you have all you wish!   Adieu, yours.

30. TO HIS SON

BATH, MARCH 9, O.S. 1748

DEAR BOY,

I must from time to time, remind you of what I have often recommended to you, and of what you cannot attend to too much; *sacrifice to the Graces.** The different effects of the same things, said or done, when accompanied or abandoned by them, is almost inconceivable. They prepare the way to the heart; and the heart has such an influence over the understanding, that it is worth while to engage it in our interest. It is the whole of women, who are guided by nothing else; and it has so much to say, even with men, and the ablest men too, that it commonly triumphs in every struggle with the understanding. Monsieur de la Rochefoucault, in his Maxims, says, that *l'esprit est souvent la dupe du cœur.** If he had said, instead of *souvent, presque toujours*, I fear he would have been nearer the truth. This being the case, aim at the heart. Intrinsic merit alone will not do; it will gain you the general esteem of all; but not the particular affection, that is, the heart, of any. To engage the affection of any particular person, you must, over and above your general merit, have some particular merit to that person, by services done, or offered; by expressions of regard and esteem; by complaisance, attentions, etc., for him: and the graceful manner of doing all these things opens the way to the heart, and facilitates, or rather insures, their effects. From your own observation, reflect what a disagreeable impression an awkward address, a slovenly figure, an ungraceful manner of speaking, whether stuttering, muttering, monotony, or drawling, an unattentive behaviour, etc., make upon you, at first sight, in a stranger, and how they prejudice you against him, though, for ought you know, he may have great intrinsic sense and merit. And reflect, on the other hand, how much the opposites of all these things prepossess you, at first sight, in favour of those who enjoy them. You wish to find all good qualities in them, and are in some degree disappointed if you do not. A thousand little things, not separately to be defined, conspire to form these graces, this *je ne sçais quoi*, that always pleases. A pretty person, genteel motions, a proper degree of dress, an harmonious voice, something open and cheerful in the countenance, but without laughing; a distinct and properly varied manner of speaking: all these things, and many others, are necessary ingredients in the composition of the pleasing *je ne sçais quoi*, which everybody feels, though nobody can describe. Observe carefully, then, what displeases or pleases you in others, and be persuaded, that, in general, the same things will please or displease them in you. Having mentioned laughing, I must particularly warn you against it: and I could heartily wish that you may often be seen to smile, but never heard to laugh while you live. Frequent and loud laughter is the characteristic of folly and ill manners: it is the manner in which the mob express their silly joy at silly things; and they call it being merry. In my mind there is nothing so illiberal, and so ill-bred, as audible laughter. True wit, or sense, never yet made anybody laugh; they are above it: they please the mind, and give a cheerfulness to the countenance. But it is low buffoonery, or silly accidents, that always excite laughter; and that is what people of sense and breeding should show themselves above. A man's going to sit down, in the supposition that he has a chair behind him, and falling down upon his breech for want of one, sets a whole company a laughing, when all the wit in the world would not do it; a plain proof, in my mind, how low and unbecoming a thing laughing is: not to mention the disagreeable noise that it makes, and the shocking distortion of the face that it occasions. Laughter is easily restrained by a very little reflection; but as it is generally connected with the idea of gaiety, people do not enough attend to its absurdity. I am neither of a melancholy nor a cynical disposition, and am as willing and as apt to be pleased as anybody; but I am sure that since I have had the full use of my reason, nobody has ever heard me laugh. Many people, at first, from awkwardness and *mauvaise honte,* have got a very disagreeable and silly trick of laughing whenever they speak: and I know a man of very good parts, Mr. Waller,* who cannot say the commonest thing without laughing; which makes those who do not know him take him at first for a natural fool.

This, and many other very disagreeable habits, are owing to *mauvaise honte* at their first setting out in the world. They are ashamed in company, and so disconcerted, that they do not know what they do, and try a thousand tricks to keep themselves in countenance; which tricks afterwards grow habitual to them. Some put their fingers in their nose, others scratch their head, others twirl their hats; in short, every awkward, ill-bred body has his trick. But the frequency does not justify the thing, and all these vulgar habits and awkwardnesses, though not criminal indeed, are most carefully to be guarded against, as they are great bars in the way of the art of pleasing. Remember that to please is almost to prevail, or at least a necessary previous step to it. You, who have your fortune to make, should more particularly study this art. You had not, I must tell you, when you left England, *les manières prévenantes*;*and I must confess they are not very common in England; but I hope that your good sense will make you acquire them abroad. If you desire to make yourself considerable in the world (as, if you have any spirit, you do), it must be entirely your own doing; for I may very possibly be out of the world at the time you come into it. Your own rank and fortune will not assist you; your merit and your manners can alone raise you to figure and fortune. I have laid the foundations of them, by the education which I have given you; but you must build the superstructure yourself. . . .

I wish you a good Easter fair at Leipsig.* See,

with attention, all the shops, drolls, tumblers, rope-dancers, and *hoc genus omne :** but inform yourself more particularly of the several parts of trade there. Adieu!

31. TO HIS SON

LONDON, APRIL 1, O.S. 1748

DEAR BOY,

I have not received any letter, either from you or from Mr. Harte, these three posts, which I impute wholly to accidents between this place and Leipsig; and they are distant enough to admit of many. I always take it for granted that you are well, when I do not hear to the contrary; besides, as I have often told you, I am much more anxious about your doing well, than about your being well; and when you .do not write, I will suppose that you are doing something more useful. Your health will continue, while your temperance continues; and at your age Nature takes sufficient care of the body, provided she is left to herself, and that intemperance on one hand, or medicines on the other, do not break in upon her. But it is by no means so with the mind, which, at your age particularly, requires great and constant care, and some physic. Every quarter of an hour, well or ill employed, will do it essential and lasting good or harm. It requires, also, a great deal of exercise, to bring it to a state of health and vigour. Observe the difference there is between minds cultivated and minds uncultivated, and you will, I am sure, think that you cannot take too much pains, nor employ too much of your time in the culture of your own. A drayman is probably born with as good organs as Milton, Locke, or Newton; but, by culture, they are much more above him than he is above his horse. Sometimes, indeed, extraordinary geniuses have broken out by the force of nature, without the assistance of education; but those instances are too rare for anybody to trust to; and even they would make a much greater figure, if they had the advantage of education into the bargain. If Shakespeare's genius had been cultivated, those beauties, which we so justly admire in him, would have been undisgraced by those extravagancies, and that nonsense, with which they are frequently accompanied. People are, in general, what they are made, by education and company, from fifteen to five-and-twenty; consider well, therefore, the importance of your next eight or nine years; your whole depends upon them. I will tell you sincerely my hopes and fears concerning you. I think you will be a good scholar, and that you will acquire a considerable stock of knowledge of various kinds; but I fear that you neglect what are called little, though, in truth, they are very material things; I mean, a gentleness of manners, an engaging address, and an insinuating behaviour: they are real and solid advantages, and none but those who do not know the world treat them as trifles. I am told that you speak very quick, and not distinctly; this is a most ungraceful and disagreeable trick, which you know I have told you of a thousand times; pray attend carefully to the correction of it. An agreeable and distinct manner of speaking adds greatly to the matter; and I have known many a very good speech unregarded, upon account of the disagreeable manner in which it has been delivered, and many an indifferent one applauded, for the contrary reason. Adieu!

32. TO HIS SON

DEAR BOY,

I am extremely pleased with your continuation of the history of the Reformation; which is one of those important eras that deserve your utmost attention, and of which you cannot be too minutely informed. You have, doubtless, considered the causes of that great event, and observed that disappointment and resentment had a much greater share in it, than a religious zeal or an abhorrence of the errors and abuses of popery.

Luther, an Augustin monk, enraged that his order, and consequently himself, had not the exclusive privilege of selling indulgences, but that the Dominicans were let into a share of that profitable but infamous trade, turns reformer, and exclaims against the abuses, the corruption, and the idolatry, of the Church of Rome; which were certainly gross enough for him to have seen long before, but which he had at least acquiesced in, till what he called the rights, that is the profit, of his order came to be touched. It is true, the Church of Rome furnished him ample matter for complaint and reformation, and he laid hold of it ably. This seems to me the true cause of that great and necessary work; but whatever the cause was, the effect was good; and the Reformation spread itself by its own truth and fitness; was conscientiously received by great numbers in Germany, and other countries; and was soon afterwards mixed up with the politics of princes; and, as it always happens in religious disputes, became the specious covering of injustice and ambition.

Under the pretence of crushing heresy, as it was

called, the House of Austria meant to extend and establish its power in the empire: as, on the other hand, many Protestant Princes, under the pretence of extirpating idolatry, or at least of securing toleration, meant only to enlarge their own dominions or privileges. These views respectively, among the chiefs on both sides, much more than true religious motives, continued what were called the religious wars in Germany, almost uninterruptedly, till the affairs of the two religions were finally settled by the treaty of Munster.*

Were most historical events traced up to their true causes, I fear we should not find them much more noble, nor disinterested, than Luther's disappointed avarice; and therefore I look with some contempt upon those refining and sagacious historians, who ascribe all, even the most common events, to some deep political cause; whereas mankind is made up of inconsistencies, and no man acts invariably up to his predominant character. The wisest man sometimes acts weakly, and the weakest sometimes wisely. Our jarring passions, our variable humours, nay, our greater or lesser degree of health and spirits, produce such contradictions in our conduct, that, I believe, those are the oftenest mistaken, who ascribe our actions to the most seemingly obvious motives: and I am convinced that a light supper, a good night's sleep, and a fine morning, have sometimes made a hero of the same man, who, by an indigestion, a restless night, and a rainy morning, would have proved a coward. Our best conjectures, therefore, as to the true springs of actions, are but very uncertain; and the actions themselves are all that we must pretend to know from history. That Caesar was murdered by twenty-three conspirators I make no doubt: but I very much doubt that their love of liberty and of their country was their sole, or even principal motive; and I dare say that if the truth were known, we should find that many other motives at least concurred, even in the great Brutus himself; such as pride, envy, personal pique, and disappointment. Nay, I cannot help carrying my Pyrrhonism* still farther, and extending it often to historical facts themselves, at least to most of the circumstances with which they are related; and every day's experience confirms me in this historical incredulity. Do we ever hear the most recent fact related exactly in the same way by the several people who were at the same time eye-witnesses of it? No. One mistakes, another misrepresents; and others warp it a little to their own turn of mind, or private views. A man who has been concerned in a transaction, will not write it fairly; and a man who has not, cannot. But notwithstanding all this uncertainty, history is not the less necessary to be known; as the best histories are taken for granted, and are the frequent subjects both of conversation and writing. Though I am convinced that Caesar's ghost never appeared to Brutus, yet I should be much ashamed to be ignorant of that fact, as related by the historians of those times. Thus the Pagan theology is universally received as matter for writing and conversation, though believed now by nobody; and we talk of Jupiter, Mars, Apollo, etc., as gods, though we know that, if they ever existed at all, it was only as mere mortal men. This historical Pyrrhonism, then, proves nothing against the study and knowledge of history; which, of all other studies, is the most necessary for a man who is to live in the world. It only points out to us, not to be too decisive and peremptory; and to be cautious how we draw inferences, for our own practice, from remote facts, partially or ignorantly related; of which we can at best, but imperfectly guess, and certainly not know the real motives. The testimonies of ancient history must necessarily be weaker than those of modern, as all testimony grows weaker and weaker, as it is more and more remote from us. I would therefore advise you to study ancient history, in general as other people do; that is, not to be ignorant of any of those facts which are universally received upon the faith of the best historians; and whether true or false, you have them as other people have them. But modern history, I mean particularly that of the three last centuries, is what I would have you apply to with the greatest attention and exactness. There the probability of coming at the truth is much greater, as the testimonies are much more recent; besides, anecdotes, memoirs, and original letters, often come to the aid of modern history. The best Memoirs that I know of are those of Cardinal de Retz,* which I have once before recommended to you; and which I advise you to read more than once, with attention. There are many political maxims in these memoirs, most of which are printed in italics; pray attend to, and remember them. I never read them, but my own experience confirms the truth of them. Many of them seem trifling to people who are not used to business; but those who are, feel the truth of them.

It is time to put an end to this long rambling letter; in which if any one thing can be of use to you, it will more than pay the trouble I have taken to write it. Adieu! Yours.

33. TO HIS SON

LONDON, MAY 10, O.S. 1748

DEAR BOY,

I reckon that this letter will find you just returning from Dresden,* where you have made your first court *caravanne*. What inclination for courts this taste of them may have given you, I cannot tell; but this I think myself sure of, from your good sense, that in leaving Dresden, you have left dissipation too; and have resumed, at Leipsig, that application, which, if you like courts, can alone enable you to make a good figure at them. A mere courtier, without parts or knowledge, is the most frivolous and contemptible of all beings; as, on the other hand, a man of parts and knowledge, who acquires the easy and noble manners of a court, is the most perfect. It is a trite, commonplace observation, that courts are the seats of falsehood and dissimulation. That, like many, I might say most commonplace observations, is false. Falsehood and dissimulation are certainly to be found at courts; but where are they not to be found? Cottages have them, as well as courts; only with worse manners. A couple of neighbouring farmers in a village will contrive and practise as many tricks to overreach each other at the next market, or to supplant each other in the favour of the squire, as any two courtiers can do to supplant each other in the favour of their prince.

Whatever poets may write, or fools believe, of rural innocence and truth, and of the perfidy of courts, this is most undoubtedly true—that shepherds and ministers are both men; their nature and passions the same, the modes of them only different.

Having mentioned commonplace observations, I

will particularly caution you against either using, believing or approving them. They are the common topics of witlings and coxcombs; those who really have wit have the utmost contempt for them, and scorn even to laugh at the pert things that those would-be wits say upon such subjects.

Religion is one of their favourite topics; it is all priestcraft; and an invention contrived and carried on by priests of all religions for their own power and profit; from this absurd and false principle flow the commonplace insipid jokes, and insults upon the clergy. With these people, every priest, of every religion, is either a public or concealed unbeliever, drunkard, and whoremaster; whereas, I conceive, that priests are extremely like other men, and neither the better nor the worse for wearing a gown or a surplice; but if they are different from other people, probably it is rather on the side of religion and morality, or, at least, decency, from their education and manner of life.

Another common topic for false wit and cold raillery, is matrimony. Every man and his wife hate each other cordially; whatever they may pretend, in public, to the contrary. The husband certainly wishes his wife at the devil, and the wife certainly cuckolds her husband. Whereas, I presume that men and their wives neither love nor hate each other the more, upon account of the form of matrimony which has been said over them. The cohabitation, indeed, which is the consequence of matrimony, makes them either love or hate more, accordingly as they respectively deserve it; but that would be exactly the same, between any man and woman, who lived together without being married.

These and many other commonplace reflections

upon nations or professions in general (which are at least as often false as true), are the poor refuge of people who have neither wit nor invention of their own, but endeavour to shine in company by second-hand finery. I always put these pert jackanapes out of countenance, by looking extremely grave, when they expect that I should laugh at their pleasantries; and by saying *Well, and so*; as if they had not done, and that the sting were still to come. This disconcerts them; as they have no resources in themselves, and have but one set of jokes to live upon. Men of parts are not reduced to these shifts, and have the utmost contempt for them; they find proper subjects enough for either useful or lively conversations; they can be witty without satire or commonplace, and serious without being dull. The frequentation of courts checks this petulancy of manners; the good-breeding and circumspection which are necessary, and only to be learned there, correct those pertnesses. I do not doubt but that you are improved in your manners, by the short visit which you have made at Dresden; and the other courts, which I intend that you shall be better acquainted with, will gradually smooth you up to the highest polish. In courts, a versatility of genius and a softness of manners, are absolutely necessary; which some people mistake for abject flattery, and having no opinion of one's own; whereas it is only the decent and genteel manner of maintaining your own opinion, and possibly of bringing other people to it. The manner of doing things is often more important than the things themselves; and the very same thing may become either pleasing or offensive, by the manner of saying or doing it. *Materiam superabat opus*,* is often said of works of sculpture: where, though the materials were valuable,

as silver, gold, etc., the workmanship was still more
so. This holds true, applied to manners; which adorn
whatever knowledge or parts people may have; and
even make a greater impression upon nine in ten of
mankind, than the intrinsic value of the materials. On
the other hand, remember, that what Horace says of
good writing is justly applicable to those who would
make a good figure in courts, and distinguish themselves in the shining parts of life; *Sapere est principium
et fons.** A man who, without a good fund of knowledge and parts, adopts a court life, makes the most
ridiculous figure imaginable. He is a machine, little
superior to the court clock; and as this points out the
hours, he points out the frivolous employment of
them. He is, at most, a comment upon the clock; and
according to the hours that it strikes, tells you now it
is levee, now dinner, now supper time, etc. The end
which I propose by your education, and which (*if you
please*) I shall certainly attain, is to unite in you all the
knowledge of a scholar with the manners of a courtier;
and to join, what is seldom joined in any of my
countrymen, books and the world. They are commonly twenty years old before they have spoken to
anybody above their schoolmaster, and the fellows of
their college. If they happen to have learning, it is only
Greek and Latin, but not one word of modern history,
or modern languages. Thus prepared, they go abroad,
as they call it; but, in truth, they stay at home all that
while; for being very awkward, confoundedly ashamed,
and not speaking the languages, they go into no foreign
company, at least none good; but dine and sup with one
another only at the tavern. Such examples, I am sure,
you will not imitate, but even carefully avoid. You will
always take care to keep the best company in the place

where you are, which is the only use of travelling: and
(by the way) the pleasures of a gentleman are only to
be found in the best company; for that riot which low
company most falsely and impudently call pleasure,
is only the sensuality of a swine.

I ask hard and uninterrupted study from you but
one year more; after that, you shall have every day
more and more time for your amusements. A few
hours each day will then be sufficient for application,
and the others cannot be better employed than in the
pleasures of good company. Adieu!

34. TO HIS SON

LONDON, JULY I, O.S. 1748

DEAR BOY,

I am extremely well pleased with the course of studies
which Mr. Harte informs me you are now in, and with
the degree of application which he assures me you
have to them. It is your interest to do so, as the advantage will be all your own. My affection for you makes
me both wish and endeavour that you may turn out
well; and, according as you do turn out, I shall be
either proud or ashamed of you. But as to mere interest, in the common acceptation of that word, it
would be mine that you should turn out ill; for you
may depend upon it, that whatever you have from me
shall be most exactly proportioned to your desert.
Deserve a great deal, and you shall have a great deal;
deserve little, and you shall have but little; and be
good for nothing at all, and I assure you you shall have
nothing at all.

Solid knowledge, as I have often told you, is the
first and great foundation of your future fortune and

character; for I never mention to you the two much greater points of Religion and Morality, because I cannot possibly suspect you as to either of them. This solid knowledge you are in a fair way of acquiring; you may, if you please; and I will add, that nobody ever had the means of acquiring it more in their power than you have. But remember, that manners must adorn knowledge, and smooth its way through the world. Like a great rough diamond, it may do very well in a closet by way of curiosity, and also for its intrinsic value; but it will never be worn, nor shine, if it is not polished. It is upon this article, I confess, that I suspect you the most, which makes me recur to it so often; for I fear that you are apt to show too little attention to everybody, and too much contempt to many. Be convinced, that there are no persons so insignificant and inconsiderable, but may, some time or other, have it in their power to be of use to you; which they certainly will not, if you have once shown them contempt. Wrongs are often forgiven, but contempt never is. Our pride remembers it for ever. It implies a discovery of weaknesses, which we are much more careful to conceal than crimes. Many a man will confess his crimes to a common friend, but I never knew a man who would tell his silly weaknesses to his most intimate one —as many a friend will tell us our faults without reserve, who will not so much as hint at our follies. That discovery is too mortifying to our self-love, either to tell another, or to be told of one's self. You must therefore never expect to hear of your weaknesses, or your follies, from anybody but me; those I will take pains to discover, and whenever I do, shall tell you of them.

Next to manners are exterior graces of person and address; which adorn manners, as manners adorn knowledge. To say that they please, engage, and charm, as they most indisputably do, is saying, that one should do everything possible to acquire them. The graceful manner of speaking is, particularly, what I shall always holla in your ears, as Hotspur hollaed *Mortimer* to Henry the Fourth, and, like him too, I have aimed to have a starling taught to say, *Speak distinctly and gracefully*, and send him you, to replace your loss of the unfortunate Matzel;* who, by the way, I am told spoke his language very distinctly and gracefully.

As by this time you must be able to write German tolerably well, I desire you will not fail to write a German letter, in the German character, once every fortnight, to Mr. Grevenkop;* which will make it more familiar to you, and enable me to judge how you improve in it.

Do not forget to answer me the questions, which I asked you a great while ago, in relation to the constitution of Saxony; and also the meaning of the words *Landsassii* and *Amptsassii.**

I hope you do not forget to inquire into the affairs of trade and commerce, nor to get the best accounts you can of the commodities and manufactures, exports and imports, of the several countries where you may be, and their gross value.

I would likewise have you attend to the respective coins, gold, silver, copper, etc., and their value, compared with our coins; for which purpose, I would advise you to put up, in a separate piece of paper, one piece of every kind, wherever you shall be, writing upon it the name and value. Such a collection will be curious enough in itself; and that sort of knowledge will be very useful to you in your way of business, where the different value of money often comes in question.

I am going to Cheltenham to-morrow, less for my health, which is pretty good, than for the dissipation and amusement of the journey. I shall stay about a fortnight.

L'Abbé Mably's *Droit de l'Europe*, which Mr. Harte is so kind as to send me, is worth your reading. Adieu.

35. TO HIS SON

LONDON, SEPTEMBER 5, O.S. 1748

DEAR BOY,

I have received yours, with the enclosed German letter to Mr. Grevenkop, which he assures me is extremely well written, considering the little time that you have applied yourself to that language. As you have now got over the most difficult part, pray go on diligently, and make yourself absolutely master of the rest. Who-ever does not entirely possess a language will never appear to advantage, or even equal to himself, either in speaking or writing it. His ideas are fettered, and seem imperfect or confused, if he is not master of all the words and phrases necessary to express them. I therefore desire, that you will not fail writing a German letter once every fortnight to Mr. Grevenkop; which will make the writing of that language familiar to you; and moreover, when you shall have left Germany, and be arrived at Turin, I shall require you to write even to me in German; that you may not forget with ease, what you have with difficulty learned. I likewise desire that, while you are in Germany, you will take all opportunities of conversing in German, which is the only way of knowing that, or any other language accurately. You will also desire your German master to teach you the proper titles and superscriptions to be used to people of all ranks; which is a point so material, in Germany, that I have known many a letter returned unopened, because one title in twenty has been omitted in the direction.

St. Thomas's Day* now draws near, when you are to leave Saxony and go to Berlin; and I take it for granted, that if anything is yet wanting to complete your knowledge of the state of that Electorate, you will not fail to procure it before you go away. I do not mean, as you will easily believe, the number of churches, parishes, or towns; but I mean the constitution, the revenues, the troops, and the trade of that Electorate. A few questions sensibly asked, of sensible people, will procure you the necessary informations; which I desire you will enter in your little book. Berlin will be entirely a new scene to you, and I look upon it, in a manner, as your first step into the great world; take care that step be not a false one, and that you do not stumble at the threshold. You will there be in more company than you have yet been; manners and attentions will therefore be more necessary. Pleasing in company is the only way of being pleased in it yourself. Sense and knowledge are the first and necessary foundations for pleasing in company; but they will by no means do alone, and they will never be perfectly welcome, if they are not accompanied with Manners and Attentions. You will best acquire these by frequenting the companies of people of fashion; but then you must resolve to acquire them, in those companies, by proper care and observation; for I have known people who, though they have frequented good company all their lifetime, have done it in so inatten-

tive and unobserving a manner, as to be never the
better for it, and to remain as disagreeable, as awkward,
and as vulgar, as if they had never seen any person of
fashion. When you go into good company (by good
company is meant the people of the first fashion of the
place) observe carefully their turn, their manners,
their address; and conform your own to them. But
this is not all neither; go deeper still; observe their
characters, and pry, as far as you can, into both their
hearts and their heads. Seek for their particular merit,
their predominant passion, or their prevailing weakness; and you will then know what to bait your hook
with to catch them. Man is a composition of so many
and such various ingredients, that it requires both time
and care to analyse him; for though we have all the
same ingredients in our general composition, as reason,
will, passions, and appetites; yet the different proportions and combinations of them in each individual,
produce that infinite variety of characters which, in
some particular or other, distinguishes every individual
from another. Reason ought to direct the whole, but
seldom does. And he who addresses himself singly to
another man's reason, without endeavouring to engage
his heart in his interest also, is no more likely to succeed, than a man who should apply only to a King's
nominal minister, and neglect his favourite.

I will recommend to your attentive perusal, now
that you are going into the world, two books, which
will let you as much into the characters of men, as
books can do. I mean, *Les Réflexions Morales de Monsieur de la Rochefoucault,* and *Les Caractères de La
Bruyère:*but remember, at the same time, that I only
recommend them to you as the best general maps, to
assist you in your journey, and not as marking out

every particular turning and winding that you will meet with. There your own sagacity and observation must come to their aid. La Rochefoucault is, I know, blamed, but I think without reason, for deriving all our actions from the source of self-love. For my own part, I see a great deal of truth, and no harm at all, in that opinion. It is certain, that we seek our own happiness in everything we do; and it is as certain, that we can only find it in doing well, and in conforming all our actions to the rule of right reason, which is the great law of nature. It is only a mistaken self-love that is a blameable motive, when we take the immediate and indiscriminate gratification of a passion, or appetite, for real happiness. But am I blameable, if I do a good action, upon account of the happiness which that honest consciousness will give me? Surely not. On the contrary, that pleasing consciousness is a proof of my virtue. The reflection, which is the most censured in Monsieur de la Rochefoucault's book, as a very ill-natured one, is this, *On trouve dans le malheur de son meilleur ami, quelque chose qui ne déplaît pas.* And why not? Why may I not feel a very tender and real concern for the misfortune of my friend, and yet at the same time feel a pleasing consciousness at having discharged my duty to him, by comforting and assisting him to the utmost of my power in that misfortune? Give me but virtuous actions, and I will not quibble and chicane about the motives. And I will give anybody their choice of these two truths, which amount to the same thing; He who loves himself best is the honestest man; or, The honestest man loves himself best.

The characters of La Bruyère are pictures from the life; most of them finely drawn, and highly coloured.

Furnish your mind with them first, and when you meet with their likeness, as you will every day, they will strike you the more. You will compare every feature with the original; and both will reciprocally help you to discover the beauties and the blemishes.

As women are a considerable, or at least a pretty numerous part of company; and as their suffrages go a great way towards establishing a man's character in the fashionable part of the world (which is of great importance to the fortune and figure he proposes to make in it), it is necessary to please them. I will therefore, upon this subject, let you into certain *Arcana*, that will be very useful for you to know, but which you must, with the utmost care, conceal; and never seem to know. Women, then, are only children of a larger growth;* they have an entertaining tattle, and sometimes wit; but for solid, reasoning good-sense, I never knew in my life one that had it, or who reasoned or acted consequentially for four and twenty hours together. Some little passion or humour always breaks in upon their best resolutions. Their beauty neglected or controverted, their age increased, or their supposed understandings depreciated, instantly kindles their little passions, and overturns any system of consequential conduct, that in their most reasonable moments they might have been capable of forming. A man of sense only trifles with them, plays with them, humours and flatters them, as he does with a sprightly, forward child; but he neither consults them about, nor trusts them with serious matters; though he often makes them believe that he does both; which is the thing in the world that they are proud of; for they love mightily to be dabbling in business (which, by the way, they always spoil); and being justly distrustful,

that men in general look upon them in a trifling
light, they almost adore that man who talks more
seriously to them, and who seems to consult and trust
them; I say, who seems; for weak men really do, but
wise ones only seem to do it. No flattery is either too
high or too low for them. They will greedily swallow
the highest, and gratefully accept of the lowest; and
you may safely flatter any woman, from her understanding down to the exquisite taste of her fan.
Women who are either indisputably beautiful, or indisputably ugly, are best flattered upon the score of
their understandings; but those who are in a state of
mediocrity, are best flattered upon their beauty, or at
least their graces; for every woman, who is not absolutely ugly, thinks herself handsome; but not hearing
often that she is so, is the more grateful, and the more
obliged to the few who tell her so; whereas a decided
and conscious beauty looks upon every tribute paid
to her beauty only as her due; but wants to shine, and
to be considered on the side of her understanding; and
a woman who is ugly enough to know that she is so,
knows that she has nothing left for it but her understanding, which is consequently (and probably in more
senses than one) her weak side. But these are secrets,
which you must keep inviolably, if you would not,
like Orpheus, be torn to pieces by the whole sex:* on
the contrary, a man who thinks of living in the great
world, must be gallant, polite and attentive to please
the women. They have, from the weakness of men,
more or less influence in all courts; they absolutely
stamp every man's character in the *beau monde*, and
make it either current, or cry it down, and stop it in
payments. It is, therefore, absolutely necessary to
manage, please and flatter them: and never to discover

the least mark of contempt, which is what they never forgive; but in this they are not singular, for it is the same with men; who will much sooner forgive an injustice than an insult. Every man is not ambitious, or covetous, or passionate; but every man has pride enough in his composition to feel and resent the least slight and contempt. Remember, therefore, most carefully to conceal your contempt, however just, wherever you would not make an implacable enemy. Men are much more unwilling to have their weaknesses and their imperfections known, than their crimes; and, if you hint to a man that you think him silly, ignorant, or even ill bred or awkward, he will hate you more and longer, than if you tell him plainly, that you think him a rogue. Never yield to that temptation, which to most young men is very strong, of exposing other people's weaknesses and infirmities, for the sake either of diverting the company, or showing your own superiority. You may get the laugh on your side by it for the present; but you will make enemies by it for ever; and even those who laugh with you then will, upon reflection fear, and consequently hate you: besides that it is ill natured, and a good heart desires rather to conceal than expose other people's weaknesses or misfortunes. If you have wit, use it to please, and not to hurt: you may shine, like the sun in the temperate zones, without scorching. Here it is wished for: under the Line it is dreaded.

These are some of the hints which my long experience in the great world enables me to give you; and which, if you attend to them, may prove useful to you, in your journey through it. I wish it may be a prosperous one; at least, I am sure that it must be your own fault if it is not.

Make my compliments to Mr. Harte, who, I am very sorry to hear, is not well. I hope by this time he is recovered.

Adieu!

36. TO HIS SON

LONDON, SEPTEMBER 27, O.S. 1748

DEAR BOY,

I have received your Latin Lecture upon War, which though it is not exactly the same Latin that Caesar, Cicero, Horace, Virgil, and Ovid spoke is, however, as good Latin as the *erudite Germans* speak or write. I have always observed, that the most learned people, that is, those who have read the most Latin, write the worst; and this distinguishes the Latin of a gentleman scholar from that of a pedant. A gentleman has probably read no other Latin than that of the Augustan age, and therefore can write no other; whereas the pedant has read much more bad Latin than good; and consequently writes so too. He looks upon the best classical books as books for schoolboys, and consequently below him; but pores over fragments of obscure authors, treasures up the obsolete words which he meets with there, and uses them upon all occasions to show his reading at the expense of his judgment. Plautus is his favourite author, not for the sake of the wit and the *vis comica* of his comedies, but upon account of the many obsolete words, and the cant of low characters, which are to be met with nowhere else. He will rather use *olli* than *illi*, *optumè* than *optimè*, and any bad word, rather than any good one, provided he can but prove that, strictly speaking, it is Latin; that is, that it was written by a Roman. By this rule, I

might now write to you in the language of Chaucer or
Spenser, and assert that I wrote English, because it was
English in their days; but I should be a most affected
puppy if I did so, and you would not understand three
words of my letter. All these, and such-like affected
peculiarities, are the characteristics of learned coxcombs and pedants, and are carefully avoided by all
men of sense. . . .

I must now say something as to the matter of the
Lecture; in which I confess there is one doctrine laid
down that surprises me. It is this: *Quum vero hostis
sit lenta citave morte omnia dira nobis minitans quo-
cunque bellantibus negotium est, parum sane interfuerit
quo modo eum obruere et interficere satagamus, si ferociam exuere cunctetur. Ergo veneno quoque uti fas est,
etc.;*[*] whereas I cannot conceive that the use of poison
can, upon any account, come within the lawful means
of self-defence. Force may, without doubt, be justly
repelled by force, but not by treachery and fraud; for
I do not call the stratagems of war, such as ambuscades,
masked batteries, false attacks, etc., frauds or treachery;
they are mutually to be expected and guarded against;
but poisoned arrows, poisoned waters, or poison ad
ministered to your enemy (which can only be done by
treachery), I have always heard, read, and thought, to
be unlawful and infamous means of defence, be your
danger ever so great. But, *si ferociam exuere cunctetur;*
must I rather die than poison this enemy? Yes, certainly, much rather die than do a base or criminal
action; nor can I be sure, beforehand, that this enemy
may not, in the last moment, *ferociam exuere.*[*] But the
public lawyers now seem to me rather to warp the
law, in order to authorise, than to check, those unlawful proceedings of princes and states; which, by

being become common, appear less criminal; though custom can never alter the nature of good and ill.

Pray let no quibbles of Lawyers, no refinements of Casuists, break into the plain notions of right and wrong; which every man's right reason, and plain common sense, suggest to him. To do as you would be done by, is the plain, sure and undisputed rule of morality and justice. Stick to that; and be convinced, that whatever breaks into it, in any degree, however speciously it may be turned, and however puzzling it may be to answer it, is, notwithstanding, false in itself, unjust, and criminal. I do not know a crime in the world, which is not, by the Casuists among the Jesuits (especially the twenty-four collected, I think, by Escobar)* allowed, in some, or many cases, not to be criminal. The principles first laid down by them are often specious, the reasonings plausible, but the conclusion always a lie; for it is contrary to that evident and undeniable rule of justice which I have mentioned above, of not doing to any one what you would not have him do to you. But, however, these refined pieces of casuistry and sophistry, being very convenient and welcome to people's passions and appetites, they gladly accept the indulgence, without desiring to detect the fallacy of the reasoning; and, indeed many, I might say most people, are not able to do it; which makes the publication of such quibblings and refinements the more pernicious. I am no skilful casuist, nor subtle disputant; and yet I would undertake to justify and qualify the profession of a highwayman, step by step, and so plausibly, as to make many ignorant people embrace the profession, as an innocent, if not even a laudable one; and to puzzle people of some degree of knowledge, to answer me point by point. I have seen a book, intituled *Quidlibet ex Quolibet*,* or the Art of making anything out of anything; which is not so difficult as it would seem, if once one quits certain plain truths, obvious in gross to every understanding, in order to run after the ingenious refinements of warm imaginations and speculative reasonings. Doctor Berkeley, Bishop of Cloyne, a very worthy, ingenious, and learned man, has written a book to prove that there is no such thing as Matter,* and that nothing exists but in idea, that you and I only fancy ourselves eating, drinking, and sleeping; you at Leipsig, and I at London: that we think we have flesh and blood, legs, arms, etc., but that we are only spirit. His arguments are, strictly speaking, unanswerable; but yet I am so far from being convinced by them, that I am determined to go on to eat and drink, and walk and ride, in order to keep that *matter*, which I so mistakenly imagine my body at present to consist of, in as good plight as possible. Common sense (which, in truth, is very uncommon) is the best sense I know of; abide by it; it will counsel you best. Read and hear, for your amusement, ingenious systems, nice questions subtilly agitated, with all the refinements that warm imaginations suggest; but consider them only as exercitations for the mind, and return always to settle with common sense.

I stumbled, the other day, at a bookseller's, upon Comte de Gabalis, in two very little volumes, which I had formerly read. I read it over again, and with fresh astonishment. Most of the extravagances are taken from the Jewish Rabbins, who broached those wild notions, and delivered them in the unintelligible jargon which the Cabalists and Rosicrucians* deal in to this day. Their number is, I believe, much lessened, but there are still some; and I myself have known two, who studied and firmly believed in that mystical nonsense. What extravagancy is not man capable of entertaining, when once his shackled reason is led in triumph by fancy and prejudice! The ancient Alchemists gave very much into this stuff, by which they thought they should discover the philosopher's stone: and some of the most celebrated Empirics employed it in the pursuit of the universal medicine. Paracelsus, a bold Empiric and wild Cabalist, asserted that he had discovered it, and called it his *Alkahest.** Why, or wherefore, God knows; only that those madmen call nothing by an intelligible name. You may easily get this book from the Hague; read it, for it will both divert and astonish you; and at the same time teach you *nil admirari;** a very necessary lesson.

Your letters, except when upon a given subject, are exceedingly laconic, and neither answer my desires nor the purpose of letters; which should be familiar conversations, between absent friends. As I desire to live with you upon the footing of an intimate friend, and not of a parent, I could wish that your letters gave me more particular accounts of yourself, and of your lesser transactions. When you write to me, suppose yourself conversing freely with me, by the fireside. In that case, you would naturally mention the incidents of the day; as where you had been, whom you had seen, what you thought of them, etc. Do this in your letters: acquaint me sometimes with your studies, sometimes with your diversions; tell me of any new persons and characters that you meet with in company, and add your own observations upon them; in short, let me see more of You in your letters. How do you go on

with Lord Pulteney,* and how does he go on at Leipsig? Has he learning, has he parts, has he application?
Is he good or ill-natured? In short, What is he? at
least, What do you think him? You may tell me
without reserve, for I promise you secrecy. You are
now of an age, that I am desirous to begin a confidential
correspondence with you; and as I shall, on my part,
write you very freely my opinion upon men and things,
which I should often be very unwilling that anybody
but you and Mr. Harte should see; so, on your part,
if you write to me without reserve, you may depend
upon my inviolable secrecy. If you have ever looked
into the Letters of Madame de Sevigné*to her daughter,
Madame de Grignan, you must have observed the ease,
freedom, and friendship of that correspondence; and
yet, I hope, and believe, they did not love one another
better than we do. Tell me what books you are now
reading, either by way of study or amusement; how
you pass your evenings when at home, and where you
pass them when abroad. I know that you go sometimes to Madame Valentin's assembly;*what do you do
there? Do you play, or sup? or is it only *la belle
conversation*? Do you mind your dancing while your
dancing-master is with you? As you will be often
under the necessity of dancing a minuet, I would have
you dance it very well. Remember, that the graceful
motion of the arms, the giving your hand, and the
putting-on and pulling-off your hat genteelly, are the
material parts of a gentleman's dancing. But the
greatest advantage of dancing well is, that it necessarily teaches you to present yourself, to sit, stand, and
walk genteelly; all of which are of real importance to
a man of fashion.

I should wish that you were polished before you go

to Berlin; where, as you will be in a great deal of good company, I would have you have the right manners for it. It is a very considerable article to have *le ton de la bonne compagnie*,* in your destination particularly. The principal business of a foreign minister is, to get into the secrets, and to know all *les allures** of the courts at which he resides; this he can never bring about but by such a pleasing address, such engaging manners, and such an insinuating behaviour, as may make him sought for, and in some measure domestic, in the best company, and the best families of the place. He will then, indeed, be well informed of all that passes, either by the confidences made him, or by the carelessness of people in his company, who are accustomed to look upon him as one of them, and consequently not upon their guard before him. For a minister who only goes to the court he resides at, in form, to ask an audience of the prince or the minister upon his last instructions, puts them upon their guard, and will never know anything more than what they have a mind that he should know. Here women may be put to some use. A king's mistress, or a minister's wife or mistress, may give great and useful informations; and are very apt to do it, being proud to show they have been trusted. But then, in this case, the height of that sort of address, which strikes women, is requisite; I mean that easy politeness, genteel and graceful address, and that *extérieur brillant*, which they cannot withstand. There is a sort of men so like women, that they are to be taken just in the same way; I mean those who are commonly called *fine men*; who swarm at all courts; who have little reflection, and less knowledge; but who, by their good-breeding, and *train-train** of the world, are admitted into all companies; and by the imprudence or carelessness of their superiors, pick up secrets worth knowing, which are easily got out of them by proper address. Adieu!

37. TO HIS SON

BATH, OCTOBER 19, O.S. 1748

DEAR BOY,

Having, in my last, pointed out what sort of company you should keep, I will now give you some rules for your conduct in it; rules which my own experience and observation enable me to lay down, and communicate to you, with some degree of confidence. I have often given you hints of this kind before, but then it has been by snatches; I will now be more regular and methodical. I shall say nothing with regard to your bodily carriage and address, but leave them to the care of your dancing-master, and to your own attention to the best models; remember, however, that they are of consequence.

Talk often, but never long: in that case, if you do not please, at least you are sure not to tire your hearers. Pay your own reckoning, but do not treat the whole company, this being one of the very few cases in which people do not care to be treated, every one being fully convinced that he has wherewithal to pay.

Tell stories very seldom, and absolutely never but where they are very apt and very short. Omit every circumstance that is not material, and beware of digressions. To have frequent recourse to narrative betrays great want of imagination.

Never hold anybody by the button, or the hand, in order to be heard out; for if people are not willing to hear you, you had much better hold your tongue than them.

Most long talkers single out some one unfortunate man in company (commonly him whom they observe to be the most silent, or their next neighbour), to whisper, or at least, in a half voice, to convey a continuity of words to. This is excessively ill bred, and in some degree a fraud; conversation-stock being a joint and common property. But on the other hand, if one of these unmerciful talkers lays hold of you, hear him with patience (and at least seeming attention), if he is worth obliging; for nothing will oblige him more than a patient hearing; as nothing would hurt him more than either to leave him in the midst of his discourse, or to discover your impatience under your affliction.

Take, rather than give, the tone of the company you are in. If you have parts, you will show them, more or less, upon every subject; and if you have not, you had better talk sillily upon a subject of other people's than of your own choosing.

Avoid as much as you can, in mixed companies, argumentative, polemical conversations; which though they should not, yet certainly do, indispose, for a time, the contending parties to each other; and if the controversy grows warm and noisy, endeavour to put an end to it, by some genteel levity or joke. I quieted such a conversation-hubbub once, by representing to them that though I was persuaded none there present would repeat, out of company, what passed in it, yet I could not answer for the discretion of the passengers in the street, who must necessarily hear all that was said.

Above all things, and upon all occasions, avoid speaking of yourself, if it be possible. Such is the natural pride and vanity of our hearts, that it perpetually breaks out, even in people of the best parts, in all the various modes and figures of the egotism.

Some, abruptly, speak advantageously of themselves, without either pretence or provocation. They are impudent. Others proceed more artfully, as they imagine; and forge accusations against themselves, complain of calumnies which they never heard, in order to justify themselves, by exhibiting a catalogue of their many virtues. *They acknowledge it may, indeed, seem odd, that they should talk in that manner of themselves; it is what they do not like, and what they never would have done; no, no tortures should ever have forced it from them, if they had not been thus unjustly and monstrously accused. But, in these cases, justice is surely due to one's self, as well as to others; and when our character is attacked, we may say, in our own justification, what otherwise we never would have said.* This thin veil of Modesty drawn before Vanity, is much too transparent to conceal it, even from very moderate discernment.

Others go more modestly and more slyly still (as they think) to work; but, in my mind, still more ridiculously. They confess themselves (not without some degree of shame and confusion) into all the Cardinal Virtues; by first degrading them into weaknesses, and then owning their misfortune, in being made up of those weaknesses. *They cannot see people suffer, without sympathizing with, and endeavouring to help them. They cannot see people want, without relieving them, though, truly, their own circumstances cannot very well afford it. They cannot help speaking truth, though they know all the imprudence of it. In short, they know that, with all these weaknesses, they are not fit to live in the world, much less to thrive in it. But they are now too old to change, and must rub on as well as they can.* This sounds too ridiculous and *outré*, almost, for the stage; and yet, take my word for it, you will frequently meet with it upon the common stage of the world. And here I will observe, by-the-bye, that you will often meet with characters in nature, so extravagant, that a discreet poet would not venture to set them upon the stage in their true and high colouring.

This principle of vanity and pride is so strong in human nature, that it descends even to the lowest objects; and one often sees people angling for praise, where, admitting all they say to be true (which, by the way, it seldom is), no just praise is to be caught. One man affirms that he has rode post an hundred miles in six hours; probably it is a lie; but supposing it to be true, what then? Why he is a very good post-boy, that is all. Another asserts, and probably not without oaths, that he has drunk six or eight bottles of wine at a sitting; out of charity, I will believe him a liar; for if I do not, I must think him a beast.

Such, and a thousand more, are the follies and extra-vagancies, which vanity draws people into, and which always defeat their own purpose; and as Waller says, upon another subject,

> Make the wretch the most despised,
> Where most he wishes to be prized.*

The only sure way of avoiding these evils is never to speak of yourself at all. But when, historically, you are obliged to mention yourself, take care not to drop one single word, that can directly or indirectly be con-strued as fishing for applause. Be your character what it will, it will be known; and nobody will take it upon your own word. Never imagine that anything you can say yourself will varnish your defects, or add lustre to your perfections! but, on the contrary, it may, and nine times in ten will, make the former more glaring, and the latter obscure. If you are silent upon your own subject, neither envy, indignation, nor ridicule, will obstruct or allay the applause which you may really deserve; but if you publish your own panegyric upon any occasion, or in any shape whatsoever, and however artfully dressed or disguised, they will all conspire against you, and you will be disappointed of the very end you aim at.

Take care never to seem dark and mysterious; which is not only a very unamiable character, but a very suspicious one too; if you seem mysterious with others, they will be really so with you, and you will know nothing. The height of abilities is, to have *volto sciolto* and *pensieri stretti*;* that is, a frank, open, and ingenuous exterior, with a prudent and reserved interior; to be upon your own guard, and yet, by a seeming natural openness, to put people off theirs. Depend upon it nine in ten of every company you are in will avail themselves of every indiscreet and unguarded expression of yours, if they can turn it to their own advantage. A prudent reserve is therefore as necessary, as a seeming openness is prudent. Always look people in the face when you speak to them: the not doing it is thought to imply conscious guilt; besides that you lose the advantage of observing by their countenances what impression your discourse makes upon them. In order to know people's real sentiments, I trust much more to my eyes than to my ears: for they can say whatever they have a mind I should hear; but they can seldom help looking what they have no intention that I should know.

Neither retail nor receive scandal willingly; for

though the defamation of others may for the present gratify the malignity of the pride of our hearts, cool reflection will draw very disadvantageous conclusions from such a disposition; and in the case of scandal, as in that of robbery, the receiver is always thought as bad as the thief.

Mimicry, which is the common and favourite amusement of little, low minds, is in the utmost contempt with great ones. It is the lowest and most illiberal of all buffoonery. Pray, neither practise it yourself, nor applaud it in others. Besides that the person mimicked is insulted; and as I have often observed to you before, an insult is never forgiven.

I need not (I believe) advise you to adapt your conversation to the people you are conversing with: for I suppose you would not, without this caution, have talked upon the same subject, and in the same manner, to a minister of state, a bishop, a philosopher, a captain, and a woman. A man of the world must, like the Cameleon, be able to take every different hue; which is by no means a criminal or abject, but a necessary complaisance; for it relates only to manners, and not to morals.

One word only, as to swearing, and that, I hope and believe, is more than is necessary. You may sometimes hear some people in good company interlard their discourse with oaths, by way of embellishment, as they think; but you must observe, too, that those who do so are never those who contribute, in any degree, to give that company the denomination of good company. They are always subalterns, or people of low education; for that practice, besides that it has no one temptation to plead, is as silly, and as illiberal, as it is wicked.

Loud laughter is the mirth of the mob, who are only pleased with silly things; for true wit or good sense never excited a laugh, since the creation of the world. A man of parts and fashion is therefore only seen to smile, but never heard to laugh.

But to conclude this long letter; all the above-mentioned rules, however carefully you may observe them, will lose half their effect, if unaccompanied by the Graces. Whatever you say, if you say it with a supercilious, cynical face, or an embarrassed countenance, or a silly, disconcerted grin, will be ill received. If, into the bargain, *you mutter it, or utter it, indistinctly and ungracefully*, it will be still worse received. If your air and address are vulgar, awkward, and *gauche*, you may be esteemed indeed, if you have great intrinsic merit; but you will never please; and without pleasing, you will rise but heavily. Venus, among the ancients, was synonymous with the Graces, who were always supposed to accompany her; and Horace tells us, that even Youth, and Mercury, the God of Arts and Eloquence would not do without her.

—Parum comis *sine te Iuventas*
Mercuriusque.

They are not inexorable Ladies, and may be had, if properly and diligently pursued. Adieu!

38. TO HIS SON

BATH, OCTOBER 29, O.S. 1748

DEAR BOY,

My anxiety for your success increases in proportion as the time approaches of your taking your part upon the great stage of the world. The audience will form their

opinion of you upon your first appearance (making
the proper allowance for your inexperience), and so
far it will be final, that, though it may vary as to the
degrees, it will never totally change. This consideration excites that restless attention with which I am
constantly examining how I can best contribute to the
perfection of that character, in which the least spot
or blemish would give me more real concern, than I
am now capable of feeling upon any other account
whatsoever.

I have long since done mentioning your great
religious and moral duties, because I could not make
your understanding so bad a compliment, as to suppose that you wanted, or could receive, any new instructions upon those two important points. Mr.
Harte, I am sure, has not neglected them; besides, they
are so obvious to common sense and reason, that com-
mentators may (as they often do) perplex, but cannot
make them clearer. My province, therefore, is to
supply, by my experience, your hitherto inevitable
inexperience in the ways of the world. People at your
age are in a state of natural ebriety; and want rails, and
gardefous,* wherever they go, to hinder them from
breaking their necks. This drunkenness of youth is
not only tolerated, but even pleases if kept within certain bounds of discretion and decency. Those bounds
are the point which it is difficult for the drunken man
himself to find out; and there it is that the experience
of a friend may not only serve, but save him.

Carry with you, and welcome, into company, all
the gaiety and spirits, but as little of the giddiness, of
youth as you can. The former will charm; but the
latter will often, though innocently, implacably offend.
Inform yourself of the characters and situations of the

company, before you give way to what your imagination may prompt you to say. There are, in all companies, more wrong heads than right ones, and many more who deserve, than who like censure. Should you therefore expatiate in the praise of some virtue, which some in company notoriously want; or declaim against any vice, which others are notoriously infected with, your reflections, however general and unapplied, will, by being applicable, be thought personal, and levelled at those people. This consideration points out to you, sufficiently, not to be suspicious and captious yourself, nor to suppose that things, because they may, are therefore meant at you. The manners of well-bred people secure one from those indirect and mean attacks; but if, by chance, a flippant woman, or a pert coxcomb, lets off anything of that kind, it is much better not to seem to understand, than to reply to it.

Cautiously avoid talking of either your own or other people's domestic affairs. Yours are nothing to them but tedious; theirs are nothing to you. The subject is a tender one; and it is odds but you touch somebody or other's sore place; for in this case, there is no trusting to specious appearances, which may be, and often are, so contrary to the real situation of things between men and their wives, parents and their children, seeming friends, etc., that with the best intentions in the world, one often blunders disagreeably.

Remember that the wit, humour, and jokes of most mixed companies are local. They thrive in that particular soil, but will not often bear transplanting. Every company is differently circumstanced, has its particular cant and jargon which may give occasion to wit and mirth within that circle, but would seem flat and insipid in any other, and therefore, will not bear repeating. Nothing makes a man look sillier, than a pleasantry not relished or not understood; and if he meets with a profound silence when he expected a general applause, or, what is worse, if he is desired to explain the *bon mot*, his awkward and embarrassed situation is easier imagined than described. *A propos* of repeating; take great care never to repeat (I do not mean here the pleasantries) in one company what you hear in another. Things, seemingly indifferent, may, by circulation, have much graver consequences than you would imagine. Besides, there is a general tacit trust in conversation by which a man is obliged not to report anything out of it, though he is not immediately enjoined secrecy. A retailer of this kind is sure to draw himself into a thousand scrapes and discussions, and to be shyly and uncomfortably received wherever he goes.

You will find, in most good company, some people who only keep their place there by a contemptible title enough; these are what we call *very good-natured fellows*, and the French, *bons diables*. The truth is, they are people without any parts or fancy, and who, having no will of their own, readily assent to, concur in, and applaud, whatever is said or done in the company, and adopt, with the same alacrity, the most virtuous or the most criminal, the wisest or the silliest scheme, that happens to be entertained by the majority of the company. This foolish and often criminal complaisance flows from a foolish cause, the want of any other merit. I hope that you will hold your place in company by a noble tenure, and that you will hold it (you can bear a quibble, I believe, yet) *in capite.** Have a will and an opinion of your own, and adhere to them steadily; but then do it with good-humour, good-breeding, and (if you have it) with urbanity; for you have not yet beard enough either to preach or censure.

All other kinds of complaisance are not only blameless, but necessary in good company. Not to seem to perceive the little weaknesses, and the idle but innocent affectations of the company, but even to flatter them, in a certain manner, is not only very allowable, but, in truth, a sort of polite duty. They will be pleased with you, if you do; and will certainly not be reformed by you if you do not. For instance; you will find, in every *groupe* of company, two principal figures, *viz*. the fine lady and the fine gentleman; who absolutely give the law of wit, language, fashion, and taste, to the rest of that society. There is always a strict, and often for the time being, a tender alliance between these two figures. The lady looks upon her empire as founded upon the divine right of beauty (and full as good a divine right it is, as any king, emperor or pope can pretend to); she requires, and commonly meets with, unlimited passive obedience. And why should she not meet with it? Her demands go no higher than to have her unquestioned pre-eminence in beauty, wit, and fashion, firmly established. Few sovereigns (by the way) are so reasonable. The fine gentleman's claims of right are, *mutatis mutandis*, the same; and though, indeed, he is not always a wit *de jure*, yet, as he is the wit *de facto* of that company, he is entitled to a share of your allegiance; and everybody expects at least as much as they are entitled to, if not something more. Prudence bids you make your court to these joint sovereigns; and no duty, that I know of, forbids it. Rebellion here is exceedingly dangerous, and inevitably punished by banishment, and immediate forfeiture of all your wit, manners, taste, and fashion;

as, on the other hand, a cheerful submission, not without some flattery, is sure to procure you a strong recommendation, and most effectual pass throughout all their, and probably the neighbouring dominions. With a moderate share of sagacity, you will, before you have been half an hour in their company, easily discover those two principal figures; both by the deference which you will observe the whole company pay them, and by that easy, careless, and serene air, which their consciousness of power gives them. As in this case, so in all others, aim always at the highest; get always into the highest company, and address yourself particularly to the highest in it. The search after the unattainable philosopher's stone has occasioned a thousand useful discoveries, which otherwise would never have been made.

What the French justly call _les manières nobles_ are only to be acquired in the very best companies. They are the distinguishing characteristics of men of fashion; people of low education never wear them so close, but that some part or other of the original vulgarism appears. _Les manières nobles_ equally forbid insolent contempt, or low envy and jealousy. Low people in good circumstances, fine clothes, and equipages, will insolently show contempt for all those who cannot afford as fine clothes, as good an equipage, and who have not (as their term is) as much money in their pockets: on the other hand, they are gnawed with envy, and cannot help discovering it, of those who surpass them in any of these articles, which are far from being sure criterions of merit. They are likewise jealous of being slighted; and consequently suspicious and captious; they are eager and hot about trifles because trifles were, at first, their affairs of consequence. _Les_ *manières nobles* imply exactly the reverse of all this. Study them early; you cannot make them too habitual and familiar to you.

Just as I had written what goes before, I received your letter of the 24th, N.S., but I have not received that which you mention for Mr. Harte. Yours is of the kind that I desire; for I want to see your private picture, drawn by yourself, at different sittings; for though, as it is drawn by yourself, I presume you will take the most advantageous likeness; yet I think that I have skill enough in that kind of painting to discover the true features, though ever so artfully coloured, or thrown into skilful lights and shades.

By your account of the German play,* which I do not know whether I should call tragedy or comedy, the only shining part of it (since I am in a way of quibbling) seems to have been the fox's tail. I presume, too, that the play has had the same fate with the squib, and has gone off no more. I remember a squib much better applied, when it was made the device of the colours of a French regiment of grenadiers; it was represented bursting with this motto under it: *Peream dum luceam.*

I like the description of your *pic-nic*,* where I take it for granted, that your cards are only to break the formality of a circle, and your *Symposion* intended more to promote conversation than drinking. Such an *amicable collision*, as Lord Shaftesbury very prettily calls it, rubs off and smooths those rough corners, which mere nature has given to the smoothest of us.* I hope some part, at least, of the conversation is in German. *A propos*; tell me, do you speak that language correctly, and do you write it with ease? I have no doubt of your mastering the other modern languages, which are much easier, and occur much oftener; for which reason, I desire that you will apply most diligently to German, while you are in Germany, that you may speak and write that language most correctly.

I expect to meet Mr. Eliot*in London, in about three weeks, after which you will soon see him at Leipsig. Adieu!

39. TO HIS SON

LONDON, NOVEMBER 18, O.S. 1748

DEAR BOY,

Whatever I see, or whatever I hear, my first consideration is, whether it can in any way be useful to you. As a proof of this, I went accidentally the other day into a print-shop, where, among many others, I found one print from a famous design of Carlo Maratti,* who died about thirty years ago, and was the last eminent painter in Europe: the subject is *il Studio del Disegno*; or, the School of Drawing. An old man, supposed to be the master, points to his scholars, who are variously employed in perspective, geometry, and the observation of the statues of antiquity. With regard to perspective, of which there are some little specimens, he has wrote, *Tanto che basti*, that is, *As much as is sufficient*; with regard to Geometry, *Tanto che basti*, again: with regard to contemplation of the ancient statues, there is written, *Non mai a bastanza; There never can be enough*. But in the clouds, at top of the piece, are represented the three Graces; with this just sentence written over them, *Senza di noi ogni fatica è vana*; that is, *Without us, all labour is vain*. This everybody allows to be true in painting; but all people do not consider, as I hope you will, that this truth is full as applicable to every other art or science; indeed to everything that is to be said or done. I will send you the print itself by Mr. Eliot, when he returns; and I will advise you to make the same use of it that the Roman Catholics say they do of the pictures and images of their Saints, which is, only to remind them of those; for the adoration they disclaim. Nay, I will go farther, and, as the transition from Popery to Paganism is short and easy, I will classically and poetically advise you to invoke, and sacrifice to them every day, and all the day. It must be owned, that the Graces do not seem to be natives of Great Britain; and, I doubt, the best of us here have more of rough than polished diamond. Since barbarism drove them out of Greece and Rome, they seem to have taken refuge in France, where their temples are numerous, and their worship the established one. Examine yourself seriously, why such and such people please and engage you, more than such and such others of equal merit; and you will always find that it is because the former have the Graces and the latter not. I have known many a woman, with an exact shape, and a symmetrical assemblage of beautiful features, please nobody; while others, with very moderate shapes and features, have charmed everybody. Why? because Venus will not charm so much, without her attendant Graces, as they will without her. Among men, how often have I seen the most solid merit and knowledge neglected, unwelcome, or even rejected, for want of them! While flimsy parts, little knowledge, and less merit, introduced by the Graces, have been received, cherished, and admired. Even virtue, which is moral beauty, wants some of its charms, if unaccompanied by them.

If you ask me how you shall acquire what neither

you nor I can define or ascertain; I can only answer, *by observation*. Form yourself, with regard to others, upon what you feel pleases you in them. I can tell you the importance, the advantage, of having the Graces; but I cannot give them you: I heartily wish I could, and I certainly would; for I do not know a better present that I could make you. To show you that a very wise, philosophical, and retired man thinks upon that subject as I do, who have always lived in the world, I send you, by Mr. Eliot, the famous Mr. Locke's book upon education, in which you will find the stress that he lays upon the Graces, which he calls (and very truly) good-breeding. I have marked all the parts of that book which are worth your attention; for as he begins with the child, almost from its birth, the parts relative to its infancy would be useless to you. Germany is, still less than England, the seat of the Graces; however, you had as good not say so while you are there. But the place which you are going to, in a great degree, is; for I have known as many well-bred, pretty men come from Turin as from any part of Europe. The late King Victor Amédée* took great pains to form such of his subjects as were of any consideration both to business and manners; the present king, I am told, follows his example: this, however, is certain, that in all Courts and Congresses where there are various foreign ministers, those of the King of Sardinia are generally the ablest, the politest, and *les plus déliés*.* You will, therefore, at Turin, have very good models to form yourself upon: and remember, that with regard to the best models, as well as to the antique Greek statues in the print, *non mai a bastanza*. Observe every word, look, and motion of those who are allowed to be the most accomplished persons there. Observe their natural and careless, but genteel air; their unembarrassed good-breeding; their unassuming, but yet unprostituted dignity. Mind their decent mirth, their discreet frankness, and that *entregent** which, as much above the frivolous as below the important and the secret, is the proper medium for conversation in mixed companies. I will observe, by-the-bye, that the talent of that light *entregent* is often of great use to a foreign minister; not only as it helps him to domesticate himself in many families, but also as it enables him to put by and parry some subjects of conversation, which might possibly lay him under difficulties both what to say and how to look.

Of all the men that ever I knew in my life (and I knew him extremely well), the late Duke of Marlborough* possessed the Graces in the highest degree, not to say engrossed them; and indeed he got the most by them, for I will venture (contrary to the custom of profound historians, who always assign deep causes for great events), to ascribe the better half of the Duke of Marlborough's greatness and riches to those Graces. He was eminently illiterate; wrote bad English and spelled it still worse. He had no share of what is commonly called *Parts*: that is, he had no brightness, nothing shining in his genius. He had, most undoubtedly, an excellent good plain understanding, with sound judgment. But these alone would probably have raised him but something higher than they found him; which was Page to King James the Second's Queen. There the Graces protected and promoted him; for, while he was an Ensign of the Guards, the Duchess of Cleveland, then favourite mistress to King Charles the Second, struck by those very Graces, gave him five thousand pounds, with which he immediately bought an annuity for his life, of five hundred pounds a year, of my grandfather, Halifax, which was the foundation of his subsequent fortune. His figure was beautiful; but his manner was irresistible, by either man or woman. It was by this engaging, graceful manner, that he was enabled, during all his war, to connect the various and jarring Powers of the Grand Alliance, and to carry them on to the main object of the war, notwithstanding their private and separate views, jealousies, and wrongheadednesses. Whatever Court he went to (and he was often obliged to go himself to some resty and refractory ones), he as constantly prevailed, and brought them into his measures. The Pensionary Heinsius, a venerable old minister, grown grey in business, and who had governed the republic of the United Provinces for more than forty years, was absolutely governed by the Duke of Marlborough, as that republic feels to this day.* He was always cool; and nobody ever observed the least variation in his countenance: he could refuse more gracefully than other people could grant; and those who went away from him the most dissatisfied as to the substance of their business, were yet personally charmed with him, and, in some degree, comforted by his manner. With all his gentleness and gracefulness, no man living was more conscious of his situation, nor maintained his dignity better.

With the share of knowledge which you have already gotten, and with the much greater which I hope you will soon acquire, what may you not expect to arrive at, if you join all these Graces to it! In your destination particularly, they are in truth, half your business: for if you can once gain the affections as well as the esteem of the prince or minister of the court to which you are sent, I will answer for it, that will effectually do the business of the Court that sent you; otherwise it is up-hill work. Do not mistake, and think that these graces, which I so often and so earnestly recommend to you should only accompany important transactions, and be worn only *les jours de gala*; no, they should, if possible, accompany every the least thing that you do or say; for if you neglect them in little things, they will leave you in great ones. I should, for instance, be extremely concerned to see you even drink a cup of coffee ungracefully, and slop yourself with it, by your awkward manner of holding it; nor should I like to see your coat buttoned, or your shoes buckled awry. But I should be outrageous, if I heard you mutter your words unintelligibly, stammer in your speech, or hesitate, misplace, and mistake in your narrations; and I should run away from you with greater rapidity, if possible, than I should now run to embrace you, if I found you destitute of all those graces, which I have set my heart upon their making you one day, *omnibus ornatum excellere rebus.*[*]

This subject is inexhaustible, as it extends to everything that is to be said or done; but I will leave it for the present, as this letter is already pretty long. Such is my desire, my anxiety for your perfection, that I never think I have said enough, though you may possibly think that I have said too much; and though, in truth, if your own good sense is not sufficient to direct you in many of these plain points, all that I or anybody else can say will be insufficient. But where you are concerned, I am the insatiable man in Horace,[*] who covets still a little corner more to complete the figure of his field. I dread every little corner that may deform mine, in which I would have (if possible) no one defect.

I this moment received yours of the 17th, N.S., and cannot condole with you upon the secession of your German *Commensaux*; who both by your and Mr. Harte's description, seem to be *des gens d'une aimable absence;*[*] and if you can replace them by any other German conversation, you will be a gainer by the bargain. I cannot conceive, if you understand German well enough to read any German book, how the writing of the German character can be so difficult and tedious to you, the twenty-four letters being very soon learned; and I do not expect that you should write yet with the utmost purity and correctness, as to the language: what I meant by your writing once a fortnight to Grevenkop, was only to make the written character familiar to you. However, I will be content with one in three weeks or so.

I believe you are not likely to see Mr. Eliot again soon, he being still in Cornwall with his father;[*] who, I hear, is not likely to recover. Adieu!

40. TO HIS SON

LONDON, DECEMBER 6, O.S. 1748

DEAR BOY,

I am at present under very great concern for the loss of a most affectionate brother, with whom I had always lived in the closest friendship. My brother John[*] died last Friday night, of a fit of the gout, which he had had for about a month in his hands and feet, and which fell at last upon his stomach and head. As he grew towards the last lethargic, his end was not painful to himself. At the distance which you are at from hence, you need not go into mourning upon this occasion, as the time of your mourning would be near over, before you could put it on.

By a ship which sails this week for Hamburgh, I shall send you those things which I proposed to have sent you by Mr. Eliot, viz., a little box from your mamma, a less box for Mr. Harte; Mr. Locke's book upon Education; the print of Carlo Maratti, which I mentioned to you some time ago; and two letters of recommendation, one to Monsieur Andrié, and the other to Comte Algarotti,*at Berlin. Both those gentlemen will, I am sure, be as willing as they are able, to introduce you into the best company; and I hope you will not (as many of your countrymen are apt to do) decline it. It is in the best companies only, that you can learn the best manners, and that *tournure*, and those graces, which I have so often recommended to you, as the necessary means of making a figure in the world.

I am most extremely pleased with the account which Mr. Harte gives me of your progress in Greek, and of your having read Hesiod, almost critically. Upon this subject I suggest but one thing to you, of many that I might suggest; which is, that you have now got over the difficulties of that language, and therefore it would be unpardonable not to persevere to your journey's end, now that all the rest of your way is down-hill.

I am also very well pleased to hear that you have such a knowledge of, and taste for curious books, and scarce and valuable tracts. This is a kind of knowledge which very well becomes a man of sound and solid learning, but which only exposes a man of slight and superficial reading; therefore, pray make the substance and matter of such books your first object, and their title-pages, indexes, letter, and binding, but your second. It is the characteristic of a man of parts and good judgment to know, and give that degree of attention that each object deserves; whereas little minds mistake little objects for great ones, and lavish away upon the former that time and attention which only the latter deserve. To such mistakes we owe the numerous and frivolous tribe of insect-mongers, shell-mongers, and pursuers and driers of butterflies, etc. The strong mind distinguishes, not only between the useful and the useless, but likewise between the useful and the curious. He applies himself intensely to the former; he only amuses himself with the latter. Of this little sort of knowledge, which I have just hinted at, you will find at least as much as you need wish to know, in a superficial but pretty French book entitled *Spectacle de la Nature;** which will amuse you while you read it, and give you a sufficient notion of the various parts of nature; I would advise you to read it at leisure hours. But that part of nature, which Mr. Harte tells me you have begun to study with the *Rector magnificus,** is of much greater importance, and deserves much more attention; I mean Astronomy. The vast and immense planetary system, the astonishing order and regularity of those innumerable worlds, will open a scene to you, which not only deserves your attention as a matter of curiosity, or rather astonishment; but still more, as it will give you greater, and consequently juster ideas of that eternal and omnipotent Being, who contrived, made, and still preserves that universe, than all the contemplation of this, comparatively, very little orb, which we at present inhabit, could possibly give you. Upon this subject, Monsieur Fontenelle's *Pluralité des Mondes,** which you may read in two hours' time, will both inform and please you. God bless you! Yours.

41. TO HIS SON

LONDON, DECEMBER 20, O.S. 1748

DEAR BOY,

I received, last Saturday, by three mails which came in at once, two letters from Mr. Harte, and yours of the 8th, N.S.

It was I who mistook your meaning, with regard to your German letters, and not you who expressed it ill. I thought it was the writing of the German character that took up so much of your time, and therefore I advised you, by the frequent writing of that character, to make it easy and familiar to you. But since it is only the propriety and purity of the German language, which make your writing it so tedious and laborious, I will tell you I shall not be nice upon that article; and did not expect that you should yet be master of all the idioms, delicacies, and peculiarities of that difficult language. That can only come by use, especially frequent speaking; therefore, when you shall be at Berlin, and afterwards at Turin, where you will meet many Germans, pray take all opportunities of conversing in German, in order not only to keep what you have got of that language, but likewise to improve and perfect yourself in it. As to the characters, you form them very well, and as you yourself own, better than your English ones; but then let me ask you this question; why do you not form your Roman characters better? for I maintain, that it is in every man's power to write what hand he pleases; and consequently, that he ought to write a good one. You form particularly your *εε* and your *εε* in zig-zag, instead of making them straight as thus *ee, ff*; a fault very easily mended. You will not, I believe, be angry with this little criticism, when I tell you, that by all the accounts I have had of late, from Mr. Harte and others, this is the only criticism that you give me occasion to make. Mr. Harte's last letter, of the 14th, N.S., particularly, makes me extremely happy, by assuring me that in every respect you do extremely well. I am not afraid, by what I now say, of making you too vain; because I do not think that a just consciousness, and an honest pride of doing well, can be called vanity; for vanity is either the silly affectation of good qualities which one has not, or the sillier pride of what does not deserve commendation in itself. By Mr. Harte's account, you are got very near the goal of Greek and Latin; and therefore I cannot suppose that as your sense increases, your endeavours and your speed will slacken, in finishing the small remains of your course. Consider what lustre and *éclat* it will give you, when you return here, to be allowed to be the best scholar, of a gentleman, in England; not to mention the real pleasure and solid comfort which such knowledge will give you throughout your whole life. Mr. Harte tells me another thing, which I own I did not expect; it is, that when you read aloud, or repeat part of plays, you speak very properly and distinctly. This relieves me from great uneasiness, which I was under upon account of your former bad enunciation. Go on, and attend most diligently to this important article. It is, of all the Graces (and they are all necessary), the most necessary one.

Comte Pertingue, who has been here about a fortnight, far from disavowing, confirms all that Mr. Harte has said to your advantage. He thinks that he shall be at Turin much about the time of your arrival there, and pleases himself with the hopes of being useful to you: though, should you get there before him, he says that Comte du Perron,* with whom you are a favourite, will take that care. You see, by this one instance, and in the course of your life you will see by a million of instances, of what use a good reputation is, and how swift and advantageous a harbinger it is, wherever one goes. Upon this point, too, Mr. Harte does you justice, and tells me that you are desirous of praise from the praiseworthy: this is a right and generous ambition, and without which, I fear, few people would deserve praise.

But here let me, as an old stager upon the theatre of the world, suggest one consideration to you; which is, to extend your desire of praise a little beyond the strictly praiseworthy; or else you may be apt to discover too much contempt for at least three parts in five of the world; who will never forgive it you. In the mass of mankind, I fear, there is too great a majority of fools and knaves; who, singly from their number, must to a certain degree be respected, though they are by no means respectable. And a man who will show every knave or fool that he thinks him such, will engage in a most ruinous war, against numbers much superior to those that he and his allies can bring into the field. Abhor a knave, and pity a fool in your heart; but let neither of them unnecessarily see that you do so. Some complaisance and attention to fools is prudent, and not mean: as a silent abhorrence of individual knaves is often necessary, and not criminal.

As you will now soon part with Lord Pulteney, with whom, during your stay together at Leipsig, I suppose you have formed a connection; I imagine that you will continue it by letters, which I would advise you to do. They tell me he is good-natured, and does not want parts; which are of themselves two good reasons for keeping it up; but there is also a third reason, which, in the course of the world, is not to be despised: his father cannot live long, and will leave him an immense fortune:* which, in all events, will make him of some consequence, and if he has parts into the bargain, of very great consequence; so that his friendship may be extremely well worth your cultivating, especially as it will not cost you above one letter in one month.

I do not know whether this letter will find you at Leipsig: at least, it is the last that I shall direct there. My next to either you or Mr. Harte, will be directed to Berlin; but as I do not know to what house or street there, I suppose it will remain at the post-house till you send for it. Upon your arrival at Berlin, you will send me your particular direction; and also, pray be minute in your accounts of your reception there, by those whom I recommend you to, as well as by those to whom they present you. Remember, too, that you are going to a polite and literate Court, where the Graces will best introduce you.

Adieu. God bless you, and may you continue to deserve my love, as much as you now enjoy it!

P.S.—Lady Chesterfield* bids me tell you, that she decides entirely in your favour, against Mr. Grevenkop, and even against herself: for she does not think that she could, at this time, write either so good a character, or so good German. Pray write her a German letter upon that subject; in which you may tell her that, like the rest of the world, you approve of her judgment, because it is in your favour; and that you true Germans cannot allow Danes to be competent judges of your language, etc.

42. TO HIS SON

LONDON, DECEMBER 30, O.S. 1748

DEAR BOY,

I direct this letter to Berlin, where, I suppose, it will either find you, or at least wait but a very little time for you. I cannot help being anxious for your success, at this your first appearance upon the great stage of the world; for though the spectators are always candid enough to give great allowances, and to show great indulgence to a new actor; yet, from the first impressions which he makes upon them, they are apt to decide, in their own minds at least, whether he will ever be a good one, or not: if he seems to understand what he says, by speaking it properly; if he is attentive to his part, instead of staring negligently about; and if, upon the whole, he seems ambitious to please, they willingly pass over little awkwardnesses and inaccuracies, which they ascribe to a commendable modesty in a young and unexperienced actor. They pronounce that he will be a good one in time; and by the encouragement which they give him, make him so the sooner. This, I hope, will be your case: you have sense enough to understand your part; a constant attention, and ambition to excel in it, with a careful observation of the best actors, will inevitably qualify you, if not for the first, at least for considerable parts.

Your dress (as insignificant a thing as dress is in itself) is now become an object worthy of some attention; for, I confess, I cannot help forming some opinion of a man's sense and character from his dress; and I believe, most people do as well as myself. Any affectation whatsoever in dress implies, in my mind, a flaw in the understanding. Most of our young fellows here display some character or other by their dress; some affect the tremendous, and wear a great and fiercely cocked hat, an enormous sword, a short waistcoat and a black cravat; these I should be almost tempted to swear the peace against, in my own defence, if I were not convinced that they are but meek asses in lions' skins. Others go in brown frocks, leather breeches, great oaken cudgels in their hands, their hats uncocked, and their hair unpowdered; and imitate grooms, stage-coachmen, and country bumpkins so well, in their outsides, that I do not make the least doubt of their resembling them equally in their insides. A man of sense carefully avoids any particular character in his dress; he is accurately clean for his own sake; but all the rest is for other people's. He dresses as well, and in the same manner, as the people of sense and fashion of the place where he is. If he dresses better, as he thinks, that is, more than they, he is a fop; if he dresses worse, he is unpardonably negligent: but, of the two, I would rather have a young fellow too much than too little dressed; the excess on that side will wear off, with a little age and reflection; but if he is negligent at twenty, he will be a sloven at forty, and stink at fifty years old. Dress yourselves fine, where others are fine; and plain where others are plain; but take care always that your clothes are well made, and fit you, for otherwise they will give you a very awkward air. When you are once well dressed for the day think no more of it afterwards; and without any stiffness for fear of discomposing that dress, let all your motions be as easy and natural as if you had no clothes on at all. So much for dress, which I maintain to be a thing of consequence in the polite world.

As to manners, good-breeding, and the Graces, I have so often entertained you upon these important subjects, that I can add nothing to what I have formerly said. Your own good sense will suggest to you the substance of them; and observation, experience, and good company, the several modes of them. Your great vivacity, which I hear of from many people, will be no hindrance to your pleasing in good company: on the contrary, will be of use to you, if tempered by good-breeding, and accompanied by the Graces. But then, I suppose your vivacity to be a vivacity of parts, and not a constitutional restlessness; for the most disagreeable composition that I know in the world, is that of strong animal spirits with a cold genius. Such a fellow is troublesomely active, frivolously busy, foolishly lively; talks much with little meaning, and laughs more, with less reason: whereas, in my opinion, a warm and lively genius, with a cool constitution, is the perfection of human nature.

Do what you will at Berlin, provided you do but do something all day long. All I desire of you is, that you will never slattern away one minute in idleness, and in doing nothing. When you are not in company, learn what either books, masters, or Mr. Harte can teach you; and, when you are in company, learn (what company only can teach you) the characters and manners of mankind. I really ask your pardon for giving you this advice; because, if you are a rational creature, and a thinking being, as I suppose, and verily believe you are, it must be unnecessary, and to a certain degree injurious. If I did not know by experience, that some men pass their whole time in doing nothing, I should not think it possible for any being, superior to

M. Descartes's automatons,* to squander away, in absolute idleness, one single minute of that small portion of time which is allotted us in this world.

I have lately seen one Mr. Cranmer, a very sensible merchant; who told me he had dined with you, and seen you often at Leipsig. And, yesterday, I saw an old footman of mine, whom I made a messenger; who told me that he had seen you last August. You will easily imagine, that I was not the less glad to see them because they had seen you; and I examined them both narrowly, in their respective departments; the former as to your mind, the latter, as to your body. Mr. Cranmer gave me great satisfaction, not only by what he told me of himself concerning you, but by what he was commissioned to tell me from Mr. Mascow.* As he speaks German perfectly himself, I asked him how you spoke it; and he assured me, very well for the time, and that a very little more practice would make you perfectly master of it. The messenger told me, you were much grown, and, to the best of his guess, within two inches as tall as I am; that you were plump, and looked healthy and strong; which was all I could expect, or hope, from the sagacity of the person.

I send you, my dear child (and you will not doubt) very sincerely, the wishes of the season. May you deserve a great number of happy New Years; and, if you deserve, may you have them. Many New Years, indeed, you may see, but happy ones you cannot see without deserving them. These, virtue, honour, and knowledge, alone can merit, alone can procure. *Dii tibi dent annos, de te nam caetera sumes,** was a pretty piece of poetical flattery, where it was said: I hope that, in time, it may be no flattery when said to you.

But I assure you, that whenever I cannot apply the latter part of the line to you with truth, I shall neither say, think, nor wish the former. Adieu!

43. TO HIS SON

LONDON, JANUARY 10, O.S. 1749

DEAR BOY,

I have received your letter of the 31st December, N.S· Your thanks for my present, as you call it, exceed the value of the present; but the use, which you assure me that you will make of it is the thanks which I desire to receive. Due attention to the inside of books, and due contempt for the outside, is the proper relation between a man of sense and his books.

Now that you are going a little more into the world, I will take this occasion to explain my intentions as to your future expenses, that you may know what you have to expect from me, and make your plan accordingly. I shall neither deny nor grudge you any money that may be necessary for either your improvement or your pleasures; I mean the pleasures of a rational being. Under the head of improvement, I mean the best books, and the best masters, cost what they will; I also mean, all the expense of lodgings, coach, dress, servants, etc., which, according to the several places where you may be, shall be respectively necessary to enable you to keep the best company. Under the head of rational pleasures, I comprehend, first, proper charities, to real and compassionate objects of it; secondly, proper presents to those to whom you are obliged, or whom you desire to oblige; thirdly, a conformity of expense to that of the company which you keep; as in public spectacles; your share of little entertainments; a few pistoles at games of mere commerce; and other incidental calls of good company. The only two articles which I will never supply are, the profusion of low riot, and the idle lavishness of negligence and laziness. A fool squanders away, without credit or advantage to himself, more than a man of sense spends with both. The latter employs his money as he does his time, and never spends a shilling of the one, nor a minute of the other, but in something that is either useful or rationally pleasing to himself or others. The former buys whatever he does not want, and does not pay for what he does want. He cannot withstand the charms of a toy-shop; snuff-boxes, watches, heads of canes, etc., are his destruction. His servants and tradesmen conspire with his own indolence to cheat him; and in a very little time, he is astonished, in the midst of all the ridiculous superfluities, to find himself in want of all the real comforts and necessaries of life. Without care and method, the largest fortune will not, and with them almost the smallest will, supply all necessary expenses. As far as you can possibly, pay ready money for everything you buy, and avoid bills. Pay that money too yourself, and not through the hands of any servant, who always either stipulates poundage, or requires a present for his good word, as they call it. Where you must have bills (as for meat and drink, clothes, etc.), pay them regularly every month, and with your own hand. Never, from a mistaken economy, buy a thing you do not want, because it is cheap; or from a silly pride, because it is dear. Keep an account, in a book, of all that you receive, and of all that you pay; for no man who knows what he receives and what he pays, ever runs out. I do not mean that you should keep an account of the shillings and half-crowns which you may spend in chair-hire, operas, etc.: they are unworthy of the time, and of the ink that they would consume; leave such *minutiae* to dull, penny-wise fellows; but remember, in economy, as well as in every other part of life, to have the proper attention to proper objects, and the proper contempt for little ones. A strong mind sees things in their true proportion; a weak one views them through a magnifying medium; which, like the microscope, makes an elephant of a flea; magnifies all little objects, but cannot receive great ones. I have known many a man pass for a miser, by saving a penny, and wrangling for twopence, who was undoing himself at the same time by living above his income, and not attending to essential articles, which were above his *portée*.* The sure characteristic of a sound and strong mind, is to find in everything, those certain bounds, *quos ultra citrave nequit consistere rectum*.* These boundaries are marked out by a very fine line, which only good sense and attention can discover; it is much too fine for vulgar eyes. In manners, this line is good-breeding; beyond it, is troublesome ceremony; short of it, is unbecoming negligence and inattention. In morals, it divides ostentatious puritanism from criminal relaxation; in religion, superstition from impiety: and in short, every virtue from its kindred vice or weakness. I think you have sense enough to discover the line; keep it always in your eye, and learn to walk upon it; rest upon Mr. Harte, and he will poise you, till you are able to go alone. By the way, there are fewer people who walk well upon that line than upon the slack rope, and therefore a good performer shines so much the more. . . .

Remember to take the best dancing-master at

Berlin, more to teach you to sit, stand, and walk gracefully, than to dance finely. The Graces, the Graces; remember the Graces! Adieu!

44. TO SOLOMON DAYROLLES, ESQ.

LONDON, APRIL 25, O.S. 1749

DEAR DAYROLLES,

I am now three letters in your debt, which I would have paid more punctually, if I had any tolerable current species to have paid you in: but I have nothing but farthings to offer, and most of them, too, counterfeit; for being, thank God, no longer concerned in the coinage, I cannot answer for the weight of the coin. I hear, as everybody does, more lies than truth, and am not in a situation of knowing which is which. It is said, for example, that our great men are reconciled, and I believe that they say so themselves; but I believe at the same time *que le diable n'y perd rien*. One *Grace* is too jealous not to suspect his best friend, and the other *Grace* too obstinate to forgive or forget the least injury. Lord Sandwich, who governs the latter, and detests the former, who in return abhors him, takes care to keep this fire alive, so that he may blow it into a flame whenever it may serve his purpose to do so; and I am much mistaken, if he does not make it blaze often.*

The Prince of Wales gains strength in Parliament in proportion as the King grows older; and Mr. Pelham loses ground there from the public conviction that he has but little power, which indeed I believe is true; the Army being entirely in the Duke of Cumberland, the Navy in Lord Sandwich, and the whole Church in the Duke of Newcastle. All other employments are scrambled for; and sometimes one Minister, and sometimes another, gets one. The situation of things little enables Mr. Pelham to satisfy the hungry and greedy rascals of the House of Commons, and consequently creates schisms and subdivisions in the Court party.* The next Session will produce events.

However disjointedly business may go on, pleasures, I can assure you, go roundly. To-morrow there is to be, at Ranelagh Garden, a masquerade in the Venetian manner. It is to begin at three o'clock in the afternoon; the several *loges* are to be shops for toys, *limonades*, *glaces*, and other *rafraîchissemens*. The next day come the fireworks, at which hundreds of people will certainly lose their lives or their limbs, from the tumbling of scaffolds, the fall of rockets, and other accidents inseparable from such crowds. In order to repair this loss to society, there will be a subscription masquerade on the Monday following, which, upon calculation, it is thought, will be the occasion of getting about the same number of people as were destroyed at the fireworks.*

I hear nothing yet of Lord Holderness* going to Holland, and therefore do not ask you when I may hope to see you here; for I suppose that his arrival must be previous to your departure: moreover, I am told that you are so busy in moving from one house to another, that you could not yet move from one country to another. Where is your new dwelling at the Hague?

I am glad to hear that Madame de Berkenroodt* goes Ambassadress to Paris; she will pass her time well there, and she deserves it. Pray make her my compliments of congratulation, and tell her that I am strongly tempted to pay my respects to her at Paris myself; but that, if I cannot, I will at least do it by proxy this winter twelvemonth, and send her an Ambassador about forty years younger, and consequently forty times better than myself. My boy will then be at Paris; he is now at Venice, goes to Turin till November, and then to Rome till the October following, when I shall emancipate him at Paris. I hear so well of him from all quarters, that I think he will do. *Adieu; portez vous bien, et aimez moi toujours.**

45 TO HIS SON

LONDON, JULY 20, O.S. 1749.

DEAR BOY,

I wrote to Mr. Harte last Monday, the 17th, O.S., in answer to his letter of the 20th June, N.S., which I had received but the day before, after an interval of eight posts, during which I did not know whether you or he existed, and indeed I began to think that you did not. By that letter you ought at this time to be at Venice; where I hope you are arrived in perfect health, after the baths of Tieffer,* in case you have made use of them. I hope they are not hot baths, if your lungs are still tender.

Your friend, the Comte d'Einsiedlen, is arrived here; he has been at my door, and I have been at his; but we have not yet met. He will dine with me some day this week. Comte Lascaris* inquires after you very frequently, and with great affection; pray answer the letter which I forwarded to you a great while ago from him. You may enclose your answer to me, and I will take care to give it him. Those attentions ought never to be omitted; they cost little, and please a great deal; but the neglect of them offends more than you can yet imagine. Great merit, or great failings, will make you respected or despised; but trifles, little attentions, mere nothings, either done, or neglected, will make you either liked or disliked, in the general run of the world. Examine youself why you like such and such people, and dislike such and such others; and you will find, that those different sentiments proceed from very slight causes. Moral virtues are the foundation of society in general, and of friendship in particular; but attentions, manners, and graces both adorn and strengthen them. My heart is so set upon your pleasing, and consequently succeeding, in the world, that possibly I have already (and probably shall again) repeat the same things over and over to you. However, to err, if I do err, on the surer side, I shall continue to communicate to you those observations upon the world which long experience has enabled me to make, and which I have generally found to hold true. Your youth and talents, armed with my experience, may go a great way; and that armour is very much at your service, if you please to wear it. I premise that it is not my imagination, but my memory, that gives you these rules: I am not writing pretty, but useful reflections. A man of sense soon discovers, because he carefully observes, where, and how long, he is welcome; and takes care to leave the company, at least as soon as he is wished out of it. Fools never perceive where they are either ill-timed or ill-placed.

I am this moment agreeably stopped, in the course of my reflections, by the arrival of Mr. Harte's letter of the 13th July, N.S., to Mr. Grevenkop, with one enclosed for your Mamma. I find by it that many of his and your letters to me must have miscarried; for he says, that I have had regular accounts of you: whereas all those accounts have been only, his letter of the 6th and yours of the 7th June, N.S.; his of the 20th June, N.S., to me; and now his of the 13th July, N.S., to Mr. Grevenkop. However, since you are so well, as Mr. Harte says you are, all is well. I am extremely glad you have no complaint upon your lungs; but I desire that you will think you have, for three or four months to come. Keep in a course of asses' or goats' milk, for one is as good as the other, and possibly the latter is the best; and let your common food be as pectoral as you can conveniently make it. Pray tell Mr. Harte that, according to his desire, I have wrote a letter of thanks to Mr. Firmian.* I hope you write to him too, from time to time. The letters of recommendation of a man of his merit and learning will, to be sure, be of great use to you among the learned world in Italy; that is, provided you take care to keep up the character he gives you in them; otherwise they will only add to your disgrace.

Consider that you have lost a good deal of time by your illness; fetch it up now you are well. At present you should be a good economist of your moments, of which company and sights will claim a considerable share; so that those which remain for study must be not only attentively, but greedily employed. But indeed I do not suspect you of one single moment's idleness in the whole day. Idleness is only the refuge of weak minds, and the holiday of fools. I do not call good company and liberal pleasures, idleness; far from it: I recommend to you a good share of both.

I send you here enclosed a letter for Cardinal Alexander Albani, which you will give him as soon as you get to Rome, and before you deliver any others; the Purple expects that preference; go next to the Duc de Nivernois,* to whom you are recommended by several people at Paris, as well as by myself. Then you may carry your other letters occasionally.

Remember to pry narrowly into every part of the government of Venice; inform yourself of the History of that Republic, especially of its most remarkable aeras; such as the *Ligue de Cambray*, in 1509, by which it had like to have been destroyed; and the conspiracy formed by the Marquis de Bedmar, the Spanish Ambassador, to subject it to the Crown of Spain.* The famous disputes between that Republic and the Pope are worth your knowledge; and the writings of the celebrated and learned *Frà Paolo di Sarpi*,* upon that occasion, worth your reading. It was once the greatest commercial Power in Europe, and in the 14th and 15th centuries, made a considerable figure; but at present its commerce is decayed, and its riches consequently decreased; and far from meddling now with the affairs of the Continent, it owes its security to its neutrality and inefficiency; and that security will last no longer than till one of the great Powers in Europe engrosses the rest of Italy; an event which this century possibly may, but which the next probably will see.*

Your friend Comte d'Einsiedlen, and his Governor, have been with me this moment, and delivered me your letter from Berlin, of February the 28th, N.S. I like them both so well, that I am glad you did; and still more glad to hear what they say of you. Go on, and continue to deserve the praises of those who deserve praises themselves. Adieu!

I break open this letter to acknowledge yours of the 30th June, N.S., which I have but this instant received, though thirteen days antecedent in date to Mr. Harte's last. I never in my life heard of bathing four hours a day; and I am impatient to hear of your safe arrival at Venice, after so extraordinary an operation.

46. TO HIS SON

LONDON, AUGUST 10, O.S. 1749

DEAR BOY,

Let us resume our reflections upon men, their characters, their manners, in a word, our reflections upon the world. They may help you to form yourself and to know others; a knowledge very useful at all ages, very rare at yours. It seems as if it were nobody's business to communicate it to young men. Their masters teach them, singly, the languages, or the sciences of their several departments; and are indeed generally incapable of teaching them the world; their parents are often so too, or at least neglect doing it; either from avocations, indifference, or from an opinion, that throwing them into the world (as they call it) is the best way of teaching it them. This last notion is in a great degree true; that is, the world can doubtless never be well known by theory; practice is absolutely necessary; but surely, it is of great use to a young man, before he sets out for that country, full of mazes, windings, and turnings, to have at least a general map of it, made by some experienced traveller.

There is a certain dignity of manners absolutely necessary, to make even the most valuable character either respected or respectable.

Horse-play, romping, frequent and loud fits of laughter, jokes, waggery, and indiscriminate familiarity, will sink both merit and knowledge into a degree of contempt. They compose at most a merry fellow; and a merry fellow was never yet a respectable man.

Indiscrimate familiarity either offends your superiors, or else dubs you their dependant, and led captain. It gives your inferiors just, but troublesome and improper claims of equality. A joker is near akin to a buffoon; and neither of them is the least related to wit. Whoever is admitted or sought for, in company, upon any other account than that of his merit and manners, is never respected there, but only made use of. We will have such-a-one, for he sings prettily; we will invite such-a-one to a ball, for he dances well; we will have such-a-one at supper, for he is always joking and laughing; we will ask another, because he plays deep at all games, or because he can drink a great deal. These are all vilifying distinctions, mortifying preferences, and exclude all ideas of esteem and regard. Whoever *is had* (as it is called) in company for the sake of any one thing singly, is singly that thing, and will never be considered in any other light; consequently never respected, let his merits be what they will.

This dignity of manners, which I recommend so much to you, is not only as different from pride, as true courage is from blustering, or true wit from joking; but is absolutely inconsistent with it; for nothing vilifies and degrades more than pride. The pretensions of the proud man are oftener treated with sneer and contempt than with indignation; as we offer ridiculously too little to a tradesman who asks ridiculously too much for his goods; but we do not haggle with one who only asks a just and reasonable price.

Abject flattery and indiscriminate assentation degrade as much as indiscriminate contradiction and noisy debate disgust. But a modest assertion of one's own opinion, and a complaisant acquiescence in other people's, preserve dignity.

Vulgar, low expressions, awkward motions and address, vilify, as they imply, either a very low turn of mind, or low education and low company.

Frivolous curiosity about trifles, and a laborious attention to little objects, which neither require nor deserve a moment's thought, lower a man; who from thence is thought (and not unjustly) incapable of greater matters. Cardinal de Retz, very sagaciously, marked out Cardinal Chigi for a little mind, from the moment he told him he had wrote three years with the same pen,* and that it was an excellent good one still.

A certain degree of exterior seriousness in looks and motions gives dignity, without excluding wit and decent cheerfulness, which are always serious themselves. A constant smirk upon the face, and a whiffling activity of the body, are strong indications of futility. Whoever is in a hurry, shows that the thing he is about is too big for him. Haste and hurry are very different things.

I have only mentioned some of those things which may, and do, in the opinion of the world, lower and sink characters in other respects valuable enough, but I have taken no notice of those that affect and sink the moral characters. They are sufficiently obvious. A man who has patiently been kicked may as well pretend to courage as a man blasted by vices and crimes may to dignity of any kind. But an exterior decency and dignity of manners will even keep such a man longer from sinking than otherwise he would be: of such consequence is the τό πρέπον, even though affected and put on! Pray read frequently, and with the utmost attention, nay, get by heart, if you can, that incomparable chapter in Cicero's Offices, upon the τό πρέπον, or the *Decorum*.* It contains whatever is necessary for the dignity of manners.

In my next I will send you a general map of courts; a region yet unexplored by you; but which you are one day to inhabit. The ways are generally crooked and full of turnings, sometimes strewed with flowers, sometimes choked up with briars; rotten ground and deep pits frequently lie concealed under a smooth and pleasing surface; all the paths are slippery, and every slip is dangerous. Sense and discretion must accompany you at your first setting out; but notwithstanding those, till experience is your guide, you will every now and then step out of your way or stumble.

Lady Chesterfield has just now received your German letter, for which she thanks you; she says the language is very correct; and I can plainly see that the character is well formed, not to say better than your English character. Continue to write German frequently, that it may become quite familiar to you. Adieu!

47. TO HIS SON

LONDON, AUGUST 21, O.S. 1749

DEAR BOY,

By the last letter that I received from Mr. Harte, of the 31st July, N.S., I suppose you are now either at Venice or Verona, and perfectly recovered of your late illness: which, I am daily more and more convinced, had no consumptive tendency; however, for some time still, *faites comme s'il y en avoit*,* be regular, and live pectorally.

You will soon be at courts, where, though you will not be concerned, yet reflection and observation upon what you see and hear there may be of use to you, when hereafter you may come to be concerned in courts yourself. Nothing in courts is exactly as it appears to be; often very different; sometimes directly contrary. Interest, which is the real spring of everything there, equally creates and dissolves friendships, produces and reconciles enmities; or rather, allows of neither real friendships nor enmities; for as Dryden very justly observes, *Politicians neither love nor hate.* This is so true, that you may think you connect yourself with two friends to-day, and be obliged to-morrow to make your option between them as enemies: observe, therefore, such a degree of reserve with your friends, as not to put yourself in their power, if they should become your enemies; and such a degree of moderation with your enemies, as not to make it impossible for them to become your friends.

Courts are, unquestionably, the seats of politeness and good-breeding; were they not so, they would be the seats of slaughter and desolation. Those who now smile upon and embrace, would affront and stab each other, if manners did not interpose; but ambition and avarice, the two prevailing passions at courts, found dissimulation more effectual than violence; and dissimulation introduced that habit of politeness, which distinguishes the courtier from the country gentleman. In the former case the strongest body would prevail; in the latter, the strongest mind.

A man of parts and efficiency need not flatter everybody at court; but he must take great care to offend nobody personally; it being in the power of very many to hurt him, who cannot serve him. Homer supposes a chain let down from Jupiter to the earth, to connect him with mortals.* There is, at all courts, a chain which connects the prince or the minister with the page of the back-stairs or the chambermaid. The king's wife, or mistress, has an influence over him; a lover has an influence over her; the chambermaid, or the *valet de chambre* has an influence over both; and so *ad infinitum*. You must, therefore, not break a link of that chain, by which you hope to climb up to the Prince.

You must renounce courts, if you will not connive at knaves, and tolerate fools. Their number makes them considerable. You should as little quarrel as connect yourself with either.

Whatever you say or do at court, you may depend upon it, will be known; the business of most of those who crowd levees and antichambers being to repeat all that they see or hear, and a great deal that they neither see nor hear, according as they are inclined to the persons concerned, or according to the wishes of those to whom they hope to make their court. Great caution is therefore necessary; and if, to great caution you can join seeming frankness and openness, you will unite what Machiavel reckons very difficult, but very necessary to be united; *volto sciolto e pensieri stretti.*

Women are very apt to be mingled in court intrigues; but they deserve attention better than confidence; to hold by them is a very precarious tenure.

I am agreeably interrupted in these reflections by a letter which I have this moment received from Baron Firmian. It contains your panegyric, and with the strongest protestations imaginable that he does you only justice. I received this favourable account of you with pleasure, and I communicate it to you with as much. While you deserve praise, it is reasonable you should know that you meet with it; and I make no doubt, but it will encourage you in persevering to deserve it. This is one paragraph of the Baron's letter. '*Ses mœurs dans un âge si tendre, réglées selon toutes les lois d'une morale exacte et sensée; son application* (that is what I like) *à tout ce qui s'appelle étude sérieuse, et Belles-Lettres, éloignée de l'ombre même d'un Faste Pédantesque, le rendent très digne de vos tendres soins; et j'ai l'honneur de vous assurer que chacun se louera beaucoup de son commerce aisé, et de son amitié: j'en ai profité avec plaisir ici et à Vienne, et je me crois très heureux de la permission, qu'il m'a accordée, de la continuer par la voïe de lettres.*'*—Reputation, like health, is preserved and increased by the same means by which it is acquired. Continue to desire and deserve praise, and you will certainly find it. Knowledge, adorned by manners, will infallibly procure it. Consider, that you have but a little way farther to get to your journey's end; therefore, for God's sake, do not slacken your pace: one year and a half more of sound application, Mr. Harte assures me, will finish his work; and when his work is finished well, your own will be very easily done afterwards. *Les Manières et les Graces* are no immaterial parts of that work; and I beg that you will give as much of your attention to them as to your books. Everything depends upon them; *senza di noi ogni fatica è vana.** The various companies you now go into will procure them you, if you will carefully observe, and form yourself upon those who have them.

Adieu! God bless you! and may you ever deserve that affection with which I am now Yours!

48. TO HIS SON

LONDON, SEPTEMBER 12, O.S. 1749

DEAR BOY,

It seems extraordinary, but it is very true, that my anxiety for you increases in proportion to the good accounts which I receive of you from all hands. I promise myself so much from you, that I dread the least disappointment. You are now so near the port which I have so long wished and laboured to bring you safe into, that my concern would be doubled, should you be shipwrecked within sight of it. The object, therefore, of this letter is (laying aside all the authority of a parent), to conjure you as a friend, by the affection you have for me (and surely you have reason to have some), and by the regard you have for yourself, to go on, with assiduity and attention, to complete that work which, of late, you have carried on so well, and which is now so near being finished. My wishes and my plan were to make you shine, and distinguish yourself equally in the learned and the polite world. Few have been able to do it. Deep learning is generally tainted with pedantry, or at least unadorned by manners: as, on the other hand, polite manners, and the turn of the world, are too often unsupported by knowledge, and consequently end contemptibly, in the frivolous dissipation of drawing-rooms and *ruelles*. You are now got over the dry and difficult parts of learning; what remains requires much more time than trouble. You have lost time by your illness; you must regain it now or never. I therefore most earnestly desire, for your own sake, that for these next six months, at least six hours every morning, uninterruptedly, may be inviolably sacred to your studies with

Mr. Harte. I do not know whether he will require so much; but I know that I do, and hope you will, and consequently prevail with him to give you that time; I own it is a good deal: but when both you and he consider that the work will be so much better, and so much sooner done, by such an assiduous and continued application, you will neither of you think it too much, and each will find his account in it. So much for the mornings, which from your own good sense, and Mr. Harte's tenderness and care of you, will, I am sure, be thus well employed. It is not only reasonable, but useful too, that your evenings should be devoted to amusements and pleasures: and therefore I not only allow, but recommend, that they should be employed at assemblies, balls, *spectacles*,* and in the best companies; with this restriction only, that the consequences of the evening's diversions may not break in upon the morning's studies, by breakfastings, visits, and idle parties into the country. At your age, you need not be ashamed when any of these morning parties are proposed, to say you must beg to be excused, for you are obliged to devote your mornings to Mr. Harte; that I will have it so; and that you dare not do otherwise. Lay it all upon me; though I am persuaded it will be as much your own inclination as it is mine. But those frivolous, idle people, whose time hangs upon their own hands, and who desire to make others lose theirs too, are not to be reasoned with: and indeed it would be doing them too much honour. The shortest civil answers are the best; *I cannot, I dare not*, instead of *I will not*; for if you were to enter with them into the necessity of study, and the usefulness of knowledge, it would only furnish them with matter for their silly jests; which, though I would not have you mind,

I would not have you invite. I will suppose you at Rome studying six hours uninterruptedly with Mr. Harte every morning, and passing your evenings with the best company of Rome, observing their manners and forming your own; and I will suppose a number of idle, sauntering, illiterate English, as there commonly is there, living entirely with one another, supping, drinking, and sitting up late at each other's lodgings; commonly in riots and scrapes when drunk; and never in good company when sober. I will take one of these pretty fellows, and give you the dialogue between him and yourself; such as, I dare say, it will be on his side; and such as, I hope, it will be on yours.

Englishman.—Will you come and breakfast with me to-morrow; there will be four or five of our countrymen; we have provided chaises, and we will drive somewhere out of town after breakfast?

Stanhope.—I am very sorry I cannot; but I am obliged to be at home all morning.

Englishman.—Why then we will come and breakfast with you.

Stanhope.—I can't do that neither; I am engaged.

Englishman.—Well, then, let it be the next day.

Stanhope.—To tell you the truth, it can be no day in the morning; for I neither go out nor see anybody at home before twelve.

Englishman.—And what the devil do you do with yourself till twelve o'clock?

Stanhope.—I am not by myself, I am with Mr. Harte.

Englishman.—Then what the devil do you do with him?

Stanhope.—We study different things; we read, we converse.

Englishman.—Very pretty amusement indeed! Are you to take Orders then?

Stanhope.—Yes, my father's orders, I believe I must take.

Englishman.—Why hast thou no more spirit than to mind an old fellow a thousand miles off?

Stanhope.—If I don't mind his orders he won't mind my draughts.

Englishman.—What, does the old prig threaten then? threatened folks live long: never mind threats.

Stanhope.—No, I can't say that he has ever threatened me in his life; but I believe I had best not provoke him.

Englishman.—Pooh! you would have one angry letter from the old fellow, and there would be an end of it.

Stanhope.—You mistake him mightily; he always does more than he says. He has never been angry with me yet, that I remember, in his life; but if I were to provoke him, I am sure he would never forgive me; he would be coolly immovable, and I might beg and pray, and write my heart out to no purpose.

Englishman.—Why then he is an odd dog, that's all I can say; and pray are you to obey your dry-nurse too, this same, what's his name—Mr. Harte?

Stanhope.—Yes.

Englishman.—So he stuffs you all morning with Greek, and Latin, and Logic, and all that. Egad, I have a dry-nurse too, but I never looked into a book with him in my life; I have not so much as seen the face of him this week, and don't care a louse if I never see it again.

Stanhope.—My dry-nurse never desires anything of me that is not reasonable, and for my own good; and therefore I like to be with him.

Englishman.—Very sententious and edifying, upon my word! At this rate you will be reckoned a very good young man.

Stanhope.—Why, that will do me no harm.

Englishman.—Will you be with us to-morrow in the evening then? We shall be ten with you; and I have got some excellent good wine; and we'll be very merry.

Stanhope.—I am very much obliged to you, but I am engaged for all the evening, to-morrow; first at Cardinal Albani's; and then to sup at the Venetian Ambassadress's.

Englishman.—How the devil can you like being always with these foreigners? I never go amongst them, with all their formalities and ceremonies. I am never easy in company with them, and I don't know why, but I am ashamed.

Stanhope.—I am neither ashamed nor afraid; I am very easy with them; they are very easy with me; I get the language, and I see their characters, by conversing with them; and that is what we are sent abroad for, is it not?

Englishman.—I hate your modest women's company; your woman of fashion as they call 'em; I don't know what to say to them for my part.

Stanhope.—Have you ever conversed with them?

Englishman.—No; I never conversed with them; but I have been sometimes in their company, though much against my will.

Stanhope.—But at least they have done you no hurt; which is probably more than you can say of the women you do converse with.

Englishman.—That's true, I own; but for all that, I would rather keep company with my surgeon half the year, than with your women of fashion the year round.

Stanhope.—Tastes are different, you know, and every man follows his own.

Englishman.—That's true; but thine's a devilish odd one, Stanhope. All morning with thy dry-nurse; all the evening in formal fine company; and all day long afraid of old Daddy in England. Thou art a queer fellow, and I am afraid there's nothing to be made of thee.

Stanhope.—I am afraid so too.

Englishman.—Well then: good night to you: you have no objection, I hope, to my being drunk to-night, which I certainly will be.

Stanhope.—Not in the least; nor to your being sick to-morrow, which you as certainly will be; and so good night too.

You will observe, that I have not put into your mouth those good arguments, which upon such an occasion would, I am sure, occur to you; as piety and affection towards me; regard and friendship for Mr. Harte; respect for your own moral character, and for all the relative duties of man, son, pupil, and citizen. Such solid arguments would be thrown away upon such shallow puppies. Leave them to their ignorance, and to their dirty, disgraceful vices. They will severely feel the effects of them, when it will be too late. Without the comfortable refuge of learning, and with all the sickness and pains of a ruined stomach, and a rotten carcase, if they happen to arrive at old age, it is an uneasy and ignominious one. The ridicule which such fellows endeavour to throw upon those who are not like them, is, in the opinion of all men of sense, the most authentic panegyric. Go on, then, my dear child, in the way you are in, only for a year and a half more; that is all I ask of you. After that, I promise that you shall be your own master, and that I will pretend to no other title than that of your best and truest friend. You shall receive advice, but no orders, from me; and in truth you will want no other advice but such as youth and inexperience must necessarily require. You shall certainly want nothing that is requisite, not only for your conveniency, but also for your pleasures, which I always desire should be gratified. You will suppose that I mean the pleasures *d'un honnête homme.*

While you are learning Italian, which I hope you do with diligence, pray take care to continue your German, which you may have frequent opportunities of speaking. I would also have you keep up your knowledge of the *Ius Publicum Imperii*, by looking over, now and then, those *inestimable manuscripts*, which Sir Charles Williams,* who arrived here last week, assures me you have made upon that subject. It will be of very great use to you, when you come to be concerned in foreign affairs; as you shall be (if you qualify yourself for them) younger than ever any other was: I mean before you are twenty. Sir Charles tells me, that he will answer for your learning; and that he believes you will acquire that address, and those graces, which are so necessary to give it its full lustre and value. But he confesses, that he doubts more of the latter than of the former. The justice which he does Mr. Harte, in his panegyrics of him, makes me hope, that there is likewise a great deal of truth in his encomiums of you. Are you pleased with, and proud of the reputation which you have already acquired? Surely you are, for I am sure I am. Will you do anything to lessen or forfeit it? Surely you will not. And will you not do all you can to extend and increase it? Surely you will. It is only going on for a year and a half longer, as you have gone on for the two years last past, and devoting half the day only to application; and you will be sure to make the earliest figure and fortune in the world, that ever man made. Adieu.

49. TO HIS SON

LONDON, SEPTEMBER 22, O.S. 1749

DEAR BOY,

If I had faith in philters and love potions, I should suspect that you had given Sir Charles Williams some, by the manner in which he speaks of you, not only to me, but to everybody else. I will not repeat to you what he says of the extent and correctness of your knowledge, as it might either make you vain, or persuade you that you had already enough of what nobody can have too much. You will easily imagine how many questions I asked, and how narrowly I sifted him upon your subject; he answered me, and I dare say with truth, just as I could have wished; till, satisfied entirely with his accounts of your character and learning, I inquired into other matters, intrinsically indeed of less consequence, but still of great consequence to every man, and of more to you than to almost any man: I mean your address, manners, and air. To these questions, the same truth which he had observed before, obliged him to give me much less satisfactory answers. And as he thought himself, in friendship both to you and me, obliged to tell me the disagreeable as well as the agreeable truths, upon the same principle I think myself obliged to repeat them to you.

He told me then, that in company you were frequently most *provokingly* inattentive, absent, and *distrait*. That you came into a room and presented yourself, very awkwardly: that at table you constantly threw down knives, forks, napkins, bread, etc., and that you neglected your person and dress, to a degree unpardonable at any age, and much more so at yours.

These things, how immaterial soever they may seem to people who do not know the world, and the nature of mankind, give me who know them to be exceedingly material, very great concern. I have long distrusted you, and therefore frequently admonished you, upon these articles; and I tell you plainly, that I shall not be easy till I hear a very different account of them. I know no one thing more offensive to a company, than that inattention and *distraction*. It is showing them the utmost contempt; and people never forgive contempt. No man is *distrait* with the man he fears, or the women he loves; which is a proof that every man can get the better of that *distraction*, when he thinks it worth his while to do so; and take my word for it, it is always worth his while. For my own part, I would rather be in company with a dead man, than with an absent one; for if the dead man gives me no pleasure, at least he shows me no contempt; whereas the absent man, silently indeed, but very plainly, tells me that he does not think me worth his attention. Besides, can an absent man make any observations upon the characters, customs, and manners of the company? No. He may be in the best companies all his lifetime (if they will admit him, which, if I were they, I would not) and never be one jot the wiser. I never will converse with an absent man; one may as well talk to a deaf one. It is, in truth, a practical blunder, to address ourselves to a man who we see plainly neither hears, minds, nor understands us. Moreover I aver, that no man is in any degree fit for either business or conversation, who cannot and does not direct and command his attention to the present object, be that what it will. You know, by experience, that I grudge no expense in your education, but I will positively not keep you a Flapper. You may read, in Dr. Swift, the description of these flappers,* and the use they were of to your friends the Laputans; whose minds (Gulliver says) are so taken up with intense speculations, that they neither can speak nor attend to the discourses of others, without being roused by some external taction upon the organs of speech and hearing; for which reason, those people who are able to afford it, always keep a flapper in their family, as one of their domestics: nor ever walk about, or make visits without him. This flapper is likewise employed diligently to attend his master in his walks; and, upon occasion, to give a soft flap upon his eyes, because he is always so wrapped up in cogitation, that he is in manifest danger of falling down every precipice, and bouncing his head against every post, and in the streets, of jostling others, or being jostled into the kennel himself. If *Christian**will undertake this province into the bargain, with all my heart; but I will not allow him any increase of wages upon that score.

In short, I give you fair warning, that when we meet, if you are absent in mind, I will soon be absent in body; for it will be impossible for me to stay in the room; and if at table you throw down your knife, plate, bread, etc., and hack the wing of a chicken for half an hour, without being able to cut it off, and your sleeve all the time in another dish, I must rise from table to escape the fever you would certainly give me. Good God! how I should be shocked, if you came into my room, for the first time, with two left legs, presenting yourself with all the graces and dignity of a tailor, and your clothes hanging upon you, like those in Monmouth Street, upon tenter-hooks!* whereas I expect, nay require, to see you present yourself with the easy and genteel air of a man of fashion, who has kept good company. I expect you not only well dressed but very well dressed; I expect a gracefulness in all your motions, and something particularly engaging in your address. All this I expect, and all this it is in your power, by care and attention, to make me find; but to tell you the plain truth, if I do not find it, we shall not converse very much together; for I cannot stand inattention and awkwardness; it would endanger my health. You have often seen and I have as often made you observe Lyttelton's distinguished inattention and awkwardness.* Wrapped up, like a Laputan, in intense thought, and possibly sometimes in no thought at all (which, I believe, is very often the case of absent people), he does not know his most intimate acquaintance by sight, or answers them as if they were at cross purposes. He leaves his hat in one room, his sword in another, and would leave his shoes in a third, if his buckles though awry, did not save them; his legs and arms by his awkward management of them, seem to have undergone the *question extraordinaire;** and his head, always hanging upon one or other of his shoulders, seems to have received the first stroke upon a block. I sincerely value and esteem him for his parts, learning, and virtue; but for the soul of me, I cannot love him in company. This will be universally the case, in common life, of every inattentive, awkward man, let his real merit and knowledge be ever so great.

When I was of your age, I desired to shine, as far as I was able, in every part of life; and was as attentive to my manners, my dress, and my air, in company on evenings, as to my books and my tutor in the mornings. A young fellow should be ambitious to shine in everything; and, of the two, always rather overdo than underdo. These things are by no means trifles: they are of infinite consequence to those who are to be thrown into the great world, and who would make a figure or a fortune in it. It is not sufficient to deserve well; one must please well too. Awkward disagreeable merit will never carry anybody far. Wherever you find a good dancing-master, pray let him put you upon your haunches; not so much for the sake of dancing, as for coming into a room, and presenting yourself genteelly and gracefully. Women, whom you ought to endeavour to please, cannot forgive a vulgar and awkward air and gestures; *il leur faut du brillant.* The generality of men are pretty like them, and are equally taken by the same exterior graces.

I am very glad that you have received the diamond buckles safe: all I desire in return for them is, that they may be buckled even upon your feet, and that your stockings may not hide them. I should be sorry you were an egregious fop; but I protest that, of the two, I would rather have you a fop than a sloven. I think negligence in my own dress, even at my age, when certainly I expect no advantages from my dress, would be indecent with regard to others. I have done with fine clothes; but I will have my plain clothes fit me, and made like other people's. In the evenings, I recommend to you the company of women of fashion, who have a right to attention, and will be paid it. Their company will smooth your manners, and give you a habit of attention and respect, of which you will find the advantage among men.

My plan for you, from the beginning, has been to make you shine equally in the learned and in the polite world; the former part is almost completed to my wishes, and will, I am persuaded, in a little time more, be quite so. The latter part is still in your power to complete; and I flatter myself that you will do it, or else the former part will avail you very little; especially in your department, where the exterior address and graces do half the business; they must be the harbingers of your merit, or your merit will be very coldly received; all can, and do judge of the former, few of the latter.

Mr. Harte tells me that you have grown very much since your illness; if you get up to five feet ten, or even nine inches, your figure will probably be a good one; and, if well dressed and genteel, will probably please; which is a much greater advantage to a man than people commonly think. Lord Bacon calls it a letter of recommendation.*

I would wish you to be the *omnis homo, l'homme universel*. You are nearer it, if you please, than ever anybody was at your age; and if you will but for the course of this next year only, exert your whole attention to your studies in the morning, and to your address, manners, air, and *tournure** in the evenings, you will be the man I wish you, and the man that is rarely seen.

Our letters go, at best, so irregularly and so often miscarry totally, that for greater security I repeat the same things. So, though I acknowledged by last post Mr. Harte's letter of the 8th September, N.S., I acknowledge it again by this to you. If this should find you still at Verona, let it inform you that I wish you would set out soon for Naples; unless Mr. Harte should think it better for you to stay at Verona, or any other place on this side Rome, till you go there for the Jubilee.* Nay, if he likes it better, I am very willing that you should go directly from Verona to Rome; for you cannot have too much of Rome, whether upon account of the language, the curiosities, or the company. My only reason for mentioning Naples, is for the sake of the climate, upon account of your health; but if Mr. Harte thinks your health is now so well restored as to be above climate, he may steer your course wherever he thinks proper; and, for aught I know, your going directly to Rome, and consequently staying there so much the longer, may be as well as anything else. I think you and I cannot put our affairs into better hands than in Mr. Harte's; and I will stake his infallibility against the Pope's, with some odds on his side. *A propos* of the Pope; remember to be presented to him before you leave Rome, and go through the necessary ceremonies for it, whether of kissing his slipper or his b——h;* for I would never deprive myself of anything that I wanted to do or see, by refusing to comply with an established custom. When I was in Catholic countries, I never declined kneeling in their churches at their elevation, nor elsewhere, when the Host went by. It is a complaisance due to the custom of the place, and by no means, as some silly people have imagined, an implied approbation of their doctrine. Bodily attitudes and situations are things so very indifferent in themselves, that I would quarrel with nobody about them. It may, indeed, be improper for Mr. Harte to pay that tribute of complaisance, upon account of his character.

This letter is a very long, and possibly a very tedious one; but my anxiety for your perfection is so great, and particularly at this critical and decisive period of your life, that I am only afraid of omitting, but never of repeating, or dwelling too long upon anything that I think may be of the least use to you. Have the same anxiety for yourself, that I have for you, and all will do well. Adieu, my dear child.

50. TO HIS SON

LONDON, SEPTEMBER 27, O.S. 1749

DEAR BOY,

A vulgar, ordinary way of thinking, acting, or speaking, implies a low education, and a habit of low company. Young people contract it at school, or among servants, with whom they are too often used to converse; but after they frequent good company, they must want attention and observation very much, if they do not lay it quite aside; and indeed, if they do not, good company will be very apt to lay them aside. The various kinds of vulgarisms are infinite: I cannot pretend to point them out to you; but I will give some samples, by which you may guess at the rest.

A vulgar man is captious and jealous; eager and impetuous about trifles. He suspects himself to be slighted, thinks everything that is said meant at him: if the company happens to laugh, he is persuaded they laugh at him; he grows angry and testy, says something very impertinent, and draws himself into a scrape, by showing what he calls a proper spirit, and asserting himself. A man of fashion does not suppose himself to be either the sole or principal object of the thoughts, looks, or words of the company; and never suspects that he is either slighted or laughed at, unless he is conscious that he deserves it. And if (which very seldom happens) the company is absurd or ill-bred enough to do either, he does not care two-pence, unless the insult be so gross and plain as to require satisfaction of another kind. As he is above trifles, he is never vehement and eager about them; and wherever they are concerned, rather acquiesces than wrangles. A vulgar man's conversation always savours strongly of the lowness of his education and company. It turns chiefly upon his domestic affairs, his servants, the excellent order he keeps in his own family, and the little anecdotes of the neighbourhood; all which he relates with emphasis, as interesting matters. He is a man-gossip.

Vulgarism in language is the next and distinguishing characteristic of bad company, and a bad education. A man of fashion avoids nothing with more care than that. Proverbial expressions and trite sayings are the flowers of the rhetoric of a vulgar man. Would he say that men differ in their tastes; he both supports and adorns that opinion by the good old saying, as he respectfully calls it, that *what is one man's meat, is another man's poison*. If anybody attempts being *smart*, as he calls it, upon him, he gives them *tit for tat*, ay, that he does. He has always some favourite word for the time being; which, for the sake of using often, he commonly abuses. Such as *vastly* angry, *vastly* kind, *vastly* handsome, and *vastly* ugly. Even his pronunciation of proper words carries the mark of the beast along with it. He calls the earth *yearth*; he is *obleiged*, not *obliged* to you. He goes *to wards*, and not *towards*, such a place.* He sometimes affects hard words by way of ornament, which he always mangles like a learned woman. A man of fashion never has recourse to proverbs, and vulgar aphorisms; uses neither favourite words nor hard words; but takes great care to speak very correctly and grammatically, and to pronounce properly; that is, according to the usage of the best companies.

An awkward address, ungraceful attitudes and actions, and a certain left-handiness (if I may use that word) loudly proclaim low education and low company; for it is impossible to suppose that a man can have frequented good company, without having catched something, at least, of their air and motions. A new-raised man is distinguished in a regiment by his awkwardness; but he must be impenetrably dull, if, in a month or two's time, he cannot perform at least the common manual exercise, and look like a soldier. The very accoutrements of a man of fashion are grievous incumbrances to a vulgar man. He is at a loss what to do with his hat, when it is not upon his head; his cane (if unfortunately he wears one) is at perpetual war with every cup of tea or coffee he drinks; destroys them first, and then accompanies them in their fall. His sword is formidable only to his own legs, which would possibly carry him fast enough out of the way of any sword but his own. His clothes fit him so ill, and constrain him so much, that he seems rather their prisoner than their proprietor. He presents himself in company like a criminal in a court of justice; his very air condemns him; and people of fashion will no more connect themselves with the one, than people of character will with the other. This repulse drives and sinks him into low company; a gulf from whence no man, after a certain age, ever emerged.

Les manières nobles et aisées, la tournure d'un homme de condition, le ton de la bonne compagnie, les Graces, le je ne sçais quoi qui plait, are as necessary to adorn and introduce your intrinsic merit and knowledge, as the polish is to the diamond; which, without that polish, would never be worn, whatever it might weigh. Do not imagine that these accomplishments are only useful with women; they are much more so with men. In a public assembly, what an advantage has a graceful speaker, with genteel motions, a handsome figure, and a liberal air, over one who shall speak full as much good sense, but destitute of these ornaments! In business, how prevalent are the Graces, how detrimental is the want of them! By the help of these I have known some men refuse favours less offensively than others granted them. The utility of them in Courts and negotiations is inconceivable. You gain the hearts, and consequently the secrets, of nine in ten that you have to do with, in spite even of their prudence; which will, nine times in ten, be the dupe of their hearts and of their senses. Consider the importance of these things as they deserve, and you will not lose one minute in the pursuit of them.

You are travelling now in a country once so famous both for arts and arms, that (however degenerated at present) it still deserves your attention and reflection. View it therefore with care, compare its former with its present state, and examine into the causes of its rise and its decay. Consider it classically and politically, and do not run through it, as too many of your young countrymen do, musically, and (to use a ridiculous word) *knick-knackically*.* No piping nor fiddling, I beseech you; no days lost in poring upon almost imperceptible *Intaglios* and *Cameos*; and do not become a Virtuoso* of small wares. Form a taste of Painting, Sculpture, and Architecture, if you please, by a careful examination of the works of the best ancient and modern artists; those are liberal arts, and a real taste and knowledge of them become a man of fashion very well. But beyond certain bounds, the Man of Taste ends, and the frivolous Virtuoso begins.

Your friend Mendes, the good Samaritan, dined with me yesterday. He has more good-nature and generosity than parts. However I will show him all the civilities that his kindness to you so justly deserves. He tells me that you are taller than I am, which I am very glad of: I desire that you may excel me in everything else too; and far from repining, I shall rejoice at your superiority. He commends your friend Mr. Stevens* extremely; of whom too I have heard so good a character from other people, that I am very glad of your connection with him. It may prove of use to you hereafter. When you meet with such sort of Englishmen abroad, who, either from their parts or their rank, are likely to make a figure at home, I would advise you to cultivate them, and get their favourable testimony of you here, especially those who are to return to England before you. Sir Charles Williams has puffed*you (as the mob call it) here extremely. If three or four more people of parts do the same, before you come back, your first appearance in London will be to great advantage. Many people do, and indeed ought to, take things upon trust; many more do, who need not; and few dare dissent from an established opinion. Adieu!

51. TO HIS SON

DEAR BOY,

If this letter finds you at all, of which I am very doubtful, it will find you at Venice, preparing for your journey to Rome; which, by my last letter to Mr. Harte, I advised you to make along the coast of the Adriatic, through Rimini, Loretto, Ancona, etc., places that are all worth seeing, but not worth staying at. And such I reckon all places where the eyes only are employed. Remains of antiquity, public buildings, paintings, sculptures, etc., ought to be seen, and that with a proper degree of attention; but this is soon done, for they are only outsides. It is not so with more important objects; the insides of which must be seen; and they require and deserve much more attention. The characters, the heads, and the hearts of men, are the useful science of which I would have you perfect master. That science is best taught and best learnt in capitals, where every human passion has its object, and exerts all its force or all its art in the pursuit. I believe there is no place in the world where every passion is busier, appears in more shapes, and is conducted with more art, than at Rome. Therefore, when you are there, do not imagine that the Capitol, the Vatican, and the Pantheon are the principal objects of your curiosity; but for one minute that you bestow upon those, employ ten days in informing yourself of the nature of that government, the rise and decay of the Papal power, the politics of that Court, the *brigues** of the Cardinals, the tricks of the Conclaves; and, in general, everything that relates to the interior of that extraordinary government, founded originally upon the ignorance and superstition of mankind, extended by the weakness of some princes and the ambition of others; declining of late in proportion as knowledge has increased; and owing its present precarious security, not to the religion, the affection, or the fear of the Temporal Powers, but to the jealousy of each other. The Pope's excommunications are no longer dreaded; his indulgences little solicited, and sell very cheap; and his territories, formidable to no Power, are coveted by many, and will, most undoubtedly, within a century, be scantled out among the great Powers, who have now a footing in Italy, whenever they can agree upon the division of the bear's skin. Pray inform yourself thoroughly of the history of the Popes and of the Popedom; which, for many centuries, is interwoven with the history of all Europe. Read the best authors who treat of these matters, and especially *Fra Paolo, de Beneficiis*,* a short but very material book. You will find at Rome some of all the religious Orders in the Christian world. Inform yourself carefully of their origin, their founders, their rules, their reforms, and even their dresses: get acquainted with some of all of them, but particularly with the Jesuits; whose Society I look upon to be the most able and best governed society in the world. Get acquainted, if you can, with their General,* who always resides at Rome; and who, though he has no seeming power out of his own Society, has (it may be) more real influence over the whole world, than any temporal Prince in it. They have almost engrossed the education of youth; they are, in general, confessors to most of the Princes in Europe; and they are the principal missionaries out of it; which three articles give them a most extensive influence, and solid advantages;

witness their settlement in Paraguay.* The Catholics in general declaim against that Society; and yet are all governed by individuals of it. They have, by turns, been banished, and with infamy, almost every country in Europe; and have always found means to be restored, even with triumph. In short, I know no government in the world that is carried on upon such deep principles of policy, I will not add morality. Converse with them, frequent them, court them; but know them.

Inform yourself too of that infernal court, the Inquisition;* which, though not so considerable at Rome as in Spain and Portugal will, however, be a good sample to you of what the villainy of some men can contrive, the folly of others receive, and both together establish; in spite of the first natural principles of reason, justice and equity.

These are the proper and useful objects of the attention of a man of sense, when he travels; and these are the objects for which I have sent you abroad; and I hope you will return thoroughly informed of them.

I receive this very moment Mr. Harte's letter of the 1st October, N.S., but I have never received his former, to which he refers in this, and you refer in your last; in which he gave me the reasons for your leaving Verona so soon; nor have I ever received that letter in which your case was stated by your physicians. Letters to and from me have worse luck than other people's: for you have written to me, and I to you, for these last three months, by way of Germany, with as little success as before.

I am edified with your morning applications, and your evening gallantries at Venice, of which Mr. Harte gives me an account. Pray go on with both there, and afterwards at Rome; where, provided you arrive in the beginning of December, you may stay at Venice as much longer as you please.

Make my compliments to Sir James Gray and Mr. Smith,* with my acknowledgments for the great civilities they show you.

I wrote to Mr. Harte by the last post, October the 6th, o.s., and will write to him in a post or two upon the contents of his last. Adieu. *Point de distractions;* and remember the *Graces*.

52. TO HIS SON

LONDON, NOVEMBER 3, O.S., 1749

DEAR BOY,

From the time that you have had life, it has been the principal and favourite object of mine, to make you as perfect as the imperfections of human nature will allow; in this view, I have grudged no pains nor expense in your education; convinced that education, more than nature, is the cause of that great difference which you see in the characters of men. While you were a child, I endeavoured to form your heart habitually to virtue and honour, before your understanding was capable of showing you their beauty and utility. Those principles, which you then got, like your grammar rules, only by rote, are now, I am persuaded fixed and confirmed by reason. And indeed they are so plain and clear, that they require but a very moderate degree of understanding, either to comprehend or practise them.

Lord Shaftesbury says, very prettily, that he would be virtuous for his own sake, though nobody were to know it; as he would be clean for his own sake, though nobody were to see him.* I have therefore, since you have had the use of your reason, never written to you upon those subjects: they speak best for themselves; and I should now just as soon think of warning you gravely not to fall into the dirt or the fire, as into dishonour or vice. This view of mine, I consider as fully attained. My next object was sound and useful learning. My own care first, Mr. Harte's afterwards, and *of late* (I will own it to your praise) your own application, have more than answered my expectations in that particular; and I have reason to believe, will answer even my wishes. All that remains for me then to wish, to recommend, to inculcate, to order, and to insist upon, is good-breeding; without which, all your other qualifications will be lame, unadorned, and to a certain degree unavailing. And here I fear, and have too much reason to believe, that you are greatly deficient. The remainder of this letter, therefore shall be (and it will not be the last by a great many) upon that subject.

A friend of yours and mine has very justly defined good-breeding to be, *the result of much good-sense, some good-nature, and a little self-denial for the sake of others, and with a view to obtain the same indulgence from them.* Taking this for granted (as I think it cannot be disputed), it is astonishing to me, that anybody who has good sense and good-nature (and I believe you have both), can essentially fail in good-breeding. As to the modes of it, indeed, they vary according to persons, places, and circumstances; and are only to be acquired by observation and experience; but the substance of it is everywhere and eternally the same. Good manners are, to particular societies, what good morals are to society in general; their cement and their security.

And as laws are enacted to enforce good morals, or at least to prevent the ill effects of bad ones; so there are certain rules of civility, universally implied and received, to enforce good manners, and punish bad ones. And indeed there seems to me to be less difference, both between the crimes and punishments, than at first one would imagine. The immoral man, who invades another man's property, is justly hanged for it; and the ill-bred man, who by his ill manners invades and disturbs the quiet and comforts of private life, is by common consent as justly banished society. Mutual complaisances, attentions, and sacrifices of little conveniences, are as natural an implied compact between civilized people, as protection and obedience are between Kings and subjects: whoever in either case violates that compact, justly forfeits all advantages arising from it. For my own part I really think, that next to the consciousness of doing a good action, that of doing a civil one is the most pleasing; and the epithet which I should covet the most, next to that of Aristides,* would be that of well-bred. Thus much for good-breeding in general; I will now consider some of the various modes and degrees of it.

Very few, scarcely any, are wanting in the respect which they should show to those whom they acknowledge to be infinitely their superiors; such as crowned heads, princes, and public persons of distinguished and eminent posts. It is the manner of showing that respect which is different. The man of fashion, and of the world, expresses it in its fullest extent; but naturally, easily, and without concern: whereas a man who is not used to keep good company, expresses it awkwardly; one sees that he is not used to it, and that it cost him a great deal; but I never saw the worst-bred man living guilty of lolling, whistling, scratching his head, and such-like indecencies, in company that he respected. In such companies, therefore, the only point to be attended to is, to show that respect, which everybody means to show, in an easy, unembarrassed, and graceful manner. This is what observation and experience must teach you.

In mixed companies, whoever is admitted to make part of them, is, for the time at least, supposed to be upon a footing of equality with the rest: and consequently, as there is no one principal object of awe and respect, people are apt to take a greater latitude in their behaviour, and to be less upon their guard; and so they may, provided it be within certain bounds, which are upon no occasion to be transgressed. But upon these occasions, though no one is entitled to distinguished marks of respect, every one claims, and very justly, every mark of civility and good-breeding. Ease is allowed, but carelessness and negligence are strictly forbidden. If a man accosts you, and talks to you ever so dully or frivolously, it is worse than rudeness, it is brutality, to show him, by a manifest inattention to what he says, that you think him a fool or a blockhead, and not worth hearing. It is much more so with regard to women; who, of whatever rank they are, are entitled, in consideration of their sex, not only to an attentive, but an officious good-breeding from men. Their little wants, likings, dislikes, preferences, antipathies, fancies, whims, and even impertinences, must be officiously attended to, flattered, and if possible, guessed at and anticipated by a well-bred man.

You must never usurp to yourself those conveniencies and *agrémens*⃰ which are of common right; such as the best places, the best dishes, etc.; but on the con-

trary, always decline them yourself, and offer them
to others; who, in their turns, will offer them to you;
so that upon the whole, you will in your turn enjoy
your share of the common right. It would be endless
for me to enumerate all the particular instances in which
a well-bred man shows his good-breeding in good company; and it would be injurious to you to suppose
that your own good-sense will not point them out to
you; and then your own good-nature will recommend,
and your self-interest enforce the practice.

There is a third sort of good-breeding, in which
people are most apt to fail, from a very mistaken
notion that they cannot fail at all. I mean with regard
to one's most familiar friends and acquaintances, or
those who really are our inferiors; and there, undoubtedly, a greater degree of ease is not only allowed,
but proper, and contributes much to the comforts of
a private, social life. But that ease and freedom have
their bounds too, which must by no means be violated.
A certain degree of negligence and carelessness becomes injurious and insulting, from the real or supposed inferiority of the persons; and that delightful
liberty of conversation among a few friends is soon
destroyed, as liberty often has been, by being carried
to licentiousness. But example explains things best,
and I will put a pretty strong case. Suppose you and
me alone together; I believe you will allow that I have
as good a right to unlimited freedom in your company
as either you or I can possibly have in any other; and
I am apt to believe too, that you would indulge me in
that freedom, as far as anybody would. But notwithstanding this, do you imagine that I should think there
were no bounds to that freedom? I assure you I
should not think so; and I take myself to be as much

tied down by a certain degree of good manners to you, as by other degrees of them to other people. Were I to show you, by a manifest inattention to what you said to me, that I was thinking of something else the whole time; were I to yawn extremely, snore, or break wind, in your company, I should think that I behaved myself to you like a beast, and should not expect that you would care to frequent me. No. The most familiar and intimate habitudes, connections, and friendships, require a degree of good-breeding, both to preserve and cement them. If ever a man and his wife, or a man and his mistress, who pass nights as well as days together, absolutely lay aside all good-breeding, their intimacy will soon degenerate into a coarse familiarity, infallibly productive of contempt or disgust. The best of us have our bad sides; and it is as imprudent as it is ill-bred to exhibit them. I shall certainly not use ceremony with you; it would be misplaced between us; but I shall certainly observe that degree of good-breeding with you which is, in the first place, decent, and which, I am sure, is absolutely necessary to make us like one another's company long.

I will say no more now upon this important subject of good-breeding, upon which I have already dwelt too long, it may be, for one letter; and upon which I shall frequently refresh your memory hereafter; but I will conclude with these axioms:

That the deepest learning, without good-breeding, is unwelcome and tiresome pedantry, and of use nowhere but in a man's own closet—and, consequently of little or no use at all.

That a man who is not perfectly well-bred, is unfit for good company, and unwelcome in it; will consequently dislike it soon, afterwards renounce it; and be reduced to solitude, or (what is worse) low and bad company.

That a man who is not well-bred, is full as unfit for business as for company.

Make then, my dear child, I conjure you, good-breeding the great object of your thoughts and actions, at least half the day. Observe carefully the behaviour and manners of those who are distinguished by their good-breeding; imitate, nay, endeavour to excel, that you may at least reach them, and be convinced that good-breeding is, to all worldly qualifications, what charity is to all Christian virtues. Observe how it adorns merit, and how often it covers the want of it. May you wear it to adorn, and not to cover you! Adieu.

53. TO HIS SON

LONDON, NOVEMBER 24, O.S. 1749

DEAR BOY,

Every rational being (I take it for granted) proposes to himself some object more important than mere respiration and obscure animal existence. He desires to distinguish himself among his fellow-creatures; and, *alicui negotio intentus, praeclari facinoris, aut artis bonae, famam quaerit.* Caesar, when embarking in a storm, said that it was not necessary he should live, but that it was absolutely necessary he should get to the place to which he was going. And Pliny leaves mankind this only alternative; either of doing what deserves to be written, or of writing what deserves to be read. As for those who do neither, *eorum vitam mortemque juxta existimo; quoniam de utraque siletur.* You have, I am convinced, one or both of these objects in view; but you must know and use the necessary means, or your pursuit will be vain and frivolous. In either case, *sapere est principium et fons*,* but it is by no means all. That knowledge must be adorned, it must have lustre as well as weight, or it will be oftener taken for lead than for gold. Knowledge you have, and will have: I am easy upon that article. But my business, as your friend, is not to compliment you upon what you have, but to tell you with freedom what you want; and I must tell you plainly, that I fear you want everything but knowledge.

I have written to you so often of late upon goodbreeding, address, *les manières liantes*,* the graces, etc., that I shall confine this letter to another subject, pretty near akin to them, and which, I am sure, you are full as deficient in; I mean style.

Style is the dress of thoughts; and let them be ever so just, if your style is homely, coarse, and vulgar, they will appear to as much disadvantage, and be as ill received as your person, though ever so well proportioned, would, if dressed in rags, dirt, and tatters. It is not every understanding that can judge of matter; but every ear can and does judge, more or less, of style: and were I either to speak or write to the public, I should prefer moderate matter, adorned with all the beauties and elegances of style, to the strongest matter in the world, ill-worded and ill-delivered. Your business is negotiation abroad, and oratory in the House of Commons at home. What figure can you make, in either case if your style be inelegant, I do not say bad? Imagine yourself writing an office-letter to a Secretary of State, which letter is to be read by the whole Cabinet Council, and very possibly afterwards laid before Parliament; any one barbarism, solecism, or vulgarism in it, would, in a very few days, circulate through the whole kingdom, to your disgrace and ridicule. For instance I will suppose you had written the following letter from the Hague, to the Secretary of State at London; and leave you to suppose the consequences of it.

THE SECRETARY OF STATE, LONDON.

THE HAGUE.

MY LORD:

I *had*, last night, the honour of your Lordship's letter of the 24th; and will *set about doing* the orders contained *therein*; and *if so be* that I can get that affair done by the next post, I will not fail *for to* give your Lordship an account of it by *next post*. I have told the French Minister, *as how that if* that affair be not soon concluded, your Lordship would think it *all long of him*; and that he must have neglected *for to* have wrote to his court about it. I must beg leave to put your Lordship in mind, *as how*, that I am now full three quarters in arrear; and if *so be* that I do not very soon receive at least one half year, I shall *cut a very bad figure*; for *this here* place is very dear. I shall be *vastly beholden* to your Lordship for *that there* mark of your favour; and so I *rest*, or *remain*, Your, etc.

You will tell me, possibly, that this is a *caricatura* of an illiberal and inelegant style: I will admit it; but assure you, at the same time, that a despatch with less than half these faults would blow you up for ever. It is by no means sufficient to be free from faults in speaking and writing; you must do both correctly and elegantly. In faults of this kind, it is not *ille optimus qui minimis urgetur*;* but he is unpardonable who has any at all, because it is his own fault: he need only attend to, observe, and imitate the best authors.

It is a very true saying, that a man must be born a poet, but that he may make himself an orator; and the very first principle of an orator is, to speak his own language particularly, with the utmost purity and elegancy. A man will be forgiven even great errors in a foreign language; but in his own, even the least slips are justly laid hold of and ridiculed.

A person of the House of Commons, speaking two years ago upon naval affairs, asserted that we had then the finest navy *upon the face of the yearth*. This happy mixture of blunder and vulgarism, you may easily imagine, was matter of immediate ridicule; but I can assure you, that it continues so still, and will be remembered as long as he lives and speaks. Another, speaking in defence of a gentleman upon whom a censure was moved, happily said, that he thought that gentleman was more *liable* to be thanked and rewarded, than censured. You know, I presume, that *liable* can never be used in a good sense.

You have with you three or four of the best English authors, Dryden, Atterbury,* and Swift: read them with the utmost care, and with a particular view to their language, and they may possibly correct that *curious infelicity of diction* which you acquired at Westminster.* Mr. Harte excepted, I will admit that you have met with very few English abroad, who could improve your style; and with many, I dare say, who speak as ill as yourself, and it may be worse; you must therefore take the more pains, and consult your authors and Mr. Harte the more. I need not tell you how attentive the Romans and Greeks, particularly the Athenians, were to this object. It is also a study among the Italians and the French; witness their respective Academies and Dictionaries* for improving and fixing their languages. To our shame be it spoken, it is less attended to here than in any polite country; but that is no reason why you should not attend to it; on the contrary, it will distinguish you the more. Cicero says, very truly, that it is glorious to excel other men in that very article, in which men excel brutes; *speech.*

Constant experience has shown me, that great purity and elegance of style, with a graceful elocution, cover a multitude of faults, in either a speaker or a writer. For my own part, I confess (and I believe most people are of my mind) that if a speaker should ungracefully mutter or stammer out to me the sense of an angel, deformed by barbarisms and solecisms, or larded with vulgarisms, he should never speak to me a second time, if I could help it. Gain the heart, or you gain nothing; the eyes and the ears are the only roads to the heart. Merit and knowledge will not gain hearts, though they will secure them when gained. Pray have that truth ever in your mind. Engage the eyes by your address, air, and motions: soothe the ears by the elegancy and harmony of your diction; the heart will certainly follow; and the whole man, or woman, will as certainly follow the heart. I must repeat it to you, over and over again, that with all the knowledge which you may have at present, or hereafter acquire, and with all the merit that ever man had, if you have not a graceful address, liberal and engaging manners, a pre-possessing air, and a good degree of eloquence in speaking and writing, you will be nobody; but will have the daily mortification of seeing people with not one-tenth part of your merit or knowledge, get the start of you, and disgrace you, both in company and in business.

You have read Quintilian, the best book in the world to form an orator;*pray read Cicero *de Oratore*; the best book in the world to finish one. Translate and retranslate from and to Latin, Greek, and English; make yourself a pure and elegant English style; it requires nothing but application. I do not find that God has made you a poet; and I am very glad that he has not: therefore, for God's sake, make yourself an orator, which you may do. Though I still call you boy, I consider you no longer as such; and when I reflect upon the prodigious quantity of manure that has been laid upon you, I expect you should produce more at eighteen, than uncultivated soils do at eight-and-twenty.

Pray tell Mr. Harte I have received his letter of the 13th, N.S. Mr. Smith was much in the right not to let you go, at this time of the year, by sea; in the summer you may navigate as much as you please; as for example, from Leghorn to Genoa etc. Adieu!

54. TO HIS SON

LONDON, NOVEMBER 26, O.S. 1749

DEAR BOY,

While the Roman Republic flourished, while glory was pursued, and virtue practised, and while even little irregularities and indecencies, not cognizable by law were, however, not thought below the public care; censors were established, discretionally to supply, in particular cases, the inevitable defects of the law, which must, and can only be general. This employment I assume to myself, with regard to your little republic,

leaving the legislative power entirely to Mr. Harte;
I hope and believe that he will seldom, or rather never,
have occasion to exert his supreme authority; and I
do by no means suspect you of any faults that may
require that interposition. But, to tell you the plain
truth, I am of opinion, that my censorial power will
not be useless to you, nor a *sinecure* to me. The sooner
you make it both, the better for us both. I can now
exercise this employment only upon hearsay, or at
most, written evidence; and therefore shall exercise it
with great lenity and some diffidence; but when we
meet, and that I can form my judgment upon ocular
and auricular evidence, I shall no more let the least
impropriety, indecorum, or irregularity, pass uncen-
sured, than my predecessor Cato* did. I shall read you
with the attention of a critic, not with the partiality
of an author: different in this respect, indeed, from
most critics, that I shall seek for faults, only to correct,
and not to expose them. I have often thought, and
still think, that there are few things which people in
general know less, than how to love and how to hate.
They hurt those they love, by a mistaken indulgence,
by a blindness, nay, often a partiality to their faults.
where they hate, they hurt themselves, by ill-timed
passion and rage. Fortunately for you, I never loved
you in that mistaken manner. From your infancy, I
made you the object of my most serious attention, and
not my plaything; I consulted your real good, not
your humours or fancies; and I shall continue to do so
while you want it, which will probably be the case
during our joint lives; for considering the difference
of our ages, in the course of nature, you will hardly
have acquired experience enough of your own, while
I shall be in a condition of lending you any of mine.

People in general will much better bear being told of their vices or crimes, than of their little failings and weaknesses. They, in some degree, justify or excuse (as they think) the former, by strong passions, seduction, and artifices of others; but to be told of, or to confess, their little failings and weaknesses, implies an inferiority of parts, too mortifying to that self-love and vanity, which are inseparable from our natures. I have been intimate enough with several people to tell them that they had said or done a very criminal thing; but I never was intimate enough with any man to tell him, very seriously, that he had said or done a very foolish one. Nothing less than the relation between you and me can possibly authorise that freedom; but fortunately for you, my parental rights, joined to my censorial powers, give it me in its fullest extent, and my concern for you will make me exert it. Rejoice, therefore, that there is one person in the world who can and will tell you what will be very useful to you to know, and yet what no other man living could or would tell you. Whatever I shall tell you of this kind, you are very sure, can have no other motive than your interest; I can neither be jealous nor envious of your reputation or your fortune, which I must be both desirous and proud to establish and promote; I cannot be your rival either in love or in business, on the contrary, I want the rays of your rising, to reflect new lustre upon my setting light. In order to this, I shall analyse you minutely, and censure you freely, that you may not (if possible) have one single spot when in your meridian.

There is nothing that a young fellow, at his first appearance in the world, has more reason to dread, and consequently should take more pains to avoid, than having any ridicule fixed upon him. It degrades him with the most reasonable part of mankind; but it ruins him with the rest; and I have known many a man undone, by acquiring a ridiculous nick-name: I would not, for all the riches in the world, that you should acquire one when you return to England. Vices and crimes excite hatred and reproach; failings, weaknesses, and awkwardnesses, excite ridicule; they are laid hold of by mimics, who, though very contemptible wretches themselves, often by their buffoonery fix ridicule upon their betters. The little defects in manners, elocution, address, and air (and even of figure, though very unjustly), are the objects of ridicule, and the cause of nick-names. You cannot imagine the grief it would give me, and the prejudice it would do you, if by way of distinguishing you from others of your name, you should happen to be called Muttering Stanhope, Absent Stanhope, Ill-bred Stanhope, or Awkward, Left-legged Stanhope: therefore, take great care to put it out of the power of Ridicule itself to give you any of these ridiculous epithets; for, if you get one, it will stick to you, like the envenomed shirt. The very first day that I see you, I shall be able to tell you, and certainly shall tell you, what degree of danger you are in; and I hope that my admonitions as Censor may prevent the censures of the public. Admonitions are always useful; is this one or not? You are the best judge; it is your own picture which I send you, drawn, at my request by a lady at Venice: pray let me know how far, in your conscience, you think it like; for there are some parts of it which I wish may, and others, which I should be sorry were. I send you, literally, the copy of that part of her letter to her friend here which relates to you.

Tell Mr. Harte that I have this moment received his letter of the 22nd, N.S., and that I approve extremely of the long stay you have made at Venice. I love long residences at capitals; running post through different places is a most unprofitable way of travelling, and admits of no application.   Adieu!

'Selon vos ordres, j'ai soigneusement examiné le jeune Stanhope, et je crois l'avoir approfondi. En voici le portrait, que je crois très fidèle. Il a le visage joli, l'air spirituel, et le regard fin. Sa figure est à present trop quarrée, mais s'il grandit, comme il en a encore et le tems et l'étoffe, elle sera bonne. Il a certainement beaucoup d'acquit, et on m'assure qu'il sçait à fond les langues sçavantes. Pour le François, je sçais qu'il le parle parfaitement bien; et l'on dit qu'il en est de même de l'Allemand. Les questions qu'il fait sont judicieuses, et marquent qu'il cherche à s'instruire. Je ne vous dirai pas qu'il cherche autant à plaire; puisqu'il paroit négliger les attentions et les graces. Il se présente mal, et n'a rien moins que l'air et la tournure aisée et noble qu'il lui faudroit. Il est vrai qu'il est encore jeune et neuf, de sorte qu'on a lieu d'espérer que ses exercices, qu'il n'a pas encore faits, et la bonne compagnie où il est encore novice, le décrotteront, et lui donneront tout ce qui lui manque à present. Un arrangement avec quelque femme de condition et qui a du monde, quelque Madame de l'Ursay, est précisément ce qu'il lui faut. Enfin j'ose vous assurer qu'il a tout ce que Monsieur de Chesterfield pourroit lui souhaiter, à l'exception des manières, des graces, et du ton de la bonne compagnie, qu'il prendra surement avec le tems, et l'usage du grand monde. Ce seroit bien dommage au moins qu'il ne

les prit point, puisqu'il mérite tant de les avoir. Et
vous sçavez bien de quelle importance elles sont. Monsieur son Père le sçait aussi, les possédant lui même
comme il fait. Bref, si le petit Stanhope acquiert les
graces, il ira loin, je vous en réponds; si non, il
s'arrêtera court dans une belle carrière, qu'il pourroit
autrement fournir."*

You see, by this extract, of what consequence other
people think these things; therefore, I hope you will
no longer look upon them as trifles. It is the character
of an able man to despise little things in great business:
but then he knows what things are little, and what not.
He does not suppose things little because they are
commonly called so: but by the consequences that
may or may not attend them. If gaining people's
affections, and interesting their hearts in your favour,
be of consequence, as it undoubtedly is, he knows very
well that a happy concurrence of all these, commonly
called little things, manners, air, address, graces, etc.,
is of the utmost consequence, and will never be at rest
till he has acquired them. The world is taken by the
outside of things, and we must take the world as
it is; you or I cannot set it right. I know at this time
a man of great quality and station, who has not the
parts of a porter, but raised himself to the station he
is in singly by having a graceful figure, polite manners,
and an engaging address: which, by the way, he only
acquired by habit, for he had not sense enough to get
them by reflection. Parts and habit should conspire to
complete you. You will have the habit of good company, and you have reflection in your power.

55. TO HIS SON

LONDON, DECEMBER 19, O.S. 1749

DEAR BOY,

The knowledge of mankind is a very useful knowledge for everybody; a most necessary one for you, who are destined to an active, public life. You will have to do with all sorts of characters; you should therefore know them thoroughly, in order to manage them ably. This knowledge is not to be gotten systematically; you must acquire it yourself by your own observation and sagacity: I will give you such hints as I think may be useful landmarks in your intended progress.

I have often told you (and it is most true) that, with regard to mankind, we must not draw general conclusions from certain particular principles, though, in the main, true ones. We must not suppose that because a man is a rational animal, he will therefore always act rationally; or because he has such or such a predominant passion, that he will act invariably and consequentially in the pursuit of it. No; we are complicated machines: and though we have one mainspring, that gives motion to the whole, we have an infinity of little wheels, which, in their turns, retard, precipitate, and sometimes stop that motion. Let us exemplify. I will suppose ambition to be (as it commonly is) the predominant passion of a minister of state; and I will suppose that minister to be an able one. Will he, therefore, invariably pursue the object of that predominant passion? May I be sure that he will do so and so, because he ought? Nothing less. Sickness, or low spirits, may damp this predominant passion; humour and peevishness may triumph over it; inferior passions may, at times, surprise it, and pre-

vail. Is this ambitious statesman amorous? indiscreet
and unguarded confidences, made in tender moments
to his wife or his mistress, may defeat all his schemes.
Is he avaricious? some great lucrative object, suddenly presenting itself, may unravel all the work of
his ambition. Is he passionate? contradiction and provocation (sometimes, it may be, too, artfully intended)
may extort rash and inconsiderate expressions, or
actions destructive of his main object. Is he vain, and
open to flattery? an artful, flattering favourite may
mislead him; and even laziness may, at certain
moments, make him neglect or omit the necessary
steps to that height at which he wants to arrive. Seek
first, then, for the predominant passion of the character
which you mean to engage and influence, and address
yourself to it; but without defying or despising the
inferior passions; get them in your interest too, for
now and then they will have their turns. In many
cases, you may not have it in your power to contribute
to the gratification of the prevailing passion; then take
the next best to your aid. There are many avenues to
every man; and when you cannot get at him through
the great one, try the serpentine ones, and you will
arrive at last.

There are two inconsistent passions which, however, frequently accompany each other, like man and
wife; and which, like man and wife too, are commonly clogs upon each other. I mean ambition and
avarice: the latter is often the true cause of the former,
and then is the predominant passion. It seems to have
been so in Cardinal Mazarin,* who did anything, submitted to anything, and forgave anything, for the sake
of plunder. He loved and courted power, like an
usurer, because it carried profit along with it. Who-

ever should have formed his opinion or taken his measures singly, from the ambitious part of Cardinal Mazarin's character, would have found himself often mistaken. Some who had found this out, made their fortunes by letting him cheat them at play. On the contrary, Cardinal Richelieu's prevailing passion seems to have been ambition, and his immense riches only the natural consequences of that ambition gratified; and yet I make no doubt but that ambition had now and then its turn with the former, and avarice with the latter. Richelieu (by the way) is so strong a proof of the inconsistency of human nature, that I cannot help observing to you, that while he absolutely governed both his King and his country, and was, in a great degree, the arbiter of the fate of all Europe, he was more jealous of the great reputation of Corneille than of the power of Spain; and more flattered with being thought (what he was not) the best poet, than with being thought (what he certainly was) the greatest statesman in Europe; and affairs stood still while he was concerting the criticism upon the *Cid*.* Could one think this possible, if one did not know it to be true? Though men are all of one composition, the several ingredients are so differently proportioned in each individual, that no two are exactly alike; and no one at all times like himself. The ablest man will sometimes do weak things; the proudest man, mean things; the honestest man, ill things; and the wickedest man, good ones. Study individuals then, and if you take (as you ought to do) their outlines from their prevailing passion, suspend your last finishing strokes till you have attended to, and discovered the operations of their inferior passions, appetites, and humours. A man's general character may be that of the honestest man of the world: do not dispute it; you might be thought envious or ill-natured; but at the same time, do not take this probity upon trust, to such a degree as to put your life, fortune, or reputation, in his power. This honest man may happen to be your rival in power, in interest, or in love; three passions that often put honesty to most severe trials, in which it is too often cast: but first analyse this honest man yourself; and then only you will be able to judge how far you may, or may not, with safety trust him.

Women are much more like each other than men: they have, in truth, but two passions, vanity and love; these are their universal characteristics. An Agrippina may sacrifice them to ambition, or a Messalina*to lust; but such instances are rare; and in general, all they say and all they do, tends to the gratification of their vanity or their love. He who flatters them most, pleases them best; and they are most in love with him, who they think is the most in love with them. No adulation is too strong for them; no assiduity too great; no simulation of passion too gross; as, on the other hand, the least word or action that can possibly be construed into a slight or contempt, is unpardonable, and never forgotten. Men are, in this respect, tender too, and will sooner forgive an injury than an insult. Some men are more captious than others: some are always wrong-headed; but every man living has such a share of vanity, as to be hurt by marks of slight and contempt. Every man does not pretend to be a poet, a mathematician, or a statesman, and considered as such; but every man pretends to common sense, and to fill his place in the world with common decency; and consequently, does not easily forgive those negligences, inattentions, and slights which seem to call in question, or utterly deny him both these pretensions.

Suspect, in general, those who remarkably affect any one virtue; who raise it above all others, and who, in a manner, intimate that they possess it exclusively. I say suspect them, for they are commonly impostors; but do not be sure that they are always so; for I have sometimes known saints really religious, blusterers really brave, reformers of manners really honest, and prudes really chaste. Pry into the recesses of their hearts yourself, as far as you are able, and never implicitly adopt a character upon common fame; which, though generally right as to the great outlines of characters, is always wrong in some particulars.

Be upon your guard against those, who, upon very slight acquaintance, obtrude their unasked and unmerited friendship and confidence upon you; for they probably cram you with them only for their own eating: but at the same time, do not roughly reject them upon that general supposition. Examine farther, and see whether those unexpected offers flow from a warm heart and a silly head, or from a designing head and a cold heart; for knavery and folly have often the same symptoms. In the first case, there is no danger in accepting them, *valeant quantum valere possunt.** In the latter case, it may be useful to seem to accept them, and artfully to turn the battery upon him who raised it.

There is an incontinency of friendship among young fellows, who are associated by their mutual pleasures only; which has very frequently bad consequences. A parcel of warm hearts and unexperienced heads, heated by convivial mirth, and possibly a little too much wine, vow, and really mean at the time, eternal friendships to each other, and indiscreetly pour out their whole souls in common, and without the least reserve. These confidences are as indiscreetly repealed as they were made; for new pleasures and new places soon dissolve this ill-cemented connection; and then very ill uses are made of these rash confidences. Bear your part, however, in young companies; nay, excel, if you can, in all the social and convivial joy and festivity that become youth. Trust them with your love-tales, if you please; but keep your serious views secret. Trust those only to some tried friend, more experienced than yourself, and who, being in a different walk of life from you, is not likely to become your rival; for I would not advise you to depend so much upon the heroic virtue of mankind, as to hope, or believe, that your competitor will ever be your friend, as to the object of that competition.

These are reserves and cautions very necessary to have but very imprudent to show; the *volto sciolto**
should accompany them.

56. TO HIS SON

LONDON, JANUARY 8, O.S. 1750

DEAR BOY,

I have seldom or never written to you upon the subject of religion and morality; your own reason, I am persuaded, has given you true notions of both; they speak best for themselves; but if they wanted assistance, you have Mr. Harte at hand, both for precept and example; to your own reason, therefore, and to Mr. Harte, shall I refer you, for the reality of both, and confine myself in this letter to the decency, the utility, and the necessity of scrupulously preserving the appearances of both. When I say the appearances of religion, I do not mean that you should talk or act like a missionary, or an enthusiast, nor that you should take up a controversial cudgel against whoever attacks the sect you are of; this would be both useless and unbecoming your age; but I mean that you should by no means seem to approve, encourage, or applaud, those libertine notions, which strike at religions equally, and which are the poor threadbare topics of half wits, and minute philosophers. Even those who are silly enough to laugh at their jokes, are still wise enough to distrust and detest their characters; for, putting moral virtues at the highest, and religion at the lowest, religion must still be allowed to be a collateral security, at least, to virtue; and every prudent man will sooner trust to two securities than to one. Whenever, therefore, you happen to be in company with those pretended *esprits forts*, or with thoughtless libertines, who laugh at all religion, to show their wit, or disclaim it, to complete their riot; let no word or look of yours intimate the least approbation; on the contrary let a silent gravity express your dislike: but enter not into the subject, and decline such unprofitable and indecent controversies. Depend upon this truth, That every man is the worse looked upon, and the less trusted for being thought to have no religion; in spite of all the pompous and specious epithets he may assume, of *esprit fort*, freethinker, or moral philosopher; and a wise atheist (if such a thing there is) would, for his own interest and character in this world, pretend to some religion.

Your moral character must be not only pure, but, like Caesar's wife,* unsuspected. The least speck or blemish upon it is fatal. Nothing degrades and vilifies more, for it excites and unites detestation and contempt. There are, however, wretches in the world profligate enough to explode all notions of moral good and evil; to maintain that they are merely local, and depend entirely upon the customs and fashions of different countries; nay, there are still, if possible, more unaccountable wretches; I mean those who affect to preach and propagate such absurd and infamous notions without believing them themselves. These are the devil's hypocrites. Avoid, as much as possible, the company of such people; who reflect a degree of discredit and infamy upon all who converse with them. But as you may sometimes by accident fall into such company, take great care that no complaisance, no good-humour, no warmth of festal mirth, ever make you seem even to acquiesce, much less to approve or applaud, such infamous doctrines. On the other hand, do not debate nor enter into serious argument upon a subject so much below it: but content yourself with telling these *Apostles*, that you know they are not serious; that you have a much better opinion of them than they would have you have; and that, you are very sure, they would not practise the doctrine they preach. But put your private mark upon them, and shun them for ever afterwards.

There is nothing so delicate as your moral character, and nothing which it is your interest so much to preserve pure. Should you be suspected of injustice, malignity, perfidy, lying, etc., all the parts and knowledge in the world will never procure you esteem, friendship, or respect. A strange concurrence of circumstances has sometimes raised very bad men to high stations, but they have been raised like criminals to a pillory, where their persons and their crimes, by being more conspicuous, are only the more known, the more detested, and the more pelted and insulted. If, in any case whatsoever, affectation and ostentation are pardonable, it is in the case of morality; though even there, I would not advise you to a pharisaical pomp of virtue. But I will recommend to you a most scrupulous tenderness for your moral character, and the utmost care not to say or do the least thing that may ever so slightly taint it. Show yourself, upon all occasions, the advocate, the friend, but not the bully of Virtue. Colonel Chartres,* whom you have certainly heard of (who was, I believe, the most notorious blasted rascal in the world, and who had by all sorts of crimes amassed immense wealth), was so sensible of the disadvantage of a bad character, that I heard him once say, in his impudent profligate manner, that though he would not give one farthing for virtue, he would give ten thousand pounds for a character, because he should get a hundred thousand pounds by it; whereas, he was so blasted, that he had no longer an opportunity of cheating people. Is it possible then that an honest man can neglect what a wise rogue would purchase so dear?

There is one of the vices above-mentioned, into which people of good education, and in the main, of good principles, sometimes fall, from mistaken notions of skill, dexterity, and self-defence; I mean lying; though it is inseparably attended with more infamy and loss than any other. The prudence and necessity of often concealing the truth, insensibly seduces people to violate it. It is the only art of mean capacities, and the only refuge of mean spirits. Whereas, concealing the truth, upon proper occasions, is as prudent, and as innocent, as telling a lie, upon any occasion, is infamous and foolish. I will state you a case in your own department. Suppose you are employed at a foreign court, and that the minister of that court is absurd or impertinent enough to ask you what your instructions are; Will you tell him a lie, which, as soon as found out (and found out it certainly will be) must destroy your credit, blast your character, and render you useless there? No. Will you tell him the truth then, and betray your trust? As certainly, No. But you will answer with firmness, That you are surprised at such a question; that you are persuaded he does not expect an answer to it; but that, at all events, he certainly will not have one. Such an answer will give him confidence in you; he will conceive an opinion of your veracity, of which opinion you may afterwards make very honest and fair advantages. But if, in negotiations, you are looked upon as a liar and a trickster, no confidence will be placed in you, nothing will be communicated to you, and you will be in the situation of a man who has been burnt in the cheek; and who, from that mark cannot afterwards get an honest livelihood if he would, but must continue a thief.

Lord Bacon very justly makes a distinction between simulation and dissimulation; and allows the latter rather than the former; but still observes, that they are the weaker sort of politicians who have recourse to either. A man who has strength of mind, and strength of parts, wants neither of them. *Certainly* (says he) *the ablest men that ever were, have all had an openness and frankness of dealing, and a name of certainty and veracity; but then, they were like horses well-managed; for they could tell passing well when to stop or turn; and at such times, when they thought the case indeed required some dissimulation, if then they used it it came to pass, that the former opinion spread abroad, of their good faith and clearness of dealing, made them almost invisible.**

There are people who indulge themselves in a sort of lying, which they reckon innocent, and which in one sense is so; for it hurts nobody but themselves. This sort of lying is the spurious offspring of vanity, begotten upon folly: these people deal in the marvellous; they have seen some things that never existed; they have seen other things which they never really saw, though they did exist, only because they were thought worth seeing. Has anything remarkable been said or done in any place, or in any company, they immediately present and declare themselves eye or ear witnesses of it. They have done feats themselves, unattempted, or at least unperformed by others. They are always the heroes of their own fables; and think that they gain consideration, or at least present attention, by it. Whereas, in truth, all they get is ridicule and contempt, not without a good degree of distrust: for one must naturally conclude, that he who will tell any lie from idle vanity, will not scruple telling a greater for interest. Had I really seen anything so very extraordinary as to be almost incredible, I would keep it to myself, rather than by telling it give anybody room to doubt, for one minute, of my veracity. It is most certain, that the reputation of chastity is not so necessary for a woman, as that of veracity is for a man; and with reason; for it is possible for a woman to be virtuous, though not strictly chaste, but it is not possible for a man to be virtuous without strict veracity. The slips of the poor women are sometimes mere bodily frailties; but a lie in a man is a vice of the mind and of the heart. For God's sake be scrupulously jealous of the purity of your moral character; keep it immaculate, unblemished, unsullied; and it will be unsuspected. Defamation and calumny never attack, where there is no weak place; they magnify, but they do not create.

There is a very great difference between that purity of character, which I so earnestly recommend to you, and the Stoical gravity and austerity of character, which I do by no means recommend to you. At your age, I would no more wish you to be a Cato, than a Clodius.* Be, and be reckoned, a man of pleasure as well as a man of business. Enjoy this happy and giddy time of your life; shine in the pleasures, and in the company of people of your own age. This is all to be done, and indeed only can be done, without the least taint to the purity of your moral character; for those mistaken young fellows who think to shine by an impious or immoral licentiousness, shine only from their stinking, like corrupted flesh, in the dark. Without this purity, you can have no dignity of character; and without dignity of character it is impossible to rise in the world. You must be respectable, if you will be respected. I have known people slattern away their character, without really polluting it; the consequence of which has been, that they have become innocently contemptible; their merit has been dimmed, their pretensions unregarded, and all their views defeated. Character must be kept bright, as well as clean. Content yourself with mediocrity in nothing. In purity of character, and in politeness of manners, labour to excel all, if you wish to equal many. Adieu!

57. TO HIS SON

LONDON, JANUARY 25, O.S. 1750

MY DEAR FRIEND,

It is so long since I have heard from you, that I suppose Rome engrosses every moment of your time;

and if it engrosses it in the manner I could wish, I willingly give up my share of it. I would rather *prodesse quam conspici.** Put out your time but to good interest; and I do not desire to borrow much of it. Your studies, the respectable remains of antiquity, and your evening amusements cannot and indeed ought not to leave you much time to write. You will probably never see Rome again; and therefore you ought to see it well now; by seeing it well, I do not mean only the buildings, statues, and paintings, though they undoubtedly deserve your attention: but I mean seeing into the constitution and government of it. But these things certainly occur to your own common sense.

How go your pleasures at Rome? Are you in fashion there; that is, do you live with the people who are? the only way of being so yourself, in time. Are you domestic enough in any considerable house to be called *le petit Stanhope?* Has any woman of fashion and good-breeding taken the trouble of abusing and laughing at you amicably to your face? Have you found a good *décrotteuse?** For these are the steps by which you must rise to politeness. I do not presume to ask if you have any attachment, because I believe you will not make me your *confident*: but this I will say, eventually, that if you have one, *il faut bien païer d'attentions et de petits soins*, if you would have your sacrifice propitiously received. Women are not so much taken by beauty as men are, but prefer those men who show them the most attention.

> Would you engage the lovely fair?
> With gentlest manners treat her;
> With tender looks and graceful air,
> In softest accents greet her.

Verse were in vain, the Muses fail,
  Without the Graces' aid;
The God of Verse could not prevail
  To stop the flying maid.

Attention by attentions gain,
  And merit care by cares;
So shall the nymph reward your pain,
  And Venus crown your prayers.
                    —*Probatum est.**

A man's address and manner weighs much more with them than his beauty; and, without them, the *Abbati* and the *Monsignori**will get the better of you. This address and manner should be exceedingly respectful, but at the same time easy and unembarrassed. Your chit-chat or *entregent**with them neither can, nor ought to be very solid; but you should take care to turn and dress up your trifles prettily, and make them every now and then convey indirectly some little piece of flattery. A fan, a ribband, or a head-dress, are great materials for gallant dissertations, to one who has got *le ton léger et aimable de la bonne compagnie.* At all events, a man had better talk too much to women, than too little; they take silence for dulness, unless where they think the passion they have inspired occasions it; and in that case they adopt the notion, that

Silence in love betrays more woe
  Than words, though ne'er so witty:
The beggar that is dumb, we know,
  Deserves a double pity.

A propos of this subject; what progress do you make in that language, in which Charles the Fifth said, that he would choose to speak to his mistress? Have you got all the tender diminutives, in *etta*, *ina*, and *ettina;**

which, I presume, he alluded to? You already possess, and I hope, take care not to forget, that language which he reserved for his horse. You are absolutely master, too, of that language in which he said he would converse with men; French. But in every language, pray attend carefully to the choice of your words, and to the turn of your expression. Indeed, it is a point of very great consequence. To be heard with success, you must be heard with pleasure: words are the dress of thoughts; which should no more be presented in rags, tatters, and dirt, than your person should. By the way; do you mind your person and your dress sufficiently? Do you take great care of your teeth? Pray have them put in order by the best operator at Rome. Are you be-laced, be-powdered, and be-feathered, as other young fellows are, and should be? At your age, *il faut du brillant, et même un peu de fracas, mais point de médiocre; il faut un air vif, aisé et noble. Avec les hommes, un maintien respectueux et un même tems respectable; avec les femmes, un caquet léger, enjoué, et badin, mais toujours fort poli.*

To give you an opportunity of exerting your talents, I send you, here enclosed, a letter of recommendation from Monsieur Villetes to Madame de Simonetti at Milan; a woman of the first fashion and consideration there; and I shall in my next send you another from the same person to Madame Clerici,* at the same place. As these two ladies' houses are the resort of all the people of fashion at Milan, those two recommendations will introduce you to them all. Let me know, in due time, if you have received these two letters, that I may have them renewed, in case of accidents.

Adieu, my dear friend! Study hard; divert yourself

heartily; distinguish carefully between the pleasures of a man of fashion, and the vices of a scoundrel; pursue the former, and abhor the latter, like a man of sense.

58. TO HIS SON

LONDON, MARCH 19, O.S. 1750

MY DEAR FRIEND,

I acknowledge your last letter of the 24th February, N.S. In return for your earthquake, I can tell you that we have had here, more than our share of earthquakes;* for we had two very strong ones in eight-and-twenty days. They really do too much honour to our cold climate; in your warm one, they are compensated by favours from the sun, which we do not enjoy. . . .

When you return here, I am apt to think that you will find something better to do than to run to Mr. Osborne's* at Gray's Inn, to pick up scarce books. Buy good books, and read them; the best books are the commonest, and the last editions are always the best, if the editors are not blockheads, for they may profit of the former. But take care not to understand editions and title pages too well. It always smells of pedantry, and not always of learning. What curious books I have, they are indeed but few, shall be at your service. I have some of the old *Collana*, and the Macchiavel* of 1550. Beware of the *Bibliomanie*.

In the midst of either your studies or your pleasures, pray never lose view of the object of your destination: I mean the political affairs of Europe. Follow them politically, chronologically, and geographically, through the newspapers, and trace up the facts which you meet with there to their sources: as, for example, consult the treaties of *Neustadt* and *Abo*,* with regard to the disputes, which you read of every day in the public papers, between Russia and Sweden. For the affairs of Italy,* which are reported to be the objects of present negotiations, recur to the quadruple alliance of the year 1718, and follow them down through their several variations to the treaty of Aix-la-Chapelle, 1748; in which (by-the-bye) you will find the very different tenures by which the infant Don Philip, your namesake, holds Parma and Placentia. Consult, also, the Emperor Charles the Sixth's Act of Cession of the kingdoms of Naples and Sicily, in 1736. The succession to the kingdoms of Naples and Sicily being a point which, upon the death of the present King of Spain, is likely to occasion some disputes; do not lose the thread of these matters; which is carried on with great ease, but, if once broken, is resumed with difficulty.

Pray tell Mr. Harte, that I have sent his packet to Baron Firmian by Count Einsiedlen, who is gone from hence this day for Germany, and passes through Vienna in his way to Italy; where he is in hopes of crossing upon you somewhere or other. Adieu, my friend. Χαριτες, Χαριτες.*

59. TO SOLOMON DAYROLLES, ESQ.

LONDON, MAY 25, O.S. 1750

DEAR DAYROLLES,

I find your journey through Flanders has been, like every man's journey through the world, some good and some bad; but, upon the whole, it was as well as being at the Hague. By what you observed, it is evident that the Court of Vienna will not lay out a shilling upon the barrier towns;* but throw that burthen, as they do every other, upon the Maritime Powers; saying, that they get nothing by Flanders, but that it is our business to take care of it. I am an Austrian in my politics, and would support that House, if I could; but then I would be their ally, not their bubble; their friend, but not their victim.

With your leave, Sir, it is none of Boden's trumpery that is to hang over against the Rubens, but a Holy Family, the masterpiece of Titian; for which the late Regent had agreed to give forty thousand livres to the Chapter at Rheims. It was accordingly sent him; but when it arrived at Paris he was dead and gone, not to the Holy Family, I believe. His son, the present Duke of Orleans, chose rather to return the picture than the money; the Chapter was obliged to take it back, and there it has remained ever since. I accidently heard of this, and that the Chapter was special poor; upon which, I determined to try what I could do, and I have succeeded. As this picture was brought from Italy by the famous Cardinal de Lorraine, after he had been at the Council of Trent, and given by him to the Cathedral of Rheims, of which he was Archbishop, he gave them at the same time his own picture, a whole length, done by Titian; which I have likewise got; they are both arrived at Paris, and I expect them here very soon. This, you will allow, is no trumpery, and I have now done with pictures; I am brimfull, and not ill filled.*

Comte Obdam's *virtu** will, I think, for the reason you give, go very cheap; few people in Holland understanding those things, or even thinking that they do. I would not give sixpence for his bronzes, nor a shilling for his books; but for some of his antique marbles, I would give reasonably. Those which, upon the face of the catalogue, I should choose, are the following ones.

297. *Hermes* (Buste) *iuvenis Romani cum lorica et sago, in marmore. Ant.*

298. *Bacchus, cum corona hederacea. Ant.*

302. *Caput iuvenis Romani, supra basin. Ant.*

305. *Statua cum anaglyphis, sacrificium in honorem Priapi efformantibus. Ant.**

There are also in the appendix two bustos, one of Homer, the other of Apollo, by Girardon;* which, if they go extremely cheap, as possibly they may, I should be glad of them; by extremely cheap, I mean about ten pounds a-piece. For the four antiques above-marked, *l'un portant l'autre;** if they are fine, I would go as far as five and twenty pounds a-piece. But should these which I have mentioned have great faults, and others which I have not mentioned have great beauties, I refer to your decision, who are upon the place, and have *un coup d'œil vif et pénétrant.**

You will see Hop* at the Hague next week; it is sooner than he proposed to go, but he is ordered, which gives him some apprehensions. You will also see the famous Madame du Boccage, who sets out from hence with her husband, and Abbé Guasco* *de l'Académie des Inscriptions*, next Tuesday. She has translated Milton into French verse, and gave a tragedy last winter at Paris, called *les Amazones*. She has good parts, *n'affiche pas le bel esprit*. Pray, give them *un petit diner*, and let them know that I did them justice with you; they stay but a few days at the Hague, so cannot be very troublesome to you. But I possibly shall, if I lengthen this letter; so, *bon soir*.

60. TO SOLOMON DAYROLLES, ESQ.

DEAR DAYROLLES,

I must say, as most fools do, *who would have thought it?* My fine Titian has turned out an execrable bad copy. By good luck, the condition of the obligation was such, that, if certain good judges at Paris should declare it either a copy, or essentially damaged, the Chapter of Rheims was to take it back again, I paying the carriage. This has happened; and the best painters in Paris pronounced it not only a copy, but a damned one; so that I am only in for the carriage back. The Chapter must have been more fools than knaves in the affair; for, had they known it to be a copy, they might have known, at the same time, that it would be returned them; by which they would get nothing but discrediting of their picture for ever.

I have received a letter from Madame du Boccage, containing a panegyric of his Majesty's Resident at the Hague. *Il est très aimable, très poli, il est au mieux avec tout ce qu'il y a de meilleur ici, et il fait très-bonne chère.* *Faire bonne chère,* you know, always sums up a French panegyric. She says, that by your means she received a thousand civilities at the Hague. She did so here, notwithstanding that Madame de Mirepoix*and she had a quarrel, in which they both contrived, as all ladies when they quarrel do, to be both extremely in the wrong.

I do not know whether my friend Abbé Guasco's judgment in *virtu* will be of any great service to us at Comte Obdam's, and I would sooner trust to your own *coup d'œil, qui est mordieu vif et perçant*!

I am very much *par voies, et par chemins,* between

London and Blackheath,* but much more at the latter, which is now in great beauty. The shell of my gallery is finished, which, by three bow-windows, gives me three different, and the finest, prospects in the world. I have already two or three of your Cantelupe melons, which are admirable; I have covered those, which are not yet ripe, with frames of oiled paper, which I am assured will do much better than glasses.

I am glad that Hop is better than he thinks himself, for he received his orders to go to Hanover, with some uneasiness, knowing that Bentinck was to be there also, in his way from Vienna.* When Bentinck returns to the Hague, some new scene or other will open. He must be either Caesar or nobody. I rather expect to see him soon the latter; combining all the circumstances that you and I know.

The Prince of Wales's last child was at last christened the day before yesterday, after having been kept at least a fortnight longer than it should have been out of a state of salvation, by the jumble of the two Secretaries of State, whose reciprocal despatches carried, nor brought, nothing decisive. Our English Atlas has carried our part of the globe with him to Woburn, *ou il s'ébaudit, et se délecte.** Adieu.

61. TO HIS SON

LONDON, OCTOBER 22, O.S. 1750

MY DEAR FRIEND,

This letter will, I am persuaded, find you, and I hope safely, arrived at Montpellier; from whence I trust that Mr. Harte's indisposition will, by being totally removed, allow you to get to Paris before Christmas. You will there find two people, who, though both

English, I recommend in the strongest manner possible to your attention; and advise you to form the most intimate connections with them both, in their different ways. The one is a man whom you already know something of, but not near enough: it is the Earl of Huntingdon;* who, next to you, is the truest object of my affection and esteem; and who (I am proud to say it) calls me, and considers me as his adopted father. His parts are as quick as his knowledge is extensive; and if quality were worth putting into an account, where every other item is so much more valuable, he is the first almost in this country: the figure he will make, soon after he returns to it, will, if I am not more mistaken than ever I was in my life, equal his birth and my hopes. Such a connection will be of infinite advantage to you; and I can assure you that he is extremely disposed to form it upon my account; and will, I hope and believe, desire to improve and cement it upon your own.

In our parliamentary government, connections are absolutely necessary; and if prudently formed and ably maintained, the success of them is infallible. There are two sorts of connections, which I would always advise you to have in view. The first I will call equal ones; by which I mean those, where the two connecting parties reciprocally find their account, from pretty near an equal degree of parts and abilities. In those there must be a freer communication; each must see that the other is able, and be convinced that he is willing to be of use to him. Honour must be the principle of such connections; and there must be a mutual dependance, that present and separate interest shall not be able to break them. There must be a joint system of action; and in case of different opinions, each must recede a little, in order at last to form an unanimous one. Such, I hope, will be your connection with Lord Huntingdon. You will both come into Parliament at the same time; and if you have an equal share of abilities and application, you and he, with other young people, whom you will naturally associate, may form a band which will be respected by any administration, and make a figure in the public. The other sort of connections I call unequal ones; that is, where the parts are all on one side, and the rank and fortune on the other. Here, the advantage is all on one side; but that advantage must be ably and artfully concealed. Complaisance, an engaging manner, and a patient toleration of certain airs of superiority, must cement them. The weaker party must be taken by the heart, his head giving no hold; and he must be governed, by being made to believe that he governs. These people, skilfully led, give great weight to their leader. I have formerly pointed out to you a couple that I take to be proper objects for your skill: and you will meet with twenty more, for they are very rife.

The other person whom I recommend to you is a woman; not as a woman, for that is not immediately my business; besides, I fear she is turned of fifty. It is Lady Hervey,* whom I directed you to call upon at Dijon, but who, to my great joy, because to your great advantage, passes all this winter at Paris. She has been bred all her life at courts; of which she has acquired all the easy good-breeding and politeness, without the frivolousness. She has all the reading that a woman should have; and more than any woman need have; for she understands Latin perfectly well, though she wisely conceals it. As she will look upon you as her son, I desire that you will look upon her as my delegate: trust, consult, and apply to her without reserve. No woman ever had more than she has *le ton de la parfaitement bonne compagnie, les manières engageantes, et le je ne sçais quoi qui plait*. Desire her to reprove and correct any, and every, the least error and inaccuracy in your manner, air, address, etc. No woman in Europe can do it so well; none will do it more willingly, or in a more proper and obliging manner. In such a case, she will not put you out of countenance, by telling you of it in company; but either intimate it by some sign, or wait for an opportunity when you are alone together. She is also in the best French company, where she will not only introduce, but *puff* you, if I may use so low a word. And I can assure you that it is no little help, in the *beau monde*, to be puffed there by a fashionable woman. I send you the enclosed billet to carry her, only as a certificate of the identity of your person, which I take it for granted she could not know again.

You would be so much surprised to receive a whole letter from me without any mention of the exterior ornaments necessary for a gentleman, as manners, elocution, air, address, graces, etc., that, to comply with your expectations, I will touch upon them; and tell you, that, when you come to England, I will show you some people, whom I do not now care to name, raised to the highest stations singly by those exterior and adventitious ornaments; whose parts would never have entitled them to the smallest office in the excise. Are they then necessary, and worth acquiring, or not? You will see many instances of this kind at Paris, particularly a glaring one, of a person raised to the highest posts and dignities in France, as well as to be absolute sovereign of the *beau monde*, singly by the graces of his person and address; by woman's chit-chat, accompanied with important gestures; by an imposing air, and pleasing *abord*.* Nay, by these helps, he even passes for a wit, though he hath certainly no uncommon share of it. I will not name him, because it would be very imprudent in you to do it. A young fellow, at his first entrance into the *beau monde*, must not offend the king *de facto* there. It is very often more necessary to conceal contempt then resentment, the former being never forgiven, but the latter sometimes forgot.

There is a small quarto book, intitled *Histoire Chronologique de la France*, lately published by le Président Hénault;* a man of parts and learning, with whom you will probably get acquainted at Paris. I desire that it may always lie upon your table, for your recourse as often as you read history. The chronology, though chiefly relative to the history of France, is not singly confined to it; but the most interesting events of all the rest of Europe are also inserted, and many of them adorned by short, pretty, and just reflections. The new edition of *les Mémoires de Sully*,* in three quarto volumes, is also extremely well worth your reading, as it will give you a clearer and truer notion of one of the most interesting periods of the French history, than you can yet have formed from all the other books you may have read upon the subject. That prince, I mean Henry the Fourth, had all the accomplishments and virtues of a hero, and of a king, and almost of a man. The last are the most rarely seen. May you possess them all! Adieu!

Pray make my compliments to Mr. Harte, and let him know that I have this moment received his letter of the 12th, N.S., from Antibes. It requires no immediate answer; I shall therefore delay mine till I have another from him. Give him the enclosed, which I have received from Mr. Elliot.

62. TO HIS SON

LONDON, NOVEMBER 8, O.S. 1750

MY DEAR FRIEND,

Before you get to Paris, where you will soon be left to your own discretion, if you have any, it is necessary that we should understand one another thoroughly; which is the most probable way of preventing disputes. Money, the cause of much mischief in the world, is the cause of most quarrels between fathers and sons; the former commonly thinking, that they cannot give too little, and the latter, that they cannot have enough; both equally in the wrong. You must do me the justice to acknowledge that I have hitherto neither stinted nor grudged any expense that could be of use, or real pleasure to you; and I can assure you, by the way, that you have travelled at a much more considerable expense than I did myself; but I never so much as thought of that, while Mr. Harte was at the head of your finances; being very sure that the sums granted were scrupulously applied to the uses for which they were intended. But the case will soon be altered, and you will be your own receiver and treasurer. However, I promise you, that we will not quarrel singly upon the *quantum,** which shall be cheerfully and freely granted; the application and appropriation of it will be the material point, which I am now going to clear up and finally settle with you. I will fix, or even name, no settled allowance; though I well know in my own mind what would be the proper one; but I will first try your drafts, by which I can in a good degree judge of your conduct. This only I tell you in general, that, if the channels through which my money is to go are the proper ones, the source shall not be scanty; but should it deviate into dirty, muddy, and obscure ones (which by-the-bye, it cannot do for a week without my knowing it), I give you fair and timely notice, that the source will instantly be dry. Mr. Harte, in establishing you at Paris, will point out to you those proper channels: he will leave you there* upon the foot of a man of fashion, and I will continue you upon the same; you will have your coach, your *valet de chambre*, your own footman, and a *valet de place*, which, by the way, is one servant more than I had. I would have you very well dressed, by which I mean dressed as the generality of people of fashion are; that is, not to be taken notice of for being either more or less fine than other prople: it is by being well dressed, not finely dressed, that a gentleman should be distinguished. You must frequent *les spectacles*, which expense I shall willingly supply. You must play *à des petits jeux de commerce* in mixed companies; that article is trifling; I shall pay it cheerfully. All the other articles of pocket money are very inconsiderable at Paris, in comparison of what they are here, the silly custom of giving money wherever one dines or sups, and the expensive importunity of subscriptions, not being yet introduced there. Having thus reckoned up all the decent expenses of a gentleman, which, I will most readily defray, I come now to those which I will neither bear nor supply. The first of these is gaming, of which, though I have not the least reason to suspect you, I think it necessary eventually to assure you, that no consideration in the world shall ever make me pay your play-debts; should you ever urge to me that your honour is pawned, I should most immoveably answer you, that it was your honour, not mine, that was pawned; and that your creditor might e'en take the pawn for the debt.

Low company, and low pleasures, are always much more costly than liberal and elegant ones. The disgraceful riots of a tavern are much more expensive, as well as honourable, than the sometimes pardonable excesses in good company. I must absolutely hear of no tavern scrapes and squabbles.

I come now to another and very material point; I mean women; and I will not address myself to you upon this subject, either in a religious, a moral, or a parental style. I will even lay aside my age, remember yours, and speak to you, as one man of pleasure, if he had parts too, would speak to another. I will, by no means, pay for whores, and their never-failing consequences, surgeons; nor will I, upon any account, keep singers, dancers, actresses, and *id genus omne;**and, independently of the expense, I must tell you, that such connections would give me, and all sensible people, the utmost contempt for your parts and address: a young fellow must have as little sense as address, to venture, or more properly to sacrifice his health, and ruin his fortune, with such sort of creatures; in such a place as Paris especially, where gallantry is both the profession and the practice of every woman of fashion. To speak plainly, I will not forgive your understanding c——s and p——s;*nor will your constitution forgive them you. These distempers, as well as their cures, fall nine times in ten upon the lungs. This argument, I am sure, ought to have weight with you; for I protest to you, that if you meet with any such accident, I would not give one year's purchase for your life.

Lastly, there is another sort of expense that I will not allow, only because it is a silly one; I mean the fooling away your money in baubles at toy-shops. Have one handsome snuff-box (if you take snuff), and one handsome sword; but then no more very pretty and very useless things.

By what goes before, you will easily perceive that I mean to allow you whatever is necessary, not only for the figure, but for the pleasures of a gentleman, and not to supply the profusion of a rake. This, you must confess, does not savour of either the severity or parsimony of old age. I consider this agreement between us as a subsidiary treaty on my part, for services to be performed on yours. I promise you, that I will be as punctual in the payment of the subsidies, as England has been during the last war;* but then I give you notice at the same time, that I require a much more scrupulous execution of the treaty on your part, than we met with on that of our allies; or else that payment will be stopped. I hope that all I have now said was absolutely unnecessary, and that sentiments more worthy and more noble than pecuniary ones, would of themselves have pointed out to you the conduct I recommend; but in all events, I resolved to be once for all explicit with you, that in the worst that can happen, you may not plead ignorance, and complain that I had not sufficiently explained to you my intentions.

Having mentioned the word Rake, I must say a word or two more on that subject, because young people too frequently, and always fatally, are apt to mistake that character for that of a man of pleasure; whereas, there are not in the world two characters more different. A rake is a composition of all the lowest, most ignoble, degrading, and shameful vices;

they all conspire to disgrace his character, and to ruin his fortune; while wine and the pox contend which shall soonest and most effectually destroy his constitution. A dissolute, flagitious footman, or porter makes full as good a rake as a man of the first quality. By-the-bye, let me tell you, that in the wildest part of my youth, I never was a rake, but, on the contrary, always detested and despised the character.

A man of pleasure, though not always so scrupulous as he should be, and as one day he will wish he had been, refines at least his pleasures by taste, accompanies them with decency, and enjoys them with dignity. Few man can be men of pleasure, every man may be a rake. Remember that I shall know everything you say or do at Paris, as exactly as if, by the force of magic, I could follow you everywhere, like a Sylph or a Gnome,* invisible myself. Seneca says, very prettily, that one should ask nothing of God, but what one should be willing that men should know; nor of men, but what one should be willing that God should know;* I advise you to say and do nothing at Paris, but what you would be willing that I should know. I hope, nay, I believe, that will be the case. Sense, I dare say, you do not want; instruction, I am sure, you have never wanted: experience you are daily gaining: all which together must inevitably (I should think) make you both *respectable et aimable*, the perfection of a human character. In that case nothing shall be wanting on my part, and you shall solidly experience all the extent and tenderness of my affection for you; but dread the reverse of both! Adieu.

P.S. When you get to Paris, after you have been to wait on Lord Albemarle, go to see Mr. Yorke,* whom I have particular reasons for desiring that you should be well with, as I shall hereafter explain to you. Let him know that my orders, and your own inclinations, conspired to make you desire his friendship and protection.

63. TO HIS SON

LONDON, JANUARY 21, O.S. 1751

MY DEAR FRIEND,

In all my letters from Paris, I have the pleasure of finding, among many other good things, your docility mentioned with emphasis: this is the sure way of improving in those things, which you only want. It is true they are little, but it is as true too that they are necessary things. As they are mere matters of usage and mode, it is no disgrace for anybody of your age to be ignorant of them; and the most compendious way of learning them is, fairly to avow your ignorance, and to consult those who, from long usage and experience, know them best. Good sense, and good nature, suggest civility in general; but, in good breeding there are a thousand little delicacies, which are established only by custom; and it is these little elegances of manners, which distinguish a courtier and a man of fashion from the vulgar. I am assured, by different people, that your air is already much improved; and one of my correspondents makes you the true French compliment of saying, *J'ose vous promettre qu'il sera bientôt comme un de nous autres.*[*] However unbecoming this speech may be in the mouth of a Frenchman, I am very glad that they think it applicable to you; for I would have you not only adopt, but rival, the best manners and usages of the place you are at, be they what they will, that is the versatility of manners, which is so useful in the course of the world. Choose your models well at Paris, and then rival them in their own way. . . .

Pleasing and governing women, may, in time, be of great service to you. They often please and govern others. *A pròpos*, are you in love with Madame de Berkenrode still, or has some other taken her place in your affections? I take it for granted, that *quae te cumque domat Venus, non erubescendis adurit ignibus. Un arrangement honnête sied bien à un galant homme.* In that case, I recommend to you the utmost discretion, and the profoundest silence. Bragging of, hinting at, intimating, or even affectedly disclaiming and denying such an *arrangement*, will equally discredit you among men and women. An unaffected silence upon that subject is the only true medium.

In your commerce with women, and indeed with men too, *une certaine douceur* is particularly engaging; it is that which constitutes that character which the French talk of so much, and so justly value, I mean *l'aimable*. This *douceur* is not so easily described as felt. It is the compound result of different things; a complaisance, a flexibility, but not a servility of manners; an air of softness in the countenance, gesture, and expression; equally, whether you concur or differ with the person you converse with. Observe those carefully who have that *douceur* which charms you and others; and your own good sense will soon enable you to discover the different ingredients of which it is composed. You must be more particularly attentive to this *douceur*, whenever you are obliged to refuse what is asked of you, or to say what in itself cannot be very agreeable to those to whom you say it. It is then the necessary gilding of a disagreeable pill. *L'aimable* consists in a thousand of these little things aggregately.

It is the *suaviter in modo*,* which I have so often re-commended to you. The *respectable*, Mr. Harte assures carefully, me, you do not want, and I believe him. Study then and acquire perfectly, the *aimable*, and you will have everything. . . .

You have now got a footing in a great many good houses at Paris, in which I advise you to make your-self domestic. This is to be done by a certain easiness of carriage, and a decent familiarity. Not by way of putting yourself upon the frivolous footing of being *sans conséquence*, but by doing in some degree, the honours of the house and table, calling yourself *en badinant*, *le galopin d'ici*,* saying to the master or mis-tress, *ceci est de mon département; je m'en charge; avouez que je m'en acquitte à merveille*. That sort of *badinage* has something engaging and *liant** in it, and begets that decent familiarity, which it is both agree-able and useful to establish in good houses, and with people of fashion. Mere formal visits, dinners, and suppers, upon formal invitations, are not the thing; they add to no connection nor information; but it is the easy, careless ingress and egress, at all hours, that forms the pleasing and profitable commerce of life.

The post is so negligent, that I lose some letters from Paris entirely, and receive others much later than I should. To this I ascribe my having received no letter from you for above a fortnight, which, to my impatience, seems a long time. I expect to hear from you once a week. Mr. Harte is gone to Cornwall, and will be back in about three weeks. I have a packet of books to send you by the first opportunity, which I believe will be Mr. Yorke's return to Paris. The Greek books come from Mr. Harte, and the English ones from your humble servant. Read Lord Boling-*

broke's* with great attention, as well to the style as to the matter. I wish you could form yourself such a style in every language. Style is the dress of thoughts; and a well-dressed thought, like a well-dressed man, appears to great advantage. Yours. Adieu.

64. TO HIS SON

MY DEAR FRIEND:

This epigram in Martial,

> Non amo te, Sabidi, nec possum dicere quare;
> Hoc tantum possum dicere, non amo te,*

has puzzled a great many people, who cannot conceive how it is possible not to love anybody, and yet not to know the reason why. I think I conceive Martial's meaning very clearly, though the nature of epigram, which is to be short, would not allow him to explain it more fully; and I take it to be this: *O Sabidis, you are a very worthy deserving man; you have a thousand good qualities, you have a great deal of learning; I esteem, I respect, but for the soul of me I cannot love you, though I cannot particularly say why. You are not* amiable; *you have not those engaging manners, those pleasing attentions, those graces, and that address, which are absolutely necessary to please, though impossible to define. I cannot say it is this or that particular thing that hinders me from loving you, it is the whole together; and upon the whole you are not agreeable.*

How often have I, in the course of my life, found myself in this situation, with regard to many of my acquaintance, whom I have honoured and respected, without being able to love? I did not know why, because, when one is young, one does not take the trouble, nor allow one's self the time to analyse one's sentiments, and to trace them up to their source. But subsequent observation and reflection have taught me why. There is a man whose moral character, deep learning, and superior parts, I acknowledge, admire, and respect; but whom it is impossible for me to love, that I am almost in a fever whenever I am in his company. His figure (without being deformed) seems made to disgrace or ridicule the common structure of the human body. His legs and arms are never in the position which, according to the situation of his body, they ought to be in, but constantly employed in committing acts of hostility upon the Graces. He throws anywhere but down his throat, whatever he means to drink, and only mangles what he means to carve. Inattentive to all the regards of social life, he mistimes or misplaces everything. He disputes with heat, and indiscriminately, mindless of the rank, character, and situation of those with whom he disputes; absolutely ignorant of the several gradations of familiarity or respect, he is exactly the same to his superiors, his equals, and his inferiors; and therefore, by a necessary consequence, absurd to two of the three. Is it possible to love such a man? No. The utmost I can do for him, is to consider him as a respectable Hottentot.*

I remember that when I came from Cambridge, I had acquired, among the pedants of that illiberal seminary, a sauciness of literature, a turn to satire and contempt, and a strong tendency to argumentation and contradiction.* But I had been but a very little while in the world, before I found that this would by no means do; and I immediately adopted the opposite character; I concealed what learning I had; I applauded often without approving; and I yielded commonly, without conviction. *Suaviter in modo* was my law and my prophets; and if I pleased (between you and me) it was much more owing to that, than to any superior knowledge or merit of my own. *A propos*, the word *pleasing* puts one always in mind of Lady Hervey; pray tell her, that I declare her responsible to me for your pleasing; that I consider her as a pleasing Falstaff, who not only pleases, herself, but is the cause of pleasing in others:* that I know she can make anything of anybody; and that, as your governess, if she does not make you please, it must be only because she will not, and not because she cannot. I hope you are *du bois dont on en fait;** and if so, she is so good a sculptor, that I am sure she can give you whatever form she pleases. A versatility of manners is as necessary in social, as a versatility of parts is in political life. One must often yield, in order to prevail; one must humble one's self, to be exalted; one must, like St. Paul, become all things to all men, to gain some;* and, by the way, men are taken by the same means, *mutatis mutandis*, that women are gained—by gentleness, insinuation, and submission; and these lines of Mr. Dryden will hold to a minister as well as to a mistress:—

> The prostrate lover, when he lowest lies,
> But stoops to conquer, and but kneels to rise.*

In the course of the world, the qualifications of the cameleon are often necessary; nay, they must be carried a little farther, and exerted a little sooner; for you should, to a certain degree, take the hue of either the man or the woman that you want, and wish to be upon terms with. *A propos*, have you yet found out at Paris any friendly and hospitable Madame de Lursay, *qui veut bien se charger du soin de vous éduquer?** And have you any occasion of representing to her, *qu'elle*

*faisoit donc des nœuds?** But I ask your pardon, Sir, for
the abruptness of the question, and acknowledge that
I am meddling with matters that are out of my department. However, in matters of less importance, I
desire to be *de vos secrets le fidèle dépositaire*. Trust me
with the general turn and colour of your amusements
at Paris. Is it *le fracas du grande monde, comédies, bals,
opéras, cour, etc.*? Or is it *des petites sociétés, moins
bruïantes, mais pas pour cela moins agréables*? Where
are you the most *établi*? Where are you *le petit Stanhope? Voiez-vous encore jouer à quelque arrangement honnête?** Have you made many acquaintances among the
young Frenchmen who ride at your academy; and
who are they? Send to me this sort of chit-chat in your
letters, which, by-the-bye, I wish you would honour
me with somewhat oftener. If you frequent any of
the myriads of polite Englishmen who infest Paris,
who are they? Have you finished with Abbé Nolét,
and are you *au fait* of all the properties and effects of
air? Were I inclined to quibble, I would say, that the
effects of *air*, at least, are best to be learned of Marcel.
If you have quite done with l'Abbé Nolét, ask my
friend l'Abbé Sallier* to recommend to you some
meagre philomath, to teach you a little geometry and
astronomy; not enough to absorb your attention, and
puzzle your intellects, but only enough not to be
grossly ignorant of either. I have of late been a sort of
an *astronome malgré moi*, by bringing last Monday into
the House of Lords a bill for reforming our present
Calendar,* and taking the New Style. Upon which
occasion I was obliged to talk some astronomical jargon, of which I did not understand one word, but got
it by heart, and spoke it by rote from a master. I
wished that I had known a little more of it myself;

and so much I would have you know. But the great and necessary knowledge of all is, to know yourself and others: this knowledge requires great attention and long experience; exert the former, and may you have the latter! Adieu.

P.S. I have this moment received your letters of the 27th February, and the 2nd March, N.S. The seal shall be done as soon as possible. I am glad that you are employed in Lord Albemarle's *bureau*; it will teach you, at least, the mechanical part of that business, such as folding, entering, and docketing letters; for you must not imagine that you are let into the *fin fin** of the correspondence, nor indeed is it fit that you should, at your age. However, use yourself to secrecy as to the letters you either read or write, that in time you may be trusted with *secret*, *very secret*, *separate*, *apart*, etc. I am sorry that this business interferes with your riding; I hope it is but seldom; but I insist upon its not interfering with your dancing-master, who is at this time the most useful and necessary of all the masters you have or can have.

65. TO HIS SON

LONDON, MARCH 18, O.S. 1751

MY DEAR FRIEND,

I acquainted you in a former letter, that I had brought a bill into the House of Lords, for correcting and reforming our present calendar, which is the Julian, and for adopting the Gregorian. I will now give you a more particular account of that affair; from which reflections will naturally occur to you, that I hope may be useful, and which I fear you have not made. It was notorious, that the Julian calendar was erroneous, and had overcharged the solar year with eleven days. Pope Gregory the Thirteenth corrected this error;* his reformed calendar was immediately received by all the Catholic powers of Europe, and afterwards adopted by all the Protestant ones, except Russia, Sweden, and England. It was not, in my opinion, very honourable for England to remain in a gross and avowed error, especially in such company; the inconveniency of it was likewise felt by all those who had foreign correspondences, whether political or mercantile. I determined, therefore, to attempt the reformation; I consulted the best lawyers, and the most skilful astronomers, and we cooked up a bill for that purpose. But then my difficulty began; I was to bring in this bill, which was necessarily composed of law jargon and astronomical calculations, to both which I am an utter stranger. However, it was absolutely necessary to make the House of Lords think that I knew something of the matter; and also to make them believe that they knew something of it themselves, which they do not. For my own part, I could just as soon have talked Celtic or Sclavonian to them, as astronomy, and they would have understood me full as well: so I resolved to do better than speak to the purpose, and to please instead of informing them. I gave them, therefore, only an historical account of calendars, from the Egyptian down to the Gregorian, amusing them now and then with little episodes; but I was particularly attentive to the choice of my words, to the harmony and roundness of my periods, to my elocution, to my action. This succeeded, and ever will succeed; they thought I informed, because I pleased them; and many of them said, that I had made the whole very clear to them; when, God knows, I had not even attempted it.

Lord Macclesfield,* who had the greatest share in forming the bill, and who is one of the greatest mathematicians and astronomers in Europe, spoke afterwards with infinite knowledge, and all the clearness that so intricate a matter could admit of; but as his words, his periods, and his utterance, were not near so good as mine, the preference was most unanimously, though most unjustly, given to me. This will ever be the case; every numerous assembly is *mob*,* let the individuals who compose it be what they will. Mere reason and good sense is never to be talked to a mob; their passions, their sentiments, their senses, and their seeming interests, are alone to be applied to. Understanding they have collectively none, but they have ears, and eyes, which must be flattered and seduced; and this can only be done by eloquence, tuneful periods, graceful action, and all the various parts of oratory.

When you come into the House of Commons, if you imagine that speaking plain and unadorned sense and reason will do your business, you will find yourself most grossly mistaken. As a speaker, you will be ranked only according to your eloquence, and by no means according to your matter; everybody knows the matter almost alike, but few can adorn it. I was early convinced of the importance and powers of eloquence; and from that moment I applied myself to it. I resolved not to utter one word, even in common conversation, that should not be the expressive, and the most elegant, that the language could supply me with for that purpose; by which means I have acquired such a certain degree of habitual eloquence, that I must now really take some pains, if I would express myself very inelegantly. I want to inculcate this known truth into you, which you seem by no means to be convinced of yet, that ornaments are at present your only objects. Your sole business now, is to shine, not to weigh. Weight without lustre is lead. You had better talk trifles elegantly to the most trifling woman, than coarse inelegant sense to the most solid man: you had better return a dropped fan genteelly, than give a thousand pounds awkwardly; and you had better refuse a favour gracefully, than grant it clumsily. Manner is all, in everything: it is by manner only that you can please, and consequently rise. All your Greek will never advance you from Secretary to Envoy, or from Envoy to Ambassador; but your address, your manner, your air, if good, very probably may. Marcel can be of much more use to you than Aristotle. I would, upon my word, much rather that you had Lord Bolingbroke's style, and eloquence, in speaking and writing, than all the learning of the Academy of Sciences, the Royal Society, and the two Universities united.

Having mentioned Lord Bolingbroke's style, which is, undoubtedly, infinitely superior to anybody's, I would have you read his works, which you have, over and over again, with particular attention to his style. Transcribe, imitate, emulate it, if possible: that would be of real use to you in the House of Commons, in negotiations, in conversation; with that, you may justly hope to please, to persuade, to seduce, to impose; and you will fail in those articles, in proportion as you fall short of it. Upon the whole, lay aside, during your year's residence at Paris, all thoughts of all that dull fellows call solid, and exert your utmost care to acquire what people of fashion call shining. *Prenez l'éclat et le brillant d'un galant homme.**

Among the commonly-called little things, to which

you do not attend, your handwriting is one, which is indeed shamefully bad and illiberal; it is neither the hand of a man of business, nor of a gentleman, but of a truant school-boy; as soon, therefore, as you have done with Abbé Nolét, pray get an excellent writing master (since you think that you cannot teach yourself to write what hand you please), and let him teach you to write a genteel, legible, liberal hand, and quick; not the hand of a *procureur*, or a writing master, but that sort of hand in which the first *Commis** in foreign bureaus commonly write; for I tell you truly, that were I Lord Albemarle, nothing should remain in my bureau written in your present hand. From hand to arms the transition is natural; is the carriage and motion of your arms so too? The motion of the arms is the most material part of a man's air, especially in dancing; the feet are not near so material. If a man dances well from the waist upwards, wears his hat well, and moves his head properly, he dances well. Do the women say that you dress well? for that is necessary too for a young fellow. Have you *un goût vif*, or a passion for anybody? I do not ask for whom: an Iphigenia* would both give you the desire, and teach you the means to please.

In a fortnight or three weeks you will see Sir Charles Hotham* at Paris, in his way to Toulouse, where he is to stay a year or two. Pray be very civil to him, but do not carry him into company, except presenting him to Lord Albemarle; for as he is not to stay at Paris above a week, we do not desire that he should taste of that dissipation: you may show him a play and an opera. Adieu, my dear child!

66. TO HIS SON

MY DEAR FRIEND,

In about three months from this day, we shall probably meet. I look upon that moment as a young woman does upon her bridal night; I expect the greatest pleasure, and yet cannot help fearing some little mixture of pain. My reason bids me doubt a little, of what my imagination makes me expect. In some articles I am very sure that my most sanguine wishes will not be disappointed; and those are the most material ones. In others, I feel something or other, which I can better fear than describe. However, I will attempt it. I fear the want of that amiable and engaging *je ne sçais quoi*, which as some philosophers have, unintelligibly enough, said of the soul, is all in all, and all in every part;*it should shed its influence over every word and action. I fear the want of that air, and first *abord*, which suddenly lays hold of the heart, one does not know distinctly how or why. I fear an inaccuracy, or at least, inelegancy of diction, which will wrong and lower the best and justest matter. And lastly, I fear an ungraceful if not an unpleasant utterance, which would disgrace and vilify the whole. Should these fears be at present founded, yet the objects of them are (thank God) of such a nature, that you may, if you please, between this and our meeting, remove every one of them. All these engaging and endearing accomplishments are mechanical, and to be acquired by care and observation, as easily as turning, or any mechanical trade. A common country fellow, taken from the plough, and enlisted in an old corps, soon lays aside his shambling gait, his slouching air, his clumsy and awkward motions; and acquires the martial air, the regular motions, and whole exercise of the corps, and particularly of his right and left hand man. How so? Not from his parts; which were just the same before as after he was enlisted; but either from a commendable ambition of being like, and equal to those he is to live with; or else from the fear of being punished for not being so. If then both or either of these motives change such a fellow, in about six months' time, to such a degree, as that he is not to be known again, how much stronger should both these motives be with you, to acquire, in the utmost perfection, the whole exercise of the people of fashion, with whom you are to live all your life! Ambition should make you resolve to be at least their equal in that exercise, as well as the fear of punishment; which most inevitably will attend the want of it. By that exercise, I mean the air, the manners, the graces, and the style of people of fashion. A friend of yours, in a letter I received from him by the last post, after some other commendations of you, says, *Il est étonnant, que pensant avec tant de solidité qu'il fait, et aiant le goût aussi sûr et aussi délicat qu'il l'a, il s'exprime avec si peu d'élégance et de délicatesse. Il néglige même totalement le choix des mots et la tournure des phrases.* This I should not be so much surprised or concerned at, if it related only to the English language, which hitherto you have had no opportunity of studying, and but few of speaking, at least to those who could correct your inaccuracies. But if you do not express yourself elegantly and delicately in French and German (both which languages I know you possess perfectly and speak eternally), it can be only from an unpardonable inattention to what you most erroneously think a little object, though, in truth, it is one of the most important of your life. Solidity and delicacy of thought must be given us: it cannot be acquired, though it may be improved; but elegancy and delicacy of expression may be acquired by whoever will take the necessary care and pains. I am sure you love me so well, that you would be very sorry, when we meet, that I should be either disappointed or mortified; and I love you so well, that I assure you I should be both, if I should find you want any of those exterior accomplishments which are the indispensably necessary steps to that figure and fortune, which I so earnestly wish you may one day make in the world.

I hope you do not neglect your exercises of riding, fencing, and dancing, but particularly the latter: for they all concur to *dégourdir*,* and to give a certain air. To ride well, is not only a proper and graceful accomplishment for a gentleman, but may also save you many a fall hereafter; to fence well, may possibly save your life; and to dance well, is absolutely necessary in order to sit, stand, and walk well. To tell you the truth, my friend, I have some little suspicion, that you now and then neglect or omit your exercises, for more serious studies. But now *non est his locus*,* everything has its time; and this is yours for your exercises; for when you return to Paris I only propose your continuing your dancing; which you shall two years longer, if you happen to be where there is a good dancing-master. Here I will see you take some lessons with your old master Desnoyers,* who is our Marcel.

What says Madame Dupin* to you? I am told she is very handsome still; I know she was some few years ago. She has good parts, reading, manners, and delicacy: such an *arrangement* would be both creditable and advantageous to you. She will expect to meet with all the good breeding and delicacy that she brings; and as she is past the glare and *éclat* of youth, may be the more willing to listen to your story, if you tell it well. For an attachment I should prefer her to *la petite Blot*; and, for a mere gallantry, I should prefer *la petite Blot* to her; so that they are consistent, *et l'un n'em-pêche pas l'autre.** Adieu. Remember *la douceur et les graces*.

67. TO HIS SON

GREENWICH, JUNE 13, O.S. 1751

MY DEAR FRIEND,

Les bienséances* are a most necessary part of the knowledge of the world. They consist in the relations of persons, things, time, and place; good sense points them out, good company perfects them (supposing always an intention and a desire to please), and good policy recommends them.

Were you to converse with a King, you ought to be as easy and unembarrassed as with your own valet-de-chambre; but yet every look, word, and action, should imply the utmost respect. What would be proper and well bred with others, much your superiors, would be absurd and ill bred with one so very much so. You must wait till you are spoken to: you must receive, not give, the subject of conversation; and you must even take care that the given subject of such conversation do not lead you into any impropriety. The art would be to carry it, if possible, to some indirect flattery; such as commending those virtues in some other person, in which that Prince either thinks he does, or at least would be thought by others to excel. Almost the same precautions are necessary to be used with Ministers, Generals, etc., who expect to be treated with very near the same respect as their masters, and commonly deserve it better. There is, however, this difference, that one may begin the conversation with them, if on their side it should happen to drop, provided one does not carry it to any subject, upon which it is improper either for them to speak, or be spoken to. In these two cases; certain attitudes and actions would be extremely absurd, because too easy, and consequently disrespectful. As, for instance, if you were to put your arms across in your bosom, twirl your snuffbox, trample with your feet, scratch your head, etc., it would be shockingly ill-bred in that company; and, indeed, not extremely well-bred in any other. The great difficulty in those cases, though a very surmountable one by attention and custom, is to join perfect inward ease with perfect outward respect.

In mixed companies with your equals (for in mixed companies all people are to a certain degree equal), greater ease and liberty are allowed; but they too have their bounds within *bienséance*. There is a social respect necessary: you may start your own subject of conversation with modesty, taking great care, however, *de ne jamais parler de cordes dans la maison d'un pendu.** Your words, gestures, and attitudes, have a greater degree of latitude, though by no means an unbounded one. You may have your hands in your pockets, take snuff, sit, stand, or occasionally walk, as you like: but I believe you would not think it very *bienséant* to whistle, put on your hat, loosen your garters or your buckles, lie down upon a couch, or go to bed and welter in an easy chair. These are negligences and freedoms which one can only take when quite alone; they are injurious to superiors, shocking and offensive to equals, brutal and insulting to inferiors. That easiness of carriage and behaviour, which is exceedingly engaging, widely differs from negligence and inattention, and by no means implies that one may do whatever one pleases; it only means that one is not to be stiff, formal, embarrassed, disconcerted, and ashamed, like country bumpkins, and people who have never been in good company; but it requires great attention to, and a scrupulous observation of *les bienséances*: whatever one ought to do, is to be done with ease and unconcern; whatever is improper must not be done at all. In mixed companies also, different ages and sexes are to be differently addressed. You would not talk of your pleasures to men of a certain age, gravity, and dignity; they justly expect, from young people, a degree of deference and regard. You should be full as easy with them as with people of your own years: but your manner must be different; more respect must be implied; and it is not amiss to insinuate, that from them you expect to learn. It flatters and comforts age, for not being able to take a part in the joy and titter of youth. To women you should always address yourself with great outward respect and attention, whatever you feel inwardly; their sex is by long prescription entitled to it; and it is among the duties of *bienséance*; at the same time that respect is very properly, and very agreeably, mixed with a degree of *enjouement*, if you have it; but then, that *badinage*[*] must either directly or indirectly tend to their praise, and even not be liable to a malicious construction to their disadvantage. But here, too, great attention must be had to the difference of age, rank, and situation. A *Maréchale*[*] of fifty must not be played with like a young coquette of fifteen; respect and *serious enjouement*, if I may couple those two words, must be used with the former, and mere *badinage, ʒesté même d'un peu de polissonnerie*,* is pardonable with the latter.

Another important point of *les bienséances*, seldom enough attended to, is, not to run your own present humour and disposition indiscriminately against everybody; but to observe, conform to, and adopt theirs. For example, if you happened to be in high good humour, and a flow of spirits, would you go and sing a *pont-neuf*, or cut a caper, to la Maréchale de Coigny,* the Pope's Nuncio, or Abbé Sallier, or to any person of natural gravity and melancholy, or who at that time should be in grief? I believe not; as, on the other hand, I suppose, that if you were in low spirits, or real grief, you would not choose to bewail your situation with *la petite Blot*. If you cannot command your present humour and disposition, single out those to converse with, who happen to be in the humour the nearest to your own.

Loud laughter is extremely inconsistent with *les bienséances*, as it is only the illiberal and noisy testimony of the joy of the mob at some very silly thing. A gentleman is often seen, but very seldom heard to laugh. Nothing is more contrary to *les bienséances* than horse-play, or *jeux de main*,* of any kind whatever, and has often very serious, sometimes very fatal consequences. Romping, struggling, throwing things at one another's head, are the becoming pleasantries of the mob, but degrade a gentleman: *giuoco di mano, giuoco de villano*,* is a very true saying, among the few true sayings of the Italians.

Peremptoriness and decision in young people is *contraire aux bienséances*: they should seldom seem to assert, and always use some softening mitigating expression: such as, *s'il m'est permis de le dire, je croirois plutôt, si j'ose m'expliquer*, which softens the manner, without giving up, or even weakening the thing. People of more age and experience expect, and are entitled to, that degree of deference.

There is a *bienséance* also with regard to people of the lowest degree; a gentleman observes it with his footman, even with the beggar in the street. He considers them as objects of compassion, not of insult; he speaks to neither *d'un ton brusque*, but corrects the one coolly, and refuses the other with humanity. There is no one occasion in the world, in which *le ton brusque* is becoming a gentleman. In short, *les bienséances* are another word for *manners*, and extend to every part of life. They are propriety; the Graces should attend, in order to complete them; the Graces enable us to do, genteelly and pleasingly, what *les bienséances* require to be done at all. The latter are an obligation upon every man; the former are an infinite advantage and ornament to any man. May you unite both!

Though you dance well, do not think that you dance well enough, and consequently not endeavour to dance still better. And though you should be told that you are genteel, still aim at being genteeler. If Marcel should, do not you be satisfied. Go on, court the Graces all your life-time; you will find no better friends at court: they will speak in your favour to the hearts of princes, ministers, and mistresses.

Now that all tumultuous passions and quick sensations have subsided with me, and that I have no tormenting care nor boisterous pleasures to agitate me, my greatest joy is to consider the fair prospect you have before you, and to hope and believe you will enjoy it. You are already in the world, at an age when others have hardly heard of it. Your character is hitherto not only unblemished in its moral part, but even unsullied by any low, dirty, and ungentleman-like vice; and will, I hope, continue so. Your knowledge is sound, extensive, and avowed, especially in everything relative to your destination. With such materials to begin, what then is wanting? Not fortune, as you have found by experience. You have had, and shall have, fortune sufficient to assist your merit and your industry; and if I can help it, you never shall have enough to make you negligent of either. You have, too, *mens sana in corpore sano*,* the greatest blessing of all. All therefore that you want, is as much in your power to acquire, as to eat your breakfast when set before you; it is only that knowledge of the world, that elegancy of manners, that universal politeness, and those graces, which keeping good company, and seeing variety of places and characters, must inevitably, with the least attention on your part, give you. Your foreign destination leads to the greatest things, and your parliamentary situation will facilitate your progress. Consider then this pleasing prospect as attentively for yourself, as I consider it for you. Labour on your part to realise it, as I will on mine to assist and enable you to do it. *Nullum numen abest, si sit prudentia.*

Adieu, my dear child! I count the days till I have the pleasure of seeing you: I shall soon count the hours, and at last the minutes, with increasing impatience.

P.S. The mohairs* are this day gone from hence for Calais, recommended to the care of Madame Morel, and directed, as desired, to the Comptroller-General. The three pieces come to six hundred and eighty French livres.

68. TO HIS SON

MY DEAR FRIEND,

As this is the last, or the last letter but one, that I think I shall write before I have the pleasure of seeing you here,* it may not be amiss to prepare you a little for our interview, and for the time we shall pass together. Before kings and princes meet, ministers on each side adjust the important points of precedence, arm-chairs, right hand and left, etc., so that they know previously what they are to expect, what they have to trust to: and it is right they should; for they commonly envy or hate, but most certainly distrust each other. We shall meet upon very different terms; we want no such preliminaries: you know my tenderness, I know your affection. My only object, therefore, is to make your short stay with me as useful as I can to you; and yours, I hope, is to co-operate with me. Whether, by making it wholesome, I shall make it pleasant to you, I am not sure. Emetics and cathartics I shall not administer, because I am sure you do not want them; but for alteratives* you must expect a great many; and I can tell you, that I have a number of *nostrums*, which I shall communicate to nobody but yourself. To speak without a metaphor, I shall endeavour to assist your youth with all the experience that I have purchased at the price of seven and fifty years. In order to this, frequent reproofs, corrections, and admonitions will be necessary; but then, I promise you, that they shall be in a gentle, friendly, and secret manner; they shall not put you out of countenance in company, nor out of humour when we are alone. I do not expect that at nineteen, you should have that knowledge of the world, those manners, that dexterity, which few people have at nine and twenty. But I will endeavour to give them you; and I am sure you will endeavour to learn them, as far as your youth, my experience, and the time we shall pass together, will allow. You may have many inaccuracies (and to be sure you have, for who has not at your age?) which few people will tell you of, and some nobody can tell you of but myself. You may possibly have others, too, which eyes less interested, and less vigilant than mine, do not discover: all those you shall hear of from one whose tenderness for you will excite his curiosity and sharpen his penetration. The smallest inattention, or error in manners, the minutest inelegancy of diction, the least awkwardness in your dress and carriage, will not escape my observation, nor pass without amicable correction. Two of the most intimate friends in the world can freely tell each other their faults, and even their crimes; but cannot possibly tell each other of certain little weaknesses, awkwardnesses, and blindnesses of self-love; to authorize that unreserved freedom, the relation between us is absolutely necessary. For example, I had a very worthy friend, with whom I was intimate enough to tell him his faults; he had but few; I told him of them, he took it kindly of me, and corrected them. But then, he had some weaknesses that I could never tell him of directly, and which he was so little sensible of himself, that hints of them were lost upon him. He had a scrag neck, of about a yard long; notwithstanding which, bags* being in fashion, truly he would wear one to his wig, and did so; but never behind him, for, upon every motion of his head, his bag came forwards over one shoulder or the other. He took it into his head too, that he must occasionally dance minuets, because other people

did; and he did so, not only extremely ill, but so awkward, so disjointed, so slim, so meagre, was his figure,
that had he danced as well as ever Marcel did, it would
have been ridiculous in him to have danced at all.
I hinted these things to him as plainly as friendship
would allow, and to no purpose; but to have told him
the whole, so as to cure him, I must have been his
father, which, thank God, I am not. As fathers commonly go, it is seldom a misfortune to be fatherless;
and considering the general run of sons, as seldom a
misfortune to be childless. You and I form, I believe,
an exception to that rule; for I am persuaded that we
would neither of us change our relation, were it in
our power. You will, I both hope and believe, be not
only the comfort, but the pride of my age; and I am
sure I will be the support, the friend, the guide of your
youth. Trust me without reserve; I will advise you
without private interest, or secret envy. Mr. Harte
will do so too; but still there may be some little things
proper for you to know, and necessary for you to
correct, which even his friendship would not let him
tell you of so freely as I should; and some of which he
may possibly not be so good a judge of as I am, not
having lived so much in the great world.

One principal topic of our conversation will be, not
only the purity but the elegancy of the English language; in both which you are very deficient. Another
will be the constitution of this country, of which,
I believe, you know less of than of most other countries in Europe. Manners, attentions, and address, will
also be the frequent subjects of our lectures; and whatever I know of that important and necessary art, the
art of pleasing, I will unreservedly communicate to
you. Dress too (which, as things are, I can logically

prove, requires some attention) will not always escape our notice. Thus, my lectures will be more various, and in some respects more useful, than Professor Mascow's; and therefore, I can tell you, that I expect to be paid for them; but, as possibly you would not care to part with your ready money, and as I do not think that it would be quite handsome in me to accept it, I will compound for the payment, and take it in attention and practice.

Pray remember to part with all your friends, acquaintances, and mistresses, if you have any, at Paris, in such a manner as may make them not only willing but impatient to see you there again. Assure them of your desire of returning to them; and do it in a manner that they may think you in earnest, that is *avec onction et une espèce d'attendrissement.* All people say pretty nearly the same things upon those occasions; it is the manner only that makes the difference; and that difference is great. Avoid, however, as much as you can, charging yourself with commissions, in your return from hence to Paris; I know, by experience, that they are exceedingly troublesome, commonly expensive, and very seldom satisfactory at last, to the persons who give them; some you cannot refuse, to people to whom you are obliged, and would oblige in your turn; but as to common fiddle-faddle commissions, you may excuse yourself from them with truth, by saying that you are to return to Paris through Flanders, and see all those great towns; which I intend you shall do, and stay a week or ten days at Brussels. Adieu! A good journey to you, if this is my last; if not, I can repeat again what I shall wish constantly.

69. TO MAJOR IRWINE*(AT DUBLIN)

SIR,

Should you ever be miserable enough to want my assistance, or I unexpectedly happy enough to be able to give you any, your commands will want no pre-amble to introduce, nor excuses to attend them. My friendship and esteem for you will sufficiently incline, though your situation will not sufficiently enable, me to serve you.

Lord Albemarle is too good a courtier, and I too bad a one, for us to have met more than once, since his return to England. I have twice endeavoured to see him, but to no purpose, since you desired me to speak to him; but I will persevere till I do; not that I think I can be of any use to you there, but that you may not think that I would omit the least possible occasion of being so. If Lord George Sackville is sincerely in your interest, your affair will certainly do, as he has not only a great deal to say with his father, but as he is the Duke of Cumberland's military man of confidence in Ireland. I heartily wish that you could get to be Lieutenant-Colonel to your father's regiment, because with that rank, at your age, the rest would do itself. And if you can get the consent of the Government, I would advise you not to haggle with Pearce about the price, but to make him a *pont d'or* to go out upon.*

My young man has been with me here this fortnight, and in most respects I am very well satisfied with him; his knowledge is sound and extensive, and, by all that I have yet observed, his heart is what I could wish it. But for his airs and manners, Paris has still a great deal to do. He stoops excessively, which I have known some very pretty fellows do, though he dances very well, and as to manners, the easy and genteel turn *d'un honnête homme* is yet very much wanting. I shall carry him with me in a fortnight to Bath for the season, where I shall rub him till his re-exportation to Paris, which will be the first week in November, for near a year more. I hardly flatter myself with the hopes of seeing you at Bath this season; nor indeed would I advise you to leave Ireland till your affair is decided one way or other. The observation, *que les absens ont toujours tort*,* is in general true; and in your case, would be particularly true in regard to a certain General whom I know.

I am extremely obliged to you for your kindness to your Lieutenant Heathcote,* in which I think I have some share, though I hope and believe he deserves it personally.

I will end this abruptly, rather than employ the common words to assure you of the uncommon esteem and friendship with which I am

> Your most faithful humble servant.

P.S.—Pray make my compliments to the Primate, and to the House of Clements.*

70. TO THE BISHOP OF WATERFORD*

NOVEMBER 30, 1751

MY DEAR LORD,

My reproach by Dr. Thomas, I insist upon it, was a very just one, and your excuse a very lame one! Indifferent as I am grown about most things, you could not suppose that I was become so where the health and happiness of you and your family were concerned; on the contrary, I find that in proportion as one renounces public, one grows more sensible to private social, cares. My circle, thank God, is so much contracted, that my attention can, and does, from its centre extend itself to every point of the circumference. I am very glad to hear that your son goes on so well; and, as he does go on so well, why should you move him? The Irish schools and Universities are indisputably better than ours, with this additional advantage, that having him within your reach will be much better for him than a better place out of it: a man no more liveth by Latin and Greek than by bread alone; but a father's care of his son's morals and manners is surely more useful than the critical knowledge of Homer and Virgil, supposing that it were, which it very seldom is, acquired at schools. I do not therefore hesitate to advise you to put your son to the best school, that is, the nearest to your usual place of residence, that you may see and examine him often and strictly, and watch his progress, not only in learning, but in morals and manners, instead of trusting to interested accounts of distant schoolmasters.

His Grace of Tuam's recovery has, I find, delayed, if not broke, a long chain of Ecclesiastical promotions, of which the first link is the only one I interest myself in; I mean the translation of that good man and citizen the Bishop of Meath, to Tuam;*the more he gets, the more Ireland gets; that being your case too, pray how goes the copper mine?* Fruitful, and yet inexhaustible, I hope. If it will but supply you with riches, I will answer for your making the best use of them.

I hear with great pleasure that Ireland improves daily,* and that a spirit of industry spreads itself, to the great increase of trade and manufactures. I think I interest myself more in that country than in this;

this is past its perfection, and seems gradually declining into weakness and caducity;*that seems but tending to its vigour and perfection, and engages one's expectations and hopes. One loves a promising youth, one only esteems an old man; the former is a much quicker sentiment than the latter: both those sentiments conspire, I assure you, in forming that friendship with which I am,

My dear Lord, your most faithful humble servant.

71. TO HIS SON

LONDON, DECEMBER 19, O.S. 1751

MY DEAR FRIEND,

You are now entered upon a scene of business,* where I hope you will one day make a figure. Use does a great deal, but care and attention must be joined to it. The first thing necessary in writing letters of business, is extreme clearness and perspicuity; every paragraph should be so clear, and unambiguous, that the dullest fellow in the world may not be able to mistake it, nor obliged to read it twice in order to understand it. This necessary clearness implies a correctness, without excluding an elegancy of style. Tropes, figures, antitheses, epigrams, etc., would be as misplaced and as impertinent in letters of business as they are sometimes (if judiciously used) proper and pleasing in familiar letters, upon common and trite subjects. In business, an elegant simplicity, the result of care, not of labour, is required. Business must be well, not affectedly, dressed; but by no means negligently. Let your first attention be to clearness, and read every paragraph after you have written it, in the critical view of discovering whether it is possible that any one man can mistake the true sense of it: and correct it accordingly.

Our pronouns and relatives often create obscurity or ambiguity; be therefore exceedingly attentive to them, and take care to mark out with precision their particular relations. For example, Mr. Johnson acquainted me, that he had seen Mr. Smith, who had promised him to speak to Mr. Clarke, to return him (Mr. Johnson) those papers which he (Mr. Smith) had left some time ago with him (Mr. Clarke): it is better to repeat a name, though unnecessarily, ten times, than to have the person mistaken once. *Who*, you know, is singly relative to persons, and cannot be applied to things; *which* and *that*, are chiefly relative to things, but not absolutely exclusive of persons; for one may say, the man *that* robbed or killed such-a-one; but it is much better to say, the man *who* robbed or killed. One never says, the man or the woman *which*. *Which* and *that*, though chiefly relative to things, cannot be always used indifferently as to things; and the ευφωνια* must sometimes determine their place. For instance, The letter *which* I received from you, *which* you referred to in your last, *which* came by Lord Albemarle's messenger, and *which* I showed to such-a-one; I would change it thus—The letter *that* I received from you, *which* you referred to in your last, *that* came by Lord Albemarle's messenger, and *which* I showed to such-a-one.

Business does not exclude (as possibly you wish it did) the usual terms of politeness and good-breeding; but, on the contrary, strictly requires them: such as, *I have the honour to acquaint your Lordship; Permit me to assure you; If I may be allowed to give my opinion*, etc. For the minister abroad, who writes to the minister at home, writes to his superior; possibly to his patron, or at least to one who he desires should be so.

Letters of business will not only admit of, but be

the better for *certain graces*—but then, they must be
scattered with a sparing and skilful hand; they must
fit their place exactly. They must decently adorn without encumbering, and modestly shine without glaring.
But as this is the utmost degree of perfection in letters
of business, I would not advise you to attempt those
embellishments, till you have first laid your foundation
well.

Cardinal d'Ossat's letters are the true letters of business; those of Monsieur D'Avaux are excellent; Sir
William Temple's* are very pleasing, but, I fear, too
affected. Carefully avoid all Greek or Latin quotations; and bring no precedents from the *virtuous Spar-*
tans, the polite Athenians, and the brave Romans. Leave
all that to futile pedants. No flourishes, no declamation. But (I repeat it again) there is an elegant simplicity and dignity of style absolutely necessary for
good letters of business; attend to that carefully. Let
your periods be harmonious, without seeming to be
laboured; and let them not be too long, for that
always occasions a degree of obscurity. I should not
mention correct orthography, but that you very often
fail in that particular, which will bring ridicule upon
you; for no man is allowed to spell ill. I wish too that
your handwriting were much better; and I cannot
conceive why it is not, since every man may certainly
write whatever hand he pleases. Neatness in folding
up, sealing, and directing your packets, is by no means
to be neglected; though I dare say you think it is.
But there is something in the exterior, even of a packet,
that may please or displease; and consequently worth
some attention.

You say that your time is very well employed; and
so it is, though as yet only in the outlines, and first

routine of business. They are previously necessary to be known; they smooth the way for parts and dexterity. Business requires no conjuration nor supernatural talents, as people unacquainted with it are apt to think. Method, diligence, and discretion, will carry a man of good strong common sense, much higher than the finest parts, without them, can do. *Par negotiis, neque supra,*[*] is the true character of a man of business; but then it implies ready attention, and no *absences*, and a flexibility and versatility of attention from one object to another, without being engrossed by any one.

Be upon your guard against the pedantry and affectation of business, which young people are apt to fall into, from the pride of being concerned in it young. They look thoughtful, complain of the weight of business, throw out mysterious hints, and seem big with secrets which they do not know. Do you, on the contrary, never talk of business but to those with whom you are to transact it; and learn to seem *vacuus* and idle, when you have the most business. Of all things, the *volto sciolto,*[*] and the *pensieri stretti*, are necessary. Adieu!

72. TO HIS SON

LONDON, JANUARY 23, O.S. 1752

MY DEAR FRIEND,

Have you seen the new tragedy of *Varon,*[*] and what do you think of it? Let me know, for I am determined to form my taste upon yours. I hear that the situations and incidents are well brought on, and the catastrophe unexpected and surprising, but the verses bad. I suppose it is the subject of all the conversations at Paris, where both women and men are judges and critics of

all such performances; such conversations, that both
form and improve the taste and whet the judgment,
are surely preferable to the conversations of our mixed
companies here; which, if they happen to rise above
brag and whist, infallibly stop short of everything
either pleasing or instructive. I take the reason of this
to be, that (as women generally give the *ton* to the
conversation) our English women are not near so well
informed and cultivated as the French; besides that
they are naturally more serious and silent.

I could wish there were a treaty made between the
French and the English theatres, in which both parties
should make considerable concessions. The English
ought to give up their notorious violations of all the
unities; and all their massacres, racks, dead bodies, and
mangled carcases, which they so frequently exhibit
upon their stage. The French should engage to have
more action, and less declamation; and not to cram
and crowd things together, to almost a degree of im-
possibility, from a too scrupulous adherence to the
unities. The English should restrain the licentiousness
of their poets, and the French enlarge the liberty of
theirs; their poets are the greatest slaves in their
country, and that is a bold word; ours are the most
tumultuous subjects in England, and that is saying a
good deal. Under such regulations, one might hope
to see a play, in which one should not be lulled to sleep
by the length of a monotonical declamation, nor
frightened and shocked by the barbarity of the action.
The unity of time extended occasionally to three or
four days, and the unity of place broke into, as far
as the same street, or sometimes the same town; both
which, I will affirm, are as probable, as four-and-
twenty hours, and the same room.

More indulgence too, in my mind, should be shown, than the French are willing to allow, to bright thoughts, and to shining images; for though, I confess, it is not very natural for a hero or a princess to say fine things in all the violence of grief, love, rage, etc., yet, I can as well suppose that, as I can that they should talk to themselves for half-an-hour; which they must necessarily do, or no tragedy could be carried on, unless they had recourse to a much greater absurdity, the choruses of the ancients. Tragedy is of a nature, that one must see it with a degree of self-deception; we must lend ourselves a little to the delusion; and I am very willing to carry that complaisance a little farther than the French do.

Tragedy must be something bigger than life, or it would not affect us. In nature the most violent passions are silent; in tragedy they must speak, and speak with dignity too. Hence the necessity of their being written in verse, and unfortunately for the French, from the weakness of their language, in rhymes. And for the same reason, Cato the Stoic, expiring at Utica, rhymes masculine and feminine at Paris; and fetches his last breath at London, in most harmonious and correct blank verse.*

It is quite otherwise with Comedy, which should be mere common life, and not one jot bigger. Every character should speak upon the stage, not only what it would utter in the situation there represented, but in the same manner in which it would express it. For which reason I cannot allow rhymes in comedy, unless they were put into the mouth, and came out of the mouth, of a mad poet. But it is impossible to deceive one's self enough (nor is it the least necessary in comedy), to suppose a dull rogue of an usurer cheating, or *gros Jean** blundering in the finest rhymes in the world.

As for Operas, they are essentially too absurd and extravagant to mention: I look upon them as a magic scene, contrived to please the eyes and the ears, at the expense of the understanding; and I consider singing, rhyming, and chiming heroes, and princesses, and philosophers, as I do the hills, the trees, the birds, and the beasts, who amicably joined in one common country dance, to the irresistible tune of Orpheus's lyre. Whenever I go to an Opera, I leave my sense and reason at the door with my half-guinea,* and deliver myself up to my eyes and my ears.

Thus I have made you my poetical confession; in which I have acknowledged as many sins against the established taste in both countries, as a frank heretic could have owned against the established Church in either, but I am now privileged by my age to taste and think for myself, and not to care what other people think of me in those respects; an advantage which youth, among its many advantages, hath not. It must occasionally and outwardly conform, to a certain degree, to established tastes, fashions, and decisions. A young man may, with a becoming modesty, dissent, in private companies, from public opinions and prejudices: but he must not attack them with warmth, nor magisterially set up his own sentiments against them. Endeavour to hear and know all opinions; receive them with complaisance; form your own with coolness, and give it with modesty.

I have received a letter from Sir John Lambert, in which he requests me to use my interest to procure him the remittance of Mr. Spencer's* money, when he goes abroad: and also desires to know to whose account he is to place the postage of my letters. I do not trouble him with a letter in answer, since you can execute the commission. Pray make my compliments to him, and assure him, that I will do all I can to procure him Mr. Spencer's business; but that his most effectual way will be by Messrs. Hoare, who are Mr. Spencer's cashiers, and who will undoubtedly have their choice upon whom they will give him his credit. As for the postage of the letters, your purse and mine being pretty near the same, do you pay it, over and above your next draft.

Your relations, the Princes Borghese,* will soon be with you at Paris; for they leave London this week; whenever you converse with them, I desire it may be in Italian; that language not being yet familiar enough to you.

By our printed papers, there seems to be a sort of compromise between the King and the Parliament, with regard to the affairs of the hospitals, by taking them out of the hands of the Archbishop of Paris, and placing them in Monsieur d'Argenson's: if this be true, that compromise, as it is called, is clearly a victory on the side of the court, and a defeat on the part of the parliament; for if the parliament had a right, they had it as much to the exclusion of Monsieur d'Argenson as of the Archbishop.*

Adieu.

73. TO HIS SON

LONDON, MARCH 2, O.S. 1752

MY DEAR FRIEND,

Whereabouts are you in Ariosto? Or have you gone through that most ingenious contexture of truth and lies, of serious and extravagant, of knights-errant, magicians, and all that various matter, which he announces in the beginning of his poem:—

> Le Donne, i Cavalier, l'arme, gli amori,
> Le cortesie, l'audaci imprese io canto.*

I am by no means sure that Homer had superior invention, or excelled more in description than Ariosto. What can be more seducing and voluptuous, than the description of Alcina's person and palace? What more ingeniously extravagant, than the search made in the moon for Orlando's lost wits,* and the account of other people's that were found there? The whole is worth your attention, not only as an ingenious poem, but as the source of all modern tales, novels, fables, and romances; as Ovid's Metamorphoses was of the ancient ones; besides that, when you have read this work, nothing will be difficult to you in the Italian language. You will read Tasso's *Gierusalemme*, and the *Decamerone di Boccaccio* with great facility afterwards; and when you have read these three authors, you will, in my opinion, have read all the works of invention that are worth reading in that language; though the Italians would be very angry at me for saying so.

A gentleman should know those which I call classical works, in every language; such as Boileau, Corneille, Racine, Molière, etc, in French; Milton, Dryden, Pope, Swift, etc., in English; and the three authors above-mentioned in Italian; whether you have any such in German, I am not quite sure, nor, indeed, am I inquisitive. These sort of books adorn the mind, improve the fancy, are frequently alluded to by, and are often the subjects of conversations of, the best companies. As you have languages to read, and memory to retain them, the knowledge of them is very well worth the little pains it will cost you, and will enable you to shine in company. It is not pedantic to quote and allude to them, which it would be with regard to the ancients.

Among the many advantages which you have had in your education, I do not consider your knowledge of several languages as the least. You need not trust to translations: you can go to the source: you can both converse and negotiate with people of all nations, upon equal terms; which is by no means the case of a man who converses or negotiates in a language which those with whom he hath to do know much better than himself. In business, a great deal may depend upon the force and extent of one word; and in conversation, a moderate thought may gain, or a good one lose, by the propriety or impropriety, the elegancy or inelegancy, of one single word. As therefore you now know four modern languages well, I would have you study (and, by the way, it will be very little trouble to you), to know them correctly, accurately, and delicately. Read some little books that treat of them, and ask questions concerning their delicacies, of those who are able to answer you. As, for instance, should I say in French, *la lettre que je vous ai* écrit, or *la lettre que je vous ai* écrite? in which, I think, the French differ among themselves. There is a short French Grammar by the Port Royal, and another by Père Buffier, both which are worth your reading; as is also a little book called *Les Synonimes François.** There are books of that kind upon the Italian language, into some of which I would advise you to dip; possibly the German language may have something of the same sort, and since you already speak it, the more properly you speak it the better; one would, I think, as far as possible, do all one does correctly and elegantly. It is extremely engaging, to people of every nation, to meet with a foreigner who hath taken pains enough to speak their language correctly; it flatters that local and national pride and prejudice of which everybody hath some share.

Francis's Eugenia,* which I will send you, pleased most people of good taste here; the boxes were crowded till the sixth night; when the pit and gallery were totally deserted, and it was dropped. Distress, without death, was not sufficient to affect a true British audience, so long accustomed to daggers, racks, and bowls of poison; contrary to Horace's rule,* they desire to see Medea murder her children upon the stage. The sentiments were too delicate to move them; and their hearts are to be taken by storm, not by parley.

Have you got the things, which were taken from you at Calais, restored? and, among them, the little packet which my sister gave you for Sir Charles Hotham? In this case, have you forwarded it to him? If you have not yet had an opportunity, you will have one soon; which I desire you will not omit; it is by Monsieur D'Aillon,* whom you will see in a few days at Paris, in his way to Geneva, where Sir Charles now is, and will remain some time. Adieu!

74. TO HIS SON

LONDON, APRIL 13, O.S. 1752

MY DEAR FRIEND,

I receive this moment your letter of the 19th, N.S., with the enclosed pieces relative to the present dispute between the King and the Parliament. I shall return them by Lord Huntingdon, whom you will soon see at Paris, and who will likewise carry you the piece which I forgot in making up the packet I sent you by the Spanish Ambassador. The representation of the Parliament is very well drawn, *suaviter in modo, fortiter in re.* They tell the King very respectfully that, in a certain case, *which they should think it criminal to suppose,* they would not obey him. This has a tendency to what we call here Revolution principles.* I do not know what the Lord's anointed, his Vicegerent upon earth, divinely appointed by him, and accountable to none but him for his actions, will either think or do, upon these symptoms of reason and good sense, which seem to be breaking out all over France: but this I foresee, that, before the end of this century, the trade of both King and Priest will not be half so good a one as it has been. Duclos, in his Reflections, hath observed, and very truly, *qu'il y a un germe de raison qui commence à se développer en France;*—*ou développement* that must prove fatal to Regal and Papal pretensions. Prudence may, in many cases, recommend an occasional submission to either; but when that ignorance, upon which an implicit faith in both could only be founded, is once removed, God's Vicegerent, and Christ's Vicar, will only be obeyed and believed, as far as what the one orders, and the other says, is conformable to reason and truth.

I am very glad (to use a vulgar expression) that *you make as if you were not well,* though you really are; I am sure it is the likeliest way to keep so. Pray leave off entirely your greasy, heavy pastry, fat creams, and indigestible dumplings; and then you need not confine yourself to white meats, which I do not take to be one jot wholesomer than beef, mutton, and partridge.

Voltaire sent me from Berlin, his History *du Siècle de Louis XIV*. It came at a very proper time; Lord Bolingbroke*had just taught me how History should be read; Voltaire shows me how it should be written. I am sensible that it will meet with almost as many critics as readers. Voltaire must be criticised; besides, every man's favourite is attacked; for every prejudice is exposed, and our prejudices are our mistresses; reason is at best our wife, very often heard indeed, but seldom minded. It is the history of the human understanding, written by a man of parts, for the use of men of parts. Weak minds will not like it, even though they do not understand it; which is commonly the measure of their admiration. Dull ones will want those minute and uninteresting details, with which most other histories are encumbered. He tells me all I want to know, and nothing more. His reflections are short, just, and produce others in his readers. Free from religious, philosophical, political, and national prejudices, beyond any historian I ever met with, he relates all those matters as truly and as impartially, as certain regards, which must always be to some degree observed, will allow him: for one sees plainly, that he often says much less than he would say, if he might. He hath made me much better acquainted with the times of Louis the Fourteenth, than the innumerable volumes which I had read could do; and hath suggested this reflection to me, which I had never made before—His vanity, not his knowledge, made him encourage all, and introduce many arts and sciences in his country. He opened in a manner the human understanding in France, and brought it to its utmost perfection; his age equalled in all, and greatly exceeded in many things (pardon me, Pedants!) the Augustan.

This was great and rapid; but still it might be done, by the encouragement, the applause, and the rewards of a vain, liberal, and magnificent Prince. What is much more surprising is, that he stopped the operations of the human mind just where he pleased: and seemed to say, 'Thus far shalt thou go, and no farther.' For, a bigot to his religion, and jealous of his power, free and rational thoughts upon either never entered into a French head during his reign; and the greatest geniuses that ever any age produced, never entertained a doubt of the divine right of Kings, or the infallibility of the Church. Poets, Orators, and Philosophers, ignorant of their natural rights, cherished their chains; and blind, active faith triumphed, in those great minds, over silent and passive reason. The reverse of this seems now to be the case in France: reason opens itself; fancy and invention fade and decline.

I will send you a copy of this history by Lord Huntingdon, as I think it very probable that it is not allowed to be published and sold at Paris. Pray read it more than once, and with attention, particularly the second volume; which contains short, but very clear accounts of many very interesting things, which are talked of by everybody, though fairly understood by very few. There are two very puerile affectations, which I wish this book had been free from; the one is, the total subversion of all the old established French orthography; the other is, the not making use of any one capital letter throughout the whole book, except at the beginning of a paragraph. It offends my eyes to see rome, paris, france, caesar, henry the fourth, etc., begin with small letters; and I do not conceive that there can be any reason for doing it half so strong as the reason of long usage is to the contrary. This is an affectation below Voltaire; whom I am not ashamed to say, that I admire and delight in, as an author, equally in prose and in verse.

I had a letter a few days ago from Monsieur du Boccage; in which he says, *Monsieur Stanhope s'est jeté dans la politique, et je crois qu'il y réussira;** You do very well, it is your destination: but remember that to succeed in great things, one must first learn to please in little ones. Engaging manners and address must prepare the way for superior knowledge and abilities to act with effect. The late Duke of Marlborough's manners and address prevailed with the first King of Prussia, to let his troops remain in the army of the Allies,* when neither their representations, nor his own share in the common cause, could do it. The Duke of Marlborough had no new matter to urge to him; but had a manner, which he could not, and did not, resist. Voltaire, among a thousand little delicate strokes of that kind, says of the Duke de la Feuillade, *qu'il étoit l'homme le plus brillant et le plus aimable du Roïaume; et quoique gendre du Général et Ministre, il avoit pour lui la faveur publique.** Various little circumstances of that sort will often make a man of great real merit be hated, if he hath not address and manners to make him be loved. Consider all your own circumstances seriously; and you will find that, of all arts, the art of pleasing is the most necessary for you to study and possess. A silly tyrant said, *oderint modo timeant:** a wise man would have said, *modo ament nihil timendum est mihi.* Judge, from your own daily experience, of the efficacy of that pleasing *je ne sçais quoi*, when you feel, as you and everybody certainly does, that in men it is more engaging than knowledge, in women than beauty.

I long to see Lord and Lady Blessington*(who are not yet arrived), because they have lately seen you; and I always fancy that I can fish out something new concerning you from those who have seen you last; not that I shall much rely upon their accounts, because I distrust the judgment of Lord and Lady Blessington in those matters about which I am most inquisitive. They have ruined their own son, by what they called and thought loving him. They have made him believe that the world was made for him, not he for the world; and unless he stays abroad a great while, and falls into very good company, he will expect, what he will never find, the attentions and complaisance from others, which he has hitherto been used to from Papa and Mamma. This, I fear, is too much the case of Mr ****, who, I doubt, will be run through the body, and be near dying, before he knows how to live. However you may turn out, you can never make me any of these reproaches. I indulged no silly, womanish fondness for you: instead of inflicting my tenderness upon you, I have taken all possible methods to make you deserve it; and thank God you do; at least, I know but one article in which you are different from what I could wish you; and you very well know what that is. I want, that I and all the world should like you, as well as I love you. Adieu.

75. TO HIS SON

LONDON, APRIL 30, O.S. 1752

MY DEAR FRIEND:

Avoir du monde is, in my opinion, a very just and happy expression, for having address, manners, and for knowing how to behave properly in all companies;

and it implies very truly, that a man that hath not these accomplishments, is not of the world. Without them, the best parts are inefficient, civility is absurd, and freedom offensive. A learned parson, rusting in his cell at Oxford or Cambridge, will reason admirably well upon the nature of man; will profoundly analyse the head, the heart, the reason, the will, the passions, the senses, the sentiments, and all those subdivisions of we know not what; and yet, unfortunately, he knows nothing of man, for he hath not lived with him, and is ignorant of all the various modes, habits, prejudices, and tastes, that always influence, and often determine him. He views man as he does colours in Sir Isaac Newton's prism,* where only the capital ones are seen; but an experienced dyer knows all their various shades and gradations, together with the result of their several mixtures. Few men are of one plain, decided colour; most are mixed, shaded, and blended; and vary as much, from different situations, as changeable silks do from different lights. The man *qui a du monde* knows all this from his own experience and observation: the conceited, cloistered philosopher knows nothing of it from his own theory; his practice is absurd and improper; and he acts as awkwardly as a man would dance, who had never seen others dance, nor learned of a dancing-master; but who had only studied the notes by which dances are now pricked down as well as tunes. Observe and imitate, then, the address, the arts, and the manners of those *qui ont du monde*: see by what methods they first make, and afterwards improve impressions in their favour. Those impressions are much oftener owing to little causes, than to intrinsic merit; which is less volatile, and hath not so sudden an effect. Strong minds have undoubtedly an ascendant over weak ones, as Galigai Maréchale d'Ancre*very justly observed, when, to the disgrace and reproach of those times, she was executed for having governed Mary of Medicis by the arts of witchcraft and magic.. But then an ascendant is to be gained by degrees, and by those arts only which experience and the knowledge of the world teaches; for few are mean enough to be bullied, though most are weak enough to be bubbled. I have often seen people of superior, governed by people of much inferior parts, without knowing or even suspecting that they were so governed. This can only happen, when those people of inferior parts have more worldly dexterity and experience, than those they govern. They see the weak and unguarded part, and apply to it: they take it, and all the rest follows. Would you gain either men or women, and every man of sense desires to gain both, *il faut du monde*. You have had more opportunities than ever any man had, at your age, of acquiring *ce monde*. You have been in the best companies of most countries, at an age when others have hardly been in any company at all. You are master of all those languages, which John Trott*seldom speaks at all, and never well; consequently you need be a stranger nowhere. This is the way, and the only way, of having *du monde*, but if you have it not, and have still any coarse rusticity about you, may one not apply to you the *rusticus expectat*of Horace?

This knowledge of the world teaches us more particularly two things, both which are of infinite consequence, and to neither of which nature inclines us; I mean, the command of our temper, and of our countenance. A man who has no *monde* is inflamed with anger, or annihilated with shame, at every disagreeable incident: the one makes him act and talk like a madman, the other makes him look like a fool. But a man who has *du monde*, seems not to understand what he cannot or ought not to resent. If he makes a slip himself, he recovers it by his coolness, instead of plunging deeper by his confusion like a stumbling horse. He is firm, but gentle; and practises that most excellent maxim, *suaviter in modo, fortiter in re*. The other is the *volto sciolto* e pensieri stretti*. People unused to the world have babbling countenances; and are unskilful enough to show what they have sense enough not to tell. In the course of the world, a man must very often put on an easy, frank countenance, upon very disagreeable occasions; he must seem pleased when he is very much otherwise; he must be able to accost and receive with smiles those whom he would much rather meet with swords. In Courts he must not turn himself inside out. All this may, nay must be done, without falsehood and treachery; for it must go no farther than politeness and manners, and must stop short of assurances and professions of simulated friendship. Good manners, to those one does not love, are no more a breach of truth, than 'your humble servant' at the bottom of a challenge is; they are universally agreed upon and understood, to be things of course. They are necessary guards of the decency and peace of society; they must only act defensively; and then not with arms poisoned with perfidy. Truth, but not the whole truth, must be the invariable principle of every man who hath either religion, honour, or prudence. Those who violate it may be cunning, but they are not able. Lies and perfidy are the refuge of fools and cowards. Adieu!

P.S. I must recommend to you again, to take your leave of all your French acquaintance in such a manner

as may make them regret your departure, and wish to
see and welcome you at Paris again, where you may
possibly return before it is very long. This must not
be done in a cold, civil manner, but with at least
seeming warmth, sentiment, and concern. Acknowledge the obligations you have to them, for the kindness they have shown you during your stay at Paris:
assure them, that wherever you are, you will remember
them with gratitude; wish for opportunities of giving
them proofs of your *plus tendre et respectueux souvenir*;
beg of them in case your good fortune should carry
you to any part of the world where you could be of
any the least use to them, that they would employ you
without reserve. Say all this, and a great deal more,
emphatically and pathetically; for you know *si vis me
flere*——.* This can do you no harm, if you never
return to Paris; but if you do, as probably you may,
if will be of infinite use to you. Remember too, not to
omit going to every house where you have ever been
once, to take leave, and recommend yourself to their
remembrance. The reputation which you leave at one
place, where you have been, will circulate, and you will
meet with it at twenty places where you are to go.
That is a labour never quite lost.

This letter will show you, that the accident which
happened to me yesterday, and of which Mr. Grevenkop gives you an account, has had no bad consequences. My escape was a great one.

76. TO SOLOMON DAYROLLES, ESQ.

LONDON, MAY 19, O.S. 1752

DEAR DAYROLLES,

This goes to you from a deaf crippleman, confined to
his bed or his chair for above a fortnight past. My

little black mare, whom you have long known to be as quiet as anything of her sex can be, wanted to drink in Hyde Park. Accordingly I rode her into one of the little ponds, and in order to let her drink I loosed the bridon, which, by her stooping, fell over her head. In backing her out of the pond, her foot unluckily engaged itself in the bridon;* in endeavouring to get clear of it, she hampered herself the more, and then, in a great *saut de mouton*,* she fell backwards, and threw me with great violence about six feet from her. I pitched directly upon my hip-bone, which, by unaccountable good fortune, was neither fractured nor dislocated; but the muscles, nerves, etc., are so extremely bruised and strained, that to this moment, and this is the nineteenth day, I feel some pain, and cannot stand upon that leg at all. This confinement, especially at this time of the year, when I long to be at Blackheath, is not, as you will easily guess, very agreeable; and what makes it still less so, is my increasing deafness. I have tried a thousand infallible remedies, but all without success. I hope for some good from warm weather, for hitherto we have had none. But this is more than enough concerning my own infirmities, which I am of an age to expect, and have philosophy enough to bear without dejection. I recommend some of that philosophy to Madame Dayrolles* two months hence, and take the liberty of warning her against any rash and embarrassing vows, which present pain has sometimes, though seldom indeed, extorted from ladies upon those occasions.

I can much more easily conceive that your affairs go on very slowly, than I can that they ever will be finished; but in the meantime, *vous êtes bien, belle ville, bonne chère, et belle femme*; make the most of them all, enjoy them while you can, and remember that our pleasures, especially our best, last too little a while to be trifled with or neglected. As for your business, you and Mitchell,* to whom my compliments, have nothing else to do, but to put yourselves behind your Dutch colleagues, whose distinguishing talent is to wrangle tenaciously upon details.

I do not believe now that a King of the Romans* will be elected so soon as we thought. The Court of Vienna, long accustomed to carry its points at the expense of its allies, and sensible that we wish to bring this about, will not contribute anything to it; but truly we must satisfy the Electors and Princes, who stand out still, and form pretensions, possibly because they hope that it will fall to the share of England, who pays well, to satisfy them. My young traveller will therefore, I fear, have full time to walk about Germany before he has a call to Frankfort. He is now at Luneville, from whence he goes to Strasburg, and then follows the course of the Rhine, through Maïence,* Manheim, Bonn, etc., to Hanover.

By his last account of the present state of France, the domestic disorders are so great, and promise to be so much greater, that we have but little to fear from that quarter. The King is both hated and despised, which seldom happens to the same man. The Clergy are implacable, upon account of what he has done; and the Parliament is exasperated, because he will not do more. A spirit of licentiousness, as to all matters of religion and government, is spread throughout the whole kingdom. If the neighbours of France are wise, they will be quiet, and let these seeds of discord germinate, as they certainly will do, if no foreign object checks their growth, and unites all parties in a common cause.

Having now given you an account of my distempers, my philosophy, and my politics, I will give you quarter, which I can tell you is great lenity in me; for a man, who can neither use his legs nor his ears, is very apt to be an unmerciful correspondent, and to employ his hand and eyes at the expense of his friends. I close this letter and open a book. Adieu.

Yours affectionately.

77. TO THE BISHOP OF WATERFORD

LONDON, JULY 14, 1752

MY DEAR LORD,

I know the gentleness, the humanity, and the tenderness of your nature too well to doubt of your grief, and I know the object of it too well to blame it.* No; in such cases it is a commendable, not a blamable passion, and is always inseparable from a heart that is capable of friendship or love. I therefore offer you no trite, and always unavailing, arguments of consolation; but, as any strong and prevailing passion is apt to make us neglect or forget for the time our most important duties, I must remind you of two in particular, the neglect of which would render your grief, instead of pious, criminal: I mean your duty to your children as a father, and to your diocese as a Bishop. Your care of your children must be doubled, in order to repair as far as possible their loss, and the public trust of your flock must not suffer from a personal and private concern. These incumbent and necessary duties will sometimes suspend, and at last mitigate, that grief, which I confess mere reason would not: they are equally moral and Christian duties, which I am sure no consideration upon earth will ever make you neglect. May your assiduous discharge of them insensibly lessen that affliction, which, if indulged, would prove as fatal to you and your family, as it must be vain and unavailing to her whose loss you justly lament! I am, with the greatest truth and affection, my dear Lord,

Yours, etc.

78. TO HIS SON

LONDON, JULY 21, O.S. 1752

MY DEAR FRIEND,

By my calculation this letter may probably arrive at Hanover three or four days before you; and as I am sure of its arriving there safe, it shall contain the most material points that I have mentioned in my several letters to you since you left Paris, as if you had received but few of them, which may very probably be the case.

As for your stay at Hanover, it must not *in all events* be less than a month; but if things turn out to *your satisfaction*, it may be just as long as you please. From thence you may go wherever you like; for I have so good an opinion of your judgment, that I think you will combine and weigh all circumstances, and choose the properest places. Would you saunter at some of the small Courts, as Brunswick, Cassel, etc., till the Carnival at Berlin?* You are master. Would you pass a couple of months at Ratisbon, which might not be ill employed? *A la bonne heure.* Would you go to Brussels, stay a month or two there with Dayrolles, and from thence to Mr. Yorke, at the Hague?* With all my heart. Or, lastly, would you go to Copenhagen and Stockholm? *Ella è anche Padrone:*choose entirely for yourself, without any further instructions from me; only let me know your determination in time, that I may settle your credit, in case you go to places where at present you have none. Your object should be to see the *mores multorum hominum et urbes*; begin and end it where you please.

By what you have already seen of the German courts, I am sure you must have observed that they are much more nice and scrupulous, in points of ceremony, respect and attention, than the greater Courts of France and England. You will, therefore, I am persuaded, attend to the minutest circumstances of address and behaviour, particularly during your stay at Hanover, which (I will repeat it, though I have said it often to you already) is the most important preliminary period of your whole life. Nobody in the world is more exact, in all points of good-breeding, than the King; and it is the part of every man's character that he informs himself of first. The least negligence, or the slightest inattention, reported to him, may do you infinite prejudice; as their contraries would service.

If Lord Albemarle (as I believe he did) trusted you with the secret affairs of his department, let the Duke of Newcastle know that he did so; which will be an inducement to him to trust you too, and possibly to employ you in affairs of consequence. Tell him that, though you are young, you know the importance of secrecy in business, and can keep a secret; that I have always inculcated this doctrine into you, and have, moreover, strictly forbidden you ever to communicate, even to me, any matters of a secret nature, which you may happen to be trusted with in the course of business.

As for business, I think I can trust you to yourself; but I wish I could say as much for you with regard to those exterior accomplishments, which are absolutely necessary to smooth and shorten the way to it. Half the business is done, when one has gained the heart and the affections of those with whom one is to transact it. Air and address must begin, manners and attention must finish that work. I will let you into one secret concerning myself; which is, that I owe much more of the success which I have had in the world, to my manners, than to any superior degree of merit or knowledge. I desired to please, and I neglected none of the means. This, I can assure you, without any false modesty, is the truth. You have more knowledge than I had at your age, but then I had much more attention and good-breeding than you. Call it vanity, if you please, and possibly it was so; but my great object was to make every man I met with like me, and every woman love me. I often succeeded; but why? By taking great pains, for otherwise I never should; my figure by no means entitled me to it; and I had certainly an up-hill game; whereas your countenance would help you, if you made the most of it, and proscribed for ever the guilty, gloomy, and funereal part of it. Dress, address and air, would become your best countenance, and make your little figure pass very well.

If you have time to read at Hanover, pray let the books you read be all relative to the history and constitution of that country; which I would have you know as correctly as any Hanoverian in the whole Electorate. Inform yourself of the powers of the States, and of the nature and extent of the several Judicatures; the particular articles of trade and commerce of Bremen, Harburg, and Stade; the details and value of the mines of the Hartz.* Two or three short books will give you the outlines of all these things;

and conversation turned upon those subjects will do the rest, and better than books can.

Remember of all things to speak nothing but German there; make it (to express myself pedantically) your vernacular language; seem to prefer it to any other; call it your favourite language, and study to speak it with purity and elegancy, if it has any. This will not only make you perfect in it, but will please, and make your court there better than anything. *A propos* of languages. Did you improve your Italian while you were at Paris, or did you forget it? Had you a master there; and what Italian books did you read with him? If you are master of Italian, I would have you afterwards, by the first convenient opportunity, learn Spanish, which you may very easily, and in a very little time do; you will then, in the course of your foreign business, never be obliged to employ, pay, or trust any translator for any European language.

As I love to provide eventually for everything that can possibly happen, I will suppose the worst that can befall you at Hanover. In that case I would have you go immediately to the Duke of Newcastle, and beg his Grace's advice, or rather orders, what you should do; adding, that his advice will always be orders to you. You will tell him, that, though you are exceedingly mortified, you are much less so than you should otherwise be, from the consideration that, being utterly unknown to his Majesty, his objection could not be personal to you, and could only arise from circumstances which it was not in your power either to prevent or remedy; that if his Grace thought that your continuing any longer there would be disagreeable, you entreated him to tell you so; and that upon the whole, you referred yourself entirely to him, whose orders you should most scrupulously obey. But this precaution, I dare say, is *ex abundanti*,* and will prove unnecessary; however, it is always right to be prepared for all events, the worst as well as the best; it prevents hurry and surprise, two dangerous situations in business; for I know no one thing so useful, so necessary in all business, as great coolness, steadiness, and *sang froid*: they give an incredible advantage over whomever one has to do with.

I have received your letter of the 15th, N.S. from Maïence, where I find that you have diverted yourself much better than I expected. I am very well acquainted with Comte Cobentzel's* character, both of parts and business. He could have given you letters to Bonn, having formerly resided there himself. You will not be so agreeably *electrified*, where this letter will find you, as you were both at Manheim and Maïence; but I hope you may meet with a second German Mrs. Fitzgerald,* who may make you forget the two former ones, and practise your German. Such transient passions will do you no harm; but, on the contrary, a great deal of good; they will refine your manners, and quicken your attention; they give a young fellow *du brillant*, and bring him into fashion; which last is a great article at setting out in the world.

I have wrote, above a month ago, to Lord Albemarle, to thank him for all his kindnesses to you; but pray have you done as much? Those are the necessary attentions, which should never be omitted, especially in the beginning of life, when a character is to be established.

That ready wit, which you so partially allow me, and so justly Sir Charles Williams, may create many admirers; but, take my word for it, it makes few friends. It shines and dazzles like the noon-day sun, but, like that too, is very apt to scorch; and therefore is always feared. The milder morning and evening light and heat of that planet, soothe and calm our minds. Good sense, complaisance, gentleness of manners, attentions, and graces, are the only things that truly engage, and durably keep the heart at long run. Never seek for wit; if it presents itself, well and good; but even in that case, let your judgment interpose; and take care that it be not at the expense of any body. Pope says very truly,

> There are whom Heaven has blest with store of wit,
> Yet want as much again to govern it.

And in another place, I doubt with too much truth,

> For wit and judgment ever are at strife,
> Though meant each other's aid, like man and wife.*

The Germans are very seldom troubled with any extraordinary ebullitions or effervescences of wit, and it is not prudent to try it upon them; whoever does, *offendet solido.**

Remember to write me very minute accounts of all your transactions at Hanover, for they excite both my impatience and anxiety. Adieu.

79. TO SOLOMON DAYROLLES, ESQ.

LONDON, SEPTEMBER 15, 1752

DEAR DAYROLLES,

In the first place I make my compliments to my godson,* who I hope sucks and sleeps heartily, and evacuates properly, which is all that can yet be desired or expected from him. Though you, like a prudent father, I find, carry your thoughts a great deal farther, and are already forming the plan of his education, you have still time to consider of it, but yet not so much as people commonly think, for I am very sure that children are capable of a certain degree of education long before they are commonly thought to be so. At a year and a half old, I am persuaded that a child might be made to comprehend the injustice of torturing flies and strangling birds; whereas, they are commonly encouraged in both, and their hearts hardened by habit. There is another thing, which, as your family is, I suppose, constituted, may be taught him very early, and save him trouble and you expense—I mean languages. You have certainly some French servants, men or maids, in your house. Let them be chiefly about him when he is six or seven months older, and speak nothing but French to him, while you and Madame Dayrolles speak nothing to him but English; by which means those two languages will be equally familiar to him.

By the time that he is three years old, he will be too heavy and too active for a maid to carry or to follow him, and one of your footmen must necessarily be appointed to attend him. Let that footman be a Saxon, who speaks nothing but German, and who will, of course, teach him German without any trouble. A Saxon footman costs no more than one of any other country, and you have two or three years to provide yourself with one upon a vacancy. German will, I fear, be always a useful language for an Englishman to know, and it is a very difficult one to learn any other way than by habit. Some silly people will, I am sure, tell you that you will confound the poor child so with these different languages, that he will jumble them altogether, and speak no one well; and this will be true for five or six years; but then he will separate them of himself, and speak them all perfectly. This plan, I am sure, is a right one for the first seven years; and before the expiration of that time we will think farther.

My boy has been a good while at Hanover: he kissed the King's hand, which was all I expected or desired. *Visage de bois*, you take for granted, *et c'etoit dans les formes.** But the Duke of Newcastle has been most excessively kind and friendly to him: had him always to dine with him, even *en famille*; and has even suggested to me a very advantageous foreign commission for him, which I hope and believe will take place. Between you and me (pray do not mention it yet to any mortal living), it is to succeed Sir James Gray at Venice, as Resident,* Sir James being appointed the King's Envoy at Naples. This is a much better thing than I either asked or could have hoped for. It will initiate him in the trade and routine of business, without exposing him to the ill consequences of any slips, errors, or inadvertencies of youth and inexperience; for there will be little for him to do there, and nothing of importance, and yet it will teach him the forms, the *trin-tran,** and the outlines of his trade. Besides, that to be able to date from Resident at twenty years old, will give him a very early rank and seniority in his profession. I am really most extremely obliged to the Duke of Newcastle, and will show him that I am so if ever I have an opportunity. He is now gone to Brunswick, and from thence goes to pass the Carnival at Berlin.

He will kiss your hands at Brussels in March or April, unless the Venetian affair should require his return here before that time, or an election of a King of the Romans should call him to Frankfort; for I cannot help thinking, notwithstanding what I read in the newspapers, and what you hint in your last, but that there will be a King of the Romans elected before it is long. That affair has been too eagerly and publicly pursued to be now dropped without ridicule and disgrace. At bottom, the Court of Vienna must earnestly wish it, and its pretended indifference was merely to throw the whole expense upon us. We have been haggling all this time about it with the Court of Vienna, which, I suppose, will at last be prevailed with to do something, and we shall, according to custom, do all the rest. The Electors, who are to be paid for it, as those of Palatine and Cologne will be paid, in a few ducats and a great many guineas!

I leave my hermitage at Blackheath next week for Bath, where I am to bathe and pump my head; but I doubt it is with deaf people as with poets, when the head must be pumped little good comes of it. However, I will try everything, just as I take a chance in every lottery, not expecting the great prize, but only to be within the possibility of having it. My compliments to Madame Dayrolles, who, I am told, looks next May.* Adieu, *mon cher enfant*!

I have paid the ten guineas, for which you gave me credit, to your treasurer.

80. TO SOLOMON DAYROLLES, ESQ.

BATH, OCTOBER 18, 1752

DEAR DAYROLLES,

Your last letter of the 6th, and my last of the 10th, crossed one another somewhere upon the road, for I received yours four days after I had sent mine. I think I rather gain ground by the waters and other medicines; but, if I do, it is but slowly, and by inches. I hear the person who sits or stands near me, and who directs his voice in a straight line to me; but I hear no part of a mixed conversation, and consequently am no part of society. However, I bear my misfortune better than I believe most other people would; whether from reason, philosophy, or constitution, I will not pretend to decide. If I have no very cheerful, at least I have no melancholy, moments. Books employ most of my hours agreeably; and some few objects, within my own narrow circle, excite my attention enough to preserve me from *ennui*.

The chief of those objects is now with you; and I am very glad that he is, because I expect, from your friendship, a true and confidential account of him. You will have time to analyse him; and I do beg of you to tell me the worst, as well as the best, of your discoveries. When evils are incurable, it may be the part of one friend to conceal them from another; but at his age, when no defect can have taken so deep a root as to be immoveable, if proper care be taken, the friendly part is rather to tell me his defects than his perfections. I promise you, upon my honour, the most inviolable secrecy. Among the defects, that possibly he may have, I know one that I am sure he has; it is, indeed, a negative fault, a fault of omission; but still it is a very great fault, with regard to the world. He wants that engaging address, those pleasing manners, those little attentions, that air, that *abord*,* and those graces which all conspire to make that first advantageous impression upon people's minds, which is of such infinite use through the whole course of life. It is a sort of magic power, which prepossesses one at first sight in favour of that person, makes one wish to be acquainted with him, and partial to all he says and does. I will maintain it to be more useful in business than in love. This most necessary varnish we want too much: pray recommend it strongly.

I have heard no more of the Venetian affair, nor do I suppose that I shall till the Duke of Newcastle comes over. I hope it will do, and have but one reason to fear that it will not. I look upon it as the making of his fortune, and putting him early in a situation from whence he may in time hope to climb up to any.

He has, I dare say, already told you himself, how exceedingly kind the Duke of Newcastle was to him at Hanover, for he wrote me word with transports of it. *Faites un peu valoir cela,** when you happen either to see or to write to his Grace, but only as from yourself and historically. Add too, that you observe that I was extremely affected with it. In truth, I do intend to give him to the two brothers* for their own; and have nothing else to ask of either, but their acceptance of him. In time he may possibly not be quite useless to them. I have given him such an education that he may be of use to any Court; and I will give him such a provision that he shall be a burthen to none.

As for my godson, who, I assure you without compliment, enjoys my next warmest wishes, you go a little too fast, and think too far beforehand. No plan can possibly be now laid down for the second seven years. His own natural turn and temper must be first discovered, and your then situation will and ought to decide his destination. But I will add one consideration with regard to these first seven years. It is this. Pray let my godson never know what a blow or a whipping is, unless for those things for which, were he a man, he would deserve them; such as lying, cheating, making mischief, and meditated malice. In any of those cases, however young, let him be most severely whipped. But either to threaten or whip him for falling down, or not standing still to have his head combed, and his face washed, is a most unjust and absurd severity; and yet all these are the common causes of whipping. This hardens them to punishment, and confounds them as to the causes of it; for, if a poor child is to be whipped equally for telling a lie, or for a snotty nose, he must of course think them equally criminal. Reason him, by fair means, out of all those things, for which he will not be the worse man; and flog him severely for those things only, for which the law would punish him as a man.

I have ordered Mr. Stanhope to pass six weeks in Flanders, making Brussels his head quarters. I think he cannot know it as he should do in less time; for I would have him see all the considerable towns there, and be acquainted and *faufilé** at Brussels, where there is a great deal of good company, and, as I hear, a very polite Court.—From thence he is to go to Holland for three months. Pray put him *au fait* of the Hague, which nobody can do better than you. I shall put him into Kreuningen's* hand there, for the reading, and the constitutional part of the Republic, of which I would have him most thoroughly informed. If, by any letters, you can be of use to him there, I know you will. I would fain have him know everything of that country, of that Government, of that Court, and of that people, perfectly well. Their affairs and ours always have been, and always will be, intimately blended; and I should be very sorry that, like nine in ten of his countrymen, he should take Holland to be the Republic of the seven

United Provinces, and the States-General for the Sovereign.*

Lord Coventry has used your friend Lady Coventry very brutally at Paris, and made her cry more than once in public. On the contrary, your other friend, Lady Caroline, has *si bien morigéné* my kinsman, that no French husband ever behaved better. *Mais à force d'être sourd je deviens bavard;* so a good night to you with Madame Dayrolles; and I think that is wishing you both very well. Yours.

81. TO HIS SON

BATH, OCTOBER 4, 1752

MY DEAR FRIEND:

I consider you now as at the Court of Augustus, where, if ever the desire of pleasing animated you, it must make you exert all the means of doing it. You will see there, full as well, I dare say, as Horace did at Rome, how States are defended by arms, adorned by manners, and improved by laws.* Nay, you have an Horace there, as well as an Augustus; I need not name Voltaire, *qui nil molitur inepte,* as Horace himself said of another poet. I have lately read over all his works that are published, though I had read them more than once before. I was induced to this by his *Siècle de Louis XIV*, which I have yet read but four times. In reading over all his works, with more attention I suppose than before, my former admiration of him is, I own, turned into astonishment. There is no one kind of writing in which he has not excelled. You are so severe a Classic, that I question whether you will allow me to call his *Henriade* an Epic poem, for want of the proper number of gods, devils, witches and other absurdities, requisite for the machinery; which machinery is, it seems, necessary to constitute the Epopée.* But whether you do or not, I will declare (though possibly to my own shame) that I never read any Epic poem with near so much pleasure. I am grown old, and have possibly lost a great deal of that fire, which formerly made me love fire in others at any rate, and however attended with smoke; but now I must have all sense, and cannot, for the sake of five righteous lines, forgive a thousand absurd ones.

In this disposition of mind, judge whether I can read all Homer through *tout de suite*. I admire his beauties; but, to tell you the truth, when he slumbers, I sleep.* Virgil, I confess, is all sense, and therefore I like him better than his model; but he is often languid, especially in his five or six last books, during which I am obliged to take a good deal of snuff. Besides, I profess myself an ally of Turnus's* against the pious Æneas, who, like many *soi disant* pious people, does the most flagrant injustice and violence in order to execute what they impudently call the will of Heaven. But what will you say, when I tell you truly, that I cannot possibly read our countryman Milton through? I acknowledge him to have some most sublime passages, some prodigious flashes of light; but then you must acknowledge that light is often followed by *darkness visible,* to use his own expression. Besides, not having the honour to be acquainted with any of the parties in his Poem, except the Man and the Woman, the characters and speeches of a dozen or two of angels, and of as many devils, are as much above my reach as my entertainment. Keep this secret for me: for if it should be known, I should be abused by every tasteless pedant, and every solid divine in England.

Whatever I have said to the disadvantage of these three poems, holds much stronger against Tasso's Gierusalemme: it is true he has very fine and glaring rays of poetry; but then they are only meteors, they dazzle, then disappear, and are succeeded by false thoughts, poor *concetti*, and absurd impossibilities; witness the Fish and Parrot; extravagances unworthy of an Heroic Poem, and would much better have become Ariosto, who professes *le coglionerie*.*

I have never read the Lusiade of Camoens,* except in a prose translation, consequently I have never read it at all, so shall say nothing of it; but the *Henriade* is all sense from the beginning to the end, often adorned by the justest and liveliest reflections, the most beautiful descriptions, the noblest images, and the sublimest sentiments; not to mention the harmony of the verse, in which Voltaire undoubtedly exceeds all the French poets: should you insist upon an exception in favour of Racine, I must insist, on my part, that he at least equals him. What hero ever interested more than Henry IV; who, according to the rules of Epic poetry, carries on one great and long action,* and succeeds in it at last? What description ever excited more horror than those, first of the Massacre, and then of the Famine, at Paris? Was love ever painted with more truth and *morbidezza* than in the ninth book! Not better, in my mind, even in the fourth of Virgil. Upon the whole, with all your classical rigour, if you will but suppose St. Louis a god, a devil, or a witch, and that he appears in person, and not in a dream, the *Henriade* will be an Epic poem, according to the strictest statute laws of the Epopée; but in my court of equity it is one as it is.*

I could expatiate as much upon all his different

works, but that I should exceed the bounds of a letter, and run into a dissertation. How delightful is his history of that northern brute, the King of Sweden!* for I cannot call him a man; and I should be sorry to have him pass for a hero, out of regard to those true heroes, such as Julius Caesar, Titus, Trajan, and the present King of Prussia,* who cultivated and encouraged arts and sciences; whose animal courage was accompanied by the tender and social sentiments of humanity; and who had more pleasure in improving, than in destroying their fellow creatures. What can be more touching, or more interesting; what more nobly thought, or more happily expressed, than all his dramatic pieces? What can be more clear and rational than all his philosophical letters:* and what ever was so graceful, and gentle, as all his little poetical trifles? You are fortunately *à portée** of verifying, by your knowledge of the man, all that I have said of his works.

Monsieur de Maupertuis*(whom I hope you will get acquainted with) is, what one rarely meets with, deep in philosophy and mathematics, and yet *honnête et aimable homme*: Algarotti is young Fontenelle. Such men must necessarily give you the desire of pleasing them; and if you can frequent them, their acquaintance will furnish you the means of pleasing everybody else.

A propos of pleasing, your pleasing Mrs. Fitzgerald is expected here in two or three days; I will do all that I can for you with her: I think you carried on the romance to the third or fourth volume; I will continue it to the eleventh; but as for the twelfth and last, you must come and conclude it yourself. *Non sum qualis eram.**

Good-night to you, child; for I am going to bed, just at the hour at which I suppose you are beginning to live, at Berlin.

82. TO HIS SON

MY DEAR FRIEND,

Since my last to you, I have read Madame Maintenon's letters;* I am sure they are genuine, and they both entertained and informed me. They have brought me acquainted with the character of that able and artful lady; whom I am convinced that I now know much better than her *directeur* the Abbé de Fénelon (afterwards Archbishop of Cambray) did, when he wrote her the 185th letter;* and I know him the better too for that letter. The *Abbé* though brimful of the divine love, had a great mind to be first Minister and Cardinal, in order, *no doubt*, to have an opportunity of doing the more good. His being *directeur* at that time to Madame Maintenon, seemed to be a good step towards those views. She put herself upon him for a saint, and he was weak enough to believe it; he, on the other hand, would have put himself upon her for a saint too, which, I daresay, she did not believe; both of them knew that it was necessary for them to appear saints to Louis the Fourteenth, who they were very sure was a bigot. It is to be presumed, nay, indeed, it is plain by that 185th letter, that Madame Maintenon had hinted to her *directeur* some scruples of conscience, with relation to her commerce with the King; and which I humbly apprehend to have been only some scruples of prudence, at once to flatter the bigot character, and increase the desires of the King. The pious *Abbé*, frightened out of his wits, lest the King should impute to the *directeur* any scruples or difficulties which he might meet with on the part of the lady, writes her the above-mentioned letter; in which he not only bids her not teaze the King by advice and exhortations, but to have the utmost submission to his will; and, that she may not mistake the nature of that submission, he tells her, it is the same that Sarah had for Abraham; to which submission Isaac perhaps was owing.* No bawd could have written a more seducing letter to an innocent country girl, than the *directeur* did to his *pénitente*; who I dare say had no occasion for his good advice. Those who would justify the good *directeur*, alias the pimp, in this affair, must not attempt to do it by saying, that the King and Madame Maintenon were at that time privately married; that the *directeur* knew it; and that this was the meaning of his *énigme*. That is absolutely impossible; for that private marriage must have removed all scruples between the parties; nay, could not have been contracted upon any other principle, since it was kept private, and consequently prevented no public scandal. It is therefore extremely evident, that Madame Maintenon could not be married to the King, at the time when she scrupled granting, and when the *directeur* advised her to grant, those favours which Sarah with so much submission granted to Abraham: and what the *directeur* is pleased to call *le mystère de Dieu*, was most evidently a state of concubinage. The letters are very well worth your reading; they throw light upon many things of those times.

I have just received a letter from Sir William Stanhope,* from Lyons; in which he tells me that he saw you at Paris, that he thinks you a little grown, but that you do not make the most of it, for that you stoop still; *d'ailleurs* his letter was a panegyric of you.

The young Comte de Schullemburg,* the Chambellan whom you knew at Hanover, is come over with the King, *et fait aussi vos éloges.*

Though, as I told you in my last, I have done buying pictures by way of *virtù*,* yet there are some portraits of remarkable people that would tempt me. For instance, if you could by chance pick up at Paris, at a reasonable price, and undoubted originals (whether heads, half-lengths, or whole-lengths, no matter) of Cardinals Richelieu, Mazarin, and Retz, Monsieur de Turenne, le grand Prince de Condé; Mesdames de Montespan, de Fontanges, de Montbazon, de Sévigné, de Maintenon, de Chevreuse, de Mogueville, d'Olonne,* etc., I should be tempted to purchase them. I am sensible that they can only be met with by great accident, at family sales and auctions, so I only mention the affair to you eventually.

I do not understand, or else I do not remember, what affair you mean in your last letter; which you think will come to nothing, and for which, you say, I had once a mind that you should take the road again. Explain it to me.

I shall go to town in four or five days, and carry back with me a little more hearing than I brought; but yet not half enough for common use. One wants ready pocket-money much oftener than one wants great sums; and, to use a very odd expression, I want to hear at sight. I love everyday senses, everyday wit and entertainment; a man who is only good on holidays is good for very little. Adieu!

83. TO THE KING'S MOST EXCELLENT MAJESTY *

THE HUMBLE PETITION OF PHILIP EARL OF CHESTER-
FIELD, KNIGHT OF THE MOST NOBLE ORDER OF
THE GARTER,

SHEWETH,

That your Petitioner, being rendered, by deafness, as
useless and insignificant as most of his equals and contemporaries are by nature, hopes, in common with
them, to share your Majesty's Royal favour and
bounty; whereby he may be enabled either to save or
spend, as he shall think proper, more than he can do at
present.

That your Petitioner, having had the honour of
serving your Majesty in several very lucrative employments, seems thereby entitled to a lucrative re-
treat from business, and to enjoy *otium cum dignitate*; *
that is, leisure and a large pension.

Your Petitioner humbly presumes, that he has, at
least, a common claim to such a pension: he has a vote
in the most august assembly in the world; he has an
estate that puts him above wanting it; but he has, at
the same time (though he says it) an elevation of sentiment, that makes him not only desire, but (pardon,
dread Sir, an expression you are used to) *insist* upon it.

That your Petitioner is little apt, and always unwilling, to speak advantageously of himself; but as,
after all, some justice is due to one's self, as well as to
others, he begs leave to represent: That his loyalty to
your Majesty has always been unshaken, even in the
worst of times; That, particularly, in the late un-

natural rebellion, when the Pretender advanced as far as Derby,* at the head of, at least, three thousand undisciplined men, the flower of the Scottish nobility and gentry, your Petitioner did not join him, as, unquestionably, he might have done, had he been so inclined; but, on the contrary, raised sixteen companies, of one hundred men each, at the public expense, in support of your Majesty's undoubted right to the Imperial Crown of these Realms; which distinguished proof of his loyalty is, to this hour, unrewarded.

Your Majesty's Petitioner is well aware, that your Civil List must necessarily be in a low and languid state, after the various, frequent, and profuse evacuations, which it has of late years undergone; but, at the same time, he presumes to hope, that this argument, which seems not to have been made use of against any other person whatsoever, shall not, in this single case, be urged against him; and the less so, as he has good reasons to believe, that the deficiencies of the Pension-fund are, by no means, the last that will be made good by Parliament.

Your Petitioner begs leave to observe, That a small pension is disgraceful and opprobrious, as it intimates a shameful necessity on one part, and a degrading sort of charity on the other: but that a great one implies dignity and affluence on one side; on the other, regard and esteem; which, doubtless, your Majesty must entertain in the highest degree, for those great personages whose respectable names stand upon your Eleemosynary list. Your Petitioner, therefore, humbly persuades himself, upon this principle, that less than three thousand pounds a year will not be proposed to him: if made up of gold, the more agreeable; if for life, the more marketable.

Your Petitioner persuades himself, that your Majesty will not suspect this his humble application to proceed from any mean, interested motive, of which he has always had the utmost abhorrence. No, Sir, he confesses his own weakness; Honour alone is his object; Honour is his passion; Honour is dearer to him than life.* To Honour he has always sacrificed all other considerations; and upon this general principle, singly, he now solicits that honour, which in the most shining times distinguished the greatest men of Greece, who were fed at the expense of the public.

Upon this Honour, so sacred to him as a Peer, so tender to him as a man, he most solemnly assures your Majesty, that, in case you shall be pleased to grant him this his humble request, he will gratefully and honourably support, and promote with zeal and vigour, the worst measure that the worst Minister can ever suggest to your Majesty: but, on the other hand, should he be singled out, marked, and branded by a refusal, he thinks himself obliged in Honour to declare, that he will, to the utmost of his power, oppose the best and wisest measures that your Majesty yourself can ever dictate.

And your Majesty's Petitioner will ever pray, etc.

84. TO HIS SON

BATH, OCTOBER 19, 1753

MY DEAR FRIEND,

Of all the various ingredients that compose the useful and necessary art of pleasing, no one is so effectual and engaging, as that gentleness, that *douceur* of countenance and manners, to which you are no stranger, though (God knows why) a sworn enemy. Other people take great pains to conceal or disguise their natural imperfections; some, by the make of their clothes, and other arts, endeavour to conceal the defects of their shape; women who unfortunately have natural bad complexions, lay on good ones; and both men and women, upon whom unkind nature has inflicted a surliness and ferocity of countenance, do at least all they can, though often without success, to soften and mitigate it; they affect *douceur*, and aim at smiles, though often in the attempt, like the Devil in *Milton*, they *grin horribly, a ghastly smile.** But you are the only person I ever knew in the whole course of my life, who not only disdain, but absolutely reject and disguise a great advantage that nature has kindly granted. You easily guess I mean *countenance*; for she has given you a very pleasing one; but you beg to be excused, you will not accept it; on the contrary, take singular pains to put on the most *funeste*, forbidding, and unpleasing one, that can possibly be imagined. This one would think impossible; but you know it to be true. If you imagine that it gives you a manly, thoughtful, and decisive air, as some, though very few of your countrymen do, you are most exceedingly mistaken; for it is at best the air of a German corporal, part of whose exercise is to look fierce, and to *blasemeer-op*.* You will say, perhaps, What, am I always to be studying my countenance, in order to wear this *douceur*? I answer, No; do it but for a fortnight, and you will never have occasion to think of it more. Take but half the pains to recover the countenance that nature gave you, that you must have taken to disguise and deform it as you have, and the business will be done. Accustom your eyes to a certain softness, of which they are very capable, and your face to smiles, which become it more than most faces I know. Give all your motions, too, an air of *douceur*, which is directly the reverse of their present celerity and rapidity. I wish you would adopt a little of *l'air du Couvent* (you very well know what I mean) to a certain degree; it has something extremely engaging; there is a mixture of benevolence, affection, and unction in it: it is frequently really sincere, but is almost always thought so, and consequently pleasing. Will you call this trouble? It will not be half an hour's trouble to you in a week's time. But suppose it be, pray tell me, why did you give yourself the trouble of learning to dance so well as you do? It is neither a religious, moral, or civil duty. You must own, that you did it then singly to please, and you were in the right on't. Why do you wear your fine clothes, and curl your hair? Both are troublesome; lank locks, and plain flimsy rags, are much easier. This then you also do in order to please, and you do very right. But then, for God's sake, reason and act consequentially; and endeavour to please in other things too, still more essential; and without which the trouble you have taken in those is wholly thrown away. You show your dancing, perhaps, six times a year at most; but you show your countenance, and your common motions every day, and all day. Which, then, I appeal to yourself, ought you to think of the most, and care to render easy, graceful, and engaging? *Douceur* of countenance and gesture can alone make them so. You are by no means ill-natured; and would you then most unjustly be reckoned so? Yet your common countenance intimates, and would make anybody, who did not know you, believe it. *A propos* of this, I must tell you what was said the other day to a fine lady whom you know, who is very good-natured in truth, but whose common countenance implies ill-nature, even to brutality.

It was Miss Hamilton, Lady Murray's niece,* whom you have seen, both at Blackheath and at Lady Hervey's. Lady Murray was saying to me, that you had a very engaging countenance, when you had a mind to it, but that you had not always that mind; upon which Miss Hamilton said, that she liked your countenance best, when it was as glum as her own. Why then, replied Lady Murray, you two should marry; for while you both wear your worst countenances, nobody else will venture upon either of you; and they call her now Mrs. Stanhope. To complete this *douceur* of countenance and motions, which I so earnestly recommend to you, you should carry it also to your expressions and manner of thinking, *mettez-y toujours de l'affectueux, de l'onction*; take the gentle, the favourable, the indulgent side of most questions. I own that the manly and sublime John Trott,* your countryman, seldom does; but, to show his spirit and decision, takes the rough and harsh side, which he generally adorns with an oath, to seem more formidable. This he only thinks fine; for to do John justice, he is commonly as good-natured as anybody. These are among the many little things which you have not, and I have lived long enough in the world to know of what infinite consequence they are in the course of life. Reason then, I repeat it again, within yourself *consequently*; and let not the pains you have taken, and still take, to please in some things, be *à pure perte,* by your negligence of, and inattention to, others, of much less trouble, and much more consequence.

I have been of late much engaged, or rather bewildered, in Oriental history, particularly that of the Jews, since the destruction of their temple, and their dispersion by Titus;* but the confusion and uncertainty of the whole, and the monstrous extravagances and falsehoods of the greatest part of it, disgusted me extremely. Their Thalmud, their Mischna, their Targums,* and other traditions and writings of their Rabbins and Doctors, who were most of them Cabalists, are really more extravagant and absurd, if possible, than all that you have read in Comte de Gabalis; and indeed most of his stuff is taken from them. Take this sample of their nonsense, which is transmitted in the writings of one of their most considerable Rabbins. 'One Abas Saul, a man of ten feet high, was digging a grave, and happened to find the eye of Goliath, in which he thought proper to bury himself; and so he did, all but his head, which the giant's eye was unfortunately not quite deep enough to receive.'* This, I assure you, is the most modest lie of ten thousand. I have also read the Turkish History, which, excepting the religious part, is not fabulous, though very possibly not true. For the Turks, having no notion of letters, and being even by their religion forbid the use of them, except for reading and transcribing the Koran they have no historians of their own, nor any authentic records or memorials for other historians to work upon; so that what histories we have of that country, are written by foreigners; as Platina, Sir Paul Rycaut, Prince Cantemir, &c., or else snatches of particular and short periods, by some who happened to reside there at those times: such as Busbequius,* whom I have just finished. I like him, as far as he goes, much the best of any of them: but then his account is, properly, only an account of his own Embassy from the Emperor Charles the Fifth to Solyman the Magnificent. However, there he gives, episodically, the best account I know of the customs and manners of the Turks, and of the nature of that government, which is a most extraordinary one. For, despotic as it always seems, and sometimes is, it is in truth a military republic; and the real power resides in the Janissaries; who sometimes order their Sultan to strangle his Vizar, and sometimes the Vizar* to depose or strangle his Sultan, according as they happen to be angry at the one or the other. I own, I am glad that the capital strangler should, in his turn, be *strangle-able*, and now and then strangled; for I know of no brute so fierce, nor no criminal so guilty, as the creature called a Sovereign, whether King, Sultan, or Sophy, who thinks himself, either by divine or human right, vested with an absolute power of destroying his fellow-creatures; or who, without enquiring into his right, lawlessly exerts that power. The most excusable of all those human monsters are the Turks, whose religion teaches them inevitable fatalism. *A propos* of the Turks, my Loyola, I pretend, is superior to your Sultan. Perhaps you think this impossible, and wonder who this Loyola is. Know then, that I have had a Barbet brought me from France, so exactly like Sultan, that he has been mistaken for him several times; only his snout is shorter, and his ears longer than Sultan's. He has also the acquired knowledge of Sultan; and I am apt to think that he studied under the same master at Paris. His habit and his white band show him to be an ecclesiastic; and his begging, which he does very earnestly, proves him to be of a Mendicant Order; which, added to his flattery and insinuation, make him supposed to be a Jesuit, and have acquired him the name of Loyola. I must not omit too, that when he breaks wind he smells exactly like Sultan.*

I do not yet hear one jot the better for all my bath-

ings and pumpings, though I have been here already
full half my time; I consequently go very little into
company, being very little fit for any. I hope you
keep company enough for us both; you will get more
by that, than I shall by all my reading. I read singly
to amuse myself, and fill up my time, of which I have
too much; but you have two much better reasons for
going into company, Pleasure and Profit. May you
find a great deal of both, in a great deal of company!
Adieu.

85. TO SOLOMON DAYROLLES, ESQ.

LONDON, JANUARY 1, 1754

DEAR DAYROLLES,

You fine gentlemen, who have never committed the
sin or the folly of scribbling, think that all those who
have, can do it again whenever they please, but you
are much mistaken; the pen has not only its moments,
but its hours, its days of impotence, and is no more
obedient to the will, than other things have been since
the fall. Unsuccessful and ineffectual attempts are in
both cases alike disagreeable and disgraceful. It is
true, I have nothing else to do but to write, and for
that very reason perhaps I should do it worse than
ever; what was formerly an act of choice, is now become the refuge of necessity. I used to snatch up the
pen with momentary raptures, because by choice, but
now I am married to it. . . . Though I keep up a
certain equality of spirits, better I believe than most
people would do in my unfortunate situation, yet you
must not suppose that I have ever that flow of active
spirits which is so necessary to enable one to do anything well. Besides, as the pride of the human heart
extends itself beyond the short span of our lives, all

people are anxious and jealous, authors perhaps more so than any others, of what will be thought and said of them at a time when they cannot know, and therefore ought not reasonably to care for, either. Notwithstanding all these difficulties, I will confess to you that I often scribble, but at the same time protest to you that I almost as often burn. I judge myself as impartially and I hope more severely, than I do others; and upon an appeal from myself to myself, I frequently condemn the next day, what I had approved and applauded the former. What will finally come of all this I do not know; nothing I am sure, that shall appear while I am alive, except by chance some short trifling essays, like the *Spectators*, upon some new folly or absurdity that may happen to strike me, as I have now and then helped Mr. Fitz-Adam in his weekly paper called the *World.* . . .*

This is the season of well-bred lies indiscriminately told by all to all; professions and wishes unfelt and unmeant, degraded by use, and profaned by falsehood, are lavished with profusion. Mine for you, Mrs. Dayrolles, and my godson, are too honest and sincere to keep such company, or to wear their dress. Judge of them then yourselves; without my saying anything more, than that I am most heartily and faithfully   Yours.

86. TO HIS SON

LONDON, FEBRUARY 12, 1754

MY DEAR FRIEND,

I take my aim, and let off this letter at you at Berlin; I should be sorry it missed you, because you will read it with as much pleasure as I write it. It is to inform you, that, after some difficulties and dangers, your seat in the new Parliament is at last absolutely secured, and that without opposition, or the least necessity of your personal trouble or appearance. This success, I must further inform you, is, in a great degree owing to Mr. Eliot's friendship to us both; for he brings you in with himself at his surest borough. As it was impossible to act with more zeal and friendship than Mr. Eliot has acted in this whole affair, I desire that you will, by the very next post, write him a letter of thanks; warm and young thanks, not old and cold ones. You may enclose it in yours to me, and I will send it to him, for he is now in Cornwall.*

Thus, sure of being a senator, I daresay you do not propose to be one of the *pedarii senatores, et pedibus ire in sententiam;* for, as the House of Commons is the theatre where you must make your fortune and figure in the world, you must resolve to be an actor, and not a *persona muta,* which is just equivalent to a candle-snuffer upon other theatres. Whoever does not shine there, is obscure, insignificant, and contemptible; and you cannot conceive how easy it is for a man of half your sense and knowledge to shine there if he pleases. The receipt to make a speaker, and an applauded one too, is short and easy—Take of common sense *quantum sufficit;* add a little application to the rules and orders of the House, throw obvious thoughts in a new light, and make up the whole with a large quantity of purity, correctness, and elegancy of style—Take it for granted, that by far the greatest part of mankind do neither analyse nor search to the bottom; they are incapable of penetrating deeper than the surface. All have senses to be gratified, very few have reason to be applied to. Graceful utterance and action please their eyes, elegant diction tickles their ears; but strong reason would be thrown away upon them. I am not only persuaded by theory, but convinced by my experience, that (supposing a certain degree of common sense) what is called a good speaker is as much a mechanic as a good shoemaker; and that the two trades are equally to be learned by the same degree of application. Therefore, for God's sake, let this trade be the principal object of your thoughts; never lose sight of it. Attend minutely to your style, whatever language you speak or write in; seek for the best words, and think of the best turns. Whenever you doubt of the propriety or elegancy of any word, search the dictionary or some good author for it, or inquire of somebody who is master of that language; and, in a little time, propriety and elegancy of diction will become so habitual to you, that they will cost you no more trouble. As I have laid this down to be mechanical and attainable by whoever will take the necessary pains, there will be no great vanity in my saying, that I saw the importance of the object so early, and attended to it so young, that it would now cost me more trouble to speak or write ungrammatically, vulgarly, and inelegantly, than ever it did to avoid doing so. The late Lord Bolingbroke, without the least trouble, talked all day long full as elegantly as he wrote. Why? Not by a peculiar gift from heaven; but, as he has often told me himself, by an early and constant attention to his style. The present Solicitor-General, Murray,* has less law than many lawyers, but has more practice than any; merely upon account of his eloquence, of which he has a never-failing stream. I remember so long ago as when I was at Cambridge, whenever I read pieces of eloquence (and indeed they were my chief study) whether ancient or modern, I used to write down the shining passages, and then translate them, as well and as elegantly as ever I could; if Latin or French, into English; if English, into French. This, which I practised for some years, not only improved and formed my style, but imprinted in my mind and memory the best thoughts of the best authors. The trouble was little, but the advantage I have experienced was great. While you are abroad, you can neither have time nor opportunity to read pieces of English or Parliamentary eloquence, as I hope you will carefully do when you return; but, in the meantime, whenever pieces of French eloquence come in your way, such as the speeches of persons received into the Academy, *oraisons funèbres,* representations of the several Parliaments to the king, etc., read them in that view, in that spirit; observe the harmony, the turn and elegancy of the style; examine in what you think it might have been better; and consider in what, had you written it yourself, you might have done worse. Compare the different manners of expressing the same thoughts, in different authors; and observe how differently the same things appear in different dresses. Vulgar, coarse, and ill-chosen words will deform and degrade the best thoughts, as much as rags and dirt will the best figure. In short, you now know your object; pursue it steadily, and have no digressions that are not relative to, and connected with, the main action. Your success in Parliament will effectually remove all *other objections*; either a foreign or a domestic destination will no longer be refused you, if you make your way to it through Westminster.

I think I may now say, that I am quite recovered from my late illness, strength and spirits excepted, which are not yet restored. Aix-la-Chapelle and Spa will, I believe, answer all my purposes.

I long to hear an account of your reception at Berlin, which I fancy will be a most gracious one. Adieu.

86. TO HIS SON.

LONDON, MARCH 8, 1754

MY DEAR FRIEND:

A great and unexpected event has lately happened in our ministerial world—Mr. Pelham died last Monday, of a fever and mortification; occasioned by a general corruption of his whole mass of blood, which had broke out into sores in his back. I regret him as an old acquaintance, a pretty near relation, and a private man, with whom I have lived many years in a social and friendly way. He meaned well to the public; and was incorrupt in a post where corruption is commonly contagious. If he was no shining, enterprising Minister, he was a safe one, which I like better. Very shining Ministers, like the sun, are apt to scorch, when they shine the brightest: in our constitution, I prefer the milder light of a less glaring Minister.

His successor is not yet, at least publicly, *designatus*. You will easily suppose that many are very willing, and very few able, to fill that post. Various persons are talked of, by different people, for it, according as their interest prompts them to wish, or their ignorance to conjecture. Mr. Fox is the most talked of; he is strongly supported by the Duke of Cumberland. Mr. Legge, the Solicitor-General, and Dr. Lee, are likewise all spoken of, upon the foot of the Duke of Newcastle's and the Chancellor's interest. Should it be any one of the three last, I think no great alterations will ensue; but, should Mr. Fox prevail, it would, in my opinion, soon produce changes, by no means favourable to the Duke of Newcastle. In the mean time, the wild conjectures of volunteer politicians, and the ridiculous importance which, upon these occasions, blockheads always endeavour to give themselves, by grave looks, significant shrugs, and insignificant whispers, are very entertaining to a bystander, as, thank God, I now am. One *knows something*, but is not yet at liberty to tell it; another has heard something from a very good hand; a third congratulates himself upon a certain degree of intimacy, which he has long had with every one of the candidates, though perhaps he has never spoken twice to any one of them. In short, in these sort of intervals, vanity, interest, and absurdity, always display themselves in the most ridiculous light. One who has been so long behind the scenes, as I have, is much more diverted with the entertainment, than those can be who only see it from the pit and boxes. I know the whole machinery of the interior, and can laugh the better at the silly wonder and wild conjectures of the uninformed spectators. This accident, I think, cannot in the least affect your election, which is finally settled with your friend Mr. Eliot. For, let who will prevail, I presume he will consider me enough not to overturn an arrangement of that sort, in which he cannot possibly be personally interested. So pray go on with your parliamentary preparations. Have that object always in your view, and pursue it with attention.

I take it for granted, that your late residence in Germany has made you as perfect and correct in German, as you were before in French: at least it is worth your while to be so; because it is worth every man's while to be perfectly master of whatever language he may ever have occasion to speak. A man is not himself, in a language which he does not thoroughly possess; his thoughts are degraded, when inelegantly or imperfectly expressed; he is cramped and confined, and consequently can never appear to advantage. Examine and analyse those thoughts that strike you the most, either in conversation or in books; and you will find, that they owe at least half their merit to the turn and expression of them. There is nothing truer than that old saying *Nihil dictum quod non prius dictum.* It is only the manner of saying or writing it, that makes it appear new. Convince yourself, that Manner is almost every thing, in every thing, and study it accordingly.

I am this moment informed, and I believe truly, that Mr. Fox is to succeed Mr. Pelham, as First Commissioner of the Treasury and Chancellor of the Exchequer; and your friend Mr. Yorke, of the Hague, to succeed Mr. Fox, as Secretary at War. I am not sorry for this promotion of Mr. Fox, as I have always been upon civil terms with him, and found him ready to do me any little services. He is frank and gentlemanlike in his manner; and, to a certain degree, I really believe, will be your friend upon my account; if you can afterwards make him yours, upon your own, *tant mieux.* I have nothing more to say now, but Adieu.

87. TO HIS SON

LONDON, MARCH 26, 1754

MY DEAR FRIEND,

Yesterday I received your letter of the 15th from Manheim, where I find you have been received in the usual gracious manner; which I hope you return in a *graceful* one. As this is a season of great devotion and solemnity, in all Catholic countries, pray inform yourself of, and constantly attend to, all their silly and pompous Church ceremonies: one ought to know them.

I am very glad that you wrote the letter to Lord ——, which, in every different case that can possibly be supposed, was, I am sure, both a decent and a prudent step. You will find it very difficult, whenever we meet, to convince me that you could have any good reasons for not doing it; for I will, for argument's sake, suppose, what I cannot in reality believe, that he has both said and done the worst he could, of and by you; what then? How will you help yourself? Are you in a situation to hurt him? Certainly not; but he certainly is in a situation to hurt you.* Would you show a sullen, pouting, impotent resentment? I hope not: leave that silly, unavailing sort of resentment to women, and men like them, who are always guided by humour, never by reason and prudence. That pettish, pouting conduct is a great deal too young, and implies too little knowledge of the world, for one who has seen so much of it as you have. Let this be one invariable rule of your conduct—Never to show the least symptom of resentment, which you cannot, to a certain degree, gratify; but always to smile, where you cannot strike. There would be no living in Courts, nor indeed in the world, if one could not conceal, and even dissemble, the just causes of resentment, which one meets with every day in active and busy life. Whoever cannot master his humour enough, *pour faire bonne mine à mauvais jeu,*,* should leave the world, and retire to some hermitage, in an unfrequented desert. By showing an unavailing and sullen resentment, you authorize the resentment of those who cannot hurt you, and whom you cannot hurt; and give them that very pretence, which perhaps they wished for, of breaking with, and injuring you; whereas the contrary behaviour would lay them under the restraints of decency at least; and either shackle or expose their malice. Besides, captiousness, sullenness, and pouting, are exceedingly illiberal and vulgar. *Un honnête homme ne les connoît point*.*

I am extremely glad to hear that you are soon to have Voltaire at Manheim: immediately upon his arrival, pray make him a thousand compliments from me. I admire him most exceedingly; and whether as an epic, dramatic, or lyric poet, or prose-writer, I think I justly apply to him the *Nil molitur inepté*. I long to read his own correct edition of *Les Annales de l'Empire*,* of which the *Abrégé Chronologique de l'Histoire Universelle*, which I have read, is, I suppose, a stolen and imperfect part; however, imperfect as it is, it has explained to me that chaos of history of seven hundred years more clearly than any other book had done before. You judge very rightly, that I love *le style léger et fleuri*.* I do, and so does everybody who has any parts and taste. It should, I confess, be more or less *fleuri*, according to the subject; but at the same time I assert, that there is no subject that may not properly, and which ought not to be adorned, by a certain elegancy and beauty of style. What can be more adorned than Cicero's philosophical works? What more than Plato's? It is their eloquence only, that has preserved and transmitted them down to us, through so many centuries; for the philosophy of them is wretched, and the reasoning part miserable.

But eloquence will always please, and has always pleased. Study it therefore; make it the object of your thoughts and attention. Use yourself to relate elegantly; that is a good step towards speaking well in Parliament. Take some political subject, turn it in your thoughts, consider what may be said, both for and against it, then put those arguments into writing, in the most correct and elegant English you can. For instance, a Standing Army, a Place-Bill,* etc.; as to the former, consider, on one side, the dangers arising to a free country from a great standing military force; on the other side, consider the necessity of a force to repel force with. Examine whether a standing army, though in itself an evil, may not, from circumstances, become a necessary evil, and preventive of greater dangers. As to the latter, consider how far places may bias and warp the conduct of men, from the service of their country, into an unwarrantable complaisance to the Court; and, on the other hand, consider whether they can be supposed to have that effect upon the conduct of people of probity and property, who are more solidly interested in the permanent good of their country, than they can be in an uncertain and precarious employment. Seek for, and answer in your own mind, all the arguments that can be urged on either side, and write them down in an elegant style. This will prepare you for debating, and give you an habitual eloquence; for I would not give a farthing for a mere holiday eloquence, displayed once or twice in a session, in a set declamation; but I want an every-day, ready, and habitual eloquence, to adorn *extempore* and debating speeches; to make business not only clear but agreeable, and to please even those whom you cannot inform, and who do not desire to be informed. All this you may acquire, and make habitual to you, with as little trouble as it cost you to dance a minuet as well as you do. You now dance it mechanically, and well, without thinking of it.

I am surprise that you found but one letter from me

at Manheim, for you ought to have found four or five; there are as many lying for you, at your banker's at Berlin, which I wish you had, because I always endeavoured to put something into them, which, I hope, may be of use to you.

When we meet at Spa, next July, we must have a great many serious conversations; in which I will pour out all my experience of the world, and which, I hope, you will trust to, more than to your own young notions of men and things. You will, in time, discover most of them to have been erroneous; and, if you follow them long, you will perceive your error too late; but, if you will be led by a guide, who, you are sure does not mean to mislead you, you will unite two things, seldom united in the same person: the vivacity and spirit of youth, with the caution and experience of age.

Last Saturday, Sir Thomas Robinson,* who had been the King's Minister at Vienna, was declared Secretary of State for the southern department, Lord Holderness having taken the northern. Sir Thomas accepted it unwillingly, and, as I hear, with a promise that he shall not keep it long. Both his health and spirits are bad, two very disqualifying circumstances for that employment; yours, I hope, will enable you, some time or other, to go through with it. In all events, aim at it, and if you fail or fall, let it, at least, be said of you, *Magnis tamen excidit ausis.** Adieu.

88. TO HIS SON

LONDON, APRIL 5, 1754

MY DEAR FRIEND,

I received, yesterday, your letter of the 20th March, from Manheim, with the enclosed for Mr. Eliot; it was a very proper one, and I have forwarded it to him by Mr. Harte, who sets out for Cornwall to-morrow morning.

I am very glad that you use yourself to translations; and I do not care of what, provided you study the correctness and elegancy of your style. The Life of Sextus Quintus is the best book, of the innumerable books written by Gregorio Leti, whom the Italians, very justly, call *Leti caca libri*.* But I would rather that you chose some pieces of oratory for your translations; whether ancient or modern, Latin or French; which would give you a more oratorial train of thoughts, and turn of expression. In your letter to me, you make use of two words, which, though true and correct English, are, however, from long disuse, become inelegant, and seem now to be stiff, formal, and, in some degree, scriptural: the first is the word *namely*, which you introduce thus, '*You inform me of a very agreeable piece of news*, namely, *that my election is secured.*' Instead of *namely*, I would always use, *which is*, or *that is*, that my election is secured. The other word is, *Mine own inclinations*: this is certainly correct, before a subsequent word that begins with a vowel; but it is too correct, and is now disused as too formal, notwithstanding the *hiatus* occasioned by *my own*. Every language has its peculiarities; they are established by usage, and, whether right or wrong, they must be complied with. I could instance many very absurd ones in different languages; but so authorized by the *ius et norma loquendi*, that they must be submitted to. *Namely*, and *to wit*,* are very good words in themselves, and contribute to clearness, more than the relatives which we now substitute in their room; but, however, they cannot be used, except in a sermon, or some very grave and formal compositions. It is with language as with manners; they are both established by the usage of people of fashion; it must be imitated, it must be complied with. Singularity is only pardonable in old age and retirement; I may now be as singular as I please, but you may not. We will, when we meet, discuss these and many other points, provided you will give me attention and credit; without both which it is to no purpose to advise either you or anybody else.

I want to know your determination, where you intend to (if I may use that expression) *while* away your time, till the last week in June, when we are to meet at Spa; I continue rather in the opinion which I mentioned to you formerly, in favour of the Hague; but, however, I have not the least objection to Dresden, or to any other place that you may like better. If you prefer the Dutch scheme, you take Treves and Coblentz in your way, as also Dusseldorp: all which places I think you have not yet seen. At Manheim you may certainly get good letters of recommendation to the Courts of the two Electors of Treves and Cologne, whom you are yet unacquainted with; and I should wish you to know them all. For, as I have often told you, *olim haec meminisse juvabit.* There is an utility in having seen what other people have seen, and there is a justifiable pride in having seen what others have not seen. In the former case you are equal to others; in the latter, superior. As your stay abroad will not now be very long, pray, while it lasts, see everything, and everybody you can; and see them well, with care and attention. It is not to be conceived of what advantage it is to anybody to have seen more things, people, and countries, than other people in general have: it gives them a credit, makes them referred to, and they become the objects of the attention of the company. They are not out in any part of polite conversation; they are acquainted with all the places, customs, courts, and families, that are likely to be mentioned; they are, as Monsieur de Maupertuis justly observes, *de tous les pais comme les sçavans sont de tous les tems*. You have, fortunately, both those advantages; the only remaining point is *de sçavoir les faire valoir;* for without that, one may as well not have them. Remember that very true maxim of La Bruyère's, *Qu'on ne vaut dans ce monde que ce qu'on veut valoir.* The knowledge of the world will teach you to what degree you ought to show *ce que vous valez*. One must by no means, on one hand, be indifferent about it; as, on the other, one must not display it with affectation, and in an overbearing manner: but, of the two, it is better to show too much than too little.

Adieu.

89. TO THE EDITOR OF THE *LONDON EVENING POST*

ARTICLE FOR INSERTION

(BATH, FEBRUARY, 1755)

On the tenth of this month, died at Paris, universally and sincerely regretted, Charles Secondat, Baron de Montesquieu,* and *Président à Mortier* of the Parliament at Bourdeaux. His virtues did honour to human nature; his writings, to justice. A friend to mankind, he asserted their undoubted and inalienable rights with freedom, even in his own country, whose prejudices in matters of religion and government he had long lamented, and endeavoured, not without some success, to remove. He well knew, and justly admired, the happy constitution of this country, where fixed and known laws equally restrain monarchy from tyranny, and liberty from licentiousness. His works will illustrate his name, and survive him as long as right reason, moral obligation, and the true spirit of laws, shall be understood, respected, and maintained.

90. TO HIS SON

BLACKHEATH, NOVEMBER 17, 1755

MY DEAR FRIEND,

I heartily congratulate you upon the loss of your political maidenhead, of which I have received from others a very good account. I hear, that you were stopped for some time in your career; but recovered breath, and finished it very well. I am not surprised, nor indeed concerned, at your accident; for I remember the dreadful feeling of that situation in myself; and as it must require a most uncommon share of impudence to be unconcerned upon such an occasion, I am not sure that I am not rather glad you stopped. You must therefore now think of hardening yourself by degrees, by using yourself insensibly to the sound of your own voice, and to the act (trifling as it seems) of rising up and sitting down again. Nothing will contribute so much to this as committee work, of elections at night, and of private bills in the morning. There, asking short questions, moving for witnesses to be called in, and all that kind of small ware, will soon fit you to set up for yourself. I am told that you are much mortified at your accident; but without reason; pray let it rather be a spur than a curb to you. Persevere, and depend upon it, it will do well at last. When I say persevere, I do not mean that you should speak every day, nor in every debate.*

Moreover, I would not advise you to speak again upon public matters for some time, perhaps a month or two; but I mean never lose view of that great object; pursue it with discretion, but pursue it always. *Pelotez en attendant partie.** You know I have always told you, that speaking in public was but a knack, which those who apply to most will succeed in best. Two old Members, very good judges, have sent me compliments upon this occasion; and have assured me, that they plainly find *it will do*, though they perceived, from that natural confusion you were in, that you neither said all nor perhaps what you intended. Upon the whole, you have set out very well, and have sufficient encouragement to go on. Attend therefore assiduously, and observe carefully all that passes in the House; for it is only knowledge and experience that can make a debater. But if you still want comfort, Mrs. ——,* I hope, will administer it to you; for, in my opinion, she may, if she will, be very comfortable; and with women, as with speaking in Parliament, perseverance will most certainly prevail, sooner or later.

What little I have played for here, I have won; but that is very far from the considerable sum which you heard of. I play every evening from seven till ten, at a crown whist party, merely to save my eyes from reading or writing for three hours by candle-light. I propose being in town the week after next, and hope to carry back with me much more health than I brought down here.

Good night.   Yours.

91. TO SOLOMON DAYROLLES, ESQ.

BLACKHEATH, JUNE 17, 1756

DEAR DAYROLLES,

Could I give you better accounts of either myself or the public, I would give you more frequent ones; but the best that I can give you of either, are such as will not flatter that affection which I know you have for both. We are both going very fast, and I can hardly guess which will be gone first. I am shrunk to a skeleton, and grow weaker and weaker every day. And as for my fellow-sufferer the public, it has lost Minorca by the incapacity of the administration; and may perhaps soon lose Gilbraltar, by a secret bargain between France and Spain, which, I have reason to think, is negotiating, if not concluded. Our naval laurels are withered by the unaccountable and shameful conduct of Admiral Byng.[*]

The French are unquestionably masters to do what they please in America. Our good Ally, the Queen of Hungary, has certainly concluded some treaty, God knows what, with our and her old enemy France. The Swedish and Danish fleets are joined, undoubtedly not in our favour, since France pays both. We have an army here of threescore thousand men, under a Prince of the Blood, to defend us against an invasion which was never really intended. We cannot pay it another year, since the expense of this year amounts to twelve millions sterling; judge if we can raise that sum another year, and, to complete all, the two Courts, the old and the young one, are upon very ill terms.[*]

These are not the gloomy apprehensions of a sick man; but real facts, obvious to whoever will see and reflect. One of the chief causes of this unfortunate situation is, that we have now in truth no Minister; but the Administration is a mere Republic, and carried on by the Cabinet Council,* the individuals of which think only how to get the better of each other. Let us then turn our eyes, as much as we can, from this melancholy prospect, which neither of us can mend, and think of something else. I find my nephew Sir Charles Hotham is a true English gentleman, and does not relish your outlandish folks.

I am told that you have an infinite number of English gentlemen now at Brussels; but I hope you do not put yourself upon the foot of stuffing them with salt beef, and drenching them with claret; for I am sure your appointments will not afford that expense, and by the way, I believe, that in their hearts they would much rather you would let them alone, to be jolly together at their inns, than go to your house, where, it is ten to one, that they would meet *des honnêtes gens, et ce n'est pas là leur fait.**

Make my compliments to Mrs. Dayrolles, to my godson, to *tutti quanti,** in short, who can receive them, for *Mademoiselle* cannot yet. Adieu, my dear and faithful friend. May you, and all who belong to you, be long happy, whatever becomes of

Yours.

92. TO SOLOMON DAYROLLES, ESQ.

LONDON, FEBRUARY 28, 1757

DEAR DAYROLLES,

I have been too long in your debt; but the true reason has been, that I had no specie* to pay you in; and what I give you even now does not amount to a penny in the pound. Public matters have been long, and are still, too undecipherable for me to understand, consequently to relate. Fox, out of place, takes the lead in the House of Commons; Pitt, Secretary of State, declares that he is no minister, and has no ministerial influence.* The Duke of Newcastle and Lord Hardwicke lie by, and declare themselves for neither party, and in the meantime, I presume, negotiate with both. Byng is reprieved for a fortnight; what will become of him at last, God knows! for the late Admiralty want to shoot him, to excuse themselves; and the present Admiralty want to save him, in order to lay the blame upon their predecessors; for neither the public service, nor the life of a fellow creature, enter into the consideration on either side. The Duke of Cumberland wants extremely to go with his own Regiment of Guards, to be beaten at the head of the Army of Observation, in Lower Saxony; for that will infallibly be the case of that army as soon as Comte D'Etrées at the head of one hundred thousand men shall arrive there.*

The fright, that your friend Mr. Van-haren has put the Dutch into, by telling them the French army is intended for Cleves and Gueldres, is a most idle alarm. They are not of importance enough to be in danger; nobody thinks of them now. Hanover is evidently the object, and the only rational one, of the operations of the French army; not as Hanover, but as belonging to the King of England, and that Electorate is to be a reply to the present state of Saxony. The fields of Bohemia and Moravia will become Golgothas, or fields of blood, this year; for probably an hundred thousand human creatures will perish there this year, for the quarrel of two individuals.* The King of Prussia, will, I suppose, seek for battle, in which, I think, he will be victorious. The Austrians will,

I suppose, avoid it if they can, and endeavour to destroy his armies, as they did the French ones in the last war, by harassing, intercepting convoys, killing stragglers, and all the feats of their irregulars.* These are my political dreams, or prophecies, for perhaps they do not deserve the name of reasonings.

The Bath did me more good than I thought anything could do me; but all that good does not amount to what builders call half-repairs, and only keeps up the shattered fabric a little longer than it would have stood without them; but take my word for it, it will stand but a very little while longer. I am now in my grand climacteric, and shall not complete it. Fontenelle's last words at a hundred and three were, *Je souffre d'être;* deaf and infirm as I am, I can with truth say the same thing at sixty-three. In my mind it is only the strength of our passions, and the weakness of our reason, that makes us so fond of life; but when the former subside and give way to the latter, we grow weary of being and willing to withdraw. I do not recommend this train of serious reflections to you, nor ought you to adopt them. Our ages, our situations, are widely different. You have children to educate and provide for, you have all your senses, and can enjoy all the comforts both of domestic and social life. I am in every sense *isolé*, and have wound up all my bottoms; I may now walk off quietly, neither missing nor being missed. Till when,

Yours most sincerely.

P.S. My compliments to Mrs. Dayrolles and company, visible or invisible.*

93. TO MAJOR IRWINE

SIR,

The installation is to be at Windsor on this day fort-night, the 29th; it is a foolish piece of pageantry, but worth seeing once. The ceremony in the Chapel is the most solemn, and consequently the silliest, part of the show. The tickets for that operation are the pretended property of the Dean and Chapter. I will take care to procure you one. I will also try to procure you a ticket for the feast, though it is full late. There you will dine very ill and very inconveniently; but, however, with the comfort of hearing the style and titles of the puissant knights proclaimed by Garter King at Arms. I take it for granted that Mrs. Irwine is to be of your Windsor party, and I will endeavour to accommodate you both as far as I can.* She made you too favourable a report of my health; which you have too easily believed, from wishing it true. It is vegetation at most, and I should be very sorry if my fellow-vegetables at Blackheath were not in a more lively and promising state than   Yours, etc.

94. TO HIS SON

BLACKHEATH, SEPTEMBER 17, 1757

MY DEAR FRIEND:

Lord Holderness has been so kind as to communicate to me all the letters which he has received from you hitherto, dated the 15th, 19th, 23rd, and 26th August; and also a draught of that which he wrote to you the 9th instant. I am very well pleased with all your letters; and, what is better, I can tell you that the King is so too; and he said, but three days ago, to

Monsieur Münchausen,* *He* (meaning you) *sets out very well, and I like his letters; provided that, like most of my English Ministers abroad, he does not grow idle hereafter.* So that here is both praise to flatter, and a hint to warn you. What Lord Holderness recommends to you, being by the King's order, intimates also a degree of approbation; for the *blacker ink, and the larger character*, show that his Majesty, whose eyes are grown weaker, intends to read all your letters himself. Therefore, pray do not neglect to get the blackest ink you can; and to make your secretary enlarge his hand, though *d'ailleurs* it is a very good one.

Had I been to wish an advantageous situation for you, and a good *début* in it, I could not have wished you either, better than both have hitherto proved. The rest will depend entirely upon yourself; and I own I begin to have much better hopes than I had; for I know, by my own experience, that the more one works, the more willing one is to work. We are all, more or less, *des animaux d'habitude*. I remember very well, that when I was in business, I wrote four or five hours together every day, more willingly than I should now half an hour; and this is most certain, that when a man has applied himself to business half the day, the other half goes off the more cheerfully and agreeably. This I found so forcibly when I was at the Hague, that I never tasted company so well, nor was so good company myself, as at the suppers of my post-days. I take Hamburgh now to be *le centre du refuge Allemand*. If you have any Hanover *refugiés* among them, pray take care to be particularly attentive to them. How do you like your house? Is it a convenient one? Have the *Casserolles** been employed in it yet? You will find *les petits soupers fins* less expensive, and turn to better account, than large dinners for great companies.

I hope you have written to the Duke of Newcastle; I take it for granted that you have to all your brother Ministers of the northern department. For God's sake be diligent, alert, active, and indefatigable in your business. You want nothing but labour and industry to be, one day, whatever you please, in your own way.

We think and talk of nothing here but Brest, which is universally supposed to be the object of our great expedition.* A great and important object it is. I suppose the affair must be *brusqué*, or it will not do. If we succeed, it will make France put some water to its wine. As for my own private opinion, I own I rather wish than hope success. However, should our expedition fail, *Magnis tamen exidit ausis*,* and that will be better than our late languid manner of making war.

To mention a person to you whom I am very indifferent about, I mean myself, I vegetate still just as I did when we parted; but I think I begin to be sensible of the autumn of the year; as well as of the autumn of my own life. I feel an internal awkwardness, which, in about three weeks, I shall carry with me to the Bath, where I hope to get rid of it, as I did last year. The best cordial I could take, would be to hear, from time to time, of your industry and diligence; for in that case I should consequently hear of your success. Remember your own motto, *Nullum numen abest si sit prudentia*.* Nothing is truer. Yours.

95. TO HIS SON

MY DEAR FRIEND:

I write to you now, because I love to write to you; and hope that my letters are welcome to you; for otherwise I have very little to inform you of. The King of Prussia's late victory,* you are better informed of than we are here. It has given infinite joy to the unthinking public, who are not aware that it comes too late in the year, and too late in the war, to be attended with any very great consequence. There are six or seven thousand of the human species less than there were a month ago, and that seems to me to be all. However, I am glad of it, upon account of the pleasure and the glory which it gives the King of Prussia, to whom I wish well as a Man, more than as a King. And surely he is so great a man, that had he lived seventeen or eighteen hundred years ago, and his life been transmitted to us in a language that we could not very well understand, I mean either Greek or Latin, we should have talked of him as we do now of your Alexanders, your Caesars, and others, with whom, I believe, we have but a very slight acquaintance. *Au reste*, I do not see that his affairs are much mended by this victory. The same combination of the great powers of Europe against him still subsists, and must at last prevail. I believe the French army will melt away, as is usual, in Germany; but his army is extremely diminished by battles, fatigues, and desertion: and he will find great difficulties in recruiting it, from his own already exhausted dominions. He must therefore, and to be sure will, negotiate privately with the French, and get better terms that way than he could any other.

The report of the three General Officers,* the Duke of Marlborough, Lord George Sackville, and General Waldegrave, was laid before the King last Saturday, after their having sat four days upon Mordaunt's affair: nobody yet knows what it is; but it is generally believed, that Mordaunt will be brought to a court-martial. That you may not mistake this matter, as most people here do, I must explain to you, that this examination, before the three above-mentioned General Officers, was by no means a trial; but only a previous inquiry into his conduct, to see whether there was, or was not, cause to bring him to a regular trial before a court-martial. The case is exactly parallel to that of a grand jury; who, upon a previous and general examination, find, or do not find, a bill, to bring the matter before the petty jury; where the fact is finally tried. For my own part, my opinion is fixed upon that affair: I am convinced that the expedition was to be defeated; and nothing that can appear before a court-martial can make me alter that opinion. I have been too long acquainted with human nature, to have great regard for human testimony: and a very great degree of probability, supported by various concurrent circumstances, conspiring in one point, will have much greater weight with me, than human testimony upon oath, or even upon honour; both which I have frequently seen considerably warped by private views.

The Parliament, which now stands prorogued to the first of next month, it is thought will be put off for some time longer, till we know in what light to lay before it the state of our alliance with Prussia, since the conclusion of the Hanover neutrality;* which, if it did not quite break it, made at least a great flaw in it.

The birthday was neither fine nor crowded; and no wonder, since the King was that day seventy-five. The old Court and the young one are much better together, since the Duke's retirement; and the King has presented the Prince of Wales with a service of plate.*

I am still *unwell*, though I drink these waters very regularly. I will stay here at least six weeks longer, where I am much quieter than I should be allowed to be in town. When things are in such a miserable situation as they are at present, I desire neither to be concerned nor consulted, still less quoted. Adieu!

96. TO EARL STANHOPE*

LONDON, MAY 13, 1758

MY DEAR LORD,

I am so odd a fellow, that I have still some regard for my country, and some concern for my conscience. I cannot serve the one, and I would not hurt the other; and therefore, for its quiet and safety, give me leave to put it into your keeping, which I do by the bit of parchment here enclosed, signed, and sealed, and which your Lordship will be pleased to have filled up with your name. If I am not much mistaken, we agree entirely in opinion for the Habeas Corpus Bill* now depending in the House of Lords; and I am confirmed in that opinion by a conversation I have lately had with a very able opposer of the Bill, in which I reduced him to this one argument, that the Bill was unnecessary. If only unnecessary, why not pass it *ex abundante*,* to satisfy people's minds upon a subject of that importance? But leave it in the breasts of the Judges, and they will do what is right. I am by no means sure of that; and my doubts upon that head are warranted by the State Trials, in which there is hardly an instance of any person prosecuted by the Crown, whom the Judges have not very partially tried, and, if they could bring it about with the jury, condemned right or wrong. We have had ship-money Judges, dispensing Judges, but I never read of any patriot Judges, except in the Old Testament; and those perhaps were only so, because at that time there was no King in Israel.* There is certainly some prerogative trick in this conspiracy of the lawyers to throw out this Bill; for, as no good reason is given for it, it may fairly be presumed that the true one is a bad one. I am going next week to settle at Blackheath, in the quiet and obscurity that best become me now, where you and Lady Stanhope, when you have nothing better to do, will always find a very indifferent dinner, and

A very faithful servant.

97. TO THE BISHOP OF WATERFORD

BLACKHEATH, MAY 23, 1758

MY DEAR LORD,
I have received your letter of the 4th instant. The day afterwards I received the book which you was so kind as to send me by Major Macculough; and the day after that, by Mr. Russel,* your bill for expenses incurred and not provided for, which I have paid.

Now, first, to the first. You solicit a very poor employment so modestly, and offer your daughters as security for your good behaviour, that I cannot refuse it you, and do hereby appoint you my sole Commissioner for the kingdom of Ireland. To the second. This ninth volume of Swift will not do him so much honour, as I hope it will bring profit to my friend George Faulkner. The historical part is a party pamphlet, founded on the lie of the day, which, as Lord Bolingbroke who had read it often assured me, was coined and delivered out to him, to write *Examiners*, and other political papers upon. That spirit remarkably runs through it. Macartney, for instance, murdered Duke Hamilton; nothing is falser, for though Macartney was very capable of the vilest actions, he was guiltless of that, as I myself can testify, who was at his trial in the King's Bench, when he came over voluntarily to take it, in the late King's time. There did not appear even the least ground for a suspicion of it; nor did Hamilton, who appeared in Court, pretend to tax him with it, which would have been in truth accusing himself of the utmost baseness, in letting the murderer of his friend go off from the field of battle, without either resentment, pursuit, or even accusation, till three days afterwards. This *lie* was invented to inflame the Scotch nation against the Whigs; as the other, that Prince Eugene intended to murder Lord Oxford, by employing a set of people called Mohocks (which Society, by the way, never existed), was calculated to inflame the mob of London. Swift took those hints *de la meilleure foi du monde*, and thought them materials for history.* So far he is blameless.

Thirdly and lastly, I have paid Mr. Russel the twenty-seven pounds five shillings, for which you drew your bill. I hope you are sensible that I need not have paid it till I had received the goods, or at least till I had proofs of your having sent them; but where I have in general a good opinion of the person, I always proceed frankly, and do not stand upon forms; and I have without flattery so good an opinion of you, that I would trust you not only with twenty-seven pounds, but even as far as thirty-seven.

Your friend's letter to you, inclosed in the book, is an honest and melancholic one, but what can I do in it? He seems not to know the nature of factions in Ireland, the prevailing for the time being is absolute, and whoso transgresseth the least of their commandments is guilty of the whole.* A Lord-Lieutenant may if he pleases govern alone, but then he must, as I know by experience, take a great deal more trouble upon himself than most Lord-Lieutenants care to do, and he must not be afraid; but as they commonly prefer *otium cum dignitate*,* their guards, their battle-axes, and their trumpets, not to mention perhaps the profits of their post, to a laborious execution of it, they must necessarily rule by a faction, of which faction for the time being they are only the first slaves. The condition of the obligation is this: Your Excellency or your Grace wants to carry on his Majesty's business smoothly, and to have it to say, when you go back, that you met with no difficulties; this we have sufficient strength in Parliament to engage for, provided we appear to have the favour and countenance of the Government; the money, be it what it will, shall be cheerfully voted; as for the public you shall do what you will, or nothing at all, for we care for that no more than we suppose your Grace or Excellency does, but we repeat it again, our recommendation to places, pensions, etc. must prevail, or we shall not be able to keep our people in order. These are always the expressed, or at least the implied, conditions of these treaties, which either the indolence or the insufficiency of the Governors ratify: from that moment these *undertakers* bury the Governor alive, but indeed pompously;

different from the worshipful Company of Undertakers here, who seldom bury any body alive, or at least never without the consent and privity of the next heirs.

I am now settled here for the summer, perhaps for ever, in great tranquillity of mind, not equally of body; I make the most of it, I vegetate with the vegetables, and I crawl with the insects in my garden, and I am, such as I am, most faithfully and sincerely   Yours.

98. TO HIS SON

BLACKHEATH, MAY 30, 1758

MY DEAR FRIEND:

I have no letter from you to answer, so this goes to you unprovoked. But *à propos* of letters; you have had great honour done you, in a letter from a fair and Royal hand, no less than that of her Royal Highness the Princess of Cassel; she has written your panegyric to her sister, Princess Amelia,* who sent me a compliment upon it. This has likewise done you no harm with the King, who said gracious things upon that occasion. I suppose you had for her Royal Highness those attentions, which I wish to God you would have, in due proportions, for everybody. You see, by this instance, the effects of them; they are always repaid with interest. I am more confirmed by this in thinking that, if you can conveniently, you should ask leave to go for a week to Cassel, to return your thanks for all favours received.

I cannot expound to myself the conduct of the Russians. There must be a trick in their not marching with more expedition. They have either had a sop from the King of Prussia, or they want an animating dram from France and Austria.* The King of Prussia's conduct always explains itself by the events; and, within a very few days, we must certainly hear of some very great stroke from that quarter. I think I never in my life remember a period of time so big with great events as the present: within two months, the fate of the House of Austria will probably be decided: within the same space of time, we shall certainly hear of the taking of Cape Breton, and of our army's proceeding to Quebec: within a few days, we shall know the good or ill success of our great expedition; for it is sailed; and it cannot be long before we shall hear something of the Prince of Brunswick's operations, from whom I also expect good things. If all these things turn out, as there is good reason to believe they will, we may once, in our turn, dictate a reasonable peace to France, who now pays seventy *per cent.* insurance upon its trade, and seven *per cent.* for all the money raised for the service of the year.*

Comte Bothmar has got the small-pox, and of a bad kind. Kniphausen diverts himself much here; he sees all places and all people, and is ubiquity itself. Michel,* who was much threatened, stays at last at Berlin, at the earnest request of the King of Prussia. Lady Coventry is safely delivered of a son, to the great joy of that noble family. The expression of a woman's having brought her husband a son, seems to be a proper and cautious one; for it is never said, from whence.

I was going to ask you how you passed your time now at Hamburgh, since it is no longer the seat of strangers and of business; but I will not, because I know it is to no purpose. You have sworn not to tell me.

Sir William Stanhope told me that you promised to

send him some Old Hock from Hamburgh, and so you
did—not. If you meet with any superlatively good,
and not else, pray send over a *foudre** of it, and write
to him. I shall have a share in it. But unless you find
some, either at Hamburgh or at Bremen, uncommonly
and almost miraculously good, do not send any. *Dixi**
                                                    Yours.

99. TO HIS SON

LONDON, NEW-YEAR'S DAY, 1759

MY DEAR FRIEND,

Molti e felici,* and I have done upon that subject, one
truth being fair, upon the most lying day in the whole
year.

I have now before me your last letter of the 21st
December, which I am glad to find is a bill of health;
but, however, do not presume too much upon it, but
obey and honour your physician, 'that thy days may
be long in the land'.*

Since my last, I have heard nothing more concerning
the riband; but I take it for granted it will be disposed
of soon. By the way, upon reflection, I am not sure
that any body but a Knight can, according to form,
be employed to make a Knight. I remember that Sir
Clement Cotterel was sent to Holland, to dub the late
Prince of Orange, only because he was a Knight himself; and I know that the proxies of Knights, who cannot attend their own installations, must always be
Knights.* This did not occur to me before, and perhaps will not to the person who was to recommend
you: I am sure I will not stir it; and I only mention it
now, that you may be in all events prepared for the
disappointment, if it should happen.

Grevenkop is exceedingly flattered with your account, that three thousand of his countrymen, all as little as himself, should be thought a sufficient guard upon three and twenty thousand of all the nations in Europe;*not that he thinks himself, by any means, a little man, for when he would describe a tall handsome man, he raises himself up at least half an inch to represent him.

The private news from Hamburg is, that his Majesty's Resident there is woundily in love with Madame ——; if this be true, God send him, rather than her, a good *delivery*! She must be *étrennée**at this season, and therefore I think you should be so to; so draw upon me as soon as you please, for one hundred pounds.

Here is nothing new, except the unanimity with which the Parliament gives away a dozen of millions sterling;*and the unanimity of the public is as great in approving of it, which has stifled the usual political and polemical argumentations.

Cardinal Bernis's*disgrace is as sudden, and hitherto as little understood, as his elevation was. I have seen his poems, printed at Paris, not by a friend, I dare say; and to judge by them, I humbly conceive his Eminency is a puppy. I will say nothing of that excellent head-piece that made him and unmade him in the same month, except *O King, live for ever*.

Good-night to you, whomever you pass it with.

100. TO HIS SON

LONDON, MARCH 30, 1759

MY DEAR FRIEND:
I do not like these frequent, however short, returns of your illness; for I doubt they imply either want of skill in your physician, or want of care in his patient.

Rhubarb, soap, and chalybeate*medicínes and waters, are always specifics for obstructions of the liver; but then a very exact regimen is necessary, and that for a long countinuance. Acids are good for you, but you do not love them; and sweet things are bad for you, and you do love them. There is another thing very bad for you, and I fear you love it too much. When I was in Holland, I had a slow fever, that hung upon me a great while; I consulted Boerhaave, who prescribed me what I suppose was proper, for it cured me; but he added, by way of postscript to his prescription, *Venus rarius colatur :*which I observed, and perhaps that made the medicines more effectual.

I doubt we shall be mutually disappointed in our hopes of seeing one another this spring, as I believe you will find, by a letter which you will receive at the same time with this, from Lord Holderness; but as Lord Holderness will not tell you all, I will, between you and me, supply that defect. I must do him the justice to say, that he has acted in the most kind and friendly manner possible to us both. When the King read your letter, in which you desired leave to return, for the sake of drinking the Tunbridge waters, he said, 'If he wants steel waters, those of Pyrmont*are better than Tunbridge, and he can have them very fresh at Hamburgh. I would rather he had asked to come last autumn, and had passed the winter here; for if he returns now, I shall have nobody in those quarters to inform me of what passes; and yet it will be a very busy and important scene.' Lord Holderness, who found that it would not be liked, resolved to push it no farther; and replied, he was very sure, that when you knew his Majesty had the least objection to your return at this time, you would think of it no longer;

and he owned that he (Lord Holderness) had given you encouragement for this application, last year, then thinking and hoping that there would be little occasion for your presence at Hamburgh this year. Lord Holderness will only tell you, in his letter, that, as he had some reason to believe his moving this matter would be disagreeable to the King, he resolved, for your sake, not to mention it. You must answer his letter upon that foot singly, and thank him for this mark of his friendship, for he has really acted as your friend. I make no doubt of your having willing leave to return in autumn, for the whole winter. In the mean time, make the best of your *séjour*, where you are; drink the Pyrmont waters, and no wine but Rhenish, which, in your case, is the only proper one for you.

Next week, Mr. Harte will send you his Gustavus Adolphus* in two quartos; it will contain many new particulars of the life of that real hero, as he has had abundant and authentic materials which have never yet appeared. It will, upon the whole, be a very curious and valuable history; though, between you and me, I could have wished that he had been more correct and elegant in his style. You will find it dedicated to one of your acquaintance, who was forced to prune the luxuriant praises bestowed upon him, and yet has left enough of all conscience to satisfy a reasonable man. Harte has been very much out of order these last three or four months, but is not the less intent upon sowing his Lucerne, of which he had six crops last year, to his infinite joy, and, as he says, profit. As a gardener, I shall probably have as much joy, though not quite so much profit, by thirty or forty shillings; for there is the greatest promise of fruit this year at Blackheath, that ever I saw in my life. Vertumnus and Pomona have been very propitious to me; as for Priapus,* that tremendous garden god, as I no longer invoke him, I cannot expect his protection from the birds and the thieves.

Adieu! I will conclude like a pedant, *Levius fit patientia quicquid corrigere est nefas.**

101. TO HIS SON

LONDON, APRIL 16, 1759

MY DEAR FRIEND:

With humble submission to you, I still say, that if Prince Ferdinand can make a defensive campaign this year, he will have done a great deal, considering the great inequality of numbers. The little advantages of taking a regiment or two prisoners, or cutting another to pieces, are but trifling articles in the great account; they are only the pence, the pounds are yet to come; and I take it for granted, that neither the French, nor the Court of Vienna, will have *le démenti* of their main object, which is unquestionably Hanover; for that is the *summa summarum*; and they will certainly take care to draw a force together for this purpose, too great for any that Prince Ferdinand has, or can have, to oppose them. In short, mark the end on't, *j'en augure mal.* If France, Austria, the Empire, Russia, and Sweden, are not, at long run, too hard for the two electors of Hanover and Brandenburgh, there must be some invisible Powers, some tutelar Deities, that miraculously interpose in favour of the latter.*

You encourage me to accept all the powers that goats, asses, and bulls, can give me, by engaging for my not making an ill use of them; but I own, I cannot help distrusting myself a little, or rather human nature:

for it is an old and very true observation, that there are misers of money, but none of power; and the non-use of the one, and the abuse of the other, increase in proportion to their quantity.

I am very sorry to tell you, that Harte's Gustavus Adolphus does not take at all, and consequently sells very little: it is certainly informing, and full of good matter; but it is as certain too, that the style is execrable: where the devil he picked it up, I cannot conceive, for it is a bad style, of a new and singular kind; it is full of Latinisms, Gallicisms, Germanisms, and all *isms* but Anglicisms; in some places pompous, in others vulgar and low. Surely, before the end of the world, people, and you in particular, will discover, that the *manner*, in everything, is at least as important as the matter; and that the latter never can please, without a good degree of elegancy in the former. This holds true in everything in life: in writing, conversing, business, the help of the Graces is absolutely necessary; and whoever vainly thinks himself above them, will find he is mistaken, when it will be too late to court them, for they will not come to strangers of an advanced age. There is an History lately come out, of the Reign of Mary Queen of Scots, and her son (no matter by whom) King James, written by one Robertson, a Scotchman, which for clearness, purity, and dignity of style, I will not scruple to compare with the best historians extant, not excepting Davila, Guicciardini, and perhaps Livy.* Its success has consequently been great, and a second edition is already published and bought up. I take it for granted that it is to be had, or at least borrowed, at Hamburgh, or I would send it you.

I hope you drink the Pyrmont waters every morning. The health of the mind depends so much on the health of the body, that the latter deserves the utmost attention, independently of the senses. God send you a very great share of both! Adieu!

102. TO HIS SON

LONDON, APRIL 27, 1759

MY DEAR FRIEND,

I have received your two letters of the 10th and 13th, by the last mail; and I will begin my answer to them, by observing to you, that a wise man, without being a Stoic, considers, in all misfortunes that befall him, their best as well as their worst side; and everything has a better and a worse side. I have strictly observed that rule for many years, and have found by experience that some comfort is to be extracted, under most moral ills, by considering them in every light, instead of dwelling, as people are too apt to do, upon the gloomy side of the object. Thank God, the disappointment that you so pathetically groan under, is not a calamity which admits of no consolation. Let us simplify it, and see what it amounts to. You were pleased with the expectation of coming here next month, to see those who would have been pleased with seeing you. That, from very natural causes, cannot be; and you must pass this summer at Hamburgh, and next winter in England, instead of passing this summer in England, and next winter at Hamburgh. Now, estimating things fairly, is not the change rather to your advantage? Is not the summer more eligible, both for health and pleasure, than the winter, in that northern, frozen Zone?—and will not the winter in England supply you with more pleasures than the summer in an empty capital could have done? So far then it appears that you are rather a gainer by your misfortune.

The *tour*, too, which you propose making to Lubeck, Altona,* etc., will both amuse and inform you; for, at your age, one cannot see too many different places and people, since at the age you are now of, I take it for granted, that you will not see them superficially, as you did, when you first went abroad.

This whole matter then, summed up, amounts to no more than this—that you will be here next winter, instead of this summer. Do not think that all I have said is the consolation only of an old philosophical fellow, almost insensible of pleasure or pain, offered to a young fellow, who has quick sensations of both. No; it is the rational philosophy taught me by experience and knowledge of the world, and which I have practised above thirty years. I always made the best of the best, and never made bad worse, by fretting. This enabled me to go through the various scenes of life, in which I have been an actor, with more pleasure, and less pain, than most people. You will say perhaps, one cannot change one's nature; and that, if a person is born of a very sensible gloomy temper, and apt to see things in the worst light, they cannot help it, nor new-make themselves. I will admit it to a certain degree, and but to a certain degree; for, though we cannot totally change our nature, we may in a great measure correct it, by reflection and philosophy; and some philosophy is a very necessary companion in this world, where, even to the most fortunate, the chances are greatly against happiness.

I am not old enough, nor tenacious enough, to pretend not to understand the main purport of your last letter; and to show you that I do, you may draw upon me for two hundred pounds, which I hope will more than clear you.

Good-night! *aequam memento rebus in arduis servare mentem;** be neither transported nor depressed by the accidents of life.

103. TO HIS SON

BLACKHEATH, MAY 16, 1759

MY DEAR FRIEND,

Your secretary's last letter of the 4th, which I received yesterday, has quieted my fears a good deal, but has not entirely dissipated them. *Your fever still continues,* he says, *though in a less degree.* Is it a continued fever, or an intermitting one? If the former, no wonder that you are weak, and that your head aches. If the latter, why has not the bark,* in substance and large doses, been administered? for, if it had, it must have stopped it by this time. Next post, I hope, will set me quite at ease. Surely you have not been so regular as you ought, either in your medicines or in your general regimen, otherwise this fever would not have returned; for the Doctor calls it, *your fever returned,* as if you had an exclusive patent for it. You have now had illnesses enough, to know the value of health, and to make you implicitly follow the prescriptions of your physician in medicines, and the rules of your own common sense in diet; in which, I can assure you, from my own experience, that quantity is often worse than quality; and I would rather eat half a pound of bacon at a meal, than two pounds of any the most wholesome food.

I have been settled here near a week, to my great satisfaction; *c'est ma place,* and I know it, which is not given to everybody. Cut off from social life by my deafness, as well as other physical ills, and being at best but the ghost of my former self, I walk here in silence and solitude as becomes a ghost: with this only difference, that I walk by day, whereas, you know, to be sure, that other ghosts only appear by night. My health, however, is better than it was last year, thanks to my almost total milk diet. This enables me to vary my solitary amusements, and alternately to scribble as well as read, which I could not do last year. Thus I saunter away the remainder, be it more or less, of an agitated and active life, now reduced (and I am not sure I am a loser by the change) to so quiet and serene a one, that it may properly be called, still life.

The French whisper in confidence, in order that it may be the more known and the more credited, that they intend to invade us this year, in no less than three places; that is, England, Scotland, and Ireland. Some of our great men, like the Devils, believe and tremble; others, and one little one, whom I know, laugh at it; and in general, it seems to be but a poor, instead of a formidable scarecrow. While somebody was at the head of a moderate army, and wanted (I know why) to be at the head of a great one, intended invasions were made an article of political faith;* and the belief of them was required, as in the Church the belief of some absurdities, and even impossibilities, is required upon pain of heresy, excommunication, and consequently damnation, if they tend to the power and interest of the Heads of the Church. But now there is a general toleration, and that the best Subjects, as well as the best Christians, may believe what their reason and their consciences suggest. It is generally and rationally supposed, the French will threaten and not strike, since we are so well prepared, both by armies and fleets, to receive, and, I may add, to destroy them. Adieu! God bless you.

104. TO ARTHUR CHARLES STANHOPE,* ESQ.

BLACKHEATH, SEPTEMBER 29, 1764

SIR,

I have forwarded your letters to their respective owners. That to Edwyn Stanhope was a very proper one. You must know that our kinsman has very strong and warm animal spirits, with a genius not quite so warm, and having nothing to do, is of course busy about trifles, which he takes for business, and sits upon them assiduously, as a certain bird, much in request upon this day particularly, does upon a piece of chalk, taking it for an egg. My boy [1] was with me on Thursday for the last time this season. He was very well, but had a little breaking out about his lips, for which I made him take a little manna,* which has done him good. He has an excellent appetite, and prefers the *haut gout*, when he can get it: and the more so, I believe, because he cannot get it at school. I indulge him but little in it, when he dines with me; for you know that I do not deal much in it myself. But when he spies anything in that taste at table, he begs so hard, that I dare not refuse him, having promised him, provided he learns well, not to refuse him anything he asks for: which promise he often puts me in mind of, without putting me to any great expense; for his last demand was a hoop to drive, value twopence. It is certain that there is a great deal of stuff put into his noddle by snatches and starts, and by no means digested as it ought to be, and will certainly be in time. When you write to him, pray tell him that his sister's application and knowledge often make you wish that she were your son, and he your daughter; for I have hinted to him, that I was informed you had said something like it to Dr. Plumptre.*

I am, etc.

105. TO ARTHUR CHARLES STANHOPE, ESQ.

LONDON, OCTOBER 12, 1765

SIR,

In answer to the favour of your last letter, in which you desire my opinion concerning your third marriage,* I must freely tell you, that in matters of religion and matrimony I never give any advice; because I will not have anybody's torments in this world or the next laid to my charge. You say that you find yourself lonely and melancholic at Mansfield, and I believe it; but then the point for your mature consideration is, whether it is not better to be alone than in bad company, which may very probably be your case with a wife. I may possibly be in the wrong, but I tell you very sincerely, with all due regard to the sex, that I never thought a woman good company for a man *tête-à-tête*, unless for one purpose, which, I presume, is not yours now. You had singular good fortune with your last wife, who has left you two fine children, which are as many as any prudent man would desire. And how would you provide for more? Suppose you should have five or six, what would you do for them? You have sometimes expressed concern about leaving your daughter a reasonable fortune: then what must be your anxiety, if to Miss Margaret, now existing, you should add a Miss Mary, a Miss Betty, a Miss Dolly, etc.; not to mention a Master Ferdinando, a

Master Arthur, etc. My brother gave me exactly the same reasons that you do for marrying his third wife. He was weary of being alone, and had, by God's good providence, found out a young woman of a retired disposition, and who had been bred up prudently under an old grandmother in the country; she hated and dreaded a London life, and chose to amuse herself at home with her books, her drawing, and her music. How this fine prospect turned out, I need not tell you. It turned out well, however, for my boy.*

Notwithstanding all these objections, I made your proposal to my sister and her girl, because you desired it. But it would not do: for they considered that her fortune, which is no great one, joined to yours, which is no great one neither, would not be sufficient for you both, even should you have no children; but if you should have any, which is the most probable side of the question, they could not have a decent provision. And that is true. Moreover, she has always led a town life, and cannot bear the thoughts of living in the country even in summer. Upon the whole, you will marry or not marry, as you think best; but to take a wife merely as an agreeable and rational companion, will commonly be found to be a grand mistake. Shakespeare seems to be a good deal of my opinion, when he allows them only this department,

> To suckle fools and chronicle small beer.*

I am just now come to town to settle for the winter, except an excursion to Bath. I shall see my boy on Monday or Tuesday next, and I am apt to think that we shall be very glad to meet. I shall now soon know what to trust to with Mr. Dodd.*

I am, etc.

106. TO HIS GODSON

BATH, OCT. 31, 1765

MY DEAR LITTLE BOY,

Our correspondence has hitherto been very desultory and various, my letters have had little or no relation to each other, and I endeavoured to suit them to your age and passion for variety. I considered you as a child, and trifled with you accordingly, and though I cannot yet look upon you as a man, I shall consider you as being capable of some serious reflections. You are now above half a man, for before your present age is doubled you will be quite a man: Therefore *paulo majora canamus.** You already know your religious and moral duties, which indeed are exceedingly simple and plain; the former consist in fearing and loving your Creator, and in observing His laws which He has writ in every man's heart, and which your conscience will always remind you of, if you will but give it a fair hearing. The latter, I mean your moral duties, are fully contained in these few words *do as you would wish to be done by.** Your Classical Knowledge, others more able than myself, will instruct you in. There remains therefore nothing in which I can be useful to you, except to communicate to your youth and inexperience, what a long observation and knowledge of the world enables me to give you. I shall then for the future write you a series of letters, which I desire you will read over twice and keep by you, upon the *Duty*, the *Utility*, and the *Means* of pleasing, that is, of being what the French call *Aimable*, an art, which, it must be owned, they possess almost exclusively. They have studied it the most, and they practise it the best. I shall therefore often borrow their expressions in my following letters, as answering my ideas better than any I can find in my own language. Remember then and fix it well in your mind, that whoever is not *Aimable* is in truth no body at all with regard to the general intercourse of life. His learning is Pedantry, and even his virtues have no Lustre.

Perhaps my subject may sometimes oblige me to say things above your present *portée*, but in proportion as your understanding opens and extends itself, you will understand them, and then *haec olim meminisse juvabit*.* I presume you will not expect elegancy, or even accuracy, in letters of this kind which I write singly for your use. I give you my matter just as it occurs to me. May it be useful to you, for I do not mean it for public perusal.

If you were in this place it would quite turn your little head, here would be so much of your dear variety, that you would think rather less if possible than most of the company, who saunter away their whole time, and do nothing.

107. TO HIS SON

BATH, NOVEMBER 28, 1765

MY DEAR FRIEND,

I have this moment received your letter of the 10th. I have now been here near a month, bathing and drinking the waters, for complaints much of the same kind as yours, I mean pains in my legs, hips, and arms; whether gouty or rheumatic, God knows; but, I believe, both, that fight without a decision in favour of either, and have absolutely reduced me to the miserable situation of the Sphynx's riddle,* to walk upon three legs; that is, with the assistance of my stick, to walk, or rather hobble, very indifferently.

I wish it were a declared gout, which is the distemper
of a gentleman; whereas the rheumatism is the distemper of a hackney-coachman or chairman, who are
obliged to be out in all weathers and at all hours.

I think you will do very right to ask leave, and I
dare say you will easily get it, to go to the baths in
Suabia;*that is, supposing you have consulted some
skilful physician, if such a one there be, either at
Dresden or at Leipsig, about the nature of your distemper, and the nature of those baths; but, *suos quisque
patimur manes.* We have but a bad bargain, God
knows, of this life, and patience is the only way not
to make bad worse. Mr. Pitt keeps his bed here, with
a very real gout, and not a political one, as is often
suspected.

Here has been a Congress of most of the *ex
Ministres,* as the Duke of Bedford, George Grenville,
Lord Sandwich, Lord Gower; in short, all of them but
Lord Halifax. If they have raised a battery, as I suppose they have, it is a masked one, for nothing has
transpired; only they confess that they intend a most
vigorous attack. *D'ailleurs*, there seems to be a total
suspension of all business, till the meeting of the
Parliament, and then *Signa canant.* I am very glad
that, at this time, you are out of it; and for reasons
that I need not mention: you would certainly have
been sent for over, and, as before, not paid for your
journey.

Poor Harte is very ill, and condemned to the Hot-
well at Bristol. He is a better poet than philosopher;*
for all this illness and melancholy proceeds originally
from the ill success of his Gustavus Adolphus. He is
grown extremely devout, which I am very glad of,
because that is always a comfort to the afflicted.

I cannot present Mr. Larpent* with my New-year's gift till I come to town, which will be before Christmas at farthest; till when, God bless you! Adieu.

108. TO HIS GODSON

BATH, DEC. 12, 1765

MY DEAR LITTLE BOY,

If you have not command enough over yourself to conquer your humour, as I hope you will, and as I am sure every rational creature may have, never go into company while the fit of ill humour is upon you. Instead of companies diverting you in those moments, you will displease and probably shock them, and you will part worse friends than you met. But whenever you find in yourself a disposition to sullenness, contradiction, or testiness, it will be in vain to seek for a cure abroad; stay at home, let your humour ferment and work itself off. Cheerfulness and good humour are of all qualifications the most amiable in company, for though they do not necessarily imply good nature and good breeding, they act them at least very well, and that is all that is required in mixed company. I have indeed known some very ill-natured people who are very good humoured in company, but I never knew any body generally ill humoured in company, who was not essentially ill natured. Where there is no malevolence in the heart, there is always a cheerfulness and ease in the countenance and the manners. By good humour and cheerfulness, I am far from meaning noisy mirth and loud peals of laughter, which art the distinguishing characteristics of the vulgar and of the ill-bred, whose mirth is a kind of a storm. Observe it, the vulgar often laugh, but never smile, whereas well-bred people often smile, and seldom or never laugh. A witty thing never excited laughter, it pleases only the mind and never distorts the countenance. A glaring absurdity, a blunder, a silly accident, and those things that are generally called Comical may excite a momentary laugh, though never a loud nor a long one among well bred people. Sudden passion is called a short lived madness; it is a madness indeed, but the fits of it generally return so often in choleric people that it may well be called a continual madness. Should you happen to be of this unfortunate disposition, which God forbid, make it your constant study to subdue, or at least to check it. When you find your choler rising, resolve neither to speak to, nor answer the person who excites it, but stay till you find it subsiding, and then speak deliberately. I have known many people, who by the rapidity of their speech have run away with themselves into a passion. I will mention to you a trifling and perhaps you will think a ridiculous receipt, towards checking the excess of passion, of which I think that I have experienced the utility myself. Do everything in Minuet time, speak, think, and move always in that measure, equally free from the dulness of slow, or the hurry and huddle of quick time. This movement moreover will allow you some moments to think forwards, and the Graces to accompany what you say or do, for they are never represented as either running, or dozing. Observe a man in a passion, see his eyes glaring, his face inflamed, his limbs trembling, and his tongue stammering, and faltering with rage, and then ask yourself calmly, whether you would upon any account be that human wild beast. Such creatures are hated and dreaded in all companies where they are let loose, as people do not choose to be exposed to the disagreeable

necessity of either knocking down these brutes or
being knocked down by them. Do on the contrary
endeavour to be cool and steady upon all occasions.
The advantages of such a steady calmness, are innumerable, and would be too tedious to relate. It may
be acquired by care and reflection. If it could not, that
reason which distinguishes men from brutes, would be
given us to very little purpose. As a proof of this,
I never saw, and scarcely ever heard of a quaker in a
passion. In truth there is in that sect, a decorum, a
decency, and an amiable simplicity, that I know in no
other. Having mentioned the *Graces* in this letter,
I cannot end it, without recommending to you most
earnestly the advice of the wisest of the Ancients, to
sacrifice to them devoutly and daily. When they are
propitious they adorn everything and engage everybody.—But are they to be acquired? Yes to a certain
degree they are, by attention, observation, and assiduous worship. Nature, I admit, must first have made
you capable of adopting them, and then observation
and imitation will make them in time your own.
There are *Graces* of the mind as well as of the body;
the former giving an easy engaging turn to the
thoughts and the expressions, the latter to motions,
attitude and address. No man perhaps ever possessed
them all; he would be too happy that did, but if you
will attentively observe those graceful and engaging
manners, which please you most in other people, you
may easily collect what will equally please others in
you, and engage the majority of the *Graces* on your
side, insure the casting vote, and be returned *Aimable*.
There are people whom the *Précieuse* of Molière, very
justly, though very affectedly calls, *les Antipodes des
Graces.* If these unhappy people are formed by

nature invincibly *Maussades**and awkward, they are to be pitied, rather than blamed or ridiculed, but nature has disinherited few people to that degree.

109. TO HIS GODSON

BATH, DEC. 18, 1765

MY DEAR LITTLE BOY,

If God gives you Wit, which I am not sure that I wish you, unless He gives you at the same time an equal portion at least of judgment to keep it in good order, wear it like your sword in the scabbard, and do not brandish it to the terror of the whole company. If you have real wit it will flow spontaneously and you need not aim at it, for in that case the rule of the Gospel is reversed, and it will prove, seek and you shall *not* find.* Wit is so shining a quality, that everybody admires it, most people aim at it, all people fear it, and few love it unless in themselves. A man must have a good share of wit himself to endure a great share of it in another. When wit exerts itself in satire it is a most malignant distemper; wit it is true may be shown in satire, but satire does not constitute wit, as most fools imagine it does. A man of real wit will find a thousand better occasions of showing it. Abstain therefore most carefully from satire, which though it fall upon no particular person in company, and momentarily from the malignity of the human heart, pleases all; upon reflection, it frightens all too, they think it may be their turn next, and will hate you for what they find you could say of him, more than be obliged to you for what you do not say. Fear and hatred are next door neighbours. The more wit you have the more good nature and politeness you must show, to induce people to pardon your superiority, for that is no easy matter.

Learn to shrink yourself to the size of the company you are in, take their tone whatever it may be, and excel in it if you can, but never pretend to give the tone; a free conversation will no more bear a Dictator than a free Government will. The character of a man of wit is a shining one that every man would have if he could, though it is often attended by some inconveniences; the dullest Alderman ever aims at it, cracks his dull joke, and thinks, or at least hopes that it is Wit. But the denomination of *a Wit*, is always formidable, and very often ridiculous. These titular *wits* have commonly much less wit, than petulance and presumption. They are at best *les rieurs de leur quartier*,* in which narrow sphere they are at once feared and admired. You will perhaps ask me, and justly, how considering the delusion of self-love and vanity, from which no man living is absolutely free, how you shall know whether you have Wit or not. To which the best answer I can give you is, not to trust to the voice of your own judgment, for it will deceive you. Nor to your ears, which will always greedily receive flattery, if you are worth being flattered; but trust only to your eyes, and read in the countenances of good company, their approbation, or dislike of what you say. Observe carefully too, whether you are sought for, solicited, and in a manner pressed into good company. But even all this will not absolutely ascertain your wit, therefore do not upon this encouragement flash your wit in people's faces a *ricochets*, in the shape of *bon mots*, epigrams, small repartées, etc., have rather less, than more, wit than you really have. A wise man will live at least as much within his wit as within his income. Content yourself with good sense and reason, which at long run are sure to please everybody who has either.

If wit comes into the bargain, welcome it, but never invite it. Bear this truth always in your mind, that you may be admired for your wit if you have any, but that nothing but good sense and good qualities can make you be loved. They are substantial, every day's wear. Wit is for *les jours de Gala*, where people go chiefly to be stared at.

I received your last letter which is very well writ. I shall see you next week, and bring you some pretty things from hence, because I am told that you have been a very good boy, and have learned well.

110. TO HIS SON

LONDON, DECEMBER 27, 1765

MY DEAR FRIEND,

I arrived here from Bath last Monday, rather, but not much better than when I went thither. My rheumatic pains, in my legs and hips, plague me still; and I must never expect to be quite free from them.

You have, to be sure, had from the office an account of what the Parliament did, or rather did not do, the day of their meeting; and the same point will be the great object at their next meeting; I mean the affair of our American Colonies, relatively to the late imposed Stamp-duty, which our colonists absolutely refuse to pay. The administration are for some indulgence and forbearance to those froward children of their mother country; the Opposition are for taking vigorous, as they call them, but I call them violent measures; not less than *les dragonades;**and to have the tax collected by the troops we have there. For my part, I never saw a froward child mended by whipping; and I would not have the mother country become a step-mother. Our trade to America brings in, *communibus annis,* two millions a year; and the Stamp-duty is estimated at but one hundred thousand pounds a year; which I would by no means bring into the stock of the Exchequer, at the loss or even the risk of a million a year to the national stock.

I do not tell you of the Garter given away yesterday, because the newspapers will; but I must observe that the Prince of Brunswick's riband*is a mark of great distinction to that family; which, I believe, is the first (except our own Royal family) that has ever had two blue ribands at a time; but it must be owned they deserve them.

One hears of nothing now, in town, but the separation of men and their wives. Will Finch the ex-Vice Chamberlain, Lord Warwick, your friend Lord Boling-broke.* I wonder at none of them for parting; but I wonder at many for still living together; for in this country it is certain that marriage is not well understood.

I have this day sent Mr. L'arpent two hundred pounds for your Christmas box, of which I suppose he will inform you by this post. Make this Christmas as merry a one as you can; for *pour le peu de bon tems qui nous reste, rien n'est si funeste qu'un noir chagrin*.* For the new years; God send·you many, and happy ones! Adieu.

III. TO HIS GODSON

BATH, DEC. 28, 1765

MY DEAR LITTLE BOY,

There is a species of minor wit, which is much used and much more abused, I mean Raillery. It is a most mischievous and dangerous weapon, when in unskilful or clumsy hands, and it is much safer to let it quite alone

than to play with it, and yet almost everybody does
play with it though they see daily the quarrels and
heart burnings that it occasions. In truth it implies
a supposed superiority, in the *railleur* to the *raillé*,
which no man likes even the suspicion of in his own
case, though it may divert him in other people's. An
innocent *raillerie* is often inoffensively begun, but
very seldom inoffensively ended, for that depends
upon the *Raillé* who, if he cannot defend himself well
grows brutal, and if he can, very possibly his *railleur*,
baffled and disappointed, becomes so. It is a sort of
trial of wit, in which no man can patiently bear to have
his inferiority made appear. The character of a *Railleur*
is more generally feared, and more heartily hated than
any one I know in the world. The injustice of a bad
man is sooner forgiven than the insult of a witty one.
The former only hurts one's liberty or property, but
the latter hurts and mortifies that secret pride, which
no human breast is free from. I will allow that there
is a sort of raillery which may not only be inoffensive but even flattering, as when by a genteel irony
you accuse people of those imperfections which they
are most notoriously free from, and consequently
insinuate that they possess the contrary virtues. You
may safely call Aristides* a knave, or a very handsome
woman an ugly one; but take care, that neither the
man's character, nor the Lady's beauty, be in the least
doubtful. But this sort of raillery requires a very light
and steady hand to administer it. A little too rough,
it may be mistaken into an offence, and a little too
smooth, it may be thought a sneer, which is a most
odious thing. There is another sort, I will not call it
of wit, but rather of merriment and buffoonery, which
is *mimicry*; the most successful mimic in the world is

always the most absurd fellow, and an Ape is infinitely his superior. His profession is to imitate and ridicule those natural defects and deformities for which no man is in the least accountable, and in their imitation of them, make themselves for the time as disagreeable and shocking as those they mimic. But I will say no more of those creatures, who only amuse the lowest rabble of mankind. There is another sort of human animals, called *wags*, whose profession is to make the company laugh immoderately, and who always succeed provided the company consist of fools, but who are greatly disappointed in finding that they never can alter a muscle in the face of a Man of sense. This is a most contemptible character, and never esteemed, even by those who are silly enough to be diverted by them. Be content both for yourself, with sound good sense, and good manners, and let Wit be thrown into the bargain where it is proper and inoffensive. Good sense will make you be esteemed, good manners be loved, and wit give a lustre to both. In whatever company you happen to be, whatever pleasures you are engaged in, though perhaps not of a very laudable kind, take care to preserve a great Personal dignity. I do not in the least mean a pride of birth or rank, that would be too silly, but I mean a dignity of character. Let your moral character of Honesty and Honour, be unblemished and even unsuspected; I have known some people dignify even their vices, first, by never boasting of them, and next by not practising them in an illiberal and indecent manner. . . . If they loved drinking too well, they did not practise at least that beastly vice in beastly company, but only indulged it sometimes in those companies whose wit and good humour, in some degree seemed to excuse it, though nothing can justify it. When you see a drunken man, as probably you will see many, study him with attention, and ask yourself soberly whether you would upon any account, be that Beast, that disgrace to human reason. The Lacedaemonians very wisely made their slaves drunk, to deter their children from being so, and with good effect, for nobody ever yet heard of a Lacedaemonian drunk.*

112. TO HIS GODSON

[Undated.

MY DEAR LITTLE BOY,

Carefully avoid all affectation either of mind or body. It is a very true and a very trite observation that no Man is ridiculous for being what he really is, but for affecting to be what he is not. No Man is awkward by nature, but by affecting to be genteel; and I have known many a man of common sense pass generally for a fool, because he affected a degree of wit that God had denied him. A Ploughman is by no means awkward in the exercise of his trade, but would be exceedingly ridiculous, if he attempted the air and graces of a Man of Fashion. You learned to dance but it was not for the sake of dancing, but it was to bring your air and motions back to what they would naturally have been, if they had had fair play, and had not been warped in your youth by bad examples and awkward imitations of other boys. Nature may be cultivated and improved both as to the body and as to the mind, but it is not to be extinguished by art, and all endeavours of that kind are absurd, and an inexhaustible fund for ridicule. Your body and mind must be at ease, to be agreeable; but Affectation is a perpetual constraint, under which no man can be genteel in his carriage, or pleasing in his conversation. Do you think that your motions would be easy or graceful if you wore the clothes of another Man much slenderer or taller than yourself? Certainly not; it is the same thing with the mind, if you affect a character that does not fit you, and that nature never intended for you. But here do not mistake, and think that it follows from hence that you should exhibit your whole character to the Public because it is your natural one. No. Many things must be suppressed, and many occasionally concealed in the best character. Never force Nature, but it is by no means necessary to show it all. Here discretion must come to your assistance, that sure and safe Guide through life; discretion that necessary companion to reason, and the useful *Garde-fou*,* if I may use that expression, to wit and imagination. Discretion points out the *A propos*, the *Decorum*, the *Ne quid Nimis*,* and will carry a Man of moderate parts further, than the most shining parts would without it. It is another word for *Judgment* though not quite synonymous to it. Judgment is not upon all occasions required, but discretion always is. Never affect nor assume a particular character, for it will never fit you but will probably give you a ridicule, but leave it to your conduct, your virtues, your morals and your manners, to give you one. Discretion will teach you to have particular attention to your *Mœurs* which we have no one word in our language to express exactly. *Morals*, are too much, *Manners* too little, Decency comes the nearest to it, though rather short of it. Cicero's word *Decorum* is properly the thing, and I see no reason why that expressive word, should not be adopted, and naturalized in our language, I have never scrupled using it in that sense. *A propos* of words, study your own language more carefully than most English people do. Get a habit of speaking it with propriety and elegance. For there are few things more disagreeable than to hear a Gentleman talk the barbarisms, the solecisms, and the Vulgarisms of Porters. Avoid on the other hand, a stiff and formal accuracy, especially what the women call *hard words*, when plain ones as expressive are at hand. The French make it a study to *bien narrer*, and to say the truth they are apt to *narrer trop*,* and with too affected an elegancy. The three commonest topics of conversation are Religion, Politics and News. All people think that they understand the two first perfectly, though they never studied either, and are therefore very apt to talk of them both, dogmatically and ignorantly, consequently with warmth. But Religion is by no means a proper subject of conversation in a mixed company. It should only be treated among a very few people of learning, for mutual instruction. It is too awful and respectable a subject to become a familiar one. Therefore, never mingle yourself in it, any further than to express a universal toleration and indulgence to all.errors in it, if conscientiously entertained; for every man has as good a right to think as he does, as you have to think as you do, nay in truth he cannot help it. As for Politics, they are still more universally understood, and as every one thinks his private interest more or less concerned in them, nobody hesitates to pronounce decisively upon them, not even the ladies; the copiousness of whose eloquence is more to be admired upon that subject, than the conclusiveness of their logic. It will be impossible for you to avoid engaging in these conversations, for there are hardly any others, but take care to do it very coolly and with great good humour; and whenever you find that the company begins to be heated and noisy for the good of their country, be only a patient hearer, unless you can interpose by some agreeable *badinage* and restore good-humour to the company. And here I cannot help observing to you that nothing is more useful either to put off or to parry disagreeable and puzzling affairs, than a good humoured and genteel *badinage*. I have found it so by long experience, but this *badinage* must not be carried to *mauvaise plaisanterie*. It must be light, without being frivolous, sensible without being sententious, and in short have that pleasing *je ne sçay quoy*, which everybody feels and nobody can describe.

I shall now suspend for a time the course of these letters, but as the subject is inexhaustible, I shall occasionally resume it, in the meantime believe and remember that a man who does not generally please is nobody, and that constant endeavours to please, will infallibly please, to a certain degree, at least.

113. TO HIS SON

BLACKHEATH, AUGUST 1, 1766

MY DEAR FRIEND:

The curtain was at last drawn up, the day before yesterday, and discovered the new actors, together with some of the old ones. I do not name them to you, because to-morrow's Gazette will do it full as well as I could. Mr. Pitt, who had *carte blanche* given him, named every one of them; but what would you think he named himself for? Lord Privy Seal; and (what will astonish you, as it does every mortal here) Earl of Chatham.* The joke here is, that he has had *a fall upstairs*, and has done himself so much hurt, that he will never be able to stand upon his legs again. Everybody is puzzled how to account for this step; and in my mind it can have but two causes; either he means to retire from business, or he has been the dupe of Lord Bute and a great lady.* The latter seems to me, of the two, the most probable, though it would not be the first time that great abilities have been duped by low cunning. But be it what it will, he is now certainly only Earl of Chatham; and no longer Mr. Pitt, in any respect whatever. Such an event, I believe, was never read nor heard of. To withdraw, in the fulness of his power, and in the utmost gratification of his ambition, from the House of Commons (which procured him his power, and which alone could insure it to him), and to go into that Hospital of Incurables, the House of Lords, is a measure so unaccountable, that nothing but proof positive could have made me believe it: but true it is. Hans Stanley is to go Embassador to Russia; and my nephew, Ellis, to Spain, decorated with the red riband. Lord Shelburne is your Secretary of State, which I suppose he has notified to you this post, by a circular letter. He has abilities, but is proud above them, so pray lay him on pretty thick in your answer to his circular. Charles Townshend has now the sole management of the House of Commons; but how long he will be content to be only Lord Chatham's vicegerent there, is a question which I will not pretend to decide.* There is one very bad sign for Lord Chatham, in his new dignity; which is, that all his enemies, without exception, rejoice at it; and all his friends are stupified and dumb-founded. If I mistake not much, he will, in the course of a year, enjoy perfect *otium cum dignitate*.* Enough of politics.

Is the fair, or at least the fat, Miss Chudleigh with

you still? It must be confessed that she knows the arts of Courts; to be so received at Dresden, and so connived at in Leicester-fields.*

There never was so wet a summer as this has been, in the memory of man; we have not had one single day, since March, without some rain; but most days a great deal. I hope that does not affect your health, as great cold does; for, with all these inundations, it has not been cold. God bless you!

114. TO THE COUNTESS OF SUFFOLK*

(WRITTEN IN THE CHARACTER OF HIS FOOTMAN)

BATH, NOVEMBER 6, 1766

MAY IT PLEASE YOUR LADYSHIP,

My Lord told me as how that it was your Ladyship's orders that I should write you a card to acquaint you how he did after his journey hither; but with submission to his Lordship, I thought that that would be too great a presumption in one like me, to a lady of your quality, to send you such a card as we carry twenty times a day in town, and therefore I chose the way of a letter as the most respectful of the two. For you must know that we London footmen pick up a sort of second-hand good manners from keeping good company, and especially from waiting at table, where we glean up some scraps of our master's good-breeding— if they have any.

To say the truth, I cannot very well understand why my Lord would rather employ my hand than his own in writing to your Ladyship; and, if I dare say so, I think he was a good deal out in point of breeding, which I wonder at the more, because I have heard him say that there was nobody in the world that he honoured and respected more than your Ladyship, and that you was the oldest acquaintance, friend, and fellow-servant that he had; and, indeed, I believe he spoke what he thought, for you know he could have no reason for telling an untruth in my hearing, who was not then very likely to have an opportunity of telling it you again.

But to come to the point, my Lord was very much fatigued with his journey, not being (as I heard him say) what he was *thirty* years ago—I believe he might have said *fifty*. However, he is pretty well for him, but often complains that he feels a sensible decay both of body and mind, and, between you and I, I think not without reason; for I, who see him every day, can, notwithstanding, observe a considerable alteration in him, and by no means for the better; and so I rest, with duty and respect, etc. Thomas Allen.

115. TO THE COUNTESS OF SUFFOLK
(WRITTEN IN THE CHARACTER OF HIS FOOTMAN)
BATH, NOVEMBER, 1766

MADAM,

When I made bould to write last to your Ladyship it was by my Lord's order, and, as he said, by your Ladyship's too; but I fear it is great presumption in me to trouble you now, as I do, upon my own account. The case is this: I received a letter some time agone from one Mrs. Wagstaff,* whom I am not acquainted with, and so do not know in what manner to address her, but must beg your Ladyship's directions, for fear of offending her. If she is Mrs. with a surname, she is above the livery, and belongs to the upper servants; but if she be Mrs. only with her Christian name—as,

Mrs. Betty, Mrs. Mary, Mrs. Dolly, etc., our cloth often looks as high as that, and they often condescend to look as low as us. Now, when I know Mrs. Wagstaff's station in life, I will either answer her letter, or refer it to my Lord's valet-de-chamber; for we of the cloth have lately improved very much both in style and propriety, by the great number of cards that we daily carry to and from the nobility and gentry, which are models of fine writing.

Now, Madam, it is time to give you some account of my Lord, for whom you show so friendly a regard. He is as well as can be expected in his condition; as is usually said of ladies in child-bed, or in great affliction for the death of somebody they did not care for. Now, I heard his Lordship say very lately at table, that he was seventy-three complete, with a shattered carcase, as he was pleased to call it. To say the truth, I believe my Lord did live a little too freely formerly; but I can assure your Ladyship that he is now very regular, and even more so, I believe, than I am. But he is still very cheerful; and as an instance of it, a gentleman having said at table that the women dressed their heads here three or four stories high—'Yes,' said my Lord, 'and I believe every story is inhabited, like the lodging-houses here; for I observe a great deal of scratching.' I thought this comical enough to tell it your Ladyship; and to confess the truth, I repeated it as my own to some of my brethren of the cloth, and they relished it wonderfully. My Lord often mentions your Ladyship with great regard and respect, and Miss Hotham* with great affection and warmth for an old gentleman. And so I remain, etc.   THOMAS ALLEN.

116. TO HIS SON

BLACKHEATH, JULY 9, 1767

MY DEAR FRIEND,

I have received yours of the 21st past, with the enclosed proposal from the French *réfugiés*, for a subscription towards building them *un Temple*.* I have shown it to the very few people I see, but without the least success. They told me (and with too much truth) that whilst such numbers of poor were literally starving here from the dearness of all provisions, they could not think of sending their money into another country, for a building which they reckoned useless. In truth, I never knew such misery as is here now; and it affects both the hearts and the purses of those who have either; for my own part, I never gave to a building in my life; which I reckon is only giving to masons and carpenters, and the treasurer of the undertaking.

Contrary to the expectations of all mankind here, everything still continues *in statu quo*. General Conway has been desired by the King to keep the seals till he has found a successor for him, and the Lord President*the same. Lord Chatham is relapsed, and worse than ever: he sees nobody, and nobody sees him; it is said, that a bungling physician has checked his gout, and thrown it upon his nerves; which is the worst distemper that a minister or a lover can have, as it debilitates the mind of the former, and the body of the latter. Here is at present an interregnum. We must soon see what order will be produced from this chaos. It will be what Lord Bute pleases.*

The Electorate, I believe, will find the want of Comte Flemming;* for he certainly had abilities; and was as sturdy and inexorable as a Minister at the head of

finances ought always to be. When you see Comtesse
Flemming, which I suppose cannot be of some time,
pray make her Lady Chesterfield's and my compliments of condolence.

You say that Dresden is very sickly; I am sure
London is at least as sickly now, for there reigns an
epidemical distemper, called by the genteel name of
l'influenza. It is a little fever, of which scarcely anybody dies; and it generally goes off with a little loose-
ness. I have escaped it, I believe, by being here. God
keep you from all distempers, and bless you!

117. TO HIS SON

BATH, DECEMBER 19, 1767

MY DEAR FRIEND,

Yesterday I received your letter of the 29th past, and
am very glad to find that you are well enough to think
that you may perhaps stand the winter at Dresden;
but if you do, pray take care to keep both your body
and your limbs exceedingly warm.

As to my own health, it is, in general, as good as I
could expect it, at my age; I have a good stomach, a
good digestion, and sleep well; but find that I shall
never recover the free use of my legs, which are now
full as weak as when I first came hither.

You ask me questions concerning Lord Chatham,
which neither I, nor, I believe, anybody but himself
can answer; however, I will tell you all that I do know,
and all that I guess, concerning him. This time twelvemonth he was here, and in good health and spirits,
except now and then some little twinges of the gout.
We saw one another four or five times, at our respective houses; but for these last eight months, he has

been absolutely invisible to his most intimate friends, *les sous Ministres*: he would receive no letters, nor so much as open any packet about business.

His physician, Dr. Addington,* as I am told, had very ignorantly checked a coming fit of the gout, and scattered it about his body; and it fell particularly upon his nerves, so that he continues exceedingly vapourish; and would neither see nor speak to anybody, while he was here. I sent him my compliments, and asked leave to wait upon him; but he sent me word, that he was too ill to see anybody whatsoever. I met him frequently taking the air in his post-chaise, and he looked very well. He set out from hence for London, last Tuesday; but what to do, whether to resume, or finally to resign the Administration, God knows; conjectures are various. In one of our conversations here, this time twelvemonth, I desired him to secure you a seat in the new Parliament; he assured me he would, and, I am convinced, very sincerely; he said even that he would make it his own affair; and desired I would give myself no more trouble about it. Since that, I have heard no more of it; which made me look out for some venal borough: and I spoke to a borough-jobber, and offered five and twenty hundred pounds for a secure seat in Parliament; but he laughed at my offer, and said, that there was no such thing as a borough to be had now, for that the rich East and West Indians had secured them all, at the rate of three thousand pounds at least; but many at four thousand; and two or three that he knew, at five thousand.* This, I confess, has vexed me a good deal, and made me the more impatient to know whether Lord Chatham had done anything in it; which I shall know when I go to town, as I propose to do in about a fortnight; and as soon as I know it you shall. To tell you truly what I think—I doubt, from all these *nervous disorders*, that Lord Chatham is *hors de combat*, as a Minister; but do not even hint this to anybody. God bless you!

118. TO HIS SON

LONDON, MARCH 12, 1768

MY DEAR FRIEND:

The day after I received your letter of the 21st past, I wrote to Lord Weymouth, as you desired; and I send you his answer enclosed, from which (though I have not heard from him since) I take it for granted, and so may you, that his silence signifies his Majesty's consent to your request.* Your complicated complaints give me great uneasiness, and the more, as I am convinced that the Montpellier physicians have mistaken a material part of your case; as indeed all physicians here did, except Dr. Maty.* In my opinion, you have no gout, but a very scorbutic and rheumatic habit of body, which should be treated in a very different manner from the gout; and, as I pretend to be a very good quack, at least, I would prescribe to you a strict milk diet, with the seeds, such as rice, sago, barley, millet, etc., for the three summer months at least, and without ever tasting wine. If climate signifies anything (in which, by the way, I have very little faith) you are, in my mind, in the finest climate in the world; neither too hot nor too cold, and always clear; you are with the gayest people living; be gay with them, and do not wear out your eyes with reading at home. *L'ennui* is the English distemper; and a very bad one it is, as I find by every day's experience; for my deafness deprives me of the only rational pleasure that I can have at my age, which is society; so that I read my eyes out every day, that I may not hang myself.

You will not be in this Parliament, at least not in the beginning of it. I relied too much upon Lord Chatham's promise above a year ago, at Bath. He desired that I would leave it to him; that he would make it his own affair, and give it in charge to the Duke of Grafton,* whose province it was to make the parliamentary arrangement. This I depended upon, and I think with reason; but, since that, Lord Chatham has neither seen nor spoken to anybody, and has been in the oddest way in the world. I sent to the Duke of Grafton, to know if Lord Chatham had either spoken or sent to him about it; but he assured me that he had done neither: that all was full, or rather running over, at present: but that, if he could crowd you in upon a vacancy, he would do it with great pleasure. I am extremely sorry for this accident; for I am of a very different opinion from you, about being in Parliament, as no man can be of consequence in this country, who is not in it; and, though one may not speak like a Lord Mansfield or a Lord Chatham, one may make a very good figure in a second rank. *Locus est et pluribus umbris.* I do not pretend to give you any account of the present state of this country, or Ministry, not knowing nor guessing it myself.*

God bless you, and send you health, which is the first and greatest of all blessings!

119. TO HIS SON

BATH, OCTOBER 17, 1768

MY DEAR FRIEND:

Your two last letters, to myself and Grevenkop, have alarmed me extremely; but I comfort myself a little, by hoping that you, like all people who suffer, think yourself worse than you are. A dropsy never comes so suddenly; and I flatter myself, that it is only that gouty or rheumatic humour, which has plagued you so long, that has occasioned the temporary swelling of your legs. Above forty years ago, after a violent fever, my legs were swelled as much as you describe yours to be; I immediately thought that I had a dropsy; but the Faculty* assured me, that my complaint was only the effect of my fever, and would soon be cured; and they said true. Pray let your amanuensis, whoever he may be, write an account regularly once a week, either to Grevenkop or myself, for that is the same thing, of the state of your health.

I sent you, in four successive letters, as much of the Duchess of Somerset's* snuff as a letter could well convey to you. Have you received all or any of them? and have they done you any good? Though, in your present condition, you cannot go into company, I hope you have some acquaintances that come and sit with you; for if originally it was not good for man to be alone, it is much worse for a sick man to be so; he thinks too much of his distemper, and magnifies it. Some men of learning among the Ecclesiastics, I daresay, would be glad to sit with you; and you could give them as good as they brought.

Poor Harte, who is here still, is in a most miserable condition; he has entirely lost the use of his left side, and can hardly speak intelligibly. I was with him yesterday. He inquired after you with great affection, and was in the utmost concern when I showed him your letter.

My own health is as it has been ever since I was here last year. I am neither well nor ill, but *unwell*. I have in a manner, lost the use of my legs; for though I can make a shift to crawl upon even ground for a quarter of an hour, I cannot go up or down stairs, unless supported by a servant.

God bless, and grant you a speedy recovery!*

120. TO MRS. EUGENIA STANHOPE*

(AT PARIS)

LONDON, MARCH 16, 1769

MADAM,

A troublesome and painful inflammation in my eyes obliges me to use another hand than my own, to acknowledge the receipt of your letter from Avignon, of the 27th past.

I am extremely surprised that Mrs. du Bouchet should have any objection to the manner in which your late husband desired to be buried, and which you, very properly, complied with.* All I desire, for my own burial, is not to be buried alive; but how or where, I think, must be entirely indifferent to every rational creature.

I have no commission to trouble you with, during your stay at Paris; from whence, I wish you and the boys a good journey home; where I shall be very glad to see you all, and assure you of my being, with great truth,

Your faithful, humble servant.

121. TO ALDERMAN FAULKNER*

LONDON, MARCH 25, 1769

MY WORTHY FRIEND,

A violent inflammation in my eyes, which is not yet quite removed, hindered me from acknowledging your last letter sooner; I regretted this delay the more, as I was extremely impatient to return, through you, my heartiest thanks to the Dublin Society, for the honour they have done me, by remembering in so advantageous a manner, and after so long an interval, an old and hearty friend and well-wisher.* Pray tell them, that I am much prouder of the place they have given me amongst those excellent citizens, my old friends Prior, Madden, Swift, etc., who benefited and improved mankind, than I should be of one amongst heroes, conquerors, and monarchs, who generally disturb and destroy their species. I did nothing for the Society but what everybody, in my then situation, must and would have done; so that I have not the least merit upon that score; and I was aware that jobs would creep into the Society, as they do now into every Society in England, as well as in Ireland, but neither that fear nor that danger should hinder one from founding or encouraging establishments that are in the main useful. Considering the times, I am afraid it is necessary that jobs should come; and all one can do is to say, woe be to him from whom the job cometh; and to extract what public good one can out of it. You give me great pleasure in telling me that drinking is a good deal lessened; may it diminish more and more every day! I am convinced, that could an exact calculation be made of what Ireland has lost within these last fifty years in its trade, manufactures, manners, and morals, by drunkenness, the sum total would frighten the most determined guzzler of either claret or whisky, into sobriety.

I have received, and thank you for, the volumes you sent me of Swift, whom you have enriched me with in every shape and size. Your liberality makes me ashamed, and I could wish that you would rather be my book-*seller* than my book-*giver*. Adieu, I am, very sincerely,　　　　　　　　　　　　Yours, etc.

122. TO MRS. EUGENIA STANHOPE

(IN LONDON)

WEDNESDAY (1769)

MADAM,

The last time I had the pleasure of seeing you, I was so taken up in playing with the boys, that I forgot their more important affairs. How soon would you have them placed at school? When I know your pleasure as to that, I will send to Monsieur Perny,* to prepare everything for their reception. In the mean time, I beg that you will equip them thoroughly with clothes, linen, etc., all good, but plain; and give me the account, which I will pay; for I do not intend, that, from this time forwards, the two boys should cost you one shilling.

I am with great truth, yours, etc.

123. TO MRS. EUGENIA STANHOPE

THURSDAY MORNING (1769)

MADAM,

As some day must be fixed for sending the boys to school, do you approve of the 8th of next month? by which time the weather will probably be warm and settled, and you will be able to equip them completely.

I will, upon that day, send my coach to you, to carry you and the boys to Loughborough House, with all their immense baggage. I must recommend to you, when you leave them there, to suppress, as well as you can, the overflowings of maternal tenderness; which would grieve the poor boys the more, and give them a terror of their new establishment. I am with great truth,

Yours, etc.

124. TO MRS. EUGENIA STANHOPE

BATH, OCTOBER II, 1769

MADAM,

Nobody can be more willing or ready to obey orders than I am; but then I must like the orders and the orderer. Your orders and yourself come under this description; and therefore I must give you an account of my arrival and existence, such as it is, here. I got hither last Sunday, the day after I left London, less fatigued than I expected to have been; and now crawl about this place upon my three legs, but am kept in countenance by many of my fellow crawlers: the last part of the Sphynx's riddle*approaches, and I shall soon end, as I began, upon all fours.

When you happen to see either Monsieur or Madame Perny, I beg you will give them this *melancholic* proof of my caducity, and tell them, that the last time I went to see the boys, I carried the Michaelmas quarterage in my pocket, and when I was there I totally forgot it; but assure them, that I have not the least intention to bilk them, and will pay them faithfully, the two quarters together, at Christmas.

I hope our two boys are well; for then I am sure you are so.

I am, etc.

125. TO MRS. EUGENIA STANHOPE

BATH, NOVEMBER 5, 1769

MADAM,

I remember very well the paragraph which you quote from a letter of mine to Mrs. du Bouchet, and see no reason yet to retract that opinion, *in general*, which at least nineteen widows in twenty had authorised. I had not then the pleasure of your acquaintance; I had seen you but twice or thrice; and I had no reason to think that you would deviate, as you have done, from other widows, so much, as to put perpetual shackles upon yourself, for the sake of your children; but (if I may use a vulgarism) one swallow makes no summer: five righteous were formerly necessary to save a city, and they could not be found;*so, till I find four more such righteous widows as yourself, I shall entertain my former notions of widowhood in general.

I can assure you that I drink here very soberly and cautiously, and at the same time keep so cool a diet, that I do not find the least symptom of heat, much less of inflammation. By the way, I never had that complaint, in consequence of having drank these waters; for I have had it but four times, and always in the middle of summer. Mr. Hawkins*is timorous, even to *minuties*, and my sister delights in them.

Charles will be a scholar, if you please; but our little Philip, without being one, will be something or other as good, though I do not yet guess what. I am not of the opinion generally entertained in this country, that man lives by Greek and Latin alone; that is, by knowing a great many words of two dead languages, which nobody living knows perfectly, and which are of no use in the common intercourse of life. Useful knowledge, in my opinion, consists of modern languages, history, and geography; some Latin may be thrown in to the bargain, in compliance with custom and for closet amusement.

You are, by this time, certainly tired with this long letter, which I could prove to you from Horace's own words (for I am a *scholar*) to be a bad one; he says, that water-drinkers can write nothing good;* so I am, with real truth and esteem,   Yours, etc.

126. TO THE BISHOP OF WATERFORD

LONDON, AUGUST 15, 1770

MY DEAR LORD,

The linen, which you were so kind as to procure me, dropped out of the clouds into my house in town last week, and is declared, by better judges than I am, very good, and very cheap. I shall not thank you for it; but, on the contrary, expect your thanks for giving you an opportunity of doing what always gives you pleasure, *clothing the naked.** I am sure that, could you equally relieve all my other wants, you would; but there is no relief for the miseries of a crazy old age, but patience; and, as I have many of Job's ills, I thank God, I have some of his patience too; and I consider my present wretched old age as a just compensation for the follies, not to say sins, of my youth.

I send you here inclosed some melon-seed, of the best and largest Cantelupe kind; and also of the green Persian sort, as much as I can venture at one time with the post; but, as none can be sown at this time of the year, I will from time to time send you more, so that you shall have of different kinds before the season. Adieu, my dear Lord; my eyes will have it so.

127. TO THE BISHOP OF WATERFORD

LONDON, AUGUST 12, 1771

MY DEAR LORD,

I received your kind letter three days ago, and make haste to acknowledge it, never knowing nor guessing what may happen to me from one day to another. I am most prodigiously old, and every month of the calendar adds at least a year to my age. My hand trembles to that degree that I can hardly hold my pen, my understanding stutters, and my memory fumbles. I have exhausted all the physical ills of Pandora's box,* without finding hope at the bottom of it; but who can hope at seventy-seven? One must only seek for little comforts at that age. One of mine is, that all my complaints are rather teasing than torturing; and my lot, compared with that of many other people's, who deserve a better, seems rather favourable. Philosophy, and confidence in the mercy of my Creator, mutually assist me in bearing my share of physical ills, without murmuring.

I send you here inclosed two little papers of melonseed, of the best kind I ever tasted; and I shall from time to time send you more, as you cannot sow any till February.

I had the pleasure of your son's company at dinner six weeks ago, where he met Lord Bristol,* who observed exactly his diet, in eating no animal food, and drinking no wine, and is in better health and spirits than I ever knew him. I am glad that he goes to Nice, which I have known to do a great deal of good to many people in his case. May you and he have all you wish for!

Adieu, my dear Lord; I am to you and yours, etc.

128. TO MRS. EUGENIA STANHOPE

BATH, OCTOBER 27, 1771

MADAM,

Upon my word, you interest yourself in the state of my existence more than I do myself; for it is worth the care of neither of us. I ordered my *valet de chambre*, according to your orders, to inform you of my safe arrival here; to which I can add nothing, being neither better nor worse than I was then.

I am very glad that our boys are well. Pray give them the enclosed.

I am not at all surprised at Mr. ——'s conversion;* for he was, at seventeen, the idol of old women, for his gravity, devotion, and dullness. I am, Madam,

Yours, etc.

129. TO CHARLES AND PHILIP STANHOPE

BATH, OCTOBER 27, 1771

I received, a few days ago, two of the best written letters that I ever saw in my life; the one signed Charles Stanhope, the other Philip Stanhope. As for you, Charles, I did not wonder at it; for you will take pains, and are a lover of letters; but you idle rogue, you Phil, how came you to write so well, that one can almost say of you two, *et cantare pares et respondere parati*? Charles will explain this Latin to you.

I am told, Phil, that you have got a nick-name at school, from your intimacy with Master Strangeways; and that they call you Master *Strangerways*; for to be sure, you are a strange boy. Is this true?

Tell me what you would have me bring you both from hence, and I will bring it you, when I come to town. In the mean time, God bless you both!

130. TO THE BISHOP OF WATERFORD

LONDON, DECEMBER 19, 1771

MY DEAR LORD,

I am sure you will believe me when I tell you that I am sincerely sorry for your loss, which I received the account of yesterday, and upon which I shall make you none of the trite compliments of condolence. Your grief is just; but your religion, of which I am sure you have enough, (with the addition of some philosophy,) will make you keep it within due bounds, and leave the rest to time and avocations. When your son was with me here, just before he embarked for France, I plainly saw that his consumption was too far gone to leave the least hopes of a cure; and, if he had dragged on this wretched life some few years longer, that life could have been but trouble and sorrow to you both. This consideration alone should mitigate your grief, and the care of your grandson will be a proper avocation from it. Adieu, my dear Lord. May this stroke of adversity be the last you may ever experience from the hand of Providence!

Yours most affectionately and sincerely.

131. TO SOLOMON DAYROLLES, ESQ.

BLACKHEATH, SEPTEMBER 10, 1772

DEAR DAYROLLES,

I know, by long experience of your friendship, that you will not grudge in a manner any trouble that I may desire of you, that can either be of use or pleasure to me. My present request to you is of that kind.

I have had several letters from the boy since he has been abroad, and hitherto all seems to go very well between him and M. d'Eyverdun.* But I am too old to trust to appearances, and therefore I will beg of you to write to M. d'Eyverdun, and desire him to send you a confidential letter concerning everything good or bad of his *élève*,* and I promise you upon my honour not to discover the secret correspondence to any mortal living. You must be sensible of the great importance which it is of for me, to be thoroughly informed of his faults as well as of his perfections (if he has any); and this is, if not the only one, I am sure the best, method of my knowing them really and truly.

I am rather better than I was when you saw me last, but indeed very little, and extremely weak. I hope you and *tutti quanti* are in a better plight. My compliments to them all, and believe me to be, what I sincerely am,   Yours, etc.

132. TO SOLOMON DAYROLLES, ESQ.

BLACKHEATH, SEPTEMBER 24, 1772

DEAR DAYROLLES,

I have just now received your letter, and likewise the copy of that which, at my request, you wrote to Monsieur d'Eyverdun. I think it must have its effect, and that I shall be able to find out by it how matters go on at Leipsig.

I am extremely sorry for Mrs. Dayrolles's situation, but I am a little in her case; for it is now four months since I have been labouring under a diarrhoea, which our common Doctor Warren* has not been able to cure. To be nearer him, and all other helps, I shall settle in town this day se'nnight, which is the best place for sick people, or well people, to reside at, for health, business, or pleasure. God bless you all.

133. TO HIS GODSON AND HEIR*

(TO BE DELIVERED AFTER HIS OWN DEATH)

Extracts.

MY DEAR BOY,

You will have received by my will solid proofs of my esteem and affection. This paper is not a will, and only conveys to you my most earnest requests, for your good alone, which requests, from your gratitude for my past care, from your good heart, and your good sense, I persuade myself, you will observe as punctually as if you were obliged by law to do so. They are not the dictates of a peevish, sour old fellow, who affects to give good rules, when he can no longer give bad examples, but the advice of an indulgent and tender friend (I had almost said parent), and the result of the long experience of one *hackneyed in the ways of life*, and calculated only to assist and guide your unexperienced youth.

You will probably come to my title and estate too soon, and at an age at which you will be much less fit to conduct yourself with discretion than you were at ten years old. This I know is a very unwelcome truth to a sprightly young fellow, and will hardly be believed by him, but it is nevertheless a truth, and a truth which I most sincerely wish, though I cannot reasonably hope, that you may be firmly convinced of. At that critical period of life, the dangerous passions are busy, impetuous, and stifle all reflection, the spirits high, the examples in general bad. It is a state of continual ebriety for six or seven years at least, and frequently attended by fatal and permanent consequences, both to body and mind. Believe yourself then to be drunk, and as drunken men, when reeling, catch hold of the next thing in their way to support them, do you, my dear boy, hold by the rails of my experience. I hope they will hinder you from falling, though perhaps not from staggering a little sometimes.

As to your religious and moral obligations I shall say nothing, because I know that you are thoroughly informed of them, and hope that you will scrupulously observe them, for if you do not you can neither be happy here nor hereafter.

I suppose you of the age of one-and-twenty, and just returned from your travels much fuller of fire than reflection; the first impressions you give of yourself, at your first entrance upon the great stage of life in your own country, are of infinite consequence, and to a great degree decisive of your future character. You will be tried first by the grand jury of Middlesex, and if they find a Bill against you, you must not expect a very favourable verdict from the many petty juries who will try you again in Westminster.*

Do not set up a tawdry, flaunting equipage, nor affect a grave one: let it be the equipage of a sensible young fellow, and not the gaudy one of a thoughtless young heir; a frivolous *éclat* and profusion will lower you in the opinion of the sober and sensible part of mankind. Never wear over-fine clothes; be as fine as your age and rank require, but do not distinguish yourself by any uncommon magnificence or singularity of dress. Follow the example of Martin, and equally avoid that of Peter or Jack.* Do not think of shining by any one trifling circumstance, but shine in the aggregate, by the union of great and good qualities, joined to the amiable accomplishments of manners, air and address.

At your first appearance in town, make as many acquaintances as you please, and the more the better, but for some time contract no friendships. Stay a little and inform yourself of the characters of those young fellows with whom you must necessarily live more or less, but connect yourself intimately with none but such whose moral characters are unblemished. For it is a true saying *tell me who you live with and I will tell you what you are*;*and it is equally true, that, when a man of sense makes a friend of a knave or a fool he must have something bad to do, or to conceal. A good character will be soiled at least by frequent contact with a bad one.

Do not be seduced by the fashionable word *spirit*. A man of spirit in the usual acceptation of that word is, in truth, a creature of strong and warm animal life with a weak understanding; passionate, wrong-headed, captious, jealous of his mistaken honour, and suspecting intended affronts, and, which is worse, willing to fight in support of his wrong head. Shun this kind of company, and content yourself with a cold, steady firmness and resolution. By the way, a woman of spirit is *mutatis mutandis*, the duplicate of this man of spirit; a scold and a vixen.

I shall say little to you against gaming, for my example cries aloud to you DO NOT GAME. Gaming is rather a rage than a passion; it will break in upon all your rational pleasures, and perhaps with some stain upon your character, if you should happen to win; for whoever plays deep must necessarily lose his money or his character. I have lost great sums at play, and am sorry I lost them, but I should now be much more sorry if I had won as much. As it is, I can only be accused of folly, to which I plead guilty. But as in the common intercourse of the world you will often be obliged to play at social games, observe strictly this rule: Never sit down to play with men only, but let there always be a woman or two of the party, and then the loss or the gain cannot be considerable.

Do not be in haste to marry, but look about you first, for the affair is important. There are but two objects in marriage, love or money. If you marry for love, you will certainly have some very happy days, and probably many very uneasy ones, if for money, you will have no happy days and probably no uneasy ones; in this latter case let the woman at least be such a one that you can live decently and amicably with, otherwise it is a robbery; in either case, let her be of an unblemished and unsuspected character, and of a rank not indecently below your own.

You will doubtless soon after your return to England be a Member of one of the two Houses of Parliament; there you must take pains to distinguish yourself as a speaker. The task is not very hard if you have common sense, as I think you have, and a great deal more. The *Pedarii Senatores*,* who were known only by their feet, and not by their heads, were always the objects of general contempt. If on your first, second or third attempt to speak, you should fail, or even stop short, from that trepidation and concern, which every modest man feels upon those occasions, do not be discouraged, but persevere; it will do at last. Where there is a certain fund of parts and knowledge, speaking is but a knack, which cannot fail of being acquired by frequent use. I must however add this caution, never write down your speeches beforehand; if you do you may perhaps be a good declaimer, but will never be a debater. Prepare and digest your matter well in your own thoughts, and *Verba non invita sequentur.** But if you can properly introduce into your speech a shining declamatory period or two which the audience may carry home with them, like the favourite song of an opera, it will have a good effect. The late Lord Bolingbroke had accustomed himself so much to a florid eloquence even in his common conversation (which anybody with care may do) that his real *extempore* speeches seemed to be studied. Lord Mansfield was, in my opinion, the next to him in undeviating eloquence, but Mr. Pitt carried with him, unpremeditated, the strength of thunder, and the splendour of lightning. The best matter in the world if ill-dressed and ungracefully spoken, can never please. Conviction or conversion are equally out of the question in both Houses, but he will come the nearest to them who pleases the most. In that, as in everything else, sacrifice to the Graces. Be very modest in your *exordium*, and as strong as you can be in your *peroratio.**

I can hardly bring myself to caution you against drinking, because I am persuaded that I am writing to a rational creature, a gentleman, and not to a swine. However, that you may not be insensibly drawn into that beastly custom of even sober drinking and sipping, as the sots call it, I advise you to be of no club whatsoever. The object of all clubs is either drinking or gaming, but commonly both. A sitting member of a drinking club is not indeed always drunk, perhaps seldom quite so, but he is certainly never quite sober, and is *beclareted* next morning with the guzzle of the preceding evening. A member of a gaming club should be a cheat, or he will soon be a beggar.

You will and you ought to be in some employment at Court. It is the best school for manners, and whatever ignorant people may think or say of it, no more the seat of vice than a village is; human nature is the same everywhere, the modes only are different. In the village they are coarse; in the Court they are polite; like the different clothes in the two several places, frieze in the one, and velvet in the other.

Be neither a servile courtier nor a noisy patriot; custom, that governs the world instead of reason, authorizes a certain latitude in political matters not always consistent with the strictest morality, but in all events remember *servare modum, finemque tueri*.*

Be not only tender and jealous of your moral, but of your political, character. In your political warfare, you will necessarily make yourself enemies, but make them only your political and temporary, not personal, enemies. Pursue your own principles with steadiness, but without personal reflection or acrimony, and behave yourself to those who differ from you with all the politeness and good humour of a gentleman, for in the frequent jumble of political atoms, the hostile and the amicable ones often change places.

In business be as able as you can, but do not be cunning; cunning is the dark sanctuary of incapacity. Every man can be cunning if he pleases, by simulation, dissimulation, and in short by lying. But that character is universally despised and detested, and justly too; no truly great man was ever cunning. Preserve a dignity of character by your virtue and veracity. You are by no means obliged to tell all that you know and think, but you are obliged by all the most sacred ties of morality and prudence, never to say anything contrary to what you know or think to be true. Be master of your countenance, and let not every fool who runs read it. One of the fundamental rules, and almost the only honest one of Italian politics, is *Volto sciolto*e pensieri stretti*, an open countenance and close thoughts.

Never be proud of your rank or birth, but be as proud as you please of your character. Nothing is so contrary to true dignity as the former kind of pride. You are, it is true, of a noble family, but whether of a very ancient one or not I neither know nor care, nor need you, and I dare say there are twenty fools in the House of Lords who could out-descend you in pedigree. That sort of stately pride is the standing jest of all people who can make one; but dignity of character is universally respected. Acquire and preserve that most carefully. Should you be unfortunate enough to have vices, you may, to a certain degree, even dignify them by a strict observance of decorum; at least they will lose something of their natural turpitude.

Carefully avoid every singularity that may give a handle to ridicule, for ridicule (with submission to Lord Shaftesbury), though not founded upon truth, will stick for some time, and if thrown by a skilful hand perhaps for ever.* Be wiser and better than your contemporaries, but seem to take the world as it is, and men as they are, for you are too young to be a *censor morum;** you would be an object of ridicule. Act contrary to many Churchmen, practise virtue, but do not preach it whilst you are young.

If you should ever fill a great station at Court, take care above all things to keep your hands clean and pure from the infamous vice of corruption, a vice so infamous that it degrades even the other vices that may accompany it. Accept no present whatever; let your character in that respect be transparent and without the least speck, for as avarice is the vilest and dirtiest vice in private, corruption is so in public life. I call corruption the taking of a sixpence more than the just and known salary of your employment, under any pretence whatsoever. Use what power and credit you may have at Court in the service of merit rather than of kindred, and not to get pensions and reversions for yourself or your family, for I call that also, what it really is, scandalous pollution, though of late it has been so frequent that it has almost lost its name.

Never run in debt, for it is neither honest nor prudent, but on the contrary, live so far within your annual income as to leave yourself room sufficient for acts of generosity and charity. Give nobly to indigent merit, and do not refuse your charity even to those who have no merit but their misery. Voltaire expresses my thought much better than I can myself:

> Repandez vos bienfaits avec magnificence,
>   Même aux moins vertueux ne les refusez pas,
> Ne vous informez pas de leur reconnoissance:
>   Il est grand, il est beau, de faire des ingrats.*

Such expense will do you more honour, and give you more pleasure, than the idle profusion of a modish and *erudite* luxury.

These few sheets will be delivered to you by Dr. Dodd at your return from your travels, probably long after I shall be dead; read them with deliberation and reflection, as the tender and last testimonies of my affection for you. They are not the severe and discouraging dictates of an old parent, but the friendly and practicable advice of a sincere friend, who remembers that he has been young himself and knows the indulgence that is due to youth and inexperience. Yes, I have been young, and a great deal too young. Idle dissipation and innumerable indiscretions, which I am now heartily ashamed and repent of, characterized my youth. But if my advice can make you wiser and better than I was at your age, I hope it may be some little atonement.

God bless you!   CHESTERFIELD.

EXPLANATORY NOTES

CHESTERFIELD is referred to throughout as C, his son as Stanhope, and his heir as the godson. The top government positions during his career and retirement were First Lord of the Treasury (effectively Prime Minister since Walpole's tenure) and Secretary of State, either for the Northern Department, hereafter (N) or the Southern (S). Responsibility for home affairs was divided between the three posts, but the Secretary of State (N) was responsible for European policy, and the Secretary of State (S) for the Colonies and Ireland. From 1768 to 1782 there was a separate Secretary of State for the Colonies, hereafter (C). For the convenience of the reader, a list of administrations during the years covered by the present edition is given below:

-Jan. 1742: Walpole
Feb. 1742–Nov. 1744: Carteret
Dec. 1744–Mar. 1754: Pelham
Mar. 1754–Oct. 1756: Newcastle
Nov. 1756–Apr. 1757: Pitt/Devonshire
June 1757–Oct. 1761: Pitt/Newcastle
Oct. 1761–May 1762: Bute/Newcastle
May 1762–Apr. 1763: Bute
Apr. 1763–July 1765: Grenville
July 1765–Aug. 1766: Rockingham
Aug. 1766–Oct. 1768: Grafton/Pitt
Oct. 1768–Jan. 1770: Grafton
Feb. 1770–   : North.

1 *Lord Townshend*: Charles, 2nd Viscount Townshend (1674–1738), Secretary of State (N) 1714–16 and 1721–30, when he resigned after trying to procure for C, sympathetic to his anti-Austrian policies, Newcastle's post as Secretary of State (S). He retired to cultivate turnips. His second wife was Walpole's sister. C replies to a letter *apart* from official business.

the death of the Duke of York: Ernest Augustus, Bishop of Osnabrück and George I's brother, died on 14 Aug. 1728. C had long wished to be a Knight of the Garter and was installed on 18 June 1730, following Walpole's agreement.

2 *the Pensionary . . . confidence*: the Grand Pensionary controlled Dutch

foreign policy during the 2nd Stadholderless period (1702–47), the last Stadholder (or supreme military commander) having been William III of England. In 1728 the Pensionary was Simon van Slingelandt, in office from 1727 until his death in 1736. Lt. Gen. Johan (or Jan) Rabo van Keppel (d. 1733) was Dutch ambassador extraordinary to Prussia.

the match ... best consequences: i.e. the planned marriage between Frederick, Prince of Wales, and his cousin Princess Wilhelmina of Prussia; intended as half of a diplomatic coup which would also have married Prince Frederick of Prussia (later Frederick II) to the Prince of Wales's sister, Amelia. The plan was to strengthen Prussia's commitment to the coalition with Britain and France which followed the Treaty of Hanover (1725). Supported by the Queen of Prussia, Sophia Dorothea (George II's sister), the arrangement was opposed decisively by her husband, Frederick William I, who wished to remain loyal to the anti-French interests of the Austrian Emperor, Charles VI.

3 *Prince of Orange ... vacant Garters*: i.e. Willem Karel Hendrik Friso, William IV of Orange, the son of William III's nephew. Stadholder of Friesland, Groningen, and Gelderland in 1728, he did not achieve control of the other provinces until 1747. The garter was granted, and announced to him by C in a letter of 22 May 1729.

ill effect ... his Governor: it was suspected that the garter was granted to subdue William, then aged 17, to British interests. His Governor was Dirk van Lynden van de Parck (1679–1735), sometime canon of Utrecht Cathedral, and later his chief steward.

4 *de Linden*: i.e. the Prince of Orange's Governor (see above note).

6 *the Greffier*: i.e. Dutch Secretary of State for home affairs, at this time Francis Fagel (1659–1746), in office for fifty-four years, and Pensionary Slingelandt's brother-in-law.

Don Carlos ... Orange: a match was proposed between Don Carlos (the first child of Philip V of Spain's second marriage, and later King Carlos III of Spain) and Maria Theresa, daughter of Charles VI of Austria. It did not take place; under the 1731 Treaty of Vienna it was agreed that no Austrian archduchess should marry a Bourbon, whether French or Spanish. William of Orange married Anne, eldest daughter of George II, in 1734, so increasing fears of excessive British influence in the Dutch provinces.

Vander Haym and Teinhoven: Nicolaas Ten Hove (1693–1738)

became Secretary of the State Council following Slingelandt's appointment as Grand Pensionary in 1727. Anthony van der Heim was treasurer of the Dutch provinces in 1728, and succeeded Slingelandt as Pensionary in 1736.

7 *Prince of Orange ... till then*: this did not happen until 1747, during a tide of nationalistic feeling resulting from the French invasion.

9 *Sir Matthew Decker ... the same view*: Sir Matthew Decker (1679–1749) was an Amsterdam merchant who had settled in London in 1702. He became an MP and director of the East India Co., and was sometimes an unofficial intermediary between Britain and the Dutch provinces. Willem Hyacinth, Prince of Nassau-Siegen, disputed the inheritance of King William III of England, receiving limited recognition. *Mr. Buys* is probably Willem Buys (1661–1749), First Secretary of the States of Holland, although his son Abraham (1699–1770) was also prominent as Pensionary of Amsterdam, in favour of peace and trading interests; the Prince of Orange's possible Stadholdership was seen as betokening Dutch involvement in British disputes. C's own mediation in this affair considerably enhanced his standing with the King.

10 *Geo. Tilson*: George Tilson had been under-Secretary of State (N) since 1710; his present master was William Stanhope, 1st Earl of Harrington (c.1690–1756), in office 1730–42 and again 1744–6, whom C had supported as an alternative to Walpole in the late 1730s.

silliest Minister in Europe: the French ambassador who insisted on the 'scrupulous rectitude' of the French court was Gabriel de Salignac, Marquis de la Mothe-Fénelon (1688–1746). At issue were the negotiations over the Treaty of Vienna (signed 16 Mar. 1731); Charles VI of Austria was keen to secure British recognition of Maria Theresa as his rightful heir (the so-called 'Pragmatic Sanction'), but baulked at British conditions, particularly the suspension of the Ostend Company, which he had established in 1722 to trade in the East Indies. France was cool about the clause forbidding marital alliance between its own court and that of Austria (see above, note to p. 6).

the doctrine of Predestination: in 1730 Prince Frederick, later Frederick II, 'the Great' (1712–86), was in prison on his father's orders, following an attempted escape to England. Frederick William had always disliked his son's penchant for philosophy.

11 *St James's Square*: C lived at no. 18 until his marriage in 1733.

the person ... Richmond: William Lancelot (d. 1743) was the second husband of Swift's impoverished cousin, Patty Rolt. Swift had written on 10 Nov. describing him as a servant of Lord Sussex and claimed that he had been promised a post by Lord Dorset, C's predecessor as Lord Steward of the Household. He found C's reply unsatisfactory, writing an ironic apology on 5 Jan. for not being an adequate courtier. Matthew Maty, in *Miscellaneous Works of the Earl of Chesterfield*, ed. J. O. Justamond (2 vols., London, 1777), ii. 572, reports that a minor post was eventually found for Lancelot. Swift met C during a visit to London in 1736, when they found each other's distaste for Walpole's Irish policies congenial.

13 *Sic hoc Decorum . . . atque factorum*: in a man's life, decorum is what wins the approval of those around him, which shines in its regularity and consistency, and in unfailing sobriety of speech and action. From Cicero, *De Officiis*, 1. 28. 98.

Mr. Maittaire: Michael Maittaire (1668–1747), classical scholar and former 2nd master of Westminster, became Stanhope's classics tutor in 1739. His patron, the Earl of Oxford, persuaded Pope to omit the following lines from *The Dunciad*: 'On yonder part what fogs of gathered air | Invest the scene, there museful sits Maittaire'.

14 *Curio . . . imperare*: when the Samnites had brought Curio a large amount of gold as he sat before the fire, he scorned their gift. 'For', he said, 'it seems to me that the glory is not in having the gold, but in ruling those who have it.' From Cicero, *De Senectute*, 56.

15 *Fabricius . . . vulsit*: Fabricius dined at his fireside on the roots which he, an old man who had celebrated a triumph, had dug up while clearing his land. From Seneca, *De Providentia*, 3. 6.

Eximiae . . . Victor: a virgin of the utmost beauty he returned unharmed to her parents, whom he had summoned, and to her fiancé; even though he, Scipio, was not only young but unmarried and victorious. Adapted from Valerius Maximus, *Factorum et Dictorum Memorabilia*, 4. 3. 1.

Venisse Diis . . . ac beneficiis: that he came a young man, resembling the gods, and conquered all, first by arms and then by kindness and good deeds. From Livy, *Ab Urbe Condita*, 26. 50. 13–14.

16 *Virgil . . . laborum*: from *Aeneid*, 4. 522. Dryden's translation best conveys the poetic effect described:

'Twas dead of night, when weary bodies close
Their eyes in balmy sleep and soft repose:

> The winds no longer whisper thro' the woods,
> Nor murm'ring tides disturb the gentle floods.
> The stars in silent order mov'd around;
> And Peace, with downy wings, was brooding on the
>   ground.
> The flocks and herds, and parti-colour'd fowl,
> Which haunt the woods, or swim the weedy pool,
> Stretch'd on the quiet earth, securely lay,
> Forgetting the past labours of the day.

17 *Amoto . . . ludo*: pursue serious matters, put aside play. Adapted from Horace, *Ars Poetica*, 226.

18 *Spa*: in Belgium. C had set out on a seven-month tour of Europe in March.

21 *Bubb Dodington*: George Bubb Dodington, later Baron Melcombe (1691–1762), served in the administration of Sir Robert Walpole (1676–1745) for 16 of its 20 years before turning against him in 1740 and censuring his 'infamy', to general derision. Treasurer of the Navy from 1744. C first met him in Antwerp in 1714, and they remained on friendly terms.

majority . . . labor est: this is the task, this is the labour. From Virgil, *Aeneid*, 6. 129 (the Sibyl tells Aeneas that it is easy to find the way down to hell, but harder to get out). The strength of parliamentary opposition might vary according to many factors, not least absenteeism and bribery, Walpole's particular forte. The 1741 general election had left Walpole with a nominal majority of 14 (Dodington had predicted a minority of that number), which grew to 21 by Christmas, and shrank to a minority of 1 by the end of Jan. 1742, when Walpole lost the division on the legality of the Chippenham election. Dodington put down Walpole's fall to 'our laborious attendance in Parliament' (Bod. MS Eng. Lett. c144 fo. 58).

Carteret and Pulteney: John Carteret, later 1st Earl Granville (1690–1763) had served under Walpole until 1730, when his dismissal as Ld.-Lt. of Ireland sent him into opposition. His oratory was a powerful weapon against Walpole, but intellectual arrogance and drunkenness made him unpopular in the Commons. Secretary of State (N) after Walpole's fall, he resigned in 1744. More promising in C's view was Sir William Pulteney, later Earl of Bath (1684–1764), who had been in opposition since 1725, occasionally with Bolingbroke's Tories; after securing Walpole's removal, however, he refused office and accepted a peerage, to intense criticism. C was associated with an aristocratic opposition Whig faction led by himself and the lords Stair, Bolton, and Scarborough. His disavowal of political interest with the exiled Tory leader and Jacobite Henry St John, Viscount Bolingbroke (1678–1751) is not necessarily compromised by the visit he paid to Bolingbroke's Avignon residence within days of writing to Dodington; he claimed they talked only philosophy, although some alleged that he was canvassing assistance for Walpole's removal.

22 *Sandys, Rushout and Gibbon*: Samuel Sandys (*c.*1695–1770) moved an address for Walpole's removal in 1741, became Chancellor in 1742 only to defend policies he had criticized in opposition, and resigned for a peerage in 1743. Sir John Rushout (1684–1775) and Pulteney's protégé, Phillips Gybbon (1678–1762) proved more sterling as lords of the treasury after Walpole; Rushout sat on a committee to inquire into the past ten years of his government.

23 *Committee of Privileges and Elections*: it was usual for the Opposition to challenge a small majority by contesting the choice of Speaker. Arthur Onslow (1691–1768), who was to oversee five successive parliaments and was the third of his family to hold the post, was too much respected, so the chairmanship of the Elections Committee was contested instead, the Opposition securing it for their own George Lee in Dec. 1741—a vital blow against Walpole since the post was crucial in deciding cases of electoral corruption.

Carthagena: Cartagena, a Colombian port, was one of many Spanish strongholds in the region which Britain hoped to seize when war was declared in 1739. Admiral Vernon's initial success at Porto Bello was followed by a series of failures at Cartagena, Santiago de Cuba, and Panama. The expedition was recalled in 1742. Spain prohibited British ships from sailing anywhere in the Caribbean except to and from British-held islands, and searched vessels deemed to be trespassing. Walpole's conduct of a war he had never wanted led to his fall.

24 *Sweden . . . Bender*: in 1713 Charles XII of Sweden, defeated by the Russians at Poltova, began to negotiate an alliance with the Turks, who were in fact arranging to hand him over to his old enemy the King of Poland. Charles's discovery of this led to the battle of Bendery, in Moldavia, where he did indeed lead a depleted army.

the Duke of Argyle: John Campbell, 2nd Duke of Argyll (1678–1743), leader of Scots opposition to Walpole following the latter's censure of Edinburgh for mishandling the Porteous Riot of 1737. He resented Walpole's refusing him the command of the army after his loyalty in putting down the 1715 rebellion in Scotland. His electioneering in 1741 proved vital in bringing about Walpole's fall. C lived next door to Lady Chesterfield and her mother in Grosvenor Square.

25 *Julius Caesar . . . advanced age*: see Plutarch, *Life of Caesar*, 11. 2.

27 *Rev. Dr. Chenevix*: Richard Chenevix (1698–1779) was C's chaplain at The Hague. Nominated by C, the new Ld.-Lt. of Ireland, as Bishop of Clonfert but refused because it was said that he had written anti-government pamphlets; when C threatened to resign, Killaloe was granted, whence C had him translated to Waterford a year later.

David Mallet: originally David Malloch (*c.*1705–65), Scots poet and dramatist who according to Willard Connely, *The True Chesterfield* (1939), 215, was in C's retinue during his second embassy to The Hague. Later patronized by Bolingbroke, whose *Letters on the Study and Use of History* he published in 1752.

28 *8,000 of your countrymen . . . for much*: C exaggerates the size of the Pretender's army and that of the population of England and Wales. At this stage Prince Charles Edward had captured Perth, Edinburgh, and Carlisle; C's coolness masked a contempt for the highlanders ('beggarly rascals', as he described them later) which encompassed delight at the appointment of Cumberland to pursue and exterminate them.

as Rowe does a Lord: from Nicholas Rowe's play *Jane Shore* (1714), 23 in the Scolar Press facsimile edn.

sixteen new regiments: 16 companies were raised in Ireland to combat the Jacobite threat on the mainland.

1689: C declares his allegiance to the Glorious Revolution and to a balance of the powers of monarch and parliament.

30 *The Duke of Newcastle*: Thomas Pelham-Holles, Duke of Newcastle (1693–1768), Secretary of State (S) almost continuously from 1724 until 1748, when he succeeded C in the Northern Department.

31 *the Council door . . . Legislature*: the Irish Privy Council supervised the activities of the Irish Parliament, preparing and approving bills. No decision of the Lord-Lieutenant's could be imposed without its consent. C's nominees were: James Fitzgerald, Duke of Leinster and 20th Earl of Kildare (1722–73), who had raised a

company against the Pretender; William Fitzmaurice, 2nd Earl of
Kerry (d. 1747); Somerset Butler, 8th Viscount Ikerrin and later
Earl of Carrick (1718–74), married to the daughter of Henry
Boyle, Speaker of the Commons and later Earl of Shannon;
Clotworthy Skeffington, 5th Viscount and later 1st Earl Massar-
ene (d. 1757), who like Richard Wingfield, 1st Viscount Powers-
court (d. 1751), was loyal to the seat of HM government in
Ireland, Dublin Castle; James Hamilton, Viscount Limerick and
later Earl of Clanbrassil (c.1691–1758); Wills Hill, 2nd Viscount
Hillsborough, later the Marquis of Downshire, nephew of
Arthur Hill, a landowner, and in later life Secretary of State (C),
1768–72, and (S), 1779–82; and Richard, 6th Viscount Fizwilliam
of Meryon (d. 1776).

32 *The Earl of Grandison*: i.e. John Villiers, 5th Viscount and 1st Earl
(c.1684–1766), whose application on behalf of his daughter
Elizabeth was granted.

33 *Barrack Patent . . . Board*: military barracks were placed at the
discretion of the Barrack Board, according to gentry and mercantile interests rather than military needs, and therefore also to
money offered to its members. An inquiry into barrack administration was held in 1751.

The Dublin Society. founded in 1731 by Thomas Prior, Samuel
Madden, and other philanthropists, its full title explains its
purpose—the Dublin Society for the Promotion of Agriculture,
Manufactures, Arts, and Sciences. The money C requested was
granted in 1749.

Cavan . . . Mayo: C successfully requested pensions for Ford
Lambart, 5th Earl of Cavan (d. 1772); Richard Parsons, 1st Earl
of Rosse; and Theobold Bourke, 7th Viscount Mayo (d. 1759).

34 *the embargo*: i.e. on the exporting of Irish glass. The measure was
intended to restrict a small but growing industry.

36 *Thomas Prior*: Prior (c.1682–1751) promoted industry among Irish
Protestants, co-founding the Dublin Society and writing books
on linen production and the benefits of drinking tar-water (1746,
dedicated to C).

tax upon glass: an Act of 1746 further forbade the export of Irish
glass and the importing of glass into Ireland from anywhere but
England. C's ambitions for Irish industry were in this case
contrary to government policy.

37 *starch . . . day*: potato-starch came to be used in the 1780s chiefly
for finishing fine cotton. Technology for its extraction was

developed by many hands from *c*.1720. See R. Salaman, *The History and Social Influence of the Potato*, rev. edn. (Cambridge, 1985).

Bishop of Meath: i.e. Dr Henry Maule (d. 1758), formerly Bishop of Dromore, translated to Meath in 1744, where he remained until death. In 1717 he had begun agitating for charter-schools which would attempt the conversion of Catholic children and encourage manufacturing skills. The first school opened in 1733, and there were about fifty by 1746; parliamentary subsidies had been granted in 1745. Modern historians dispute their efficiency and morality.

38 *Bishop of Cloyne ... Dr. Madden*: George Berkeley, Bishop of Cloyne (1685–1753) and author of works of sceptical philosophy. After the success of *Siris* (1744), a eulogy to tar-water, C offered to translate him to the more lucrative see of Clogher, but he declined. Samuel Madden (1686–1765) was a Dublin philanthropist and dramatist who established funds for giving prizes to Trinity College students and for improving manufacturing technology in Ireland.

39 *wine ... here*: claret was cheaper and poorer than in England. In 1736 Lord Orrery had written of the Irish gentry, 'Drunkenness is the Touch Stone by which they try every man; and he that cannot or will not drink, has a mark set upon him' (quoted by R. F. Foster, *Modern Ireland* (Harmondsworth, 1988), 177). *Communibus annis* means the yearly average.

the Linen Board: founded in 1711 to encourage and regulate linen production, but widely agreed to be of dubious benefit.

42 *Pope ... spring*: Pope, *An Essay on Criticism*, 215–16, writes,

> A little Learning is a dang'rous Thing;
> Drink deep, or taste not the *Pierian* Spring.

Cicero ... rusticantur: these tasks give sustenance in youth, pleasure in old age, elegance in prosperity, and a refuge and solace in adversity. At home they afford pleasure and don't encumber us when we are out; with us they spend the night and stay in foreign lands or in the country. From Cicero, *Pro Archia Poeta*, 7. 16.

43 *Mr. Harte ... dead*: for Moses and the Prophets, see Luke 16: 31. The Revd. Walter Harte (1709–74) was Stanhope's tutor and travelling companion, 1745–9. Ex-Vice Principal of St Mary Hall, Oxford. C's editor Maty blamed him for Stanhope's failings: 'long accustomed to college life', Harte was 'too awk-

ward both in his person and address to be able to familiarise the graces with his young pupil.'

44 *that ruling passion*: see Pope, *Epistle to Cobham*, 174—'Search then the Ruling Passion . . .'.

Schaffhausen: the northernmost canton of present-day Switzerland; also its principal city.

berline: a covered four-wheeled carriage with a hooded seat behind.

45 *like Caesar . . . agendum*: reckoning nothing done while anything remained to be done. Slightly misquoted from Lucan, *De Bello Civili*, 2. 656.

vivida vis animi: lively force of mind. From Lucretius, *De Rerum Natura*, 1. 73.

46 *Nullum . . . prudentia*: no divinity is absent if prudence is present. Adapted from Juvenal, *Satires*, 10. 365.

52 *Solomon Dayrolles*: Dayrolles (d. 1786) was at this time HM Resident at The Hague. He was C's godson and the nephew of James Dayrolles, former Resident at The Hague. He had been C's secretary at The Hague in 1745 and in Ireland later the same year.

30,000 Russians: hiring Russian troops had been C's solution to the War of the Austrian Succession (1740–8). The Dutch entered the war against France with reluctance in 1744. At one stage C made the hire of Russians a condition of becoming Secretary of State. They were *en route* to the Austrian Netherlands in 1748 when the fighting stopped.

des mercuriales: reprimands.

53 *the Dutch frontier . . . corps*: of these three towns near the border with present-day Belgium, the French captured Bergen-op-Zoom in September 1747, soon to halt their progress when Louis XV abandoned the war effort. Prince Josef of Saxen-Hildburghausen (1702–87), a favourite of Empress Maria Theresa, was a Field-Marshal and head of the Austrian high command until 1749.

55 *Spanish proverb*: already an old English proverb in 1747. Wilson, *The Oxford Dictionary of English Proverbs* (Oxford, 1970), 807, finds 'Tell me with whom thou goest, and I'll tell thee what thou doest' in 1581. C's dislike of 'vulgar' English proverbs made him prefer 'Dime con quien andas, decirte he quien eres' (see Cervantes, *Don Quixote*, ii. 10).

56 *Mr. Addison and Mr. Pope*: C had met the two authors at Hampton

Court in Sept. 1717. Addison (1672–1719) was at the time celebrated not only as an essayist and dramatist but as Secretary of State; C thought him 'the most timid and awkward man in good company I ever saw'. With Pope (1688–1744) C shared an admiration of John Gay, Henrietta Howard, Mary Lepell (later Hervey), and Dr John Arbuthnot; C's 'Attic wit' is praised in Pope's *Epilogue to the Satires: Dialogue II*, and he ranks among those who were not patrons but friends. See also Pope's *One Thousand Seven Hundred and Forty*.

57 *Arguses*: i.e. Argus Panoptes, son of Inachus, watchman over the cow into which Io had been transformed, but killed by Hermes.

59 *Cardinal Richelieu . . . the Cid*: Corneille's play appeared in 1637 to general acclaim. Richelieu, Louis XIII's first minister, supported the dramatist Georges de Scudéry in applying to the Académie française for a judgement on it, resulting in Jean Chapelain's *Sentiments de l'Académie sur le Cid* (1638), which criticized the style and grammar of the play. Richelieu also employed five hack dramatists to write plays under his direction and himself penned a justly neglected tragi-comedy, *Mirame*.

62 *scribendi cacoethes*: the incurable itch of writing. From Juvenal, *Satires*, 7. 52.

65 *an Elzevir classic*: the Elseviers were a Dutch family of publishers and booksellers active between 1581 and 1712. Their series of small duodecimo classics proved especially popular and portable.

66 *Leonidas and Curtius*: Leonidas, King of Sparta, secured the pass of Thermopylae in 480 BC with 300 men; Marcus Curtius leapt fully armed and on horseback into a chasm which had opened in the Roman forum (362 BC), and which the seers declared would never close except over Rome's most precious possession.

68 *Vittorio Siri*: a reference to Siri's 8-vol. history of France, *Memorie recondite dall'anno 1601 sino al 1640* (1677–9), published in Paris and Lyons. Siri is better known by his pseudonym, Nicocleonte.

my present . . . situation: C had resigned as Secretary of State on 6 Feb. 1748. He had wanted to end the war with France, but his colleague Newcastle was pressing for a continuation in secret talks with Bentinck, the Prince of Orange's envoy. In addition, George II had consistently refused to advance members of his family. Three days after his resignation Newcastle began to talk of peace and C's family prospered. C is presumed to have written an acerbic *Apology for a late Resignation* (4 edns., 1748); a pamphlet war followed, in which he was attacked for seeking to betray Britain's interests.

69 *Commissioner of the Admiralty*: C's younger brother John Stanhope (1705–48) was MP for Nottingham from 1727 and for Derby from 1736. He died 10 months after accepting his admiralty post.

George Stanhope: C had sought the promotion of his cousin George (1717–54) since taking office in 1746.

Countess Flemming … passablement décrotté: Karl Georg Friedrich, Graf von Flemming (1706–67) was Saxon envoy to the court of Savoy at Turin and then England. He and his wife found Stanhope 'acceptably polished' in a visit to the Leipzig *salon* of Benigna von Treiden, Duchess of Courland, in Latvia (b. 1703).

70 *Lord Sandwich … Envoy*: John Montagu, 4th Earl of Sandwich (1718–92) was plenipotentiary at peace conferences at Breda prior to the full congress of Aix-la-Chapelle, 24 Apr. 1748, where he represented Britain. Dayrolles's ambition to be promoted to ambassador remained unfulfilled; his next position was as Resident in Brussels (1751–7). In command of the French army were Comte Hermann Maurice de Saxe (1696–1750), Marshal-General of France and natural son of King Augustus II of Poland, and Ulrik Løvendal (1700–55), his Danish protégé and Maréchal de France.

Et sachez … comprise aussi: be mindful that there is a lady involved as well. Cp. Gay, 'The Hare and Many Friends': 'For when a lady's in the case, | You know all other things give place' (41–2). This lady was Anne, wife of the Prince of Orange, and in touch with her sister Emily at the English Court.

sacrifice to the Graces: Plato's advice to Xenophon. See Plutarch, *Life of Caius Marius*, 2. 3.

71 *L'esprit … du cœur*: the mind is often the dupe of the heart. C underestimates the pessimism of the French moralist, François, Duc de La Rochefoucauld (1613–80), whose Maxim 102 reads, 'L'esprit est toujours la dupe du cœur'. From *Maximes et réflections diverses*, ed. Jacques Truchet (Paris, 1972), 54.

72 *mauvaise honte*: bashfulness.

73 *Mr. Waller*: C's friend Edmund Waller, with whom he wrote pamphlets in 1743 opposing the pro-Hanover policies of Carteret. C's aversion to laughter, shared by Swift, Pope, and Voltaire, was not as eccentric as it may appear. See V. Heltzel, 'Chesterfield and the Anti-Laughter Tradition', *Modern Philology*, 26 (1928).

les manières prévenantes: prepossessing manners.

a good Easter fair at Leipsig: founded as a cloth and hide market *c.*1170. There was another fair in September.

74 *hoc genus omne*: all that tribe. From Horace, *Satires*, 1. 2. 2.

77 *Munster*: the Peace of Westphalia (1648), consisting of the two treaties of Münster and Osnabrück, put an end to the so-called Thirty Years War between France, Sweden, and the German Protestant Princes on one side, and the Austrians and German Catholics on the other.

78 *Pyrrhonism*: a belief in the relativity of all judgement, as advanced by the Greek philosopher Pyrrho of Elis (*c*.365–275 BC).

79 *Cardinal de Retz*: Paul de Gondi, Cardinal de Retz (1614–79), became Archbishop of Paris in 1653 and schemed without success for a post in Louis XIV's ministry. His *Mémoires* (1717) are notable for their scathing portraits of court rivals. It was no accident that C should have recommended them so soon after his own fall from grace.

80 *Dresden*: home of the Court of Augustus III (1696–1763), Elector of Saxony (as Frederick Augustus II) and King of Poland from 1733. An ally of Austria against Prussia. *Caravanne* means a tourist's visit.

82 *Materiam superabat opus*: the work excelled the material. From Ovid, *Metamorphoses*, 2. 5.

83 *Sapere est principium et fons*: knowledge is the foundation and source. From Horace, *Ars Poetica*, 309.

86 *Hotspur ... Matzel*: Shakespeare, 1 Henry IV:

> in his ear I'll holler 'Mortimer!'
> Nay, I'll have a starling shall be taught to speak
> Nothing but 'Mortimer'. (1. iii. 222–4)

Matzel was the name of a pet bullfinch owned by Sir Charles Hanbury Williams, British envoy at Dresden, and promised to Stanhope whenever Williams should leave. It was killed by a cat in Williams's rooms at the beginning of June, prompting a letter of apology and a six-stanza elegy from its owner (see Dobrée, p. 1171).

Mr. Grevenkop: Gaspar Grevenkop was a Dane in C's service who occasionally accompanied Stanhope on his travels.

Landsassii and Amptsassii: Ambts-sassen were people who in legal matters had to apply in the first instance to a lower court (in Saxony ambts-sassen were also defined as those who had been granted estates in return for military assistance but still had to apply to a lower court); Land-sassen were wealthy landowners permitted to appeal directly to the authority of the Duke or Prince.

87 *L'Abbé Mably*: Gabriel Bonnot de Mably (1709–85) was a Jesuit-trained legal scholar who advised his cousin, Cardinal de Temeius, Minister of State. Chief among his works on jurisprudence was *Le Droit de l'Europe, fondé sur les traités* (1746), which attracted intense criticism for its liberal sentiments.

88 *St. Thomas's Day*: i.e. 21 Dec.

89 *La Rochefoucault . . . La Bruyère*: for La Rochefoucauld, see note to p. 71. Jean de La Bruyère (1645–96) published the first version of his *Caractères de Théophraste, traduits du grec, avec les caractères ou les mœurs de ce siècle* in 1688. His pessimistic view of people and institutions exhibits, like the maxims of La Rochefoucauld, a contempt for hypocrisy which C found congenial at this time.

90 *On trouve . . . déplaît pas*: there is something in the distress of one's best friend which is not displeasing. C misquotes slightly (see *Maximes*, ed. Truchet, p. 94), and sentimentalizes his author's pessimism. La Rochefoucauld means that a friend's distress assures us of our own relative happiness, irrespective of the responsible discharge of duty to which C refers.

chicane: *OED* records only *chicane* (cp. chicanery), to equivocate.

91 *Women . . . growth*: Cp. Dryden, *All for Love*—'Men are but children of a larger growth' (IV. 43).

92 *Orpheus . . . the whole sex*: in the most commonly accepted version of his story, Orpheus, preferring the rites of Apollo to those of Dionysus, was torn apart by the women of Thrace on the orders of the angry god.

95 *Quum vero hostis . . . etc.*: but when we are at war, dealing with an enemy who threatens us with all manner of terrible things, with slow or sudden destruction, it does not matter how we endeavour to defeat and kill him as long as he lingers in his all-consuming animosity. It is therefore right to make use even of poison.

ferociam exuere: [the enemy's] animosity may at last burn itself out.

96 *collected . . . by Escobar*: Antonio Escobar Y Mendoza (1581–1669) was a Spanish Jesuit who wrote *Liber theologiae moralis* (1644), an account of truth and error, rectitude and crime. This was pilloried in Pascal's *Lettres provinciales* (1656–7) for allegedly lax morality.

97 *Quidlibet ex Quolibet*: i.e. Thomas Aquinas, *XII Quaestiones quodlibetales*, records of free-for-all debates held between 1269 and 1272.

Doctor Berkeley ... Matter: C is probably referring to Berkeley's *Treatise Concerning the Principles of Human Knowledge* (1710).

Comte de Gabalis ... Rosicrucians: Cabbalism (from *c*.1200) perpetuates Jewish oral traditions of mystical interpretation and white magic; Rosicrucianism, established by the early seventeenth century, combines Cabbalism, Gnosticism, alchemy, and other occult practices. *Le Comte de Gabalis* (1670), by the Abbé de Montfauçon de Villars, is a study of Cabbalist beliefs referred to by Pope in the dedication of *The Rape of the Lock* (see note to p. 215).

98 *Paracelsus ... Alkahest*: Paracelsus was the pseudonym of Theophrastus Bombastus von Hohenheim (*c*.1490–1541), the Swiss physician and alchemist. Alkahest is a sham Arab term for panacea, Paracelsus' own search for which centred on hot mineral baths designed to restore the balance of elements in the body. A monument was erected to him in Salzburg four years after C's letter.

nil admirari: wonder at nothing. Horace, *Epistles*, 1. 6. 1, following Pythagoras, says this is the only way to make and sustain happiness.

99 *Lord Pulteney*: i.e. Viscount Pulteney (1731–63), only son of the Whig politician. After his Grand Tour, he became MP for Old Sarum in 1754, a Lt.-Col. in 1759, and MP for Westminster in 1761.

the Letters of Madame de Sevigné: Marie de Rabutin-Chantal, Marquise de Sévigné (1626–96), wrote celebrated accounts of Louis XIV's court to her daughter, who had married the Lt.-Governor of Provence.

Madame Valentin's assembly: presumably Marie de St Simon, Comtesse de Valentinois (1728–74), a Parisian society hostess.

100 *le ton ... compagnie*: the air of polite company.

les allures: motions, ways.

train-train: routine.

104 *Waller ... to be prized*: Edmund Waller (1606–87), 'Of Love', writes:

> Postures which render him despis'd,
> Where most he wishes to be priz'd.

105 *volto sciolto ... pensieri stretti*: the passage of Machiavelli C had in mind is uncertain, but the advice resembles that of the Discourses, 3. 6 ('On Conspiracies'). The phrasing derives from Sir

Henry Wootton, letter to Milton, 13 Apr. 1638, in acknowledgement of *Comus*: '*I pensieri stretti, & il viso sciolto* will go safely over the whole World'.

107 *Parum comis . . . Mercuriusque*: youth, not pleasing without you [the Graces] and Mercury. From Horace, *Odes*, 1. 30. 7–8.

108 *gardefous*: balustrades.

110 *in capite*: C hopes that Stanhope, who had an exceptionally large head, would be at the head of whatever company he was in.

113 *the German play*: Stanhope appears to have seen an improvised harlequinade by the company of Karl Friedrich Reibehand, a travelling *commedia* actor specializing in pyrotechnic effects who gave several performances in Leipzig in October 1748, some of them advertised as tragedies.

Peream dum luceam: let me perish if I can but shine. C recalls the colours, but not the motto, of the Grenadiers de Cheval de la Maison du Roi. This 'squib' was a stylized grenade.

pic-nic: *OED* gives this as the first recorded use of the word in English. Here it means 'a fashionable entertainment in which each person present contributed a share of the provisions'.

Shaftesbury . . . of us: Shaftesbury, *An Essay on the Freedom of Wit and Humour*: 'We polish one another, and rub off our corners and rough sides by a sort of amicable collision.' (I. ii)

114 *Mr. Eliot*: Edward, Lord Eliot (1727–1804), inherited his father's huge Cornwall estates in Nov. 1748, so gaining control of three parliamentary constituencies. He accompanied Stanhope occasionally on his travels, sharing the tuition of Harte.

Carlo Maratti: Maratti (1625–1713) was a leading painter of the Roman school under the influence of the counter-reformation.

116 *Locke . . . education*: i.e. *Some thoughts concerning Education* (1693), the most widely read educational treatise of the eighteenth century.

the late King Victor Amédée: Victor Amadeus II (1666–1732), Duke of Savoy, 1st King of Sicily and then of Sardinia, greatly increased the influence of Savoy in Europe. In 1730 he abdicated in favour of his son, Charles Emmanuel III. C neglects to mention the unfilial proceedings which followed: Victor tried to revoke his abdication in 1731 and was thrown by his son into prison, where he died.

les plus déliés: the most refined.

117 *entregent*: tact.

Duke of Marlborough: John Churchill, 1st Duke of Marlborough (1650–1722), leader of the British and Dutch armies in the War of the Spanish Succession (1701–13). C's summary of his career is not completely accurate. After leaving St Paul's School (*c.*1665) he was page of honour to the Duke of York, later James II, who was having an affair with his sister, Arabella. His attachment to Barbara, Lady Castlemaine and Duchess of Cleveland, brought him a gift of £5,000, £4,500 of which he invested with C's grandfather, George Savile, Marquis of Halifax (1633–95). He enjoyed diplomatic successes at Berlin and Hanover (1704), Leipzig (1707, at the camp of Charles XII of Sweden), and Frankfurt (1707).

118 *Pensionary Heinsius . . . to this day*: Antonius Heinsius (1641–1720) was appointed Grand Pensionary, or Secretary of State, by William III in 1689, and continued in office until death. Criticized for failing to secure Dutch interests at the Treaty of Utrecht (1713) and in the Barrier Treaty of 1715, the inadequate terms of which contributed to the French invasion in 1747 (see p. 53). C's view of his negotiations with Marlborough (1701–7) is not wholly just in that Heinsius denied his ally the administration of the Belgic provinces in 1706. See *The Correspondence of John Churchill and Anthonie Heinsius* (The Hague, 1951), ed. B. van't Hoff.

119 *omnibus . . . rebus*: endowed with all gifts, at all times to excel. Adapted from Lucretius, *De Rerum Natura*, 1. 27.

the insatiable man in Horace: a reminiscence of Horace, *Odes*, 2. 18. 21–4.

120 *Commensaux . . . absence*: Stanhope's late dining companions were people whose absence gave pleasure.

Mr. Eliot . . . father: Richard Eliot died within a few days, leaving his son Edward to inherit his Cornish estates.

my brother John: see note to p. 69.

121 *Andrié . . . Algarotti*: Andrie was a former Prussian envoy to London; Conte Francesco Algarotti (1712–64), an Italian author of books on optics, opera, and architecture, had been invited to the court of Frederick II in 1740. He corresponded with C, Hervey, and Gray, and three of his books were translated into English in C's lifetime.

122 *Spectacle de la Nature*: published in 1732, by Abbé Noël-Antoine Pluché (1688–1761), author of books on linguistics and religion.

Rector magnificus: at this time the philosopher Johann Christophe Gottsched (1700–66).

Pluralité des Mondes: i.e. *Entretiens sur la pluralité des mondes* (1686), a dialogue stressing the insignificance of man and the Earth to the universe as a whole. Bernard le Bovier, Sieur de Fontenelle (1657–1757) was a philosopher and FRS, admired for his prodigious learning and sceptical intelligence. C had met him in 1741 at the salon of Madame de Tencin, a Parisian hostess and friend of Bolingbroke's.

125 *Comte Pertingue . . . Comte du Perron*: Comte Pertingue was minister to Charles Emmanuel III, King of Sardinia, at the Court of Turin; Comte du Perron was its ambassador to Hanover.

126 *an immense fortune*: Viscount Pulteney died while returning to London from Portugal, months before his father, leaving his uncle to inherit the £40,000 and property which the Earl of Bath left behind.

Lady Chesterfield: C's wife, Petronilla Melusina von der Schullenberg, Countess of Walsingham (1693–1778), natural daughter of George I by the Duchess of Kendal. C had met her in 1722 and married her for gain in 1733 (she had a fortune of £50,000 and claimed £3,000 from the Civil List). Their marital relations were accordingly frigid, if respectfully polite.

130 *Descartes's automatons*: René Descartes (1596–1650) had argued in his *Principia Philosophiae* (1644) that animals were governed solely by laws of motion, without feeling or consciousness.

Mr. Mascow: John James Mascow (1689–1762), Professor of Civil Law at Leipzig University and author of *The History of the Germans* (1726). Stanhope had lodged with him during his stay in Leipzig.

Dii tibi . . . sumes: may the gods grant you a long life, for other advantages you must secure for yourself. From Ovid, *Epistles from Pontus*, 2. 1. 53.

133 *portée*: reach, compass.

quos ultra . . . rectum: beyond and short of which rectitude has no place. Slightly misquoted from Horace, *Satires*, 1. 1. 107.

134 *blaze often*: C believed that the devil would lose nothing by the supposed reconciliation between the two Secretaries of State, the Dukes (hence 'Graces') of Newcastle and of Bedford. Soon after the appointment of John Russell, 4th Duke of Bedford (1710–71) as Secretary of State (S) in succession to C (12 Feb. 1748), the two

had frequently quarrelled, and the government split into factions, Bedford being supported by Sandwich. Newcastle's jealousy of his colleagues often caused friction, even when they were supposed, as here, to be 'best friends'; in 1751 he forced Bedford's resignation.

135 *Prince of Wales ... Court party*: also associated with Bedford was George II's third son, William Augustus, Duke of Cumberland (1721–65), 'Butcher Billy' of Culloden and captain-general of the army; the 1st Lord of the Admiralty was Sandwich, to whom Newcastle had originally offered Bedford's job. Newcastle's influence in the church and in Parliament derived from his vast landed wealth, producing a rent-roll of £25,000 per year. Henry Pelham (1695–1754), Newcastle's brother, had been 1st Lord of the Treasury and therefore first minister for the past five years. His position was weakened as much by quarrels with Newcastle as by factional disturbance, but he gained by exploiting George II's anticipated death (65 at the time), giving undertakings to those expecting preferment after the accession of Frederick, Prince of Wales, who included William Pitt. In the event the Prince died in 1751.

Ranelagh Garden ... fireworks: Ranelagh Gardens, Chelsea, opened as a pleasure-ground and place of assembly in 1742, offering vaudevilles, dancing, acrobats, and music, as well as the imitation of the Venice carnival and fireworks for the peace of Aix-la-Chapelle which took place on 26 and 27 Apr. *Loges* were boxes for spectators.

Lord Holderness: Robert D'Arcy, 4th Earl of Holderness (1718–78), was minister plenipotentiary at The Hague, 1749–51, and Secretary of State, moving between departments, from 1751 to 1761.

Madame de Berkenroodt: Catherine Windsor married Matthys Lestevenon van Berkenroodt, Dutch ambassador to Paris, and separated from him there. C had met her in The Hague in 1744 and admired her; Stanhope failed to win her favour in Paris, his friend Huntingdon (see p. 207 and note) receiving C's encouragement instead.

136 *portez vous ... toujours*: stay in good health, and love me always.

Tieffer: i.e. Tiefensee, NE of Stanhope's last stopping-point, Berlin.

Comte d'Einsiedlen ... Comte Lascaris: presumably the Comte Einsiedel, Minister to the Elector of Saxony, Augustus III, at the

Court of Dresden, where Stanhope had stayed the previous year. Lascaris had been French ambassador to the same court.

138 *Mr. Firmian*: Karl Josef, Graf von Firmian (1716–82), was Austrian envoy at Milan and Parma.

139 *Albani ... Nivernois*: Albani (1692–1779) was Pope Clement XI's nephew and librarian of the Vatican, later papal nuncio to the Holy Roman Emperor; 'the Purple' refers to the official scarlet dress of a cardinal. Louis Charles, Duc de Nivernois (1716–98), was French ambassador at Rome, 1748–52, and subsequently at Berlin and London.

Ligue de Cambray ... Crown of Spain: in 1509 Pope Julius II joined the League of Cambrai, established the year before against Venice by France, Germany, Spain, and others, inflicting defeat at Agnadello and recovering control of church appointments and taxation rights. Alfonso de la Cueva, Marqués de Bedmar (*c.*1572–1655) was appointed ambassador in 1607 at a time when Spain sought to increase its influence in other parts of Italy, a policy Venice opposed and Bedmar assisted. It is thought the conspiracy was concocted by the Venetian senate as an excuse for getting rid of Bedmar.

Pope ... Sarpi: Pope Paul V, elected in 1605, regained supremacy in Naples, Savoy, and Genoa while Venice, engaged in trying two clerics in its own courts, retained control over the building of churches and the purchase of land by the clergy. Paul excommunicated the Venetian senate and placed the city under a papal interdict, which the senate declared invalid, expelling all who observed it. In 1607 a settlement was reached on terms humiliating to the Pope. The case of Venice was put by its state theologian, the Servite Fra Paolo Sarpi (1552–1623), a physician who, although excommunicated for a series of anti-papal pamphlets including *Tractatus de Beneficiis*, carried on his priestly functions until death.

the next will probably see: an accurate prediction. Much of N. Italy fell to Napoleon during his Italian campaign, which forced the deposition of the last Doge of Venice in 1797.

142 *Cardinal de Retz ... same pen*: Fabio Chigi was elected Pope Alexander VII in 1655. Retz, *Mémoires* (1817 edn.), iv. 27, said that he had written for *two* years with the same pen.

143 *Decorum*: see note to p. 13.

faites comme ... avoit: act as if you had [a consumptive tendency]; 'pectorally' here means 'with concern for your chest'.

144 *Politicians . . . hate*: Dryden, *Absalom and Achitophel*, 223.

    Homer . . . mortals: *Iliad*, 8. 25–32.

145 *volto . . . stretti*: see note to p. 105.

146 *ses mœurs . . . de lettres*: for one so young, his manners conform to most strict and sensible standards; his application . . . to all that goes by the name of learning and polite literature, without the taint of ostentatious pedantry, makes him truly worthy of your tender regard; and I have the honour to assure you that everyone is proud to own his acquaintance and his friendship. I profited from it myself with great pleasure in Vienna, and count myself happy to have received his permission to continue it by correspondence.

    senza . . . vana: see p. 114.

147 *ruelles*: receptions in the bedrooms of fashionable ladies.

148 *spectacles*: i.e. plays, entertainments, tableaux.

153 *Ius Publicum Imperii . . . Sir Charles Williams*: the laws of the imperial state. Stanhope was lodging and studying Roman law with Professor John Mascow (see p. 130 and note). Sir Charles Hanbury Williams (1708–59) was envoy to Saxony, 1746–50 and 1751–5; in 1750–1 he was envoy to Berlin, where Voltaire admired his wit and verses. He committed suicide in 1759 after an unsuccessful attempt to negotiate an alliance between Britain, Austria, and Russia.

156 *flappers*: Swift, *Gulliver's Travels*, III. chap. 2.

    Christian: Stanhope's Swiss valet.

157 *Monmouth Street . . . tenter-hooks*: a tenter is a machine for stretching cloth so that it dries in shape; the hooks hold the articles on the frame. Monmouth Street in St Giles's was famous for its second-hand clothes shops.

    Lyttelton's . . . awkwardness: George, 1st Baron Lyttelton (1709–73), chancellor from 1755 to 1756 (when Horace Walpole remarked that 'he seemed strangely bewildered in the figures'), and patron of Pope, Thomson, Fielding, Shenstone, and others. Caricatured by Smollett as Gosling Scragg in *Peregrine Pickle*. In 1737 he and C had both written for the anti-Walpole journal, *Common Sense*.

    question extraordinaire: torture on the rack.

158 *il leur faut du brillant*: they insist upon polish.

159 *Lord Bacon . . . recommendation*: Bacon, 'Of Ceremonies and Re-

spects', writes, 'it doth much add to a man's reputation, and is (as queen Isabella said) *like perpetual letters commendatory*, to have good forms.' In *Works*, ed. J. Spedding, R. L. Lewis, and D. D. Heath (14 vols., 1857–74), vi. 500.

tournure: appearance.

160 *the Jubilee*: the Holy Year of the Catholic Church, from one Christmas Eve to the next. Since 1470 it had happened every 25 years, and to commemorate special events.

slipper or his b——h: probably 'breech', or backside, denoting sycophancy. The Pope in question was Benedict XIV.

162 *Proverbial expressions . . . such a place*: Wilson, *Dictionary of Proverbs*, 522, finds the first use of 'one man's meat' in Lucretius, while 'tit for tat' appears in Heywood's *Dialogue* of proverbs (1546). C himself was hardly averse to quoting proverbs in French, Italian, or Latin; another captivating hypocrisy for Dickens's Sir John Chester. *OED* dates the first record of 'smart' in the sense of 'affectation in wit, manners or clothing' at 1712. 'Vastly' appeared after the Restoration and was a particular bugbear of C's. In the first of his articles for the *World* on Johnson's Dictionary (28 Nov. 1754) he execrated those who found a snuff-box 'vastly pretty, because . . . vastly little'; the egregious Ann Steele in Jane Austen's *Sense and Sensibility* is fond of the word. 'Obleiged' and 'to wards' survived until the present century.

164 *les manières nobles . . . qui plait*: noble and unforced manners, the appearance of a man of quality, the air of polite company, the Graces, the indefinable something which gives pleasure. *Je ne sais quoi* was already a cliché for the designation of politeness.

knick-knackically: a nonce word of C's devising.

165 *Virtuoso*: a person of dilettante scientific or artistic interests.

Mendes . . . Stevens: Thomas Steavens (*c.*1728–59) was a friend of Horace Walpole and Sir Charles Hanbury Williams who undertook the Grand Tour in 1749; the identity of Mendes, who had evidently helped Stanhope in Rome, is not known.

puffed: praised excessively. Common since the early seventeenth century for describing the interested promotion of plays and literary works.

166 *brigues*: intrigues.

167 *Fra Paolo, de Beneficiis*: see above, p. 139 and note.

their General: at this time the head of the Jesuits was a Bohemian, Francis Retz.

168 _their settlement in Paraguay_: Jesuit missions in SE Paraguay had governed what were in effect separate states since the early seventeenth century, promoting local industry and meeting military needs. A Spanish and Portuguese attack of 1767 forced their expulsion.

the Inquisition: the papal judicial institution for inquiring into cases of heresy and witchcraft. Physical punishment of heretics had been practised for more than a thousand years before Inquisitions were established in Rome (1542), Portugal (1547), and Spain, where the idea reached its bloodiest fruition under the first Spanish Grand Inquisitor, Torquemada (1420–98).

169 _Sir James Gray and Mr. Smith_: Sir James Gray (d. 1773) was HM Resident at Venice, 1744–53, envoy at Naples until 1761, and then at Madrid. Joseph Smith (1682–1770) was British Consul at Venice, 1740–60, and a noted collector of rare books and paintings. In 1765 he sold his books to the Crown for £10,000, and his art treasures for £20,000.

170 _Lord Shaftesbury ... were to see him_: from _An Essay on the Freedom of Wit and Humour_—'Should one who had the countenance of a gentleman ask me "Why I would avoid being nasty, when nobody was present?", in the first place I should be fully satisfied that he himself was a very nasty gentleman who could ask this question, and that it would be a hard matter for me to make him ever conceive what true cleanliness was.' (III. iii)

171 _that of Aristides_: i.e. Aristides the Just, an Athenian general and statesman of the fifth century BC.

172 _agrémens_: pleasures.

175 _alicui negotio ... quaerit_: occupied with work of some kind, seeks fame either by great deeds or distinguished ability. Source unknown.

Caesar ... siletur: probably a reminiscence of Lucan, _De Bello Civili_, 5. 669–71, where Caesar, at sea in a skiff, says he can dispense with a grave as long as his appearance is dreaded in every land. _Pliny ... siletur_: their life and death are much the same to me, and nothing needs to be said of either. I can find neither the Latin quotation nor the thought preceding it in Pliny (old or young). In his _Letters_ Pliny the Younger says, 'Since we are denied a long life, let us leave behind something to show that we have lived' (3. 7. 15); C's stricter version may derive from Benjamin Franklin's _Poor Richard_ (1738)—'either write things worth reading, or do things worth the writing'.

176 *sapere . . . et fons*: see note to p. 83.

les manières liantes: engaging manners.

177 *ille optimus . . . urgetur*: he is the best who is distressed by the smallest mistakes. Horace, *Sermonum*, 1. 3. 68.

178 *Atterbury*: Francis Atterbury (1663–1732), Bishop of Rochester, was a prominent Jacobite, polemical author, member of the Scriblerus Club, and friend of Pope, Swift, and Bolingbroke. His *Sermons and Discourses on Several Subjects and Occasions* were published after his exile in 1723.

Westminster: where Stanhope had studied before his time with Harte.

179 *Academies and Dictionaries*: in the sixteenth century there were nearly 700 literary and scientific academies in Italy. Most famous for the promotion of Italian was the Accademia della Crusca, founded in 1582 by Anton Francesco Grazzini. Its *Vocabolario della Crusca* (1612) sought to stabilize literary language using Tuscan as a model. The Académie française opened officially in 1637 under the aegis of Richelieu. The *Dictionnaire de l'Académie française*, excluding all vulgar and technical expressions, first appeared in 1694. C's complaint that the improving and fixing of languages was less attended to in Britain may justify the claim that he had simply forgotten about Johnson's plea for patronage, which had taken place more than two years before.

Cicero says . . . speech: Cicero, *De Oratore*, 1. 8. 33.

180 *Quintilian . . . orator*: i.e. *Institutio oratoria* (the Training of an Orator), published in AD 95.

181 *Cato*: i.e. Marcus Porcius Cato, called Censorinus (234–149 BC), Roman statesman and orator of famed strictness in matters of morals, manners, and rhetoric.

184 *Selon vos ordres . . . fournir*: as you instructed, I have examined young Stanhope carefully, and have, I believe, understood his character completely. What follows is his portrait, which I take to be a true likeness. He has a pleasant face, a sensible manner, and a discerning look. His figure is rather square at present, but if he grows taller, for which he has both time and build, it will be well proportioned. He certainly has a good fund of knowledge, and I am assured of his deep familiarity with the ancient languages. French I know he speaks perfectly well; his German is said to be just as good. He asks intelligent questions which show his eagerness to learn. I will not say that he is as eager to please; for

he seems negligent of the proper attentions and graces. He is bad at introducing himself, and has anything but the unforced, noble manner, and appearance proper to him. It is true that he is still young and inexperienced, so there is occasion to hope that practice, which he has not had, and polite company, where he is yet a novice, will polish him, and give him all that he now lacks. An attachment to some lady of quality well-versed in the world, some Madame de l'Ursay, is just what he needs. To conclude, I venture to assure you that he has everything that My Lord Chesterfield could wish, except the manners, graces, and air of polite company which he will surely acquire given time and exposure to the fashionable world. It would be at the least a great pity if he did not acquire what he so deserves to have; you know how important these things are. My Lord his father knows too, being in full possession of them himself. In brief, if little Stanhope acquires the graces, he will, I assure you, go far; if not, he will be stopped short in what would otherwise have been a distinguished career.

Madame de l'Ursay: a middle-aged, worldly-wise coquette in *Les Égarements du Cœur et de l'Esprit* (1736) by C's acquaintance Claude-Prosper Jolyot de Crébillon, usually called Crébillon *fils*.

187 *Mazarin*: chief minister of France from 1643 until his death in 1661, the Italian cardinal acquired a fortune of several million pounds.

188 *Richelieu . . . Cid*: see note to p. 59.

189 *Agrippina . . . Messalina*: i.e. the mother of Nero and the promiscuous wife of Claudius.

190 *valeant quantum valere possunt*: let them pass for what they are worth. Proverbial.

191 *volto sciolto*: see note to p. 105.

192 *like Caesar's wife*: from Plutarch, *Life of Caesar*, 10 (also in the life of Cicero and in Suetonius, *Lives of the Caesars: Julius*, 74). The wife in question was his third, Pompeia.

194 *Colonel Chartres*: Colonel Francis Chartres, or Charteris (1675–1732) was a rapist, pimp, cheat, and usurer, expelled from the army and described in a footnote to l. 20 of Pope's *Epistle to Bathurst* as 'a man infamous for all manner of vices', and by Arbuthnot, in an epitaph appended to the same note, as 'the most unworthy of all mortals'.

195 *Certainly . . . invisible*: from Bacon's 'Of Simulation and Dissimulation', *Works*, ed. Spedding *et al.*, vi. 387.

197 *Cato ... Clodius*: i.e. Cato Censorinus (see note to p. 181) and Publius Clodius Pulcher (*c*.93–52 BC), an irresponsible and corrupt politician in late republican Rome who was once tried for entering the house of Julius Caesar during the all-female Bona Dea festival dressed as a woman harpist.

198 *prodesse quam conspici*: have progress than draw attention to myself.

décrotteuse: a lady to polish your manners.

199 *Would you ... Probatum eşt*: it is proven. These, and the lines which follow, are C's own.

Abbati ... Monsignori: abbots and prelates of the Vatican Court.

entregent: see note to p. 117.

le ton léger ... compagnie: the unforced and agreeable air of polite company.

Charles the Fifth ... ettina: Charles V, Holy Roman Emperor from 1519 to 1556, is said to have remarked, 'To God I speak Spanish, to women Italian, to men French, and to my horse German.' His knowledge of German was suitably scanty. *Etta* and *ina* added to a name signify 'dear sweet'; *ettina* enhances the effect.

200 *il faut du brillant ... fort poli*: there must be sparkle, even a little swagger, but nothing coarse: a lively, unforced, and noble air With men, a bearing at once respectful and worthy of respect; with women, a light, playful, waggish, chattering manner, but always strictly polite.

Monsieur Villettes ... Madame Clerici: Arthur Villettes (*c*.1702–76) had been HM Resident at the Court of Savoy in Turin from 1741 to 1749, and had just moved as minister to the Helvetic Cantons. The first husband of the Milanese hostess Teresa di Castalbarco (d. 1765) was called Simonetta; her second was Francis III of Modena. Mme de Clerici is cited in Dutens, *Mémoires d'un voyageur*, i. 327, as one of the first women of fashion in Milan.

201 *earthquakes*: for which some blamed Fielding's *Tom Jones* (1749).

Mr. Osborne's: Thomas Osborne jnr. (d. 1767) succeeded to the business in Gray's Inn established by his father (d. 1743), whose most notable acquisition (1742) had been the Earl of Oxford's library. See Pope, *The Dunciad*, II. 167, for his piracy of Pope's folio Homer.

Collana ... Macchiavel: *collana* means 'collection', in this case the *c*.130 Greek and Latin classics published by Aldo Manuzio ('Aldus') in Venice between 1495 and 1515, notable for their high editorial and typographical standards. The first of the so-called

'Testina' editions of Machiavelli's works, in five parts, is dated 1550.

201 *Neustadt and Abo*: during the Great Northern War (1700–21), in which Sweden fought Russia, Saxony-Poland, and Denmark-Norway, Russia occupied Finland from 1713 to 1721, forcing Sweden to cede the SE part of the country under the 1721 Treaty of Nystad (Uusikaupunki). The Treaty of Abo concluded the Russo-Swedish war of 1741–3, allowing for the return of some Finnish territory to Sweden in exchange for installing Russia's preferred candidate as Swedish Crown Prince.

202 *the affairs of Italy*: under the Treaty of Utrecht (1713), Naples, Milan, and Sardinia were ceded to Charles VI of Austria. Sicily went to Victor Amadeus II of Savoy. The 1718 Treaty of London, however, ordered the exchange of Sardinia for Sicily; this same treaty provided that the dukedoms of Parma and Piacenza in NW Italy should, in the event of the last Farnese, Duke Antonio, dying without issue, go to the first son of his niece, Isabella of Spain. Antonio duly died childless in 1731, leaving Don Carlos to inherit. During the War of the Polish Succession (1733–5), Spain sided with France against Austria and Savoy, and Don Carlos seized Naples and Sicily, declaring himself king; at the subsequent 1st Treaty of Vienna (1735) he was allowed to keep the twin crowns (Charles's 'Cession') on condition that he renounce Parma and Piacenza to Austria, which he did. The Treaty of Aix-la-Chapelle (1748), which ended the War of the Austrian Succession, returned the duchies to Spain, but to Don Carlos's younger brother, Philip. The King of Spain in 1750 was Ferdinand VI, Carlos's half-brother; when he died in 1759 and Carlos became King Carlos III, Naples and Sicily went to Carlos's third son Ferdinand, it being agreed that no one could hold the crowns of Spain and Naples.

Χαριτες, Χαριτες: *The Graces! The Graces!*

Court of Vienna ... barrier towns: during the war of the Austrian Succession (1740–8), Britain was subsidizing Austria to defend the Austrian Netherlands, regarded as a barrier against French attack on the Dutch provinces and so on British trading interests. Austria withdrew its troops when territory closer to home was threatened, and France broke through into the Dutch provinces. At the Treaty of Aix-la-Chapelle (1748) it was returned to Austria amid false expectations that it would then be adequately fortified.

203 *Boden's trumpery ... ill filled*: *Boden's trumpery* is obscure; C wrote a letter to a Capt. Charles Bodens, a wit and amateur scribbler, in

June 1753. Philippe, Duc d'Orléans (1674–1723), was regent during Louis XV's minority, a leading patron of music and painting; and his son Louis (1703–52) an austerely pious and learned man who retired to an abbey to write Christian apologetics. Charles de Lorraine (1525–74), Archbishop of Rheims from 1538, was a Grand Inquisitor and member of the King's Council under Henri II. He attended the Council of Trent, 1562–3.

Comte Obdam's virtu: Unico Wilhelm, Count Wassanaer-Obdam (1692–1766) was a leader of the Dutch republican party, opposed to the installation of William IV as Stadholder. *Virtu* is used in the Machiavellian sense of a display of manly, civic virtues.

204 *Hermes ... Ant.*: a bust of Hermes as a young Roman with a breastplate and mantle, in marble ... Bacchus, with an ivy garland ... the head of a young Roman on a pedestal ... a statue with anaglyphs, proclaiming a sacrifice in honour of Priapus. (*Ant.* is short for *antiquarius*, belonging to antiquity.)

Girardon: François Girardon (1628–1715) produced statues for Versailles, Vaux-le-Vicomte, and the Sorbonne (Richelieu's tomb).

l'un portant l'autre: likewise.

un coup d'œil vif et pénétrant: a quick and discerning glance.

Hop: Lt.-Gen. Hendrik Hop (1686–1761) was Dutch envoy to the Court of St James.

Madame du Boccage ... Abbé Guasco: Marie Anne Le Page (1710–1802), wife of Fiquet du Bocage, saw her *Paradis terrestre, poème imité de Milton* published in 1749. *Les Amazones* flopped at the Comédie française in the same year. C says she 'did not show off her wit'. Hoping to secure her patronage of Stanhope during his 1751 stay in France, C had busts made of Shakespeare, Milton, Pope, and Dryden for the du Bocage house in Normandy, observing that Shakespeare 'sometimes deserves the best [reception], and sometimes the worst'. Octavien de Guasco, Comte de Clavières (1712–81), edited the letters of his friend Montesquieu and wrote historical works.

205 *Il est très aimable ... chère*: he is most agreeable, most well-mannered, he is intimate with all that is best here, and he lives very well.

Madame de Mirepoix: Anne Margarite Beauveau, Duchesse de Mirepoix (1707–91), whose second husband, Gaston, Duc de

Mirepoix, was French ambassador to the Court of St James from 1749 to 1755.

206 *Blackheath*: i.e. the Christopher Wren house at Blackheath which C had inherited from his brother John in 1748. In the one-acre garden he grew fruit and vegetables from seeds sent by Dayrolles, keeping the house as a country residence.

Bentinck ... Vienna: Hop's position as Dutch envoy had often been undermined (like C's during his period in office) by secret negotiations between the British government and Count Willem Bentinck (1704–68), confidential minister to the Prince of Orange.

The Prince of Wales's last child ... se délecte: i.e. Frederick William (1750–65), eighth of the nine children of Frederick, Prince of Wales, who died the following year. The two Secretaries of State were Newcastle and Bedford; the latter was often criticized for shunning business at Westminster in favour of his estate at Woburn, where in C's words he 'gambolled and delighted in himself'.

207 *Earl of Huntingdon*: Francis Hastings, 10th Earl of Huntingdon (1729–89) had met Stanhope at Westminster School. Master of the Horse to the Prince of Wales, 1756–60, continuing for a year after his master's accession as George III. Made guardian to C's heir in 1772.

208 *Lady Hervey*: Mary Lepell (1700–68), maid of honour to the Princess of Wales in 1715, married John, Lord Hervey of Ickworth (Pope's 'Sporus' in the *Epistle to Dr Arbuthnot*, 305–33) in 1720. C met her at court in 1717, associated with her at Leicester House when Prince George broke from his father, George I, and was godfather to her son in 1732. Celebrated as a wit and beauty by Voltaire, Gay, and Pope.

209 *puff*: see note to p. 165.

210 *pleasing abord*: the man who prospered through his pleasing way of greeting people was Armand, Duc de Richelieu (1696–1788), great-nephew of the cardinal and a distinguished soldier who took Minorca from the British in 1756. His court gallantries became infamous after his private papers were written up as memoirs by Soulavie.

Président Hénault: i.e. *Nouvel Abrégé chronologique de l'histoire de France* (1744) by Charles-Jean Hénault (1685–1770), magistrate in the Paris *parlement* (hence 'Président', or presiding judge). His book evinces strong monarchic sympathies.

les Mémoires de Sully: i.e. the 'London' edition (1747), published in Paris, of *Économies royales* by Maximilien de Béthune, Duc de Sully (1559–1641), minister to Henri IV.

211 *quantum*: amount.

212 *Mr. Harte . . . will leave you there*: Harte had been made Canon of Windsor in 1750 and acquired the valuable living of St Austell and St Blazey, in Cornwall, where he retired to write.

valet de place: a *valet de chambre* is a manservant, a *valet de place* a courier.

les spectacles: see note to p. 148.

les petits jeux de commerces: i.e. the card-game 'commerce', popular from the early eighteenth century.

213 *id genus omne*: see note to p. 74.

c——s and p——s: presumably 'claps' and 'peppers', common colloquialisms for venereal disease.

214 *subsidies . . . during the last war*: see note to p. 202.

215 *a Sylph or a Gnome*: C may derive these terms from Pope, *The Rape of the Lock*, or from Pope's source, *Le Comte de Gabalis* (see note to p. 97). His use of them seems ironic: Pope says that gnomes are 'Daemons of Earth [which] delight in Mischief'; while sylphs are kindly and protective 'upon a Condition very easie to all true *Adepts*, an inviolate preservation of Chastity', which was hardly on Stanhope's agenda.

Seneca says . . . God should know: adapted from Seneca, *Epistles*, 10. 5.

Lord Albemarle . . . Mr. Yorke: William Anne Keppel, 2nd Earl of Albemarle (1702–54) had become ambassador extraordinary at Paris in 1748 after a military career which embraced service at Dettingen and Culloden, where he commanded the first line. A high-spending envoy, he employed Stanhope in a minor clerical post from Mar. 1751. Also at Culloden was his secretary, Joseph Yorke, later Baron Dover (1724–92), son of the Lord Chancellor, Hardwicke. Later in 1751 Yorke succeeded Solomon Dayrolles as HM Resident at The Hague, where he was ambassador from 1761 to 1780.

216 *J'ose vous promettre . . . nous autres*: I venture to promise you that he will soon be like one of us.

217 *quae te . . . homme*: whatever beautiful woman enchants you, you are not the slave of any demeaning passion. From Horace, *Odes*, 1. 27. 14. C adds that a civil attachment becomes a gentleman.

218 *suaviter in modo*: i.e. *suaviter in modo, fortiter in re*—gentle in manner, strong in performance. Derived from a maxim of Claudio Aquaviva, Jesuit General, in *Industrie ad Curandos Animae Morbos* (1606).

en badinant, le galopin d'ici: jokingly, the errand-boy of the place. C recommends that he go on to say 'this is my department; I take it upon myself; be assured that I will acquit myself superbly.'

liant: winning.

219 *Lord Bolingbroke's*: either *A Dissertation upon Parties* (1735) or *Remarks on the History of England* (1743), collections of Bolingbroke's articles for the *Craftsman*, an anti-Walpole journal begun in 1726.

Martial ... non amo te: I do not love you, Sabidis, but I can't say why. All that I can say is that I don't love you. Martial, *Epigrams*, 1. 32.

220 *respectable Hottentot*: Boswell, *Life of Johnson*, says that this was meant to be Johnson himself, although Johnson thought it was George, Lord Lyttelton, for C's similar description of whom see p. 157. For Boswell, ii. 159 (Everyman edn.).

Cambridge ... contradiction: C had left Trinity Hall, Cambridge, in 1714 after a stay of just over a year.

221 *a pleasing Falstaff ... pleasing in others*: Shakespeare, *2 Henry IV*: 'I am not only witty in myself, but the cause that wit is in other men' (1. ii. 9–10).

du bois dont on en fait: good material for Lady Hervey's attentions.

St Paul ... some: Paul's First Epistle to the Corinthians, 9: 22: 'I am made all things to all men, that I might by all means save some.'

The prostrate lover ... kneels to rise: Cp. Dryden, *Amphitryon*:
    Th'offending Lover, when he lowest lies,
    Submits, to conquer; and but kneels, to rise. (III. i. 609–10).

qui veut ... éduquer: who really wishes to assume the task of educating you. For *Madame de Lursay* see p. 184 and note.

222 *qu'elle faisoit ... nœuds*: she will thereby create bonds between you.

de vos secrets ... honnête: wishing to be the faithful keeper of his son's secrets, C asks him if he is enjoying 'the glamour of high society, plays, balls, operas, and court'; or 'small assemblies, less clamorous but no less agreeable for that'. He wants to know where Stanhope is 'established' and whether he is still considering playing at some polite attachment to a society woman.

Abbé Nolét ... l'Abbé Sallier: Jean Antoine Nollet (1700–70), a French philosopher noted for his writings on electricity; Marcel had been the leading Parisian dancing master for forty years, and is said to have remarked that while in other countries people jumped, only the French danced; Claude Sallier (1685–1761) was the author of *Mémoires de l'Académie des Inscriptions*, of which he was a member.

a bill ... Calendar: for C's own explanation, see below, pp. 223–4. C brought the bill to the House of Lords on 20 Feb. 1751, 'an astronomer in spite of [him]self', and moved the second reading on 18 Mar. Newcastle, nervous of all change, tried to dissuade him, perhaps anticipating the protests which ensued calling for the 'missing' eleven days to be restored.

223 *fin fin*: last, most secret part.

224 *Pope Gregory ... this error*: in 1582.

225 *Lord Macclesfield*: George Parker, 2nd Earl of Macclesfield (1697–1764), astronomer and colleague of William Jones, with whom he studied at his Shirburn Castle Observatory. In 1752 he was elected President of the Royal Society, to which his preliminary paper on the lunar and solar years had been submitted in 1750.

mob: *OED* has 'Without *the*: Disorderly or lower-class people forming a crowd'. C's dictum is a translation of Retz, *Maxims*, no. 36.

226 *Prenez l'éclat ... homme*: assume the lustre and polish of a gentleman.

227 *procureur ... first Commis*: respectively, attorneys and chief clerks.

an Iphigenia: daughter of Agamemnon, according to some versions of the story sacrificed to permit the passage of Greek ships to Troy; here, presumably, a type of the beautiful and willing victim.

Sir Charles Hotham: the 6th Baronet Hotham (d. 1767), son of C's sister, Gertrude, who had married the 5th Baronet in 1724. He travelled in France in 1751 and became Groom of the Bedchamber to George III in 1761.

228 *philosophers ... in every part*: probably a reference to Plato's *Timaeus*, or Plotinus's *Enneads*.

229 *Il est étonnant ... des phrases*: it is astonishing that a man of such sense, such propriety and delicacy of taste, should express himself with so little elegance and refinement. He is quite negligent of his diction and turns of phrase.

230 *dégourdir*: to remove stiffness.

non est hic locus: this is not the place for these matters.

Desnoyers: dancing master to Frederick, Prince of Wales.

Madame Dupin: Louise de Fontaine Dupin (1707–99) held literary *salons* at Paris and Chenonceaux which were attended by Fontenelle, Marivaux, and Rousseau.

231 *Blot . . . l'autre*: Mme du Blot was the 17-year-old niece of C's friend, Mme de Monconseil, maid of honour to the Duchess of Orléans and married to Gilbert de Chavigny, Baron de Blot-le-Chateau. C advises Stanhope that enjoyment of her does not prohibit enjoyment of Mme Dupin. It was at this time that Stanhope was in fact first taking an interest in his future wife.

Les bienséances: propriety, decency.

232 *jamais parler . . . pendu*: never talk of ropes in the house of a hanged man. Derived from Terence, *Phormio*, 686.

233 *badinage*: bantering. *Enjouement* means 'playfulness'.

Maréchale: the wife of a field-marshall.

234 *badinage . . . polissonerie*: bantering spiced even with a little smut.

pont-neuf . . . la Maréchale de Coigny: C hopes that Stanhope would not sing a ballad to the wife of François de Franquetot, Maréchal de Coigny (1670–1759), victor over the Austrians at Guastella (1734).

jeux de main: horseplay, practical jokes.

giuoco di mano . . . villano: horse-play is rogue's play. Recorded in E. Jones, *Dictionary of Foreign Phrases and Comical Quotations* (Edinburgh, 1910).

236 *mens sana . . . sano*: a sound mind in a healthy body. From Juvenal, *Satires*, 10. 356.

Nullum . . . prudentia: see note to p. 46.

mohairs: requested by Stanhope as presents for Mesdames du Blot, de Polignac, and Monconseil. Mme Morel may have been the wife of Stanhope's former teacher at Westminster.

237 *seeing you here*: Stanhope visited his father from Aug. to Nov. for a thorough inspection.

alteratives: medicines to alter bodily processes.

238 *bags*: a pouch, usually of silk, to contain the back part of a wig. Probably another reference to the lanky Lord Lyttelton (see p. 157).

240 *avec onction ... attendrissement*: with unction and a kind of sorrow.

241 *Major Irwine*: John Irwine (1728–88) met C in Ireland in 1746; C
     gave him letters of introduction when he toured Europe two
     years later. He reputedly suggested to C the article 'Good
     Breeding' which appeared in the *World*, 30 Oct. 1755. Later
     served under Ferdinand of Brunswick in 1760 and became both
     MP for East Grinstead and a Major-General in 1762. He
     corresponded with C between 1746 and 1766.

     Sackville ... out upon: Lord George Sackville Germain (1716–85)
     was secretary to the Ld.-Lt. of Ireland, who was his father, the
     Earl of Dorset. Irwine attained the rank of Lt.-Col. in 1752, and
     in his father's regiment, the 5th Irish foot; whether by bribing
     commissioner Pearce is not known.

242 *les absens ... tort*: the absent are always in the wrong. See also
     Wilson, *English Proverbs*, 1. C had just been reading the letters of
     Anne, 'Ninon' de Lenclos (1620–1705), who claimed to have
     quoted this proverb every time she was unfaithful to her
     husband. The general to whom C applies this proverb has not
     been identified; it is not likely to have been Irwine's father, Lt.-
     Gen. in the 5th Irish Foot.

     Lieutenant Heathcote: William Heathcote was described by C in a
     letter of Dec. 1750 to Dorset, Ld.-Lt. of Ireland, as his 'third
     page'; a younger brother and on half-pay after his company was
     disbanded.

     the Primate ... Clements: i.e. the Primate of Ireland—at this time
     George Stone (*c.*1708–64), Archbishop of Armagh—and the
     bishops.

     Bishop of Waterford: i.e. Richard Chenevix (see note to p. 27). C's
     reproach regarding his health may have been carried by Dr Noah
     Thomas (1720–92), later physician to George III, although there
     were at this time also three bishops called Dr John Thomas.

243 *promotions ... Tuam*: the health of Bishop Josiah Hort
     (*c.*1674–1751), who had lost his voice and travelled to the Riviera
     to recover it, had been a matter of controversy since his
     appointment in 1742. He was succeeded in 1752 not by Henry
     Maule, of Meath, but John Ryder.

     the copper mine: small deposits of copper were mined in Wicklow.

     Ireland improves daily: increased textile and agricultural production
     caused a 47 per cent rise in exports during the 1740s, compared
     with 26 per cent in the previous decade.

244 *caducity*: premature loss of faculties.

scene of business: a reference to Stanhope's post at the British embassy in Paris, obtained in March 1751.

245 ευφωνια: euphony.

246 *d'Ossat ... D'Avaux ... Temple*: Cardinal Arnauld d'Ossat (1537–1604), political adviser and author of letters to Henri IV and his minister the Marquis de Villeroy (pub. 1624); Jean Antoine, Comte d'Avaux, French ambassador to The Hague until 1688, where his *Lettres et Négociations* were published in 1710; Sir William Temple (1628–99), English ambassador at The Hague and patron of Swift, who published his *Letters* in 1700.

247 *Par negotiis ... supra*: equal to business and not too grand for it. Tacitus, *Annals*, 6. 39, recounts the death of Poppaeus Sabinus, a man of humble extraction who rose by friendship with emperors and succeeded not through great abilities but by efficiency— perhaps a reminder of Stanhope's ambiguous position *vis-à-vis* the family name of which he was given to boasting.

volto sciolto: see note to p. 105.

tragedy of Varon: by Jean-Hyacinthe, Vicomte de Grave, presented at the Comédie française on 20 Dec. 1751.

249 *Cato the Stoic ... blank verse*: Marcus Porcius Cato, called Uticensis (95–46 BC), committed suicide at Utica after learning of Pompey's defeat by Caesar. By 1752, five French translations of Addison's *Cato* (1713) had appeared, and one original *Caton*, by François Deschamps (1715). C's tepid compromise between French and English tragedy relies heavily on Addison, *Spectator*, nos. 39, 40, 42, and 44 (all Apr. 1711), as do his comments on p. 254, on *Eugenia*.

250 *gros Jean*: a common, vulgar person.

half-guinea: i.e. the cost of a pit or box seat. C made further disparaging remarks about opera in the *World*, 14 Nov. 1754, and *Common Sense*, 15 Jan. 1738, resembling, as here, Johnson's definition, in his life of John Hughes, of Italian opera: 'an exotick and irrational entertainment'.

Sir John Lambert ... Spencer: Sir John Lambert (1690–1772) was a British banker serving expatriates, travellers, and embassy staff in Paris; he was anxious for the account of the wealthy John Spencer, youngest son of the 5th Earl of Sunderland.

251 *Princes Borghese*: i.e. the sons of Agnese Colonna, Principessa Borghese (1702–80), a Roman society hostess who often enter-

tained English visitors, though not in the way C's 'relations' suggests.

King and the Parliament . . . Archbishop: the dispute began in 1749, when the Archbishop of Paris, Christophe de Beaumont, instructed clergy not to give the last rites to those without a certificate proving they had confessed to a priest who had accepted the anti-Jansenist papal bull of 1713, *Unigenitus*. Louis XV supported de Beaumont, but the Paris *parlement*, after protests from Jansenists, moved to arrest any priest who refused them the last rites. Beaumont had tried to install his own candidate as head of the *Salpetrière*, a home for old women, while a royal declaration of Mar. 1751 had given him control over ecclesiastical appointments at the Hôpital général, formerly a haven for Jansenists. Marc-Pierre de Paulmy, Comte d'Argenson (1696–1764), was Secretary of State for War, founder of the École militaire, and a close ally of the king.

252 *Le Donne . . . io canto*: of ladies and knights, of arms and love, of chivalry, of courageous deeds, I sing—the opening lines of Ariosto's *Orlando Furioso* (1516).

Alcina's person . . . Orlando's lost wits: *Orlando Furioso*, Canto VI. 35–60, and Canto XXXIV. 68–92 (refs. to the final version, of 1532).

253 *French Grammar . . . Synonimes François*: i.e. the *Grammaire générale* (1660) by Antoine Arnauld and Claude Lancelot, Jansenist scholars who worked in the former Cistercian convent of Port-Royal; Claude Buffier's *Grammaire* (1709); and *Synonymes françois* (1736) by Abbé Gabriel Girard.

254 *Francis's Eugenia*: the Revd Philip Francis's translation of *Cénie* by Françoise de Grafigny opened on 17 Feb. 1752 at Drury Lane with Garrick in the leading role, and closed after six showings on the 25th. C had read the play in manuscript and approved. Francis (1708–73) also translated Horace and taught Gibbon. He dedicated his play *Constantine* to C in 1754. The author of *Have at you All* (20 Feb. 1752) agreed with C's opinion of the play, declaring it 'a true tragedy, tho' nobody dies in it'.

Horace's rule: in *Ars Poetica*, 185–6—'don't let Medea murder the children in front of the audience'.

Monsieur D'Aillon: mentioned in a letter of May 1751 as 'an old friend' of C's, entrusted to report back on Stanhope's progress.

255 *The representation . . . principles*: for *suaviter in modo*, see note to p. 218. By *Revolution principles* C means those of the Glorious

Revolution of 1688, permitting resistance to a monarch acting outside the law. The *parlement* issued a series of representations against the King's religious policy (culminating in the *Grandes Remonstrances* of Apr. 1753) which stated its right to resist the King in defending the laws of the realm. See also note to p. 251.

Duclos . . . en France: there is a germ of reason beginning to unfold in France. Adapted from *Considerations sur les mœurs de ce siècle* (1751), chap. 10, by Charles Pineau Duclos (1704–72), historian, moralist, and friend of Voltaire.

256 *Voltaire . . . Bolingbroke*: C had just read Bolingbroke's *Letters on the Study and Use of History* (written 1735–8, pub. 1752), which criticizes antiquarian approaches to history in favour of finding examples of conduct useful to readers. Voltaire's *Le Siècle de Louis XIV* (1751), based on unprecedented reading of memoirs and interviews with survivors, was published in Berlin. Its praise of Louis XIV was widely taken as criticism of the present king; in 1751 Voltaire's French home had been raided by officials looking for satirical material concerning Louis XV and Mme de Pompadour.

258 *Monsieur Stanhope . . . réussira*: Mr Stanhope has thrown himself into politics, and I believe he will be successful.

Duke of Marlborough . . . Allies: i.e. in Nov. 1705, when Marlborough visited Berlin to soothe the nerves of Frederick I (1657–1713), styled King *in* Prussia from 1701, in deference to Polish interests. Prussia was allied with Britain, Austria, the Dutch provinces, and Savoy against France and Spain in the War of the Spanish Succession (1701–13).

qu'il étoit . . . publique: that he was the most distinguished and pleasant man in the kingdom, and although the minister's son-in-law, was very popular. From *Le Siècle de Louis XIV*, chap. 20. François d'Aubusson, Duc de la Feuillade (1625–91) was a Maréchal de France.

oderint modo timeant: 'let them hate as long as they fear', from *Atreus*, 203, by the Roman dramatist Accius (170–90 BC), was a favourite remark of Caligula's; according to C it would have been wiser to say, 'as long as they love me I have nothing to fear'.

259 *Lord and Lady Blessington*: William Stewart (1709–69), Viscount Mountjoy, was granted his earldom in 1745 on C's recommendation. His wife was Eleanor (d. 1774); their spoiled and only son died living it up in Paris.

260 *Sir Isaac Newton's prism*: developed in the late 1660s, it dispersed sunlight passed through a slit into its main constituent colours.

261 *Galigai Maréchale d'Ancre*: Leonora Dori, known as 'Galigai' because her mother pretended to come from a family of that name, was Lady of the Bedchamber to Henri IV's wife, Marie de Medici. Her husband, Concino Concini, Maréchal d'Ancre, was assassinated in 1617; she was executed in the same year.

John Trott: a bumpkin. See Wilson, *English Proverbs*, 413.

rusticus expectat: Horace, *Epistles*, 1. 2. 42, says that the man who puts off the hour of correct living is like 'the bumpkin who sat waiting' for the river to run out.

262 *volto sciolto*: see note to p. 105.

263 *plus ... souvenir*: most tender and respectful remembrance.

si vis me flere: if you want me to weep [you must first feel grief yourself]. Horace, *Ars Poetica*, 102.

264 *bridon*: a snaffle.

saut de mouton: bucked.

Madame Dayrolles: Dayrolles had married Christabella Peterson in 1751; their first child, Thomas, was born in July 1752.

265 *Mitchell*: i.e. Andrew Mitchell (1708–71), Dayrolles's commissary at Brussels, later knighted and made ambassador to Prussia.

King of the Romans: the title of Holy Roman Emperor had been with one exception *de facto* hereditary in the Austrian royal family for over 300 years, although the Electors of the German States still gathered to vote in Frankfurt. Both Newcastle and George II believed that Anglo-Austrian relations could be cemented by supporting Maria Theresa's son, Joseph, as the successor to the title, to which end hefty 'subsidies' were distributed to the Electors to persuade them to vote for Joseph. The absurdity of this scheme was to be the subject of C's last parliamentary speech, in 1755. Eventually Austria declined to co-operate without France's agreement, and Britain and Austria were at war four years later. Joseph did eventually succeed his father, Francis I, in 1765.

Maïence: i.e. Mainz, whose archbishop presided over the electoral college of the Holy Roman Empire. *Mayence* is the French spelling.

266 *to blame it*: the bishop's wife had died at the beginning of the month.

267 *Brunswick, Cassel ... Berlin*: the Duchy of Brunswick was bound by treaty and family ties to Prussia; Prince Ferdinand was knighted for services in the defence of Hanover during the Seven Years War. Kassel was a principal seat of the house of Hesse-Kassel; Landgrave Frederick I was married to George II's daughter Mary. Both Hesse-Kassel and Brunswick rejected Austria's call for a 'war of the Empire' against Prussia in 1756. The Berlin Carnival took place in mid-February, on the weekend before Ash Wednesday.

Ratisbon ... the Hague: Ratisbon, now Regensburg, in Bavaria, home of the Imperial Diet, at which Stanhope was to be British representative in 1763—'in good time' indeed. Dayrolles had become HM Resident at Brussels (Court of Charles of Lorraine, Maria Theresa's brother-in-law, who administered the Austrian Netherlands) in 1751. Joseph Yorke (Stanhope's former colleague from the embassy in Paris), was Resident at The Hague.

Ella è anche Padrone: you too are the master.

268 *mores ... urbes*: the ways of many men and cities. A rendering of Homer, *Odyssey*, 1. 3.

269 *powers of the States ... Hartz*: Bremen, a river port, was the second largest Hanoverian port after Hamburg (of which Harburg is now a suburb), specializing in ship-building and the processing of goods from the colonies. Stade, annexed to Hanover in 1715, was also a river port with ship-building and timber industries. The coal and potash fields of the Harz mountains were SE of the city of Hanover.

271 *ex abundanti*: from an excess [of precaution].

Comte Cobentzel: Comte Johann Karl Cobenzl (1712–70) was first minister of the Austrian Netherlands.

German Mrs. Fitzgerald: Stanhope had met Lady Mary Fitzgerald (1725–1815) in Leipzig, where she was travelling with her mother. C later became acquainted with the family (see p. 282), pronouncing Mr Fitzgerald, no doubt partly to encourage Stanhope, 'excessively awkward and vulgar' (letter to Stanhope dated 6 Jan. 1752).

272 *There are ... man and wife*: Pope, *An Essay on Criticism*, writes,
> Some, to whom Heav'n in Wit has been profuse,
> Want as much more, to turn it to its use;
> For Wit and Judgement often are at strife,
> Tho' meant each other's Aid, like Man and Wife. (80–3)

offendit solido: strikes something solid. From Horace, *Sermonum*, 2. 1. 78.

my godson: i.e. Dayrolles's son Thomas.

274 *Visage de bois . . . formes*: this was a private meeting, not an official audience (*visage de bois* means 'no one at home'); it was therefore 'according to form' for the king to meet the illegitimate Stanhope.

Venice, as Resident: this request was curtly refused by the King because of Stanhope's illegitimacy, even though other English Residents abroad had been born out of wedlock.

trin-tran: a version of *train-train*, meaning 'routine'.

275 *next May*: Christabella Dayrolles gave birth to a girl, also called Christabella, the following spring.

276 *abord*: way of greeting people.

277 *Faites un peu valoir cela*: make the most of it discreetly.

the two brothers: i.e. Pelham, first minister, and his brother, Secretary of State Newcastle.

278 *faufilé*: insinuated into favour.

Kreuningen: C had met P. A. de Huybert, Baron van Kreuningen (1693–1780), during his first embassy to The Hague. Kreuningen was then Sheriff of Muiden and an authority on the Dutch constitution.

279 *Holland . . . Sovereign*: every town in the seven provinces had a senate council which sent deputies to a provincial senate; in turn, each provincial senate sent deputies to The Hague, capital of the United Provinces. It was the deputies of the provincial senates who held sovereign power, not those at The Hague, although the latter were, as here, commonly called 'the States General'.

Lord Coventry . . . bavard: deafness makes me garrulous. 'Lady Caroline' is Lady Caroline Petersham (d. 1784), sister of Grafton, the future Secretary of State, and married to C's relation William Stanhope, later 2nd Earl of Harrington (1719–79), an eccentric and untidy man whom on this as on many other occasions she 'so thoroughly took to task' that he could only imitate the proverbial passivity of a French husband in turning a blind eye to her extra-marital exploits. Lady Coventry was the celebrated beauty Maria Gunning (1733–60), married to the 6th Earl, whose abuse of her led to her seeking refuge in an affair with Frederick, 2nd Viscount Bolingbroke.

as at the Court of Augustus ... by laws: Stanhope was in Berlin at the Court of Frederick the Great. C refers to Horace, *Odes*, 4. 15. 13–20.

qui nil molitur ineptè: who attempts nothing foolishly. Horace, *Ars Poetica*, 140. The 'other poet' is Homer, the opening of whose *Odyssey* Horace commends for its purposefulness.

Henriade: first published in 1723 as *La Ligue, ou Henri le Grand*, Voltaire's 10-canto epic of the life of Henri IV appeared in its final form in 1728, dedicated to Caroline, George II's consort. The author was in England at the time, collecting subscribers; C bought ten copies. The poem embodies the hatred of extremism and unrest which Voltaire shared with C.

280 *Epopée*: epic poem.

Homer ... I sleep: Horace, *Ars Poetica*, 360–1 — 'sometimes even the excellent Homer slumbers [i.e. has lapses]'.

Turnus: in Virgil's *Aeneid*, 7–12, Turnus is the champion of Latians who oppose Aeneas's divinely ordained mission to rebuild Troy in Italy.

darkness visible: Milton, *Paradise Lost*, 1. 63. C's subsequent judgement resembles that of Johnson, who in his *Life of Milton* wrote, 'the want of human interest is always felt'.

281 *Tasso ... coglionerìè*: in his *Gerusalemme liberata* (1581), Torquato Tasso compares Tancredi's vain attempt to escape from prison to a fish trying to avoid a whirlpool (VII. 46), while in the garden of the palace where Rinaldo is captive a parti-coloured bird speaks of the brevity of life (XVI. 13–15). *Concetti* means conceits, or more specifically here, epic similes; *le coglionerìè* the art of seizing an unexpected image.

Camoens: i.e. *Os Lusiadas* (The Portuguese) by Luis Vaz de Camoës (1524–80), published in 1572. It charts the victories of the Portuguese over the enemies of Christianity. C had probably read the French prose translation by Duperron de Castera (1735), since there was no English version between those of Richard Fanshawe (1655, in verse) and William Mickle (1776, in prose).

great and long action: Aristotle, *Poetics*, 4. 1, says that epic, like tragedy, should consist of 'one whole or complete action'.

the Massacre ... as it is: Voltaire has Henri narrate the St Bartholomew's Day Massacre to Elizabeth I, like Aeneas to Dido, in II. 175–358. The siege and famine at Paris appear in X. 179–332. Henri's amorous encounter with the fair d'Estrées is depicted in IX. 181–238 and 289–304; it is at the instigation of Discord and Henri must, like Aeneas, be reminded of his higher calling—this, and the attendance of the Graces, may explain C's interest. *Morbidezza* means delicacy of tint, while St Louis (Louis IX of France) appears to Henri in a dream throughout Canto VII, conducting him to heaven and hell and showing him his destiny. (All references are to the Geneva edition of 1970 by O. R. Taylor.)

282 *the King of Sweden*: Voltaire's *Histoire de Charles XII* appeared in 1731. Charles was a ruthless soldier who cherished private passions for eastern art, philosophy, and mathematics. Cp. his bellicose appearance in Johnson's *The Vanity of Human Wishes* (191–222).

Julius Caesar ... King of Prussia: Julius Caesar (100–44 BC) wrote incomparable descriptions of warfare in *De Bello Gallico* and *De Bello Civili*, and lavished alms upon the citizens of Rome. Titus Vespasianus (AD 39–81) captured Jerusalem in AD 70, completed the Colosseum and the Baths of Titus, and gave emergency assistance after the eruption of Vesuvius. Trajan (AD 53–117) won the Dacian and Parthian Wars and constructed the Trajan forum. As well as the military successes C reports, Frederick II encouraged industry, gave refuge to artists, philosophers, and writers including Voltaire, and wrote a good deal of music beside his *Histoire de mon temps* and *Antimachiavell*, the handbook of enlightened despotism.

dramatic pieces ... philosophical letters: 23 of Voltaire's 54 plays had by this time been performed. His *Lettres philosophiques* (1733 in England, 1734 in France), reflect upon English empiricism to the disadvantage of Pascal's penitential philosophy and were denounced by the Paris *parlement*, causing him to seek refuge. C goes on to say that to verify his estimation of Voltaire was 'within the compass' of Stanhope, since Voltaire was then at Berlin.

portée: see note to p. 133.

Monsieur de Maupertuis: Pierre Louis Moreau de Maupertuis (1698–1759), director of the Berlin Academy of Science in 1740, after travelling to Lapland to prove that the world was shaped as calculated by Newton. Satirized by Voltaire in *Diatribe du Docteur Akakia* (1752). For Algarotti and Fontenelle, see notes to pp. 121–2.

Mrs. Fitzgerald ... Non sum qualis eram: I am not the man I was. From Horace, *Odes*, 4. 1. 3. For Mrs Fitzgerald, see p. 271 and note.

283 *Madame Maintenon's letters*: Françoise d'Aubignac, Marquise de Maintenon (1635–1719), was secretly married to Louis XIV, probably in 1684.

Abbé de Fénelon . . . 185th letter: François de Salignac de la Mothe-Fénelon (1651–1715) was a theologian whose belief in 'Quietism' brought him into conflict with Louis XIV and the militantly Catholic Mme de Maintenon. C's account is wide of the mark: Fénelon almost certainly did know of her secret marriage to the King when this letter was written, in 1690. See *Lettres et opuscules de Fénelon* (Paris, 1850), 229–30.

284 *Sarah . . . owing*: Abraham and Sarah were the parents of Isaac. See Genesis 16 and 21. Fénelon advised Mme de Maintenon to have the same submission to the King as Abraham had to God.

Sir William Stanhope: C's younger brother William (1702–72) was at this time MP for Buckingham.

Comte de Schullemburg: possibly the grandson of Matthias John, elder brother of C's mother-in-law Melusina von der Schullenberg, Duchess of Kendal. He, too, sang Stanhope's praises.

285 *virtù*: in the Machiavellian sense—a display of splendour.

Richelieu . . . d'Olonne: of those not mentioned elsewhere: Henri, Vicomte de Turenne (1611–75), Louis XIV's Marshal General from 1660; Louis II de Bourbon, Prince de Condé (1621–86), general celebrated for victories over the Spanish, and a close ally of Turenne; Françoise, Marquise de Montespan (1640–1707), mistress of Louis XIV; Marie, Duchesse de Fontanges (1661–81), another mistress; Marie de Bretagne, Duchesse de Montbazon (1612–57), exiled by Louis XIII, returned to play a minor role in the rebellion, or *Fronde*, of 1648; Marie de Rohan-Montbazon, Duchesse de Chevreuse (1600–79), another opponent of Richelieu and Mazarin. *Mogueville* is presumably Françoise de Motteville (1621–89), lady-in-waiting to Louis XIII's queen and a friend of Charles I's, and author of celebrated memoirs; by *d'Olonne* C may mean the author and diarist, Marie Catherine d'Aulnoy (*c.*1650–1705).

286 *Majesty*: this complaint was written for C's own satisfaction and was never sent. It expresses some of the polished resentment he felt towards George II.

otium cum dignitate: leisure with honour. Cicero, *Pro Sestio*, 45. 98, says this is what is most desirable for all healthy, good, and prosperous people.

287 *Pretender ... Derby*: Prince Charles Edward reached Derby on 4 Dec. 1745 and retreated two days later. C raised troops from Ireland.

288 *Honour ... than life*: among many possible sources, this most closely resembles Shakespeare, *Troilus and Cressida*, v. iii. 27: 'the brave man | Holds honour far more precious-dear than life'.

289 *a ghastly smile*: *Paradise Lost*, ii. 845–6, where Death 'Grinned horrible a ghastly smile'.

blasemeer-op: C confuses two German expressions. *Blasemeer-op* was an obscenity similar to 'kiss my arse'; but *aufblasen* means to signal an order with a blow on a bugle or trumpet—here, to puff oneself up self-importantly (a common caricature of a German corporal).

291 *Miss Hamilton, Lady Murray's niece*: Sir Patrick Murray, 4th Baronet of Ochtertyre, had married Helen Hamilton (d. 1773) in 1741; it was her brother's daughter Elizabeth who liked Stanhope's countenance.

John Trott: see note to p. 261.

à pure perte: utterly lost.

dispersion by Titus: Titus, emperor from AD 79, was sent by his father Vespasian to quell the Jewish revolt. Jerusalem fell in AD 70 and was ransacked, the Temple of Herod the Great being destroyed.

292 *Thalmud ... Targums*: the Talmud ('learning') is an encyclopaedia of Jewish myths and customs, regarded as a sacred book until the eighteenth century; the Mishna ('repetition') is the part of it which deals with Jewish law. Targums are Aramaic translations of the Old Testament, made for Jews of the first century BC who no longer spoke Hebrew.

Abas Saul ... receive: apparently from the Talmud Nidda 24b— 'Abba Sha'ul says: I was a burier of the dead. Once I opened a grave and stood up to my neck in the eyesocket of a corpse. Then a voice said, "That was the eye of Absalom".' Absalom was also said to be a giant.

Platina ... Busbequius: the *History of the Growth and Decay of the Ottoman Empire* by Dmitri Cantemir, Prince of Moldavia (1673–1723), appeared in English in 1734–5, translated from the original Latin (1716). Augier de Busbecq (1522–92), a Flemish diplomat, represented the brother of Emperor Charles V at

Constantinople and wrote much admired letters in Latin which described the court of Suleiman the Magnificent. Sir Paul Rycaut published the first version of *The History of the Turkish Empire* in 1680 (this was a continuation of the history published in 1603 by Richard Knolles), and in 1685 translated as *The Lives of the Popes* the masterpiece of Bartolomeo Sacchi de Platina which was first published in 1479 and contained remarks on the history of Turkey.

293 *Janissaries ... Vizar*: Janissaries were the personal bodyguards of the monarch, or Sultan; the chief minister was usually called the Grand Vizier.

like Sultan: Stanhope's black pointer Sultan was a present from Dayrolles; Loyola greeted his master's son on his next visit with a vicious attack to the chest, perhaps objecting to his posture.

295 *Fitz-Adam ... the World*: 'Fitz-Adam' was the pseudonym of Edward Moore (1712–57), a poet and dramatist, for whose journal the *World* C wrote anonymous articles between May 1753 and Oct. 1756, including two on Johnson's Dictionary (28 Nov. and 5 Dec. 1754). C's satirical pieces, in the style of the *Spectator* articles which he had admired in his youth, covered such items as opera, social climbers, excessive drinking, and, surprisingly, francophilia.

296 *Parliament ... Cornwall*: Stanhope was elected MP for Liskeard, without opposition, the following April. Seven years later Edward Eliot also made sure of Stanhope's seat at St Germans (which C himself had occupied in 1715) on receipt of £2,000; in 1765, however, he paid his friend to vacate it.

pedarii senatores ... sententiam: senators of inferior rank who could only follow the decisions of others.

receipt ... quantum sufficit: as much as suffices. *Receipt* means recipe.

297 *Solicitor-General, Murray*: William Murray, 1st Earl of Mansfield (1705–93), was about to become Attorney-General after Pelham's death, when Newcastle came to rely on his oratory to defend the government in the Commons against Pitt and Fox. His Oxford training consisted of the method C himself used and recommended: study of Cicero through translation into and from English.

298 *oraisons funèbres*: funeral orations, often written by distinguished members of the French academies.

299 *Mr. Pelham died*: First Minister Pelham died on 6 Mar. 1754 of

erysipelas, a disease brought on by over-eating. C's estimate of his abilities was and is widely shared.

His successor ... Newcastle: Pelham was succeeded by his brother, Newcastle, formerly Secretary of State. Philip Yorke, 1st Earl of Hardwicke (1690–1764), who was Lord Chancellor, agreed with George II to keep out Henry Fox, later Baron Holland (1705–74), then Secretary for War and a close ally of the Duke of Cumberland. Newcastle offered Fox a Secretaryship of State, but with unacceptable conditions attached. After the brief, disastrous appointment of Sir Thomas Robinson (see p. 305), Fox agreed to Newcastle's renewed offer in Nov. 1755, only to resign eleven months later after the Minorca débâcle (p. 311). Henry Bilson Legge (1708–64) became the new chancellor in spite of his enmity with George II, who refused him admission to the royal presence; the next seven years saw him dismissed from office three times and recalled twice. George Lee, DCL (1700–58), had been a favourite of the late Prince of Wales, and remained Treasurer of the Household to his widow after Pelham's death.

301 *Nihil dictum ... dictum*: nothing is said which has not been said before. One of many adaptations of Terence, *Eunuchus*, prologue, l. 41.

this moment informed: all of C's information was wrong.

tant mieux: so much the better.

302 *Lord —— ... you*: the nature of this quarrel and the name of Stanhope's antagonist are not known.

pour faire ... jeu: to smile in the face of adversity.

303 *un honnête homme ... point*: a well-bred man is a stranger to them.

Les Annales de l'Empire: i.e. *Les Annales de l'empire depuis Charlemagne*, generally considered one of Voltaire's least successful books, published in Basel (1753) and, revised, in Geneva (1754). For *Nil molitur*, see note to p. 279.

le style léger et fleuri: the light and florid style.

304 *Place-Bill*: a 'placeman' was a member of parliament appointed by the Court or the government. Place bills were introduced by the Opposition to regulate their number. In 1733 C had spoken in support of Walpole's bill to maintain a standing army of *c*.18,000, only to lose favour by opposing the Excise Bill in the same year.

305 *Sir Thomas Robinson*: a career diplomat who had been ambassador at Vienna for 18 years before negotiating the Treaty of Aix-la-Chapelle jointly with Lord Sandwich, Robinson (1695–1770),

later Baron Grantham, was chosen by Newcastle as a pliant spokesman in the Commons, where for 18 months he was mauled by Pitt and Fox before being granted the less boisterous post of Keeper of the King's Wardrobe. Lord Holderness (see p. 135 and note) had been moved from the southern secretaryship.

Magnis tamen . . . ausis: he fell aiming at great things. From Ovid, *Metamorphoses*, 2. 328, or Seneca, *De Vita Beata*, 20. 5. 13.

306 *Leti caca libri*: the romantic, inexact histories of Gregorio Leti (1630–1701) earned him the nickname 'book-shitter'. His life of Sixtus V (1669), the 'iron pope' of the Counter-Reformation, was translated into English in 1704 and 1754.

Namely . . . to wit: OED cites the first uses of these at 1450 and 1577. *Ius et norma loquendi* means 'the laws and customs of speech'.

307 *Treves and Cologne*: Trier, in the Rhineland Palatinate, and Cologne were the seats of two of the archbishop Electors.

olim . . . juvabit: the memory of this sorrow will one day bring us joy. From Virgil, *Aeneid*, 1. 203.

308 *Maupertuis . . . les faire valoir*: to know how to make the most of them. The Maupertuis quotation means '[acquainted with] all countries as the learned are with all times'. Source uncertain; possibly adapted from his *Discours académiques* (*Œuvres*, iii. 265) or *Réflexions philosophiques* (*Œuvres*, ii. 275).

La Bruyère . . . veut valoir: one values nothing in this world except what one wants to value. Not by La Bruyère, but a reminiscence of Molière, *Les Précieuses Ridicules*, IX. 278: 'Les choses ne valent que ce qu'on les fait valoir.'

Montesquieu: C had met Montesquieu (1689–1755) in The Hague in 1729, and they had travelled together to London, where C introduced him at court. His most famous work is *De L'esprit des lois* (1748), a libertarian analysis of government which saw in the British parliamentary system an ideal separation of legislative, judicial, and executive powers. Like C, he knew and admired Bolingbroke. His presidency for life of the Bourdeaux parliament was granted in recognition of his writings rather than of his regular attendance.

309 *maidenhead . . . debate*: Stanhope's maiden parliamentary speech was given on 13 Nov. 1755 during the debate on the King's speech about French encroachments in America and the protection of Hanover. He lost his thread and could not find it readily in his notes; Horace Walpole (to H. Conway, 15 Nov. 1755) said

that he and most of the other speakers were 'very bad'. This maiden speech was his last.

310 *Pelotez . . . partie*: trifle while awaiting your chance.

Mrs ——: unidentified, but C's faith in Stanhope's chances with the opposite sex was as misplaced as his political ambitions for him.

311 *Minorca . . . Admiral Byng*: Admiral John Byng was dispatched in 1755 to save the British naval base at Minorca from French attack and arrived in 1756 to find the fortress already under siege. The supporting French fleet was allowed to escape, while Byng judged that his forces were too small to attack the fortress. He retreated to Gibraltar, abandoning one guarantor of Britain's trading routes but protecting another, and returned home to public outrage. Sentenced to death in Jan. 1757, he was finally executed in March. He was widely believed to have been a scapegoat for administrative incompetence. In 1757 Pitt, attempting to break the Franco-Spanish alliance, offered Gibraltar to Spain, but he was refused.

The French . . . very ill terms: in the past year, expeditions against French positions at Niagara, Crown Point, and Fort Duquesne had failed. C was correct in predicting further losses: in August 1756 Oswego fell to the new French commander, Montcalm, as did Fort William Henry in 1757. Maria Theresa of Austria-Hungary, formerly Britain's ally, approved the Treaty of Versailles with France, which envisaged a cession of the Austrian Netherlands in return for French help in recovering Silesia. This so-called 'Diplomatic Revolution' was one cause of the Seven Years War, which broke out in 1756. Sweden was subsidized by France to enter the Seven Years War against Prussia, with whom it made a separate peace in 1762. The Duke of Cumberland, George II's second son, was an autocratic captain-general of the army to whom fears of invasion meant job security and enhanced political power, while the cost of fighting the ensuing war averaged £13.7 million per year. Relations between the courts of the King and the Prince of Wales were soured by the latter's coming of age and choosing his own 'first minister', Lord Bute, promptly backed by Pitt, whom the King disliked for his anti-Hanover views.

312 *Administration . . . Council*: Newcastle's administration had been in disarray for a month, following the loss of its chief spokesman in the Commons (William Murray, elevated by his own wish to the

Lords as Lord Chief Justice Mansfield); the losses of Oswego, Minorca, and Calcutta in the summer forced the resignations of Fox and Newcastle.

ce n'est pas là leur fait: polite people, who are not for them.

tutti quanti: as many as [can receive them].

Mademoiselle: Dayrolles's first daughter, Christabella.

specie: coined money.

313 *Fox ... influence*: Newcastle and Fox gave way to William Cavendish, 4th Duke of Devonshire (*c.*1720–64), 1st Lord of the Treasury, and William Pitt (1708–78) as Secretary of State (S), who lasted until Apr. 1757. Pitt had been Fox's ally against Newcastle. The King negotiated with Fox in Mar. 1757 but was dissuaded from reappointing him. The Lord Chancellor, Hardwicke, brought together the subsequent Pitt–Newcastle administration in June, with C's assistance.

Duke of Cumberland ... arrive there: the Army of Observation was meant to protect Hanover. Cumberland allegedly went to lead it on condition that Pitt be sacked, which he was (see note above). On 26 July he was defeated at Hastenback by a French army of 80,000 commanded by Louis, Duc d'Estrées (1695–1771), Maréchal de France, who afterwards compelled him to agree to the humiliating Convention of Kloster-Zeven, which neutralized Hanoverian forces and cost him his job and his reputation.

Mr Van-haren ... individuals: presumably Onno Zwier van Haren (1713–79), President of the State Council and noted for his anti-French views. Cumberland's army was attacked by d'Estrées in retaliation for Prussia's occupation of Saxony in 1756. In the autumn of 1756 Frederick II had already marched on Bohemia to pre-empt Austrian support for Saxony; in May 1757 he defeated the Austrians at Prague and laid siege to the city, during which over 40,000 people died. The 'quarrel of two individuals' refers to the 1748 cession of Silesia from Austria to Prussia in return for Prussian recognition of Francis I as Holy Roman Emperor— what triggered the Seven Years War was Frederick II's failure to gain Maria Theresa's assurance of her good intentions towards him.

314 *French ... irregulars*: during the last year of the War of the Austrian Succession, French resources had been inadequate to support full-scale offensives; they often made use of pirates to harass ships.

Je souffre d'être: Fontenelle had died six weeks before at the age of 100. According to Maty, he said not 'I suffer from existing', but 'I feel nothing but a difficulty in existing'. He is also reported to have said that his was the first death he had seen.

wound ... bottoms: concluded, drunk up. See Wilson, *English Proverbs*, 894.

visible or invisible: Christabella Dayrolles was expecting a third child.

315 *The installation ... I can*: the new Knight of the Garter was the 1st Lord of the Treasury, Devonshire. Mrs Irwine was the second of three, Anne Barry.

316 *Münchausen*: Stanhope had from Sept. 1756 been HM Resident at Hamburg. Monsieur Münchausen is probably Philip Adolph Münchausen, Hanoverian minister in London; his brother Gerlach Adolph was minister in Hanover.

Casserolles: OED lists the first use in English as 1725.

317 *Brest ... expedition*: this fortified Brittany port housed a large proportion of the French navy, but it was to the arsenal at Rochefort that the 'great expedition' was sent. Another disaster ensued. General Sir John Mordaunt and Admiral Hawke disagreed over naval support for an attack, the latter being unable to guarantee that his ships could enter the harbour quickly enough to pre-empt French reinforcement. The mission was abandoned and Mordaunt was court-martialled (see p. 319) but cleared.

Magnis ... ausis: see note to p. 305.

Nullum numen ... prudentia: see note to p. 46.

318 *King of Prussia's late victory*: at Rossbach, 5 Nov. 1757, with the Prussians outnumbered two to one. It was as inconclusive as C observed, although followed by a greater success at Lutynia on 5 Dec.

319 *the three General Officers*: appointed to make recommendations on Mordaunt's conduct (see note to p. 317) were Charles Spencer, 5th Earl of Sunderland and 3rd Duke of Marlborough (1706–58), a Lt.-Gen. who had become Lord Privy Seal in 1755; Lord George Sackville Germain (1716–85), former secretary to the Ld.-Lt. of Ireland (see note to p. 241), Maj.-Gen. in 1755, court-martialled for his conduct at the Battle of Minden in 1759, and Secretary of State (C) from 1779; and John, 3rd Earl Waldegrave (d. 1784), Lt.-Gen. who served at Minden and was in active opposition during the 1760s.

Hanover neutrality: the Treaty of Kloster-Zeven, signed by Cumberland but subsequently repudiated by the British government, immobilized Hanoverian troops who had shielded Prussia's western borders. Frederick II was compensated with an annual subsidy of £670,000, extra troops for the Army of Observation (to be placed under Ferdinand of Brunswick), and an agreement that no separate peace would be made with France or Austria.

320 *The birthday . . . plate*: George II was born on 10 Nov. 1683 (NS). The disgrace of the Duke of Cumberland had eased relations between the King and his grandson's court, the mother of the future George III having been a bitter opponent of Cumberland's designs on the Regency in 1751.

Earl Stanhope: Philip, 2nd Earl (1717–86), son of the politician who had been Walpole's colleague until his sudden death in 1721. C's cousin was a gifted mathematician, Fellow of the Royal Society, and a fluent speaker in the Lords.

Habeas Corpus Bill: a bill to make *Habeas Corpus ad subjudiciendum* non-discretionary was passed in the Commons but rejected in the Lords, upon Newcastle's advice and George II's wishes. The act was designed to reduce the exploitation of legal vacations as a way of evading the law and to reduce judicial discretion in permitting inquiries into the legality of detention and impressment for the armed forces.

ex abundante: from largesse.

321 *ship-money Judges . . . King in Israel*: ship money became controversial when revived by Charles I, who in 1635 obtained the opinion of ten judges that it could be levied on all parts of the country in emergencies, as defined by the monarch alone. A similar abuse of monarchic power was James II's revival of the Court of High Commission in 1686, headed by Judge Jeffreys and investing responsibility for ecclesiastical and university appointments in the Crown, so dispensing with existing laws—a leading issue in the Glorious Revolution of 1688. C uses 'Patriot' in the common eighteenth-century sense of 'defender of freedoms', so suggesting that judges, never patriotic, always serve the interests of the king. Moves to strengthen the independence of the judiciary by granting judges unlimited tenure had, like the Habeas Corpus Bill, failed in 1758. The biblical reference is to Judges 21: 25 ('In those days there was no king in Israel: every man did that which was right in his own eyes'), showing C's customary distaste for absolute power.

Major Macculough ... Mr. Russel: possibly Francis Russell, MP for Armagh borough. Major Macculough remains unidentified.

322 *Swift ... history*: *The History of the Last Four Years of the Queen* was begun in 1713 and not published until 1758, when the Dublin bookseller George Faulkner (1699–1775) added it to his existing 8-vol. collection of Swift's works in response to a pirate edition. Swift claimed that Col. George Maccartney, second to Lord Mohun, had stabbed the Duke of Hamilton, envoy to Paris, after a duel in which Hamilton was wounded; also, 'with the best faith in the world' but on the slender evidence of Plunket's *Memoirs of Torcy* (1711), that Prince Eugene of Savoy's commitment to the War of the Spanish Succession induced him to plot the death of Robert Harley, Earl of Oxford, who opposed it. For references, see vol. vii of the Blackwell Swift, ed. Davis, pp. 155 and 26–7.

The Examiner was a Tory periodical started by Bolingbroke in 1710 and edited by Swift during October of that year. *Mohocks* was the name given to men who banded together to commit acts of violence (see *Spectator* no. 324, 12 Mar. 1712)—Swift mentions only 'obscure ruffians'.

323 *Your friend's letter ... of the whole*: the Irish Parliament had been divided into three factions led by the Earl of Kildare, Archbishop George Stone of Armagh, and John Ponsonby, Speaker of the Commons. Stone and Ponsonby joined forces in 1757 to compel the autocratic Ld.-Lt. Bedford to convey Irish grievances to London.

otium cum dignitate: see note to p. 286.

324 *Princess of Cassel ... Princess Amelia*: Mary (1723–72), 4th daughter of George II, was married to Frederick, Landgrave of Hesse-Kassel; her elder sister Amelia (1711–86) resided with her father.

325 *conduct of the Russians ... Austria*: in 1755 Britain had agreed to pay Russia to defend Hanover in the event of war, but was also negotiating with Russia's enemy, Prussia, to resist any attack on the German states. Russia joined the Seven Years War on the side of France and Austria, defeating the Prussian army at Gross-Jägerndorf in Aug. 1757 and suddenly retreating, perhaps because of disagreements between Empress Elizabeth and her Prussophile heir, Peter. In Jan. 1758 the Russians took Königsberg in East Prussia but again retreated, apparently because of bad weather, to be crushed by Frederick II at Zorndorf in Aug. On the accession of Peter III in 1762, Russia made peace and

entered the war against Austria, a policy revoked following Peter's murder six months later.

King of Prussia . . . of the year: neither the next two months nor the rest of the war were so decisive. Frederick II had advanced into Moravia to lay siege to Olomouc but was forced to abandon the operation when the Austrians threatened his supply lines. Austria's position was to return more or less to that of 1748, with some loss of prestige: under the Treaty of Hubertusburg (1763), Silesia and Glatz reverted to Prussia and Saxony to its own elector; Prussia consented to the election of Joseph as Holy Roman Emperor. The port of Louisburg on Cape Breton Island, off Nova Scotia, had been captured by Britain in 1745, returned to France in 1748, and was recaptured in 1758 by Amherst, opening the way for the fall of Quebec in Sept. 1759. Ferdinand, Duke of Brunswick (1721–92) defeated a French force almost twice the size of his own at Krefeld, 23 June 1758, securing NW Germany. France was paying 7 per cent on National Debt repayments to the *fermiers générales*, syndicate financiers who lent money to the government, at the same time as paying huge insurance premiums on merchant shipping; it was also committed to subsidizing Austria, while seeing its empire in America and India eroded by British successes.

Comte Bothmar . . . Michel: Hans Caspar von Bothmer (1727–87) was Danish ambassador to the Court of St James (C may have confused his name with that of a former Hanoverian envoy, Bothmar); Dodo Heinrich, Freiherr von Knyphausen (1729–89), was Prussian ambassador; his deputy, Andreas (or Abraham) Ludwig Michel (*c.*1712–82), was constantly suspected of consorting with parliamentary opposition groups throughout his 17-year posting, being recalled a number of times before his final return home in 1764.

326 *foudre*: a large tun for storing wine.

Dixi: I have said.

Molti e felice: many and happy [days].

that thy days may be long in the land: see Exodus 20: 12. Stanhope had inherited his father's susceptibility to asthma, gout, and sudden fevers, adding to them dropsy.

the riband . . . Knights: three Knighthoods of the Garter were vacant at the time, one of them that of Sir Clement Cotterel (d. 1758), Master of Ceremonies and Vice-President of the Society of Antiquaries. The Lord Privy Seal, Richard Grenville, 2nd Earl

Temple, threatened to resign if he did not get one; eventually they were bestowed in Feb. 1760 on Temple, Prince Ferdinand of Brunswick, and the Marquis of Rockingham.

327 *three thousand . . . Europe*: Stanhope had referred to a solution for detaining prisoners of the Seven Years War.

étrennée: about to receive a present, in this case for the New Year.

Parliament . . . millions sterling: recent successes had made some members more enthusiastic about the cost of the war, which was to run to about £80 million by 1763.

Cardinal Bernis: François Joachim de Bernis (1715–94), protégé of Mme de Pompadour. As confidential intermediary he negotiated the treaties with Austria which led to the Seven Years War, and became foreign minister in 1757. Soon after his creation as a cardinal in 1758 he received a curt dismissal from the King, impatient with French reverses in the war. His flowery verses also earned the scorn of Voltaire. C's 'head-piece' and comment presumably allude to the cardinal's hat, recently acquired, and the oath of fidelity which Bernis made to get it.

328 *chalybeate*: impregnated with iron salts.

Venus rarius colatur: Venus should be honoured rarely. Hermann Boerhaave (1668–1738) was Professor of Medicine, Botany, and Chemistry at the University of Leiden, and the most celebrated teacher of medical science in Europe. He had treated C in 1728.

Pyrmont: i.e. Bad Pyrmont, a spa town SW of the city of Hanover.

329 *Harte . . . Gustavus Adolphus*: Harte's *The History of the Life of Gustavus Adolphus, King of Sweden*, 2 vols. (1759), was dedicated to C with the words, 'It is moreover an addition to my good fortune, that these imperfect labours have been perused, protected, and encouraged by One, whose single approbation is a sort of universal passport throughout all Europe.'

330 *Vertumnus . . . Priapus*: Vertumnus, an Etruscan god associated with profitable trading; Pomona, Roman goddess of fruit; and Priapus, the fertility god noted for his enormous phallus, hence C's nostalgic remark. Statues of Priapus were often used as scarecrows.

Levius . . . nefas: what cannot be set right becomes easier to bear through patience. Horace, *Odes*, 1. 24. 19.

Prince Ferdinand . . . the latter: *dementi* means failure, *summa summarum* the total of totals (from Lucretius, *De Rerum Natura*, iii. 817). C was wrong to be pessimistic: although Ferdinand had been defeated by the French at Bergen, near Frankfurt-on-Main, on 13 Apr., he was to gain revenge at Minden, against great odds, on 1 Aug., when the war began to go the way of Britain and her allies. The Elector of Brandenburg was Frederick II of Prussia.

331 *an History . . . perhaps Livy*: C had just read *A History of Scotland during the Reigns of Queen Mary and James VI until his Accession to the Crown of England*, 2 vols. (1759), by William Robertson (1721–93), whose lofty style was also admired by Hume and Gibbon. His peers, in C's view, were Enrico Caterino Davila (1576–1631), author of *Historia delle guerre civili di Francia* (1630); Francesco Guicciardini (1483–1540), who wrote *Storia d'Italia* (1561); and Titus Livius (*c.*59 BC–AD 17), whose *Ab Urbe Condita* is a history of Rome in 142 books.

333 *Lübeck, Altona*: Lübeck is a Baltic port in Schleswig-Holstein; Altona a small resort outside Hamburg, now a suburb.

334 *aequam . . . mentem*: when things become difficult, remember to keep your cool. Horace, *Odes*, 2. 3. 1.

the bark: i.e. quinine, extracted from the bark of Cinchona trees, powdered, and often used to control fever.

335 *The French . . . believe and tremble*: the threat was more real than C supposed. Bernis's successor, Choiseul, planned to restore French losses by attacking England from Ostend, the Clyde from Brest and Toulon, and Ireland with the help of a privateer, Thurot. Newcastle in particular believed and trembled (see James 2: 19), while Pitt trusted coolly to the British Navy, which destroyed a large number of ships sailing from Brest, so thwarting the plan.

While somebody . . . political faith: a reference to the disgraced Duke of Cumberland, former captain-general of the army and ally of Fox in manœuvrings for political power. See also p. 311 and note.

336 *Arthur Charles Stanhope*: C's cousin, d. 1770, and father of his heir, whose mother was A. Stanhope's second wife. The Edwyn Stanhope referred to in the letter was Arthur's first cousin (b. 1729) and, like C, a great-great-grandson of the 1st Earl of Chesterfield.

My boy . . . manna: C gave his godson and heir a sweet juice often used as a laxative. Philip Stanhope, later 5th Earl of Chesterfield (1755–1815), had been under C's direction since the age of 4; his sister, favourably cited at the end of the letter, was called Margaret. Neither his career nor his manner proved much more distinguished than C's son's: Fanny Burney, *Diary*, v. 92, said he had 'as little good breeding as any man I ever met with'; and while he was friendly with George III, he never exceeded his good fortune in gaining the nominal post of ambassador extraordinary to Madrid in 1784, spending the rest of his working days in a series of minor government positions.

337 *Dr. Plumptre*: probably Dr Robert Plumptre (1723–88), like Arthur Stanhope a native of Nottinghamshire. In 1764 he was President of Queen's College, Cambridge, having been Vice-Chancellor in 1760, and had the dubious honour in 1769 of being appointed Professor of Casuistry.

your third marriage: his second wife, Margaret Headlam, had died in 1763; in Dec. 1765 he married Frances Broade, his proposal to marry C's niece, Gertrude Hotham (see p. 338), having been rejected.

338 *My brother . . . my boy*: C's younger brother, Sir William Stanhope, had in 1762 married Ann Delaval, who was forty years his junior. They separated a year later, C proclaiming this in a letter of 1 Sept. 1763 as 'the best office that can be done, to most married people'. His fear was that any offspring would disinherit his appointed heir; that his brother was turned 60 boded ill for a legitimate alternative. This was a familiar double standard among those who, like C, liberally defended the interests of any illegitimate offspring of the male line.

To suckle fools . . . beer: *Othello*, II. i. 159. C is unconcerned that the speaker is Iago; Desdemona had asked him what a woman 'ever fair and never proud' was good for.

Mr. Dodd: Dr William Dodd (1729–77) was the godson's tutor from 1765, on the recommendation of Bishop Samuel Squire of St David's, whose chaplain he then was. C had thought him of 'unexceptionable character and very great learning' and called him 'the best preacher in England'. Only a year after C's death he was found guilty of simony and in 1777 was hanged for forging his former pupil's signature on a bond for £4,200.

339 *paulo majora canamus*: we sing in celebration of a small coming-of-age.

do as . . . done by: see Matthew 7: 12.

340 *haec olim . . . juvabit*: see note to p. 307.

the Sphynx's riddle: i.e. 'What is it that has one voice and yet becomes four-footed and two-footed and three-footed?' The answer, supplied by Oedipus, is man, who crawls, walks, and leans on a staff at different times of life.

341 *Suabia*: i.e. Schwaben, in SW Bavaria.

suos quisque . . . manes: each of us suffers his own punishment. From Virgil, *Aeneid*, 6. 743: during Aeneas's visit to hell, his dead father Anchises explains that all who live there pay the penalty for their former sins.

ex Ministres: the Marquis of Rockingham's administration of July 1765 had no place for allies of George Grenville (1712–70), who had been 1st Lord of the Treasury since Apr. 1763. These included Bedford, Grenville's President of the Council; Sandwich, his Secretary of State (N); Granville Leveson-Gower, 2nd Earl Gower (1721–1803), former Lord Chamberlain of the Household; and George Montagu Dunk, 2nd Earl of Halifax (1716–71), who had been Secretary of State (S). The chief bone of contention was the Stamp Act (see p. 347), which Grenville had passed and Rockingham wanted repealed. Neither Grenville nor Bedford returned to office, even after Rockingham's fall in Aug. 1766.

Signa canant: the signal is given [to fight]. From Virgil, *Aeneid*, 10. 310. *D'ailleurs* means besides.

better poet than philosopher: in the 1730s Harte's poetry had attracted the favourable notice of Pope; during the illness to which C refers he wrote a collection of poems, *The Amaranth* (1767).

342 *Mr. Larpent*: John Larpent (1710–97) was chief clerk at the Foreign Office, overseeing the income and expenditure of Britain's embassies and residencies.

344 *les Antipodes des Graces*: in Molière's *Les Précieuses Ridicules*, IX. 34–6, Magdelon declares that anyone who does not believe Paris to be the centre of all that is polite and cultured must be 'at the Antipodes of reason'.

345 *Maussades*: surly, sullen.

rule of the Gospel . . . find: see Matthew 7: 7.

346 *les rieurs . . . quartier*: the laughers of their own circle.

347 *Stamp-duty . . . les dragonades*: *dragonades*, after Louis XIV's harrying of Protestants with dragoons, means persecution with the aid of troops. This measure was being considered to enforce Grenville's Stamp Act (Mar. 1765), which introduced a tax payable on newspapers and legal and other documents, and was to bring in *c.*£60,000 p.a. for the up-keep of British troops in America.

348 *Prince of Brunswick's riband*: granted to Charles William Ferdinand
(1735–1806), nephew of Prince Ferdinand; he too had fought
with distinction during the Seven Years War. In 1764 he married
George III's sister, Augusta. His uncle's garter had been bestowed in 1760.

Will Finch ... Lord Bolingbroke: William Finch (1691–1766), C's
successor at The Hague in 1732 and then Vice-Chamberlain of
the Household, had married Lady Charlotte Fermor in 1746;
Francis Greville, 1st Earl Brooke and Warwick (1719–73) married Elizabeth Hamilton in 1742. Frederick St John, 2nd Viscount Bolingbroke (1734–87), nephew of the politician, was an
unlucky gambler who in 1767 decided to replace his wife, Lady
Diana Spencer, with 'a rich monster'. A divorce was obtained in
1768 and Lady Diana married Sir Topham Beauclerk; her former
husband went mad in his vain, ten-year search for a replacement.

pour le peu ... chagrin: for the few good days left to us, nothing is
so baleful as a deep disappointment.

349 *Aristides*: see note to p. 171.

351 *Lacedaemonians ... drunk*: Plutarch, *Life of Lycurgus* (28. 4), says
that the Spartans made their Helot slaves drunk to be displayed at
public eating-places (not only for children).

352 *Garde-fou*: a balustrade or rail.

Ne quid Nimis: nothing in excess. From Ausonius, *Septem Sapien-
tum Sententiae*, 49.

353 *bien narrer ... narrer trop*: to relate information well, or with
excessive refinement.

354 *Mr. Pitt ... Earl of Chatham*: Pitt returned to power in Aug. 1766.
His peerage, partly dictated by his being too ill to manage the
Commons, and partly by his wife's having been made Baroness
Chatham at the end of his previous term of office (1761), was
widely seen as a betrayal comparable to Pulteney's self-elevation
after Walpole's fall in 1742. He lasted until Oct. 1768.

355 *Lord Bute and a great lady*: a reference to the liaison of John Stuart,
3rd Earl of Bute (1713–92), first minister from 1761 to 1763, with
George III's mother, the Dowager Princess Augusta; this had
begun with Bute's protection of the future king following the
death of the Prince of Wales in 1751. That Bute was the *éminence
grise* behind recent events was a popular Whig fiction in 1766.

Stanley ... to decide: Hans Stanley (*c.*1720–80), former Lord of the
Admiralty, was chosen to negotiate a secret alliance between

Britain, Prussia, and Russia, which foundered before he even left London; Welbore Ellis, 1st Baron Mendip (1713–1802), married to Elizabeth Stanhope (daughter of C's brother William), former Secretary at War, was made a Knight of the Bath in 1766 and went to Spain for talks concerning the Falkland Islands dispute of that year; William Petty, Lord Shelburne (1737–1805), went on to become first minister in 1782; Charles Townshend (1725–67) had survived under Grenville and Rockingham and was Chatham's chancellor, seeing his first budget voted out.

otium cum dignitate: see note to p. 286.

356 *Miss Chudleigh ... Leicester-fields*: Elizabeth Chudleigh (1720–88) was a sensation from the moment she made her society début, topless, at a ball attended by George II. She kept secret her marriage to Augustus Hervey, from 1775 Lord Bristol, in order to remain a Maid of Honour; all was (again) revealed when she married the Duke of Kingston in 1769, only to be tried for bigamy. Her London parties, attended by foreign dignitaries as well as the Prince of Wales (hence the disapproval of the Dowager Princess, of Leicester House), equipped her for her Continental tour of 1765–6; before Dresden she had been in Berlin, downing two bottles of wine and falling over while attempting to dance at a royal wedding reception.

The Countess of Suffolk: Henrietta Howard, Countess of Suffolk (1681–1767) had been George II's mistress but was displaced from influence soon after his coronation in 1727 by that of his wife, who disliked C partly because of his association with her, which dated back to 1716. She retired from court in 1734 and corresponded often with C, Pope, Swift, Bolingbroke, and Horace Walpole.

357 *Mrs. Wagstaff*: the Countess, unable to match C's *jeu d'esprit*, had asked Horace Walpole to reply in the name of her housemaid, Elizabeth Wagstaff.

358 *Miss Hotham*: Henrietta Gertrude Hotham (1753–1816), daughter of C's sister Gertrude, became intimate with the Countess of Suffolk and was heir to her fortune.

359 *réfugiés ... Temple*: *Temple* was the usual slang word for a Protestant church in France.

Conway ... Lord President: Fd. Marshall Henry Seymour Conway (1721–95) had been Secretary of State (S) under Rockingham and changed to the northern department under Chatham, whose factiousness and colonial policies he soon found disagreeable. On

30 May 1767 he expressed his wish to resign, but was compelled to continue until the following January, when he was succeeded by Thomas Thynne, 3rd Viscount Weymouth (1734–96). The Lord President of the Council, Robert Henley, 1st Earl Northington (*c.*1708–72), had to wait only until December to give way to Earl Gower (see note to p. 341). Chatham suffered a mental breakdown in the spring of 1767, and from May of that year until Oct. of the next, when he at last resigned, he was virtually housebound, refusing to see anyone except his doctor.

what Lord Bute pleases: see note to p. 355.

Comte Flemming: former Saxon minister to Turin and England. See p. 69 and note.

361 *Dr. Addington*: Dr Anthony Addington (1713–90) was as notorious for his mediation between his reclusive patient and other ministers as for his often unlikely prescriptions. George III tried to persuade Chatham to find him an assistant; he was finally vindicated by his appointment in 1788 as Surgeon to the King.

new Parliament ... five thousand: the election of 1768 was to see the return of nineteen 'nabob' MPs, men who had made their fortunes in the Indies and raised the price of a parliamentary seat.

362 *your request*: Stanhope had requested leave from his Residency at Dresden in order to recover from sickness. It was granted with a reduction of salary. Lord Weymouth was Secretary of State (N).

Dr. Maty: Matthew Maty (1718–76) became both MD and Ph.D. at Leiden in 1740; he attended Stanhope in 1763. Secretary of the Royal Society in 1765, he became principal librarian at the British Museum in 1772. He defended C against Johnson over the dictionary episode in his *Journal britannique*, for which Johnson described him as 'that black dog'. His *Memoirs of the Earl of Chesterfield* were completed by his son-in-law and added to C's *Miscellaneous Works* (1777).

363 *the Duke of Grafton*: Augustus Henry Fitzroy, 3rd Duke of Grafton (1735–1811), was 1st Lord of the Treasury from 1766 to 1770.

Locus ... myself: there is room for several uninvited guests. From Horace, *Epistles*, 1. 5. 28. Chatham's illness and the premature death in Sept. 1767 of his chancellor, Townshend, set off a slow decline in the Ministry: an unstable coalition was formed with the Bedford faction in Dec. 1767, while Grafton assumed more of the power which Chatham was becoming incapable of wielding,

continuing in office for 18 months after Chatham's resignation in
Oct. 1768.

364 *the Faculty*: i.e. of Medicine, at the University of Leiden. See note
to p. 328.

Duchess of Somerset: probably Anna Maria Bonnell, wife of Webb
Seymour, the 10th Duke.

365 *a speedy recovery*: Stanhope died on 16 Nov. A few days later C
found that he had been married for nine years.

Mrs. Eugenia Stanhope: Stanhope's wife since 1760, born *c.*1720 the
natural daughter of a wealthy Irishman, Domville. Under the
name of Peters, she had met Stanhope in Paris in 1750, at the
lodgings of Lord Charlemont, an Irish peer on tour; after
marriage she lived in secret lodgings both in London and
Germany. There were two children, Charles and Philip.

the manner . . . complied with: Stanhope was buried by a Catholic
priest at Vaucluse. His mother, Madelena Elizabeth du Bouchet
(b. 1702), was a Huguenot and complained to his widow, who
wrote to C for support. C had met du Bouchet in July 1731
during his embassy to The Hague; she was then governess in an
influential family, the Wassanaer-Twickells, whom C was cultivating for political reasons. She followed C to London in 1732 to
give birth to Stanhope, and became a British citizen. C left her
£500 in his will 'as a small reparation for the injury I did her'.

Alderman Faulkner: the Dublin bookseller had been elected
Alderman earlier in the year. See also note to p. 322.

366 *Dublin Society . . . well-wisher*: a bust of C had been placed in the
gallery of the Dublin Society. For Madden, Swift, and Prior, see
notes to pp. 38, 11, and 36 respectively.

367 *Monsieur Perny*: master of Loughborough House, a Marylebone
boarding school formerly under the direction of Mr and Mrs
Robert, when C's godson and heir had attended.

368 *Sphynx's riddle*: see note to p. 340.

369 *five righteous . . . found*: Genesis 18: 28. God said that if He found
fifty righteous in Sodom he would spare it; Abraham thought
there might 'lack five of the fifty righteous'.

Mr. Hawkins: possibly Caesar Hawkins (1711–86), sergeant surgeon to George III, or his brother Pennell (d. 1791), also a
surgeon.

370 *water-drinkers . . . good*: see Horace, *Epistles*, 1. 19. 2.

clothing the naked: see Matthew 25: 36.

371 *Pandora's box*: Pandora, according to Hesiod the first woman, found a jar containing all the evils of the world (*Works and Days*, 70–95). C had used the same expression when describing the 'poor crazy deformed body' of his friend Pope.

Lord Bristol: George William Hervey, 2nd Earl of Bristol (1721–75), had been Ld.-Lt. of Ireland from 1766 to 1770 without once setting foot there. In 1771 he was Groom of the Stole to George III.

372 *Mr ——'s conversion*: sometimes thought to refer to Stanhope's conversion to Catholicism, but a reference to an unknown convert to Methodism seems more likely given C's subsequent ironic remarks.

et cantare . . . parati: ready to sing as well as to reply. Virgil, *Eclogues*, 7. 5.

373 *the boy . . . d'Eyverdun*: Georges d'Eyverdun was a Swiss critic and friend of Gibbon, whom he followed to England in 1765. He and Gibbon dedicated to C a collection of their essays, *Mémoires littéraires de la Grande Bretagne* (1769). C asked him in 1771 to act as his godson's 'Governor' during a continental tour on which they embarked the following year.

374 *élève*: breeding.

Doctor Warren: Richard Warren (1731–97) had been physician to George III since 1762, succeeding his father-in-law. The wealthiest doctor in England, he attended C from 1772 and was present at his death.

375 *To his Godson and Heir*: written in 1768.

376 *Middlesex . . . Westminster*: a grand jury decides whether there is a 'probable cause' of wrong-doing, and if there is, the defendant is tried before a petty (*petit*) jury. C seems to be referring to his godson's likely chances of success in Parliament if his entrance into London society and the Court does not go well.

Martin . . . Peter or Jack: in Swift's *A Tale of a Tub* (1704), Martin, who represents the Anglican Church, shuns extravagance in dress but finds that he cannot strip too much away 'without damaging the cloth'; his compromise contrasts with the high fashion of Peter (the Catholic Church) and the zealous plainness of Jack (Calvinism).

377 *tell me . . . what you are*: see note to p. 55.

378 *Pedarii Senatores*: see note to p. 296.

379 *Verba ... sequentur*: the words will come of their own accord. Horace, *Ars Poetica*, 311.

exordium ... peroratio: the introduction and conclusion in a seven-part classical oration.

380 *servare ... tueri*: stay within bounds and watch them carefully. Adapted from Virgil, *Aeneid*, 10. 502.

381 *Volto sciolto*: see note to p. 105.

ridicule ... perhaps for ever: C is dissenting from Shaftesbury's belief that ridicule is one means of recognizing the truth. See his *An Essay on the Freedom of Wit and Humour* (1709), I. i.

censor morum: censor of morals.

383 *Repandez ... ingrats*: lavish your gifts on others royally, do not refuse them even to the least virtuous, pay no heed to whether they are acknowledged: it is noble and fine to make people ungrateful. From Voltaire's *Précis de l'ecclésiaste*, 199–202.

INDEX OF PERSONS

American Literature

British and Irish Literature

Children's Literature

Classics and Ancient Literature

Colonial Literature

Eastern Literature

European Literature

History

Medieval Literature

Oxford English Drama

Poetry

Philosophy

Politics

Religion

The Oxford Shakespeare